D1035176

MĀLAMALAMA

Mālamalama

ROBERT M. KAMINS AND ROBERT E. POTTER
AND MEMBERS OF THE UNIVERSITY COMMUNITY

A HISTORY OF THE UNIVERSITY OF HAWAI'I

UNIVERSITY OF HAWAI'I PRESS, HONOLULU

Dedicated to the memory of Beatrice H. Kapuaokalani Krauss who grew up with her University and as student, teacher, ethnobotanist, and citizen exemplified its best.

A NOTE ON HAWAIIAN DIACRITICS

History plays with everything, including diacritical marks. Only in recent years have they been applied to Hawaiian words to guide pronunciations. For most of the century covered by this book the diacritics were not in use; hence the materials quoted herein often lacked the macron and the glottal that now routinely appear. For consistency among the quotations and citations within the text, the diacritics have been omitted in this book, except when the text refers to the current University of Hawai'i system.

Printed in the United States of America

03 02 01 00 99 98 5 4 3 2 1

Library of Congress Cataloging-in-Publication Data

Kamins, Robert M.

Mālamalama : a history of the University of Hawai'i / by Robert M. Kamins and Robert E. Potter.

p. cm.

Includes bibliographical references (p.) and index.

ISBN 0-8248-2006-1 (alk. paper)

1. University of Hawaii (System)—History. 2. Community colleges—Hawaii—History. 3. Community and college—Hawaii—History. I. Potter, Robert E. II. Title.

LD2221.K35 1998

378.969—dc21 97-50348

CIP

University of Hawai'i Press books are printed on acid-free paper and meet the guidelines for permanence and durability of the Council on Library Resources.

Book design by Kenneth Miyamoto

CONTENTS

FOREWORD

THIS HISTORY of our university is written for all of us who have been influenced by it. Whether we are alumni, dropouts, or eager learners enrolled there now, or are teachers, researchers, secretaries, administrators, technicians, or custodians of its ten campuses, or are simply interested bystanders, we have been affected in countless ways by the services it performs for all the people who live in these islands of Hawaii.

Many voices join here to tell the University's story. Reflecting the many different functions of the the University, and the innumerable people who have helped to create it, this account draws upon contributions from members of the faculty, administrators, former students, and alumni. In every sense, this is a labor of love.

It tells how the idea of a university, an institution of higher learning that evolved in distant Europe, the font of Western culture, was imported to Hawaii, the newest and least Western part of the United States. And it explains how we here, in adopting this alien concept, have adapted it to our needs and interests. As is usually the case with a *hanai* (adopted) child, it resembles both the ancestral parents and the adopting ones, the while also displaying traits that are genuinely its own. The University's seal —a Roman torch of learning superimposed upon a map of the Pacific hemisphere and the Hawaiian word *Mālamalama,* meaning light of knowledge—symbolizes the hybrid creation we have made.

The writers of this book will remind you of things you know already. And they will acquaint you, too, with things that are new. All will confirm Willard Wilson's opinion, written in 1958. From his perspective, gained during four decades of service on the Manoa campus, first as a teacher of English, later as perennial vice-president and frequent acting president, he saw that, "in many respects the University of Hawai'i is Hawaii in miniature. We conduct many of the same intricate . . . operations, we share many of the same interests and aspirations, we shoulder many of the same burdens in an attempt to build a better world."

In helping us reach that noble goal, our university offers instruction in a dazzling array of courses concerned with most of the disciplines of knowledge that are valued in the complex world of today. All this variety has grown out of the tiny seed that was planted in 1907, in the College of Agriculture and Mechanic Arts, with five borrowed students, twelve valorous instructors, a token library, all gathered in a rented house on Young Street on the Waikiki side of Thomas Square.

Now on ten different campuses, from the big one at Manoa in Honolulu to adjuncts on Oahu, Kauai, Maui, and the island of Hawaii, each year it enrolls some fifty thousand students. In the ninety years since its founding, the institution has graduated more than two hundred thousand people, who have earned the kinds of recognition that a university can award, from associates' certificates to bachelors', masters', and doctors' degrees. No counts are available for part-time students, dropouts, auditors, and East-West Center scholars, but at least one hundred thousand of these must have been in attendance for one course or another during this period. The total number of people who have been directly influenced by the University's teaching is a significant part of this state's population.

In addition to offering scores of academic curricula, the University administers notable research institutes. The history of some of them is described in this volume. The statewide University system operates libraries, art galleries, theatres, music and dance centers, radio stations, an aquarium, and an arboretum. It is a publisher, with its chartered press, and a banker, through its federal credit union. It provides housing for thousands of students and hundreds of faculty members, food services, and medical and counseling care for students. It manages scores of buildings, miles of roads, acres of grounds that (when well maintained) resemble parks, and security forces for guarding its several campuses and the people who gather on them. For fans, it provides football, baseball, basketball, volleyball, swimming, and other competitive sports.

The extent of its activities is astonishing. In 1907 even the most imaginative of prophets would not have foreseen such a wealth of academic enterprise. It trains, for example, physicians, nurses, dental hygienists, lawyers, astronomers, school teachers, architects, engineers, entomologists, librarians, social workers, business administrators, travel-industry experts, and electronic theorists. Scholars in a wide range of the sciences, natural and social, are prepared for careers in Hawaii and around the world. The ten campuses together teach actors, musicians and dancers, choreographers, artists, and composers; computer programmers and technicians; food technologists and chefs; automobile and airplane mechanics; linguists, poets, essayists, journalists —writers in all genres from haiku to novels. With few exceptions, any profession, trade, or art practiced in Hawaii can be learned within the University system.

The University operates vessels for research in oceanography, geophysics, and marine biology and facilities for some of the world's major telescopes at the summit of Mauna Kea. Its agricultural research stations function on all of the state's larger islands.

Because of its location in the central Pacific, Hawaii serves as a bridge between Asia, the other Pacific islands, and the United States. This linking, both intellectual and social, is anchored in the University and in the East-West Center. These connected institutions, with their manifold interests and their inclusive ethnic representation in student body, teachers, and research staffs, have promoted interracial and international amity.

Closer to home, the University has taught many of our leaders in politics, business, the professions, and the arts and sciences. These leaders represent a wide range of ethnicity. Thanks in good measure to the ease of ethnic mixing that UH students have experienced from the earliest days of the school, Hawaii has achieved the art of comfortable and pacific living for all who join us here.

Moreover, the University, since its founding, has shared with the Bernice Pauahi Bishop Museum the responsibility for conserving the language and the history of Native Hawaiians. In great part the "Hawaiian Renaissance" we are witnessing today grew out of interests and knowledge preserved by faculty and students at the University.

Whatever criteria we may use to evaluate our University's teachings and influences, they are impressive. We should be in awe of its achievements and proud of its successes. And, to be fair, we must also acknowledge its shortcomings in failing, from time to time, to maintain the creative forces that this history celebrates. Most of these failures seem to be due to intrusions from outside the University system by those people who think they ought to be the ones to run it.

In sad truth, we in Hawaii do not give the University the appreciation it deserves. Rarely has it been accorded the support that an alma mater, a fostering mother, should receive. Most of us ignore it, or take it for granted. We treat it like an unloved stepchild—or, better still, like the proverbial Japanese daughter-in-law who is subjected to the relentless abuse of a tyrannical mother-in-law. *Auwe* for the poor thing!

Legislators of the Territory of Hawaii were grudging in the appropriations they made to the struggling new College of Hawaii. In recent years, our state legislators have not been much more supportive, choosing rather to follow the example of that fabled mother-in-law. Our University draws more recognition from agencies beyond this state, most notably from the federal government. The Carnegie Foundation for the Advancement of Teaching has ranked it among the top seventy American "research universities," judged according to the grants received for research programs and instruction in sciences that can be studied better here than in other places on earth.

But who here at home ever bothers to praise our University—or to champion it in times of stress, such as it is enduring now? Occasionally a student or a worried member of the faculty speaks up, or writes, in its defense. From the alumni, however, not a heartening sound is heard. More than two hundred thousand people have profited in one way or another from the University's presence here. And of these only about 1 percent have joined one or another of its several alumni associations. Many University graduates are distinguished in their professions, but few are distinguished for profession of loyalty and gratitude to the fostering mother who prepared them for their careers. Most of us merely got up and left the campus after the diplomas were handed out. As champions of the University we, all together, do not amount to a decibel's worth of cheer. For our indifference and inaction, we should "get one good scolding," as Hawaii's *tutus* say to their heedless grandchildren.

The reason for such apathy is no mystery. Most citizens honor athletes more than intellects. When the football team is in trouble, people speak up. Even so, having been educated—that is to say, led out of ignorance, having been enlightened by that torch of knowledge—all of us should want to avoid slipping back into medieval darkness.

The authors of this history, unreconstructed teachers still, hope that its readers will be led to prize our University, a treasure in our midst.

O. A. Bushnell
Class of 1934, UH-Mānoa

PREFACE

A UNIVERSITY is a strange institution, easier to describe than explain, particularly if it is a public university encompassing the full range of higher education from community colleges to professional schools. Its most appreciated function is to prepare people for an enormously wide range of careers, but in a democracy it also serves another purpose, less often noticed. That is to help students prepare for responsible citizenship, many in leadership roles, by sharpening their understanding of the ever-changing society in which they live. In multiethnic Hawaii this function has extended to accustoming young adults of all races to interact with ease and grace.

The University of Hawai'i, furthermore, also took on the function of relating to Asia and the island nations of the Pacific, fulfilling Hawaii's abiding ambition to be a major link between East and West. To do so, it gained preeminence in a range of academic disciplines focused on the Pacific and its western rim, as well as achieving the general distinction in graduate programs needed for recognition as a research university. From its early days, the University also took on responsibility for preserving Hawaiian as a disciplined language and in recent times has expanded that role to include the study and appreciation of Polynesian culture.

The central purpose of our history is to show how this broad agenda developed along with the institution, as a College of Agriculture and Mechanic Arts, starting up in an old house with five underqualified students, became a statewide university system teaching some fifty thousand each year in hundreds of courses and programs, its research programs of notable scope and excellence, its services to the people of Hawaii broad and varied beyond listing.

Governance, the power to create university programs and direct their operation, necessarily set the conditions for each stage of the history. Some governors held the University at arm's length, treating it like any other department of the Territory and

State of Hawaii; a few closely embraced it, generally to its benefit. Boards of Regents appointed by governors viewed their function variously: most delegated operational decision making to the president they chose, but others themselves made decisions on courses, programs, and personnel. Some presidents, particularly those who served long terms of office, shaped the future of the school, while others, short-termers, were preoccupied with immediate problems. (The exception was Thomas H. Hamilton, who in five years directed the University's most defining period of development.)

Developing and presenting the programs selected by those officeholders is the faculty, of limited influence before mid-century, then gaining influence through its Senate and union. Between and betwixt are campus administrators, growing in number and layers in the last half of the century. Their story is not closely followed here but, coincidentally and fortunately, has been told by David Yount in *Who Runs the University? The Politics of Higher Education in Hawaii, 1985–1992*. What we do document is the continuous involvement of the University with the legislature that gave it life and provides its essential support—and sometimes its severest problems.

The present authors, both retired after long service on the Manoa campus, realized the difficulty of perceptively viewing an institution as complex as the University from only two vantage points. We provide a general overview of its history in Part I. To gain other perspectives, we invited collaborators deeply knowledgeable about particular colleges and programs at Manoa and the other campuses of the University system—UH at Hilo, UH at West O'ahu, and the community colleges—to provide accounts of their history. These appear in Parts II and III.

For the same reason, to sample views of the University as seen by the young people for whose particular benefit it was created, we asked three alumni to tell about their experience as UH undergraduates. Their stories appear alongside the main text.

The whole, we trust, provides not only a history of an institution, its intentions, problems, mistakes, and achievements, but also some feeling for the people who worked for it and in it, how they were caught up in the struggles and triumphs of ninety years. Written at a time of severe budgetary constriction, it is our hope that this story of survival, of emerging again and again like the fabled phoenix from the fire, will hearten all who wish the University well.

This book of history itself has a history. It first arose in the mind of Willard Wilson about forty years ago, when he began writing short pieces about the University derived from his rich experience as member and chairman of the English Department, as dean of student personnel, dean of the College of Arts and Sciences, dean of faculties, vice-president, acting president, provost, and corporate secretary of the University. He made copious notes, summarizing meetings of the regents—with comments obviously not intended for their eyes. Over the decades, he wrote pieces on a variety of topics that caught his attentive notice. There is a draft foreword to a "History of the University," but at some time as Wilson neared retirement in 1969 he crossed out "History" and substituted "Reminiscences." After he died in 1973, colleagues preserved a score of his "musings" in *Professor's Briefcase: Wit and Wisdom of Willard Wilson*. One piece is incorporated in this book and others are quoted.

Wilson's notes were saved by David Kittelson, in charge of Hawaiiana in the Hamilton Graduate Library. Kittelson, who had written a master's thesis on the University's early history, and who had in print several journal articles on its library, picked up the torch to prepare a more complete UH history. Unhappily, he suddenly died in 1988. We have relied on his writing on the library and had access to the materials he had collected.

Stimulus to this volume was the appointment of a History of the University of Hawai'i Committee in 1989 by President Albert J. Simone. The committee, on which we both served, readily agreed that with the near approach of UH's centennial it was time for a history to be written. There was no agreement, however, on how to go about it—namely, on whether a University historian should be appointed and whether the history should be "authorized," that is, officially sponsored and therefore subject to skeptical reading as being self-serving. We decided to prepare an unauthorized history.

Reconstruction of the past depends on the record available. Over the years, only a few units of the University have written their own histories. Dean Wilfred "Jasper" Holmes, author of popular sea stories, left an account of the College of Engineering which is included in this volume. Dean Terence Rogers (Medicine), Dean David Bess (Business Administration), Professors Vincent Peterson (Physics), Robert Potter (Education), Walter Steiger (Astronomy), and Herbert Weaver (Psychology) had covered their respective fields so completely that this general history could not incorporate their narratives, although we were informed by them. The same was true of the history of the Women's Campus Club, written by Dr. Norma Carr and Lenore Johnson. Briefer accounts of a few academic departments, such as Economics and Political Science, were also helpful, as were the memoirs of emeritae professors Dorothy F. Aspinwall and Ella L. Wiswell (European Languages), Marjorie Sinclair Edel (English), and of former Lieutenant Governor Jean King.

We extend our thanks, and where appropriate an apology, to the generous colleagues who contributed to this history. To hold the book to manageable size, reductive editing was unavoidable. For the same reason, space could not be found for a few lengthy contributions. Where we received permission, manuscripts in their original form were placed in the University Archives. There they may inform future researchers into the continuing history of this university.

In addition to these persons, and the authors of sections included in this volume, we wish to acknowledge our indebtedness to others who in various ways helped us in this work. They are listed alphabetically and identified by their field of study or area of responsibility at UH.

Mitsuo Aoki (Religion), Abe Arkoff (Psychology), Steven T. Boggs (Ethnic Studies), James R. Brandon (Theatre), J. Russell Cades (former regent), University Archivist James F. Cartwright, University Photographer Robert Chinn, Bruce J. Cooil (Plant Physiology), the late A. Grove Day (English), Jean H. Ehrhorn (Library), the late Earle Ernst (Theatre), Hubert Everly (Education), Barbara J. Furstenberg (Community Service Program), Chuck Y. Gee (Travel Industry Management), Moheb A. Ghali (Research Administration), Gayle Y. Gilbert (Medicine), the late Madeleine J. Goodman (Academic Affairs), Wytze Gorter (Economics), Michael Haas (Political Science), Sandra Hammond (Dance), the late Robert W. Hiatt (Zoology), Christina Higa (PEACESAT), Judith G. Hughes (College of Arts and Humanities), Shirley R. Kamins (English), Anna M. Keppel (Education), Edgar C. Knowlton (European Languages), Mildred D. Kosaki (Institutional Research), Richard H. Kosaki (Political Science), Hazel Kraemer (Human Development), Beatrice Krauss (Ethnobotany), Edward A. Langhans (Theatre), L. Stephen Lau (Engineering), the late Richard K. C. Lee (Public Health), Leonard Mason (Anthropology), Harold E. McCarthy (Philosophy), Richard S. Miller (Law), Marty Myers (Kennedy Theatre), Colonel Robert Parker (ROTC), Abraham Piianaia (Hawaiian Studies), Patricia A. Polansky (Library), Richard L. Rapson (History), Karen M. Rehbock (Astronomy), Norman Rian (Music), Paul J. Scheuer (Chemistry), Mary Shaw and Robert D. Stevens (Library Studies), Richard S. Takasaki (Social Work), Murray Turnbull (Art), Daniel W. Tuttle (Political Science and Education), Mary Lou Wade (Nursing), Bruce E. White (Education), Elizabeth Wichmann (Theatre), Walter A. Wittich (Educational Technology).

To Ann Bystrom and Marian Kittelson we are grateful for the loan of materials left by their husbands dealing, respectively, with the University's Peace Satellite Program and with the UH libraries.

Our thanks go to others whose aid was invaluable. Charles E. Bouslog joined in planning this volume and made available his writings on mid-century days in Manoa. Incisively reacting to successive drafts of the manuscript, James R. Linn and O. A. Bushnell enlarged our understanding while shrinking the word count. Kenneth K. Lau, to our benefit, over many an hour generously shared his rich university experience as teacher and administrator. Clifford DeVries enabled us to commit these pages to computer mode without going mad.

Finally, to Pamela Kelley of the University of Hawai'i Press we are grateful for her high professional competence in editing and helping shape a book that without her would have been longer and yet less complete.

Me ke aloha pumehana.

Robert M. Kamins
Robert E. Potter

PART I

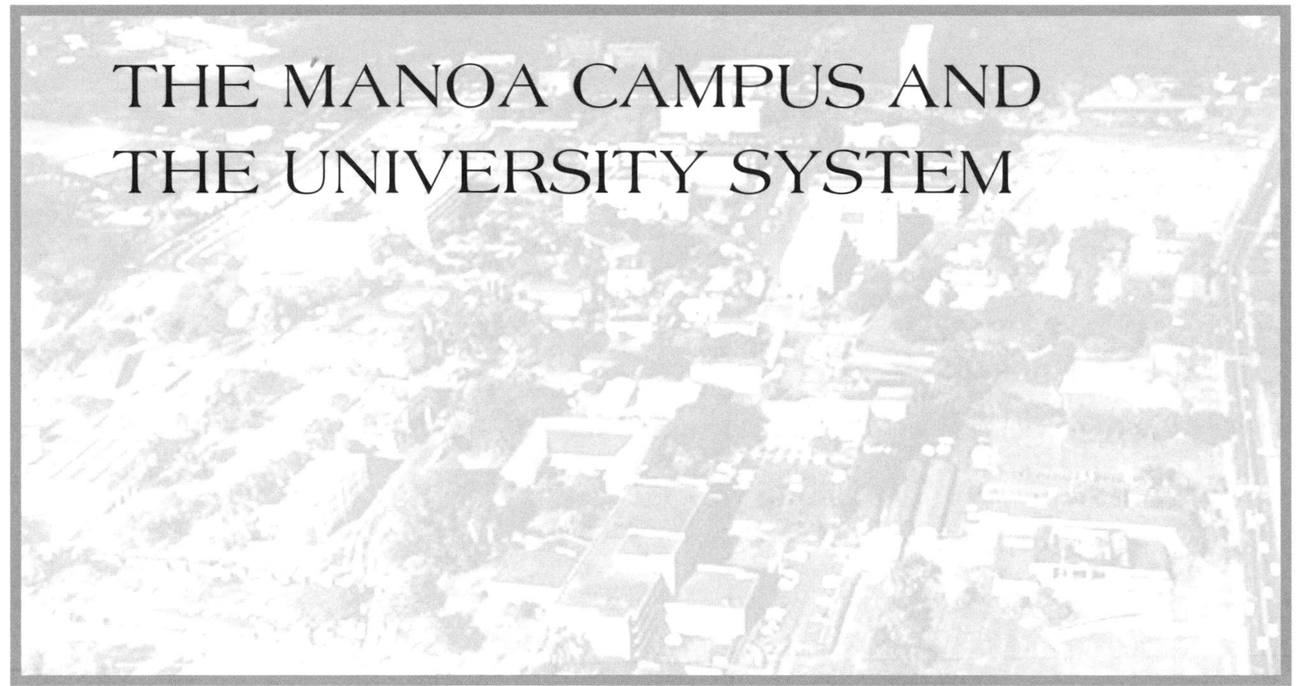

THE MANOA CAMPUS AND THE UNIVERSITY SYSTEM

1

ORIGINS AND EARLY YEARS: 1907–1946

HAWAII AT THE BEGINNING of the twentieth century needed an institution of higher learning. The further integration into the United States desired by those who had sided against the Hawaiian monarchy, if it was to work politically, required the further development of American culture here. Across the nation, every state and incorporated territory except Hawaii and Alaska had a college. Without one of its own, the far offshore Territory of Hawaii would present itself as not only remote and exotic but also as backwater and uncultured, territorial indeed.

A college would crown an Island educational establishment that already was remarkable for its time and place. Thanks in large part to the zeal for universal literacy instilled by the Calvinist missionaries from New England, at the time of annexation Hawaii already had 192 schools, 132 of them public. On Oahu there was a public high school in Honolulu with more than a hundred students and three private high schools—Punahou, St. Louis, and Iolani. Lahainaluna Seminary on Maui also offered some secondary education.

However, even though a congressional commission sent in 1898 to propose laws for the newly annexed territory recommended that the existing school system "remain in force," it was incomplete. Affluent families could afford to send their sons to universities on the mainland, and they did—frequently to Yale, Princeton, and Harvard. That, however, was expensive, and daughters were also beginning to ask for a college education. A small but growing middle class of storekeepers, school teachers, bookkeepers, supervisors, mechanics, and the like had similar ambitions for their children. On the plantations and in the villages of the Islands, a quiet hope for higher education was awaiting the opportunity.

The call to establish a college and later a university for this remote outpost of America came from three cultural groups—first in the territorial legislature by native

Hawaiian members, then by a bank employee of Chinese ancestry, with the strong support of many "Northern Europeans," to use the ethnic classifier of that time, who believed in the importance of higher education for building a good society. Once the school came into existence, it attracted students and support from all ethnic groups. Indeed it became the primary agency within Hawaii's society to foster mutual respect among its diverse cultures.

Resistance to the creation of a college came primarily from some leaders of the sugar industry. As major employers and taxpayers, they were concerned about the effects of a public college on their labor supply and on their tax burden. Underneath lay feelings about the appropriate place in society of non-Caucasian people and the desirability of providing higher education to children of plantation families. Opposition, however, was blunted by the religious background of many spokesmen for the industry, since the church that had sent their forefathers to the Islands had taught the importance of learning to achieve salvation. When a decision had to be made by a territorial legislature in which sugar was well represented, no dissent was expressed. The statutes that created first a College and then later a University of Hawai'i passed unanimously.

CREATING THE COLLEGE

Decisive to the creation of a public college in Hawaii early in the twentieth century was the availability of federal funds. As a territory, Hawaii was eligible for grants to assist colleges of "agriculture and mechanic arts"—in the language of the Morrill Act of 1890. (The first Morrill Act, passed during the American Civil War, granted federal land for the same purpose, but only to states, not territories.) The annual grant to each qualified institution, in 1900 amounting to $25,000, was attractively large.

Interest was shown at the first meeting of the new territorial legislature in 1901. Representative J. W. Kaliikoa of Keauhou, Hawaii, presented a petition from North Kona residents asking for a "territorial university" in their district. At the same legislative session, Senator Daniel Kanuha of Oahu introduced Senate Bill No. 62 to create an "Agricultural College and Model Farm." Amended to locate the proposed college at Mountain View on the island of Hawaii, the district of the Senate president, it passed the Senate, but only on the last day of a tumultuous session and so never reached the House of Representatives. The next legislature, in 1903, reversed the process. Representative David Kupihea of Oahu introduced House Bill No. 11, identical with the 1901 Senate bill. It too proposed a campus at Mountain View, but since the Speaker was from Maui the location was changed to the Lahainaluna Seminary campus on that island. Passed by the House, the bill died in the Senate.

The legislative infighting that had thwarted the first two attempts to create an agricultural college led Governor George R. Carter to consider doing so by executive order. He was advised, however, that qualifying for federal funds required legislation.

At that point, Wallace Rider Farrington, managing editor of the *Honolulu Evening Bulletin,* took the initiative by urging the legislature to commission a study of the feasibility of a land-grant college in Hawaii. With the governor's approval, Farrington drafted a resolution to that effect, which Representative William Joseph Huelani Coelho of Maui (his mother Hawaiian, his father Portuguese) introduced at the 1905 special session of the legislature. Adopted on May 25, the resolution noted that "the industries of this Territory are almost exclusively agricultural and our future development must depend for its best progress upon the education of our youth." This may have been an appeal for support by the burgeoning sugar industry, then entering its period of most rapid growth, a reminder that it would be advantageous to have a local source of the chemists, engineers, and technicians they had been recruiting from abroad. That support was slow in coming.

The 1905 resolution directed the territorial commissioners of public instruction to determine the probable expense of a College of Agriculture and Mechanic Arts and a "possible practicable site," including Lahainaluna. They were to report to the next legislative session, in 1907.

Farrington, providentially a member of the commission, wrote its report, clear and to the point. After showing how grants under the two Morrill Acts had supported the creation of colleges across the nation—including his alma mater, the University of Maine, where his father had served as professor of agriculture—he noted that the federal government also funded agricultural experiment stations, such as the one already operating in Honolulu. Perhaps a college could be bolstered by affiliation with the experiment station. Farrington's report recommended that "Hawaii should . . . have a College of Agriculture and Mechanic Arts" that should admit only students who had "completed a course of study equal to that required for graduation from Honolulu High School [later called McKinley] or Oahu College [subsequently renamed Punahou]."[1]

The report opposed putting the school at Lahainaluna, whose incomplete high school did not furnish "a proper basis for a College." It rebutted the argument that an agricultural college had to be in a rural area, explaining that such an institution would engage in intensive research, not in extensive farming. Rather, access to the Hawaii Agricultural Experiment Station near Punchbowl Crater and other scientific laboratories in Honolulu was essential. Therefore, it proposed the "vicinity of Honolulu" as the proper location

> because the capital city offers more opportunity for the student to come in touch with the practical application of theory than any other community in the Islands.

> . . . To bury an advanced institution of learning in the country should be a crime undoubtedly ending in the death of the victim.

Farrington's report addressed the underlying issue of race. In an astonishingly outspoken rebuke to those critics from the plantation oligarchy who viewed the non-white youth as potential laborers for the fields and factories, Farrington dealt with their opposition to a public institution of higher learning in the territory:

> One of the objections offered to a college for Hawaii is that we already have too much education for our cosmopolitan children, and that these children are educated away from labor. *It is useless to attempt to answer such an argument for it represents the stone age of mental development.* [Italics in original.]

The report concluded by recommending that the legislature create an appointive Board of Trustees and petition Congress for a grant of $25,000 annually, as then provided by federal law. It also proposed that public lands in Hawaii sufficient to yield another $25,000 be set aside for the college, as well as an initial start-up appropriation by the territorial government, all to be administered by the trustees.

At the opening session of the 1907 legislature, Governor Carter strongly supported the recommendations. He asked three friends, Henry E. Cooper, Charles R. Hemenway, and Ralph Hosmer—all members of the University Club of Honolulu and subsequent regents—to prepare implementing legislation. They had two bills drafted, one establishing the college, the other appropriating money to start it up, which were introduced by William J. Huelani Coelho, now serving as a Maui senator.

By good fortune, passage was eased by concurrent action in the U.S. Congress. A 1907 amendment to the college-support program added $5,000 to the annual grants for agricultural and mechanic arts colleges, increasing the subsidy to $30,000. Furthermore, it would continue to rise by increments of $5,000, to reach $50,000 a year in 1912—a substantial sum for a territory then operating on a budget of less than three million dollars. With this financial inducement, there was no legislative opposition to Act 24, which established the College of Agriculture and Mechanic Arts of the Territory of Hawaii under a five-member Board of Regents. The legislature appropriated $10,000 for college buildings and $15,000 for salaries over the ensuing biennium.

STARTING UP

Governor Carter signed Act 24 on March 25, 1907, and appointed the first College governing board: Judge Henry E. Cooper as chairman; Marston Campbell, a civil engineer; Charles F. Eckart, director of the Hawaiian Sugar Planters' Association Experiment Station; Alonzo Gartley, manager of the Hawaiian Electric Company; and Walter G. Smith, editor of the *Pacific Commercial Advertiser.* Eckart served only four months, to be replaced by Ralph Hosmer, the territorial forester.

Chairman Cooper, who had been minister of education for the Republic of Hawaii, announced that the new college would not be a trade school of manual arts. In a newspaper interview, he said:

> The college will be for the study of advanced scientific agriculture, the curriculum embracing such subjects as soil analysis, arborculture, agricultural chemistry, fertilization, drainage and irrigation and probably the advanced languages, for many of the books on these subjects are published in the French and German languages.[2]

Noting the history of other land-grant colleges that had become full-fledged universities, he predicted, "It may well be that the University of Hawaii may grow out of the agricultural college" about to be created.

Two days later, Cooper asked fellow regents to meet him at "9 am Sunday 12th at Punahou and Wilder . . . to inspect the various sites" that might serve as a campus. Attention centered almost immediately on "Highland Park and the government land of Puahia" in Manoa Valley. (Puahia was the land around the present East-West Center, and adjacent Highland Park was a proposed housing area owned by Theophilus Metcalf, remembered in the name of the street that would lead into the future campus.) Owner of the largest private estate in Manoa, Cooper was well acquainted with the land of the valley.

The campus site in lower Manoa was well chosen for a small college. Immediately adjacent was the area selected for development by Mid-Pacific Institute, a church-related private school. Its graduates would help form the student body of the new college, and its dormitories would from time to time provide housing for College students. Above the valley from Mid-Pacific a residential area was opening up. Over the years, it was to become a neighborhood favored by faculty members of the nascent University, within easy walking distance of their offices. For teachers and students living farther away, a new line of the Honolulu streetcar system coming up Oahu Avenue would provide transportation until the age of the automobile was well established in the 1930s.

Regents' minutes of January 16, 1908, report a protest made to Governor Walter F. Frear (who had just succeeded Carter) against the Board of Health's granting permission to use a portion of Highland Park as a cemetery. "To forestall such a dolorous outlook for a campus devoted to the future, the regents hastened to acquire Blocks 1, 2, 3, 5, 6, and 8," adding them to Blocks 4 and 7, purchased earlier for $1,350 an acre.[3] By September, the regents had acquired by exchange, territorial grant, or purchase forty-one acres, with another twenty-three under negotiation. That provided about one-sixth of the present Manoa campus, but five years were to pass before the land actually became the home of the College.

The Young Street Campus

In the meantime, as a temporary location, a lot in central Honolulu on Young Street, near Thomas Square, was leased from Cecil Brown for $50 a year. On adjacent ground, chosen by the Department of Public Instruction as the site of a new building for McKinley High School, was an old Victorian-style residence, known as the Maertens house, which for a time had housed the Chinese consulate. It was hauled over to the college lot to serve as its first building. The living room became the library. In it went the first collection of books, purchased with a $5,000 legislative appropriation, $350 going for Hawaiiana. In early 1908 another wooden building was added. Its fifteen rooms provided space for the educational enterprise being hastily assembled as the College of Agriculture and Mechanic Arts of the Territory of Hawaii.

Quick action was needed to qualify for the crucial grants. Governor Frear on January 16, 1908, informed the regents that the federal government would pay $30,000 as soon as the College was in operation. To qualify for the current fiscal year would mean getting classes started no later than February. Haste would prevent waste.

The regents had already taken urgent action in October 1907 to select Professor J. E. Roadhouse of the University of California to preside over the College. Unfortunately, he died in late November before leaving Berkeley. With classes scheduled to begin in two months, the regents reacted quickly. After both Regent Hosmer and ex-governor Carter declined the honor, they persuaded Willis T. Pope to take leave from his position as vice-principal of the Territorial Normal School to act as head of the College for its first semester, which would begin in February 1908.

Even before accepting the post on December 6, 1907, Pope set to work, itemizing the furniture, apparatus, and supplies needed to ready the Maertens house for classes. On December 12 the regents reviewed the list, item by item, before approving the expenditure of $1,400. On December 30 Pope presented a detailed plan for a four-year curriculum in agriculture. By January he had written and distributed a thousand copies of a "prospectus" describing the new school and its program.

Pope hurriedly recruited five young men from his agriculture class at the Normal School to form a college preparatory class. Ching Quon Amona, Simeon K. Domingo, Dewitt Gibson, Ernest K. Richardson, and Alexander R. Tulloch were to take secondary school-level classes because they were not yet qualified for college instruction. Their teachers were Pope for horticulture and botany and the Reverend W. E. Potwine for English and mathematics. Pope reported to the regents on February 27, 1908, that classes had begun on February 3, whereupon Governor Frear requested the federal funds for which the College now qualified. They arrived April 2, 1908, making Hawaii's new institution of higher learning the sixty-fourth land-grant college in the nation. In the words of a future president of the College, "The five young men who enrolled February 3 appeared to have endowed the college with $6,000 each."[4] Unfortunately, none of them went on to complete the four-year course of study.

The educational purposes of the school were broadly set forth in Pope's *Prospectus of the College of Agriculture and Mechanic Arts of the Territory of Hawaii,* dated January 1, 1908:

> The leading object shall be, without excluding other scientific and classical studies, and including military tactics, to teach such branches of learning as are related to agriculture and mechanic arts, . . . in order to promote the liberal and practical education of the industrial classes in the several pursuits and professions of life.

Devising a college curriculum to fit those goals, so specific in detail and yet so general in intent, was the responsibility of the first president, who was still being sought. Following the death of Roadhouse of California, the search turned eastward to Cornell, then the most prestigious university supported by the Morrill Acts. The selection was made by Regent Hosmer, who on April 20 was authorized by the regents "to engage a suitable man as President of the College while on his Eastern trip." On the advice of Cornell's president, Hosmer recommended the appointment of John W. Gilmore, professor of agriculture at Cornell. Gilmore had wide experience in the Pacific and Asia, having organized agricultural schools in China and advised the Indian Commission of Agriculture and the Philippine Department of Agriculture, as well as having taught agriculture for a year at Hawaii's Normal School. His appointment was quickly approved by the Board of Regents.

Authorized to do his own recruiting, Gilmore brought with him a number of faculty members when he arrived in Honolulu late in August 1908. A Cornell connection was thus established that would strongly influence the shaping of the new school.

The College opened its doors as an institution of higher learning on September 14, 1908, when five freshmen registered for a bachelor of science degree, five "preparatory" and thirty-one "special" (i.e., nondegree) students came to Young Street to begin classes under the faculty of thirteen, including Gilmore. Of that first faculty, four had studied at Cornell: Gilmore, Minnie Chipman (ceramics), John Mason Young (engineering), and Vaughn MacCaughey (botany). MacCaughey was recruited from the staff of the Territorial Normal School, along with John Donaghho, who taught mathematics. In the next few years other Cornell alumni were appointed, notably Arthur L. Andrews, who later became the first dean of arts and sciences, and David L. Crawford, who was to be Hawaii's longest-serving president. They were joined by Jerome Morgan and Raymond Severance in chemistry and physics; Arthur R. Keller, engineering; Agnes Hunt, domestic science; Briggs Porter, animal husbandry; and Warren Ross, agronomy and botany.

Choosing a nucleus of Cornell-educated faculty well served the purposes of the new College. Cornell, though a private university, was the federally supported land-

The vision of a few men guided the creation and development of the College of Hawaii. Wallace R. Farrington (top left) wrote the 1907 report recommending that the territorial legislature create a College of Agriculture and Mechanic Arts. Senator William J. Huelani Coelho (no photo available) introduced the enabling bills. Henry E. Cooper (top right), first chairman of the regents, directed selection of a campus site in Manoa Valley. Willis T. Pope (top left in the group picture in the facing page), as interim head of the College, got it started on a temporary campus in central Honolulu. John Gilmore (left) was the first president (1908–1913).

The school began college-level instruction on September 14, 1908, in the Maertens House, a private residence that had served as the Chinese consulate, where its first faculty posed. From left in back row, Willis Pope, (the next man is unidentified), Raymond Severance, Minnie Chipman, Carrie Green; front row, Agnes Hunt, (another unidentified man), bearded John Donaghho, Briggs Porter, (a third unidentified man), John Gilmore, and John Mason Young.

The first football team, practicing in front of the Maertens House in 1909, included faculty members Arthur Keller, Severance, and Porter. The College defeated neighboring McKinley High School but lost to Punahou.

grant institution of New York state. Its emphases on agriculture and mechanic arts provided a fitting model for Hawaii's school, which offered bachelor of science degrees in programs of agriculture, civil engineering, general science, and household economics.

During the first years, in order to cover all the courses offered so ambitiously, some faculty members found themselves teaching outside their disciplines, as well as in their own specialties. English instructor Mildred Yoder, for example, offered the College's first course in economics. Foreign-language teachers were hired part-time, with the result that during the first six years six different people taught French and five German.

By 1909 enrollment had increased to thirteen regular and fifty-one special students. Now there were enough males on campus, including Professors Keller, Severance, and Porter, to field a football team. The College won its first game from McKinley High School next door, then lost twice to Punahou before defeating McKinley again. Support of the fledgling athletic program was limited until 1910, when the student body organized itself into the Associated Students of the College of Hawaii (now the ASUH).

Readying Manoa

Preparing the Manoa lands acquired for the campus took enormous toil. Clearing began in 1909 and would continue for decades as the school developed. Frederick G. Krauss, who came to the College in 1910 to be its professor of agriculture, described the heavy labor.

> When the college took over the tract of land which was to become the future [experimental] farm, it was all cut up into small stone-walled fields, ranging in area from one-tenth to one-fourth of an acre. These fields were farmed by individual Chinese and Hawaiian tenants. . . . Most of the tillage was done with dynamite and crowbar! Five thousand cubic yards of stone was removed . . . from the stone walls alone. Besides that there was a large amount of surface and buried rock. Twenty-two acres were cleared during the first ten years. . . . The aggregated rocks made a pile at the future site of Hawaii Hall five feet deep, spread over an acre.[5]

Then there was the problem of evicting the people who were living on the land. The Mahele of 1848, which established a legal regime of private ownership in land, was still working its way into the social fabric. Possibly the Hawaiians working the area being tilled with dynamite felt that the usages of pre-Mahele tradition, which assured cultivators of the soil access to lands governed by overlords, were still in effect. In any case, Gilmore saw a problem to be solved before the campus could be readied. He reported to the regents in a letter of May 8, 1911:

> Rapid progress is being made in bringing the Puahia lands into service but . . . the Hawaiians now dwelling on the land are an obstacle. They are scattered over the land in about seven groups. One group tills the land. Some of them carouse and loaf a great deal.

A week later Gilmore wrote that "sanitary and moral conditions are not promoted by their presence" and asked that the attorney general be requested to "remove these people entirely from the land." In July the attorney general informed the regents of his "willingness to remove the squatters from the land . . . at once."

Building could now begin. Repeatedly, in meetings as early as 1908, the regents had discussed the need for a "comprehensive plan" for the future campus. In February 1909, Professor John Mason Young completed a design, ambitious in its inclusion of buildings for schools of law, medicine, veterinary science, and architecture, which by its geometry set the pattern of campus development. Young's design showed a large quadrangle aligned on an east-west axis running from what became University Avenue to Manoa Stream. In geometrical array, buildings were squared to the cardinal points of the compass, the whole strongly resembling the quadrangle of the campus at Cornell, where Young had last served.

Straight rows of rectangular buildings made no concession to the flowing contours of Manoa Valley. Streets and bypaths of the valley were seldom straight, but curved with the land. The layout of the new College, however, proclaimed it to be traditionally Western, using the land it required but not greatly responsive to its site in a valley of exceptional beauty. The campus buildings that were to come, columned neoclassical forms derived from the temples of Greece and Rome, asserted the culture of the Occident. And their orientation to the north, rather than to the axis of Manoa Valley, which guides the trade winds, failed to maximize the natural cooling of the campus. A pattern was set that would make for heavy dependence on air-conditioning when that technology became available in the years to come.

The first buildings at Manoa, however, were necessarily simple, with no relationship to classical temples. In 1910, a poultry shed and a cow barn with attached farm office were constructed on the new campus. Two "temporary" wooden structures were shifted from Young Street to serve as a shop and the chemistry laboratory. Students in agriculture heard their lectures on Young Street but did their "lab work" on the Manoa campus farm, helping with the clearing, plowing, and planting of the fields.

In preparation for the move to the new campus, in 1911 the legislature shortened the name of the College of Agriculture and Mechanic Arts of the Territory of Hawaii to what everyone already called it—the College of Hawaii. The change was more than merely euphonic. It implied a broadened institutional purpose, perhaps even the full university that Judge Cooper had envisaged. At the same session, $75,000 was appropriated for the first permanent building on the new campus. The cornerstone of that structure—known as Main Hall until renamed Hawaii Hall in 1922—was laid on January 22, 1912, to the accompaniment of lowing cattle wandering under the kiawe trees. Designed in part by the ubiquitous John Mason Young (his professorial tenure threatened for heading a firm that sought the construction contract), this first permanent building was to be the center of campus activities for many decades.

Main Hall provided lecture rooms for the 128 students enrolled in 1912 and offices for a faculty of twenty-three. It also housed the library; dining, sewing, and locker rooms; and laboratories for teaching about cement, electricity, farm machinery, dairy production, home economics, bacteriology, entomology, and zoology as well as the English, German, and French classes that helped provide a nucleus of liberal education.

The first College commencement was held on the steps of Main Hall, facing westward toward what would become the Quadrangle, on June 3, 1912. Baccalaureate degrees were conferred upon Leslie Clark, Louise Gulick, William S. Hartung, and Yook Fook Tong.

All classes were finally conducted on the new campus in September 1912. President Gilmore, repeatedly in conflict with the regents and perhaps exhausted by the rigors of creating a college with severely limited resources, resigned the following year. John Donaghho assumed the administrative burden until a new president was recruited in 1914. Like Gilmore, he was found in the eastern United States, at Yale. Arthur L. Dean, an assistant professor of chemistry there with his doctorate from Harvard, had the youthful energy needed to persevere through a presidency of thirteen years. It was said of him, "he found a pasture and left behind him a campus."

The Manoa site, as later described by the new president, must have made a sobering contrast to the Yale left behind. He had indeed come to a cow college.

> Immediately in front of Hawaii Hall was a strip of lawn, perhaps 75 feet wide. The wooden building moved up from Young Street, stained dark brown, was the only other building on . . . the campus. Dirt roads, which were impassable in wet weather, straggled through the grounds and disappeared among the trees and bushes in the direction of the farm. A neighboring dairyman paid a small monthly rate for the privilege of running his cows through the lands and they wandered about at all hours and places.[6]

The financial condition of the College was no less dismal. On reporting for duty, Dean found that his administration had at its disposal the sum of $6,269.88 for all purposes for which federal funds could not be used, and they were many. The annual grant from Washington, for example, could not cover administrative costs, so Dean had to teach several courses to qualify for funds to pay his own salary of $5,000.

Things turned even worse. A short-term drop in sugar prices temporarily reduced territorial tax revenues in 1914. Newly appointed Governor Lucius Pinkham, no admirer of the College, ordered severe budget cuts. The regents' report to the legislature, signed by Wallace R. Farrington as chairman, expressed sadness over the lack of support, mellowed by a sense of history.

> Appropriations necessary . . . were not available because of the enforced Territorial policy of retrenchment. The prospect was altogether discouraging. . . . The attitude of some of our people towards the College is remarkably similar to the position taken in States and Territories toward these endowed colleges of agriculture and mechanic arts forty years ago. This has made the situation at times rather discouraging because those associated with the College have apparently had to do over again that which the mainland leaders supposed settled years ago.[7]

In the meantime, the faculty and administration used their knowledge and cunning to make a campus out of the wilderness that had greeted Dean. Two remarkable pioneers stand out. One was Arthur Keller. To provide a decent road for the muddy campus, engineering professor Keller devised a research project: testing on campus different kinds of road material used by the local government. With machinery from the City and County of Honolulu and $5,000 from the territory for materials, he and his students laid down an all-weather road that came in to Hawaii Hall—freeing President Dean from the obligation of driving faculty members to campus on rainy days with his horse and buggy. Keller and his students then built a drainage system to carry off the Manoa rains that had frequently turned the campus into a quagmire.

The other memorable pioneer was Joseph Francis Charles Rock, a skilled, energetic, and resourceful botanist. His "Notes upon Hawaiian Plants with Descriptions of New Species and Varieties" was the first research publication of the College. In 1914 Rock was appointed to a faculty Buildings and Grounds Committee and asked to develop twenty acres of the campus into a garden. Over the next four years he collected from around the world the starts and seeds of a great variety of plants, about five hundred species in all, for ornamentation of the campus and the botanical instruction of its students.

Dean reported that plantings were so placed that the rarer specimens would not be displaced by future construction. Indeed, as the College developed, its flora beautified a campus not graced with exceptional architecture. Anniversaries of the school, visits of luminaries, and other special occasions were commemorated by planting trees. Before his death in 1962, Rock had gathered enough plants to create a campuswide botanical garden. Unfortunately, by that time, the flora was being pushed aside by buildings that did not begin to match its beauty.

Events changed the attitude of downtown doubters toward the school. In 1917, an upturn in sugar prices triggered by the nation's entry into World War I stimulated an interest in the College by Hawaii's sugar industry, which hitherto had not been among its enthusiasts. The College had recently added a bachelor's program in sugar technology, which attracted ten students in 1915 and another dozen the next year, comprising a fifth of the total enrollment. There was a corresponding reduction in the diversified agriculture program. Again, Wallace Farrington made things clear, this time in his 1917 report as chairman of the Board of Regents:

> It has been assumed that the moral obligation of any institution endowed by funds of the Federal government should be to lead the way toward "small farm" agriculture and away from the main corporation-controlled sugar industry of the Territory. Consequently there was, in the earlier days, indifference toward the sugar industry course, and special attention given to what might be termed a diversified agriculture course.[8]

That "indifference" was now corrected. With a shift in emphasis to sugar technology, the College's standing with decision makers within the territorial government improved markedly. For the biennium 1919–1921 its appropriation rose to $281,000, more than it had received from the legislature during the entire first decade of operation.

IMPACT OF A DISTANT WAR

During World War I, official Hawaii, like the rest of the nation, displayed strong anti-German feelings. The regents, concerned about any possible disloyalty on campus, directed President Dean to send a letter to all faculty members, probing their loyalty. Dean's letter asked if the recipient supported the "purpose of the United States as stated by President Wilson in his message to Congress on December 4, 1917"—a speech in which Wilson called for an end to antiwar talk. Nineteen of the twenty-one faculty members replied affirmatively. Elizabeth Matthews, assistant professor of household service, said she opposed America's entering the war but did not promote her beliefs in class. Maria Heuer, assistant professor of modern languages, wrote that she was a German citizen but was loyal only to her conscience and not to any government at war.

Meeting on December 14, the Board of Regents voted unanimously not to employ anyone holding allegiance to a nation at war with America. The next day Regents Charles R. Hemenway and Jennie R. Ashford changed their minds and requested reconsideration of the matter. Unable to get a unanimous vote, the board left the matter to President Dean. Regent Frederick Waldron, born in England and with a son serving in France, resigned in protest. Dean asked for Heuer's resignation and paid her $900 for the unfinished term of her contract. Matthews' contract was not renewed. German was not again taught at Manoa until 1927.

The board resolved to have the College aid the war effort by providing military training. Although the 1862 Morrill Act required land-grant schools to teach military tactics, Hawaii had no military program because the law also provided that colleges with enrollments under 150 did not have to hold military drills. President Dean wrote to the commanding general at Fort Shafter, requesting rifles, bayonets, ammunition, and a noncommissioned officer to train the students, but the Army could not spare the equipment. The College then tried to establish a Student Army Training Corps to offer military instruction for male students. To qualify, campuses had to provide cadet housing, and the regents hoped to get federal funds for barracks that would later serve as a badly needed dormitory. By the time the College got permission to start the program, however, the end of the war was anticipated. Barracks did not appear on campus until after the next world war.

BUILDING THE COLLEGE INTO A UNIVERSITY

Local support of Hawaii's college strengthened rapidly after World War I. The year 1919 was a milestone: for the first time the territorial appropriation to the school exceeded its federal grant. (Students still paid no tuition fees.) Increased enrollment in the new sugar technology program obviously pleased the industry and its proponents in the legislature. An additional $142,000 was appropriated for a chemistry, physics, and sugar technology building, later named Gartley Hall.

A development broader by far than the extension of an agricultural college to serve the chief industry of the territory was also instigated—a move to make the college a university, authorized to offer graduate degrees. Appropriately, the protagonist for change was a member of the first non-haole ethnic group that had come to the Islands in numbers, and the first to break into large-scale business and the professions. He was William Kwai Fong Yap, an assistant cashier with the Bank of Hawaii.

Yap was the father of eight sons and three daughters, and higher education was on his mind. In his autobiographical account of the origin of the University of Hawaii, he wrote of his desire to have his children benefit from an affordable education broader than that offered within the limited curriculum of the College of Hawaii: "I found that the question of providing my children with a college education was a problem not peculiar to me alone, but that thousands of other parents in the Territory had to face the same problem."[9]

Yap consulted with President Dean and Wallace Farrington, still chairman of the regents, who helped him draft a petition to the legislature requesting creation of a university on grounds that spoke to community interests and appealed to legislators:

> WHEREAS, there is great need of opportunities for a broader education for our young men and women to fit them for lives of the greatest value to Hawaii and our nation, and
> WHEREAS, these Islands are located at a point where the civilization and com-

> merce of the United States, the Orient and the Islands of the Pacific meet, and are therefore at the strategic point for a University unique in its opportunities, and WHEREAS, a University of broad scope and facilities should attract students from the Mainland and act as a promotion asset of the highest order. . . .

At its meeting of January 17, 1919, the Board of Regents "took the position that it was not prepared to press such a quest, but that if it were the desire of the people of the territory, the Board itself would give its support."[10]

Yap collected 438 signatures on his petition, including those of ex-Governor Walter Frear, Regents Farrington and Charles Hemenway, Gerrit Wilder, Charles Atherton, Harold Dillingham, and Charles W. Baldwin—all of them business and community leaders. Territorial Normal School principal Edgar Wood and McKinley High School principal M. M. Scott signed, as did several future regents. The list shows a diversity of ethnic surnames—Hawaiian, Caucasian, Chinese, and Japanese. One surprise was Dr. Syngman Rhee, then living on Oahu in political exile from Korea. Support, however, was far from universal. Yap complained that "seven of my best friends and the most influential citizens in Hawaii were not in accord with my plan . . . [and] refused to sign."[11] Edward P. Irwin editorialized in the *Pacific Commercial Advertiser* on February 26, 1919, that the time was not ripe.

> There is much more urgent need for other educational facilities now than there is for a university. . . . The expansion of vocational education in the public schools is a matter of obvious importance. Isn't it better to educate all the youth of the Territory along practical lines than a rather small number in calculus, Ovid and other branches of "higher education"?

In urging "practical" education, the newspaper spoke for the planter interest, which saw non-Caucasian youth as sugar plantation field hands and pineapple cannery workers. It did not, however, speak for the editorial writer himself. Irwin had already signed Yap's petition.

Regent Arthur Smith helped draft the enabling legislation. Senate Bill 76, a measure to create the University of Hawai'i, was introduced by Senator Charles E. King, a Kamehameha School alumnus and noted composer of Hawaiian songs, and seconded by G. P. Kamauoha. With strong backing by Senator John H. Wise, a future professor of Hawaiian at Manoa, and Education Committee chairman Stephen L. Desha, Sr. (editor of the newspaper *Ka Hoku o Hawaii*), S.B. 76 passed unanimously. In the House, the bill was guided to unanimous passage by other Hawaiian or part-Hawaiian legislators, including Henry L. Kawewehi and Henry J. Lyman, chairman of the Education Committee. Enactment came on April 29, 1919.

Senate Bill 76 set forth the purposes of the University in terms clearly indicating how they went beyond the scope of the College. The University of Hawai'i was being created, it said, to give:

William Kwai Fong Yap (above left) in 1919 successfully petitioned the legislature to expand the College of Hawaii into a university, the enabling act being supported by, among others, Senator John Wise (below left), who later taught Hawaiian at UH for twelve years. Arthur L. Dean (above right), whose presidency ran from 1914 to 1927, oversaw the transition from college to university. Charles E. Hemenway (facing camera), a regent for thirty years from 1910, is shown talking with President David A. Crawford (1929–1941).

> thorough instruction and conduct researches in and disseminate knowledge of agriculture, mechanic arts, mathematics, physical, natural, economic, political and social sciences, language, literature, history, philosophy, and such other branches of advanced learning as the Board of Regents may from time to time prescribe. . . . The standard of instruction shall be equal to that given and required in similar universities on the mainland of the United States.

Then, preserving an antidiscrimination proviso in the 1907 statute that had established the College, the legislative charter of the University declared that: "No person shall, because of sex, color or nationality, be deprived of the privileges of this institution." It was a provision that would be respected scrupulously.

Governor Charles J. McCarthy signed the bill into law on April 30, 1919, the day after it passed. Effective July 1, 1920, it gave the College more than a year to plan its transformation and recruit more faculty members. Yap had estimated costs at $32,000, and the legislature appropriated $35,000 for transformation expenses, in addition to the $104,000 already budgeted for running the school in the next biennium.

Anticipating the changeover, ten of the approximately two hundred students registering at Manoa in 1919 indicated that their goal was a bachelor of arts degree, which the new university would offer. Two were children of Yap: Charles, a sophomore, who registered as an agriculture major, and Ruth, a freshman, who later served as a mathematician on the faculty. In September 1920, when the University's first semester began, they were joined by brother David. Their father must have been pleased at the success of his efforts.

The University was now composed of two colleges. Programs in agriculture, sugar technology, home economics, and engineering were assigned to the new College of Applied Science, with Arthur Keller as dean. Arthur Andrews became dean of the new College of Arts and Sciences, which offered the bachelor of arts degree in a variety of fields. From the beginning, it had a marked orientation toward Pacific and Asian studies. In languages, for example, Chinese, Japanese, and Hawaiian could be studied, as well as French and Spanish—but not German.

Tuition continued to be free for residents and children of military families stationed in Hawaii, as had been the policy of the College. Nonresidents were assessed a charge of $25 per semester. Enrollment, still small, doubled to approximately four hundred. Faculty size increased to forty-four, including Professors Tasuku Harada and Tien Mu Wang, recruited to bolster instruction in Asian languages and literature. Ten of the forty-four were women, a proportion unusually large for American universities of the time.

The school's limited research capabilities quickly expanded to meet some of the needs of a university. In 1919 the legislature placed the Waikiki Aquarium under the regents, and the privately funded Cooke Laboratory of Marine Biology was built at

Waikiki. The regents approved institutional connections with other research agencies in Honolulu, first (in 1919) with the Bernice P. Bishop Museum, establishing reciprocal use of libraries, laboratories, and collections. Graduate students thus gained the right to work under the direction of museum staff members, a resource greatly helpful to scholarship while the University built up its own strength in research. Later, in 1930, would come a similar relationship with the Honolulu Academy of Arts. In 1924 the University accepted administrative responsibility for the research arm of the Hawaiian Pineapple Canners Association (later called the Pineapple Research Institute, or PRI for short) and its laboratory on the campus.

The delicate question of how, in a society that generally asserted the superiority of Caucasians, its public university should deal with students of Polynesian or Asian ancestry was met head on. President Dean told a faculty assembly in 1921 that the University was preparing students to "compete with members of the white community on an equal intellectual basis." If students of Japanese, Chinese, and Hawaiian parentage believed themselves to be unjustly treated while at the University, their influence later would be "detrimental." Dean urged faculty members to "use their influence in upholding democratic principles within the University."[12]

The student body reflected the ethnic variety in Hawaii's population, though not proportionately. Regents' reports to the legislature conspicuously tabulated enrollment by race. Of the approximately three hundred degree-seeking students enrolled in September 1922, one-third were Caucasian, half were of Oriental ancestry, somewhat over a tenth Hawaiian or part-Hawaiian. The 1926 enrollment of 574 showed almost exactly the same racial distribution—although the number of students of Japanese ancestry by then was double that of Chinese descent. The number of Hawaiians or part-Hawaiians on campus was sixty-five, or eighty-five if those not seeking degrees were included. (Eighty-five composed about 12 percent of the total enrollment; the percentage of Hawaiians and part-Hawaiians in the territory was then estimated at about 16.)

Campus attitudes on race may be inferred from student associations. From the beginning, leadership roles in the growing number of student organizations—the student government and newspaper, in debating, dramatic, and literary societies, and so forth—were as likely to be filled by nonhaole as by haole students. Religious group representation was less diverse. Beginning in 1921 a secretary of the Young Men's Christian Association was placed on campus, "without expense to the University through the generosity of interested members of the community." It would be some time before there was a recognized Buddhist presence, although from the beginning an appreciable number of students came from non-Christian families.

The program in military science and tactics unsuccessfully sought during the last months of World War I was established in the fall of 1921 with the organization of a Reserve Officers Training Corps unit. For many years directed by Colonel Adna G.

Clark, it became one of the most highly commended ROTC programs in the western United States. As at other land-grant schools, all male freshmen and sophomores of American citizenship and in good physical condition were required to participate. Compulsory military training would not be protested by Hawaii's students in any organized way until the Vietnam War, a half-century into the future.

The campus began to offer recreational opportunities. Students collected $20,000 for a swimming pool in 1920, raising the unrealized hope that the University of Hawai'i would become preeminent in a sport in which its students had a natural advantage. A portent of the actual shape of the athletic program to come appeared in 1921, however, when the football team met its first intercollegiate opponent, the University of Nevada. UH lost by two touchdowns, but an abiding fascination with gridiron contests against mainland schools was born.

During these formative years, it happened that advocates of a broad curriculum in the arts and sciences received encouragement from the national authority in their continuing debate with proponents of a vocational education focused on the needs of Hawaiian agriculture. In 1920 the federal commissioner of education sent investigators to survey the local schools. Starting from the premise that a major purpose of education was to stimulate a "wider range of thought and action" for the population, the survey team recommended that students in Hawaii, as elsewhere in America, be encouraged to develop career interests not only in agriculture but also in teaching, the law, medicine, languages, and research. Programs should be expanded. Indeed, the commissioner's report urged that "the University of Hawaii set for its ultimate goal the high purpose of becoming the recognized university of the Pan-Pacific States."[13]

That "ultimate goal" fired interest and ambition for the University, but first local needs had to be served. One was to provide a research facility for the agricultural programs supported by federal grants and expected by the territorial legislature. In 1921 old sugar lands at Waiakea, outside Hilo, were transferred to the University to serve as its first agricultural experiment station and first base of operations off the island of Oahu. For a number of reasons too complex for this brief history to address, the Waiakea project was not feasible. In 1929, the legislature finally responded to the University's repeated request for an alternative site by funding an experimental station at Kona, which productively studied coffee, macadamia nuts, and other tree crops. Another decade was needed fully to incorporate within the University the functions of the long-standing Hawaii Agricultural Experiment Station (see chapter 8).

The idea of serving the entire territory, an idea attractive both educationally and politically, sent President Dean and senior members of his faculty traveling among the islands to address or confer with farmers, church groups, teachers, businessmen —seemingly wherever they were invited. In mid-1921, an Extension Division was created to organize this activity, with entomology professor David Crawford as head. His motto for the division: "Making the Territory of Hawaii Our Campus." From

July 1922 faculty members gave regular talks on the Honolulu radio stations then beginning service. Broadcasts sent their lectures, however distorted in transmission, to listeners among the Islands.

In the meantime, basic campus facilities had to be provided. UH was destined to be a commuters' school, most of its students living in family homes, rented bedrooms, or private rooming houses, but it was deemed essential to house on campus at least some students coming from the Neighbor Islands or abroad. The first dormitory, a simple wooden building accommodating twenty-six men and a proctor and known familiarly as the "Boiler Factory" was built in 1921. Two years later a women's dormitory ("Chicken Inn") housed sixteen students and a matron. The cost was $36 per semester, with bedding supplied by the student. In 1921 a small cafeteria was erected on the western end of the campus. It provided lunch for thirty-seven cents, or a breakfast-dinner meal plan at $25 per month. The alternative eating place on campus was on the lanai of Hawaii Hall, where lunch was served by members of the newly formed Women's Faculty Club, assisted by student helpers.

For students and faculty staying on campus after sundown, movement became less hazardous when in 1923 the regents accepted the offer of Honolulu's government to install electric lights on the campus road and to supply at cost equipment to light up the area around Hawaii Hall. The illuminated campus was effectively doubled in size by the completion in 1925 of its first library building, later named George Hall. The new library provided more than books and study areas. Since the campus had neither auditorium nor gym, student dances were held, nine to midnight, in the library lobby, festooned with streamers and balloons.

As territorial appropriations permitted, the faculty and course offerings increased. In 1922, courses in business were introduced, including a "lab" in banking, offered downtown at the Bank of Hawaii. Classes in science and the liberal arts were expanded, especially in the English Department to help many students to make the transition from local dialects to "standard" English. The teaching of Hawaiian was early accepted as a special responsibility. Replying to a legislative inquiry, the regents in 1921 stated:

> It has been a part of the plan of the University of Hawaii to give instruction in the Hawaiian language. . . . [I]t will probably be desirable to include studies of the other Polynesian languages and the relationships of this whole group. The University should become the center for the study of Hawaiian and a strong effort made to preserve the language in its purity.[14]

The regents budgeted $1,000 for a part-time instructor in Hawaiian. Frederick W. Beckley was appointed, and in 1921 he began teaching an introductory course. In the next biennium, three more year-long courses were added, covering *mele* and legends, as well as language structure. Beckley, now full-time, in 1926 was succeeded

The new University at Manoa was photographed by an Army airplane in 1924, showing a campus largely devoted to work in argiculture. Hawaii Hall, gleaming white toward the center, flanked by Gartley and George Halls, began to form the Quadrangle. Hawaii Hall was the heart of the campus. In it, in addition to classrooms and offices, the campus library—and its patrons—were crowded (as the 1914 photo, left, demonstrates). Along its side, physical culture classes in 1924 (top, facing page) exerted themselves. Before its entrance, graduates received their diplomas. The 1919 graduating class of five (seated in the front row facing the steps) was addressed by white-bearded ex-Governor

Sanford Dole and Regent Wallace Farrington (standing).

Difficult to see in the aerial view is the first men's dormitory (right), known as the "Boiler Factory," and a similar dorm for women, "Hale Aloha" or simply "Chicken Inn." The cost: $36 per semester, bedding supplied by the student. Capacity: twenty-one men; sixteen women.

by John Wise, a sponsor in the territorial Senate of the legislation creating the University, as full professor. In 1925 a credit course in Hawaiian history was offered in tandem by thirty-two speakers from the campus and town, led by E. S. C. Handy, Polynesian specialist at the Bishop Museum (see chapter 4).

By the end of Dean's presidency in 1927, the University was pushing against its constraints. It was not yet limited in land, for the 1925 legislature had appropriated $500,000 to buy from the Bishop Estate acreage across University Avenue. The limit was space under roof for a student body approaching a thousand and a staff of more than sixty. Reporting to the regent's perennial chairman C. R. Hemenway, Dean said: "We have reached the limit of our space for classroom and laboratory purposes. . . . There is no space where [the student body] can be gotten together for any kind of a public address, except outdoors."[15]

DAVID L. CRAWFORD AND THE POLITICS OF EXPANSION

A modest construction program would soon supply the most urgent building needs of the campus, but not under the presidency of Arthur Dean. After thirteen years in office, Dean resigned in 1927 to become director of the Pineapple Research Institute. He was succeeded by entomologist David L. Crawford, who at thirty-eight was the youngest university president in the United States. During Crawford's long tenure the Manoa campus was to attain its development into a university in fact as well as in name.

In his first report to the regents and the territorial legislature, Crawford addressed the criticism that the University continued to receive—usually at second or third hand—that too many of its students were non-Caucasians.

> Already this territory is attracting into higher education a surprisingly large percentage of its youth. Notwithstanding the fact that some people seem to view with alarm this 'rising tide' of university attendance by certain racial groups, it is my firm conviction that herein is the surest road to a future of social and economic well-being for Hawaii.[16]

Reports to the legislature continued to display prominently the racial composition of the student body. Approximately half of the students enrolled in degree programs in the late 1920s were still of Oriental ancestry, with those of Japanese descent now far outnumbering students of Chinese lineage. However, the total enrollment, including students not registered as degree candidates, showed a majority of Caucasians and a small but growing number of Hawaiians. It would be some decades before increasing racial intermarriage made such listings of questionable significance. In pre–World War II Hawaii, the statistics served to demonstrate that the University was abiding by the directive of its charter not to deprive any person "of the privileges of this institution" because of color or nationality.

The Class of 1926

Robert M. Kamins

By the mid-1920s the Manoa campus had developed the essential elements of an American college of that period. It had a student body slowly approaching a thousand, a faculty of more than fifty, a proper library (later named George Hall), a student organization (ASUH), a newspaper *(Ka Leo),* a yearbook *(Ka Palapala),* an alma mater to sing ("In Green Manoa Valley"), a school band, school colors (green and white), and a football team ("The Fighting Deans"). Like other land-grant schools, it had an ROTC program, required for able-bodied underclassmen. Women had to take physical education courses.

The graduating class of 1926, representative of the first decade of the university, showed a diversity that might have surprised those who doubted a public university could attract capable students from the territory's range of social backgrounds. The first surprise was the number of women—exactly a third of the fifty-four graduates that year. Then there was the varied ethnicity. To judge from their names, photographs, and biographical references in *Ka Palapala,* the senior class included twenty-four Caucasians, fourteen of Japanese ancestry, ten Chinese, and six Hawaiians.

Eight of the haole students had come from mainland schools, perhaps accompanying their parents to military posts or civilian jobs in the territory. Most of the Japanese American students were graduates of McKinley High School in Honolulu, which strongly encouraged its pupils to prepare for college, and Hilo High School. Five of the class came from Maui High. Seven—one Hawaiian, the others haole—were Punahou graduates. Two, both Asian Americans, had come to Manoa from the adjacent campus of Mid-Pacific Institute. The single graduate from Kauai High School was Iwao Miyake, who was to have a long career in the physics faculty. Among the graduates who had attended Punahou School was Beatrice Himler Krauss, future ethnobiologist of distinction, who was beginning a lifelong association with the Manoa campus.

The small student body energetically filled all the roles felt required at a self-respecting college. In addition to student government (ASUH, a student council, and class officers), there were a score of campus organizations to be staffed, including dramatic, literary, and debating societies; ROTC drill and rifle teams; career interest clubs such as agriculture, pre-medical, and engineering; and social groups (eleven, including Theta Alpha Phi, coed, the only Greek-letter society on campus, and Ka Pueo for women and Hui Lokahi for men). There were athletic teams: nine for men, three for women; fencing was coeducational. Rough-and-tumble contests, such as an annual tug-of-war, a sandbag relay race, and a "flag rush" in which male freshmen attempted to tear down a banner from the top of a graphite-coated pole defended by sophomores, had been toned down after the accidental death of freshman George Paul in 1923, following a tussle on the steps of Hawaii Hall.

With so many campus organizations, students filled multiple roles. The same faces

(continued)

(continued)

look out again and again from the pages of *Ka Palapala.* Beatrice Krauss appears on the ASUH executive committee, as president of the Dramatic Club and vice-president of the Adelphai social and service club, as program chairman of Hawaii Quill (the literary club), librarian of the Agriculture Club, and member of the fencing team. She had edited *Ka Palapala* the preceding year.

Beatrice Himler Krauss

Equally prominent was junior classman Shunzo Sakamaki, later to serve as professor and dean at Manoa. Young Sakamaki, besides his extracurricular life as debater (winning against a visiting Oxford debate team), as student actor, secretary of the Student Council, and *Ka Leo* staffer, played the cymbals in the school band. He edited the 1926 *Ka Palapala.*

Even at this early stage of Manoa's history, intercollegiate football was already important—perhaps then more intensely followed by the students of a campus seeking its identity than by townspeople. The season of 1925–1926 was a good one for the Fighting Deans, coached by Otto Klum. Players were all local students; the athletic scholarship was not yet known in Hawaii. Play began in the fall with six victories, in which the UH team held military and town opponents to a single touchdown.

Then came the real competition, against three mainland schools. The first game was with Occidental College, reigning champions of the Southern California Conference, played on Thanksgiving Day 1925 in the Los Angeles Coliseum before a crowd estimated at fifty thousand. In downtown Honolulu, seventeen hundred students, faculty, staff, and other fans crowded into the Princess Theatre to hear the game described over shortwave radio. What they heard through the crackling static was indeed electrifying: the University gained its first mainland victory, 13 to 0!

When the team returned a week later, its ship was greeted by students and faculty members cheering the Fighting Deans, a new football power. There followed a parade to Iolani Palace, where the victors were congratulated by Governor Farrington.

More triumphs followed at home. The Deans whitewashed Colorado State, leaders of the Rocky Mountain Conference, 41 to 0. The season ended on New Year's Day with a victory over Washington State, 20 to 11. During the entire season the UH team had allowed only 17 points, while scoring 333.

Ka Palapala saluted the team, particularly its backfield, the "Four Horsemen of the Pacific," composed of William Wise (from McKinley), Eddie Fernandez and "Pump" Searle (from Punahou), and John D. Morse (the kicker, high school unknown): "The members of the famous quartet have now disbanded, but their exploits on local as well as foreign gridirons will forever be cherished in the memory of every lover of football."

Forever? Not likely, even in the collective memory of football fans. However, for a generation of University students this team, outweighed by its mainland rivals but wonderfully elusive from blocks or tackles, was recalled as the "Undefeated Champions of 1925."

A policy of keeping higher education affordable to families throughout Hawaii's social structure was supported in the territorial capitol by the University's leading advocate. The regents in 1928 proposed to impose tuition fees applicable to local residents, but the plan was stopped by Wallace Farrington, then serving as governor of the territory.

When in 1930 the school began its second decade as a university, the administration viewed its future with justifiable optimism. Space for growth was assured: at Christmas time in 1929, at the close of his term, Governor Farrington had by executive order set aside for it a 190-acre tract adjoining the farm at the far end of the campus. Academic acceptance had been achieved: accreditation by the Association of American Universities in 1928 meant that UH degrees and course credits would be generally recognized throughout the academic world. Its first doctoral program, in tropical agriculture, was in preparation. Mainland recruitment was adding graduates of leading universities to the faculty. Student enrollment well exceeded one thousand, and the number of degrees granted annually topped one hundred—numbers betokening success to the legislature and other sources of funding. Those numbers would be swelled in 1931 by the creation of the Teachers College through a merger of the Territorial Normal School with the University.

President Crawford, in his 1930 report to the regents, pondered on the expanding role of universities, including his own, in a democracy.

> The modern American university finds itself under obligations to perform more than the original function of educating a small fraction of the youth of the state. In the first place, that fraction has greatly increased until it begins to appear that higher education has become a part of the mass education program of the country, rather than the privilege of the few.

That expansionist's view of the proper scope of public education was then being contradicted by a committee appointed by Governor Lawrence M. Judd, successor to Farrington, but financed by the Honolulu Chamber of Commerce. The committee's report, written by consultant Dr. Charles A. Prosser, the head of a technical school in Minnesota, sharply opposed expanding programs of public schools at any level, except for vocational education. For the University, it recommended that the number of students in the arts and sciences be frozen for five years and the construction of campus buildings be curtailed.

In a prophetic rebuttal of the policy of restriction advocated by the Prosser Committee, Crawford's report continued:

> Lawyers, doctors, dentists, engineers, architects . . . now come chiefly from the universities, which has required the development at very great expense of professional schools. . . . Hawaii has not gone so far as the states in this broad development of its university but it is on its way.

That way was to be long and bumpy, as the further development of the University was slowed by the Great Depression and then halted during Hawaii's consuming involvement in the world war that followed.

DEPRESSION YEARS

The Great Depression that began in 1929 with a Wall Street crash came late to the Islands and in diminished force. Banks in the territory did not fail; there was no panic. Federal military expenditures helped offset declines in sugar, pineapple, and tourism. Nevertheless, tax revenues of the territorial government, on which the University depended for two-fifths of its budget, began to drop.

The University shared in the fiscal retrenchment that followed when the 1932 legislature cut its appropriation by $210,000—more than 20 percent. The appropriation for the biennium 1933–1935 "was scarcely more than half of what had been provided . . . two years earlier," President Crawford reported to the regents. Federal grants were reduced by a fourth. Austerity was imposed on the campus. Since salaries were the largest element in the budget, significant reductions were sought from the staff. Faculty members volunteered to accept a 10 percent cut in order to prevent the firing of their newest colleagues, who had not yet established any claim to tenure. The administration accepted the offer, then cut the highest salaries by additional amounts. Furthermore, those who taught in the summer sessions, as a large proportion of the faculty did, would receive no additional pay for that service. Outright severance was minimized, but several faculty and professional staff were "urged" to take a year off for advanced study.

The administration tried not to lose promising academicians recruited by Crawford himself during mainland trips. In his 1931 report the president noted that only twenty-five of the staff of approximately two hundred bore degrees from Hawaii. The rest had been trained outside the territory, and generally at highly respected schools: fifteen at the University of California; eleven each at Stanford, Yale, and Wisconsin; ten at Harvard; six at Chicago; and so forth.

Nor were the president and regents easy about imposing tuition fees, thus far required only of nonresidents, on local students. Nevertheless, in 1930 a tuition charge of $15 per semester ($40 for nonresidents) was set, this time without objection by the governor. In 1933 tuition was increased to $50 for residents and nonresidents alike. The portion of total University income derived from student fees rose from 10 to 30 percent, a degree of dependence on student payments never again experienced. Crawford justified the tuition increase in a way that reminded the community of the broad benefits conferred by the University:

> Students are required to pay fees amounting to practically one half of their instruction. This is a higher percentage than is usually placed upon the students

> by state universities, but I believe that it is an equitable and proper arrangement, for the Territory and the student share about equally in the benefits that come from his education.[17]

The administration cast about for extramural support and other ways of continuing to operate with declining government appropriations. Welcome grants from the Rockefeller Foundation helped support research in race relations, and the Carnegie Endowment for International Peace paid the salaries of visiting professors. Grants and donations from local sources were still negligible.

Cost-cutting in the campus physical plant was the economy most readily available. Construction stopped, except for privately funded projects. A men's dormitory and social center, badly needed, was provided when the Atherton family paid for the building across University Avenue that bears the name of Charles Atherton, a signer of the 1919 petition to create the University. A private facility on its own land, Atherton House functioned as a part of the campus from the time of its planning, which involved the University and the YMCA, as well as the Athertons.

Private funds also paid for campus embellishments. Contributions of a dollar, largely by students, faculty, and alumni, raised the $2,664 needed to build the Founders' Gate across University Avenue, erected to signalize the union between the University and the Normal School in 1931. (The physical connection was more evident then as the two sides of the gate spanned a narrow University Avenue. When the street was widened from two to six lanes, the halves of the gate were moved to their present locations, where in today's frenzied traffic they stand little noticed.) At the dedication of this memorial in September 1933, the thousand people in attendance, including many alumni as well as President Crawford and Governor Lawrence Judd, were greeted by student body president O. A. Bushnell.

At the opposite side of the campus, Varney Circle with its fountain was added in 1934, paid for by the Normal School's class of 1929 and by subsequent classes after the school became part of UH. A bronze plaque on the fountain's rim memorializes Ada Susan Varney, longtime history teacher in the old Normal School.

Andrews Outdoor Theatre, for many graduating classes the verdant, and frequently rainy, place of their commencement exercise, was completed in 1935 at a cost to the University of $5,000 for materials. Labor, valued at ten times that amount, provided by the Federal Emergency Relief Administration, transformed what had been a gully used as a refuse dump into a chief amenity of the campus.

Free labor, this time by inmates of Oahu Prison, also contributed to the construction of storm drains, stone retaining walls, sidewalks, and the like. "By the help of prisoners assigned for service on our campus we have made a good deal of progress in grading the land around the Teachers College building. The unsightly hill near the entrance gate on University Avenue has been completely removed and much of the area turfed."[18] Prisoners also maintained the campus lawns.

The 1930s

Willard Wilson

The year 1930 and the decade following it marked the real changing of the small, agriculturally oriented college into a bustling embryonic university. This was marked, it is true, by the assimilation of the old Territorial Normal School (in 1931) as a "Teachers College." . . . It was in 1930 that the regular enrollment first passed the 1,000 mark. But more importantly, and happily, the '30s were marked by the coalescing and growth of a truly unusual and stimulating faculty.

Particularly was this true in what had become inevitably the heart of the University—the College of Arts and Sciences, which for some years (1930 to 1939) enjoyed as its dean the brilliant, acerbic, stimulating political scientist, Dr. William George, who was affectionately and respectfully known among his faculty friends by the Hawaiian equivalent of George, "Keoki." . . .

The English department, at that time and thereafter, quite naturally, the largest in the institution, was also one of the strongest and most varied. Of the old guard headed by the chairman, Dr. A. L. Andrews, there were several who had come in the mid-twenties or before: Charles Neil, a perceptive instructor from Yale; Dr. Laura Schwartz (Korn), who had earned her doctorate from Stanford at a phenomenally early age; and Gregg M. Sinclair—a man of versatile background who after a distasteful sampling of the banking business in Minnesota had taken a graduate degree at Columbia University and spent some years in Japan, where he acquired a feeling for the Orient that was to have a profound effect on the University in the years to come. The younger contingent was made up of Carl Stroven, of Stanford, who was to develop the first true concentrations in American and Pacific literature and for many years later was University librarian; Willard Wilson (who certainly was to have a varied career in teaching and administration in the University community); and Blake Clark—an ingratiating southerner from Nashville, who was in later years an editor of the *Reader's Digest* and a business tycoon in Washington, D.C. Other bright and hardworking young men were added during the decade—Charles Bouslog, a 19th century specialist; Marshall Stearns, the jazz critic; and others. . . .

In economics, the strident and authoritarian voice of Merton Cameron resounded across the Old Quad; but he was seconded by Harold Hoflich, later of the universities of California and Arizona, and William Taylor, who was to go on and make a controversial but brilliant record in Washington in the field of international public finance. Political science was the domain of Dean George and of an encyclopedic young protege he had brought from the University of Washington, Paul S. Bachman. In chemistry, there were the two Drs. Bilger—Leonora already having attracted national attention by her analytical work

From Willard Wilson, *Professor's Briefcase: Wit and Wisdom of Willard Wilson,* edited by Amos P. Lieb, Elizabeth B. Carr, and Thomas Nickerson (Honolulu: University of Hawai'i, Office of University Relations and Development, 1975).

(continued)

(continued)

with Dr. Arthur L. Dean (former president) on the esters of chalmoogra oil, that was then thought to have curative powers on leprosy. . . .

Willard Wilson

In history, Ralph Kuykendall worked away steadily at his monumental Hawaiian history. The department also included Don Rowland, later of USC and a Latin American historian at heart, and most important of all for University purposes, Shunzo Sakamaki—brilliant young debater on the University of Hawaii team that met and defeated Oxford in the first intercollegiate debate of the University in Honolulu in 1927 [1925] when he was an undergraduate, and one of the first University graduates of Japanese ancestry to earn a doctorate at Columbia.

The Art department had Huc Luquiens, dean of all Hawaii's artists at the time, whose delicate and perceptive etchings are now collectors' items; Henry Rempel, an unconventional but exciting young chap never short on ideas, whose exploits ran the gamut from arguments with local traffic police to the designing of the controversial Varney Circle fountain with its *tiki* motifs that still adorns our campus; and Ben Norris—probably most versatile of all in style and medium. . . .

[T]here was the colorful and elegant Louis Pecker, the French department in one man, who also at one time had affixed to the office door the official seals of the consulates of France, Italy, Belgium and another that slips the mind, and who could be counted on to add color and mystery to the academic procession at Commencement time by appearing in full dress uniform with tricorn hat, gold epaulettes, and a full row of decorations. There was Maria (Mrs. Arthur) Hormann, wife of the local Lutheran minister and beloved teacher of German to scores of devoted students, ably abetted later by Dr. Bertha Mueller, translator of Goethe and specialist in scientific German. In psychology, there was Thayne Livesay, later to serve as head of the Summer Session, and still later for many years as dean of the Arts [and Sciences] College, and a bright young clinical psychologist, later eminent in national circles, Dr. Lowell Kelly. Stanley Porteus and Marjorie Babcock were adding national lustre within the Psychological Clinic. Sociology had for a time the famed Chicago teacher and writer, Romanzo Adams, followed by his disciple Andrew Lind, who even then was writing assiduously and without whose books no study of Hawaii's people is today complete. . . . Toward the late '30s John Embree, one of the most brilliant of the young American anthropologists of his time, was for a short while a stimulating presence.

In the physical sciences, Dr. Harold Palmer—geologist and general science teacher—presided over his carefully catalogued collection of rocks and volcanic bombs, and useful workshop items filed in scores of Tuxedo pipe tobacco cans that filled numerous shelves. John Wesley Coulter, geographer of the Pacific, was well on his way to becoming a world authority.

(continued)

(continued)

There were also scientists in the Agriculture College whose work was increasingly known and who rarely entered a classroom: Charles Bice for his amazing improvements in the poultry industry and control of disastrous diseases; Louis Henke for work on cattle feed; Harold Wadsworth for his contributions to general agricultural practices, such as irrigation and diversified cropping. Carey D. Miller, peripatetic and insistent dietician, was tracking down relentlessly the deficiencies of island diet leading to high incidence of tooth decay, and supplying her share of faculty gossip by stories of the doings of her white rats which she thoughtfully named for faculty members and deans.

The people "over across the road" in Teachers College were busily preparing scores of teachers annually to go into the schools of the Islands . . . [including] a crop of young irreconcilables such as Robert Clopton, sticking pins into pet theories and even needling the normally imperturbable Dean Wist with his cigarette holder akimbo. On the fringe of the academic, though exerting a disproportionate influence on students and townfolk alike, was Arthur Wyman, dynamic skin-and-bones director of the University of Hawaii Theatre, producing on the Farrington Hall stage all sorts of plays . . . some of very high quality, and some unbelievably bad, but most of them interesting and well patronized.

But the amazing and wonderful thing about the whole University in those growing years was the fact that the faculty members all knew one another—and hence they were working together at the common chore of educating young men and women. Everyone knew "Proc" Klum, the football coach, and if "one of his boys" was in trouble, Proc would appear at the office of the concerned professor to discuss the case. "He's not goofing off—the boy is just a big dumb ox," he would say. "But did you see the block that he threw on that St. Mary's guard last week? He's scared of you, Doc. Why don't you talk to him and see if you can straighten him out?"

There was good, honest, and brilliant teaching that went on constantly around the campus. There was a feeling of burgeoning destiny, of a thing that was being born and of the hard necessity obligatory on the University to assist the process. The faculty was young—it took a young and adventurous type to leap the Pacific and come to the untried school. But also these were the "depression years" and most of the young instructors and even older professors were grateful for a solid though underpaid job that would provide groceries and a weekly nip of *okolehao,* if one were so inclined, for a party. It was a good, tightly woven, and hard-working faculty, as the record of its students and subsequent productivity of its graduates themselves proved. It was a good place to be and work because the people were fun to work with, and the school was growing in purpose and solidarity of accomplishment.

In 1932, when the deep depression was beginning to affect finances of the Territory, the faculty began discussing the matter. When it became obvious that the depression had hit Hawaii to such a devastating extent that it was going to be necessary for the University budget to be reduced drastically, the faculty indicated to a harried [President] Dave Crawford that

(continued)

(continued)

they would prefer that he administer an across-the-board cut of 10 percent rather than drop from the staff the recent arrivals who had no claim to tenure. The fact that there was not yet any firm system for securing and assuring tenure probably had a reinforcing effect on the vote!

Those days, however, were golden days, whether seen through an idealistic haze or not, for we were all for the most part truly busy at our job, and also generally we knew what the job was. It is from this period more than any other that students now [in the 1950s] return to thank their professors for what they fancy they gained from the classroom.

By 1938, with the construction of a Social Science Building (later Crawford Hall), the quadrangle that was the heart of the Manoa campus for the next quarter century had been formed. The "Quad," still actually a horseshoe formed by Hawaii, Dean, Gartley, George, and Crawford halls, presented an architectural harmony that the University would retain until the building boom after statehood. The five gleaming white buildings of reinforced concrete, flat-roofed and unpretentiously neoclassical, were all low-rise structures. Against the background of green provided by the visible slopes of Manoa Valley, for a time the straight-lined Quad gave a sense of connection, of quiet and harmony, for the people of the campus.

For more architectural variety, and the livelier sounds of out-of-class campus life, behind the Quad there was the Union Building, also built in 1938. It provided a cafeteria, lounges, and offices for the student newspaper, *Ka Leo,* the Associated Students of the University of Hawai'i (ASUH), and the student council. Students, exhorted by a series of ASUH presidents, contributed $12,000 while faculty, alumni, and the Women's Campus Club gave $10,000. The rest of its $85,000 cost was contributed by regents for the building that in 1940 was renamed after Charles Hemenway, who had retired after thirty years of service on the board.

MERGER WITH TEACHERS COLLEGE

In 1931, one of the deepest years of the Depression, the University was expanded substantially by merger with the Territorial Normal School. An option in education and psychology had been offered at Manoa for a decade; the first University catalog (1922) showed one education faculty member and listed twenty-two students in that field. By 1930 more than half of the undergraduate degree candidates were in education programs, most of them preparing for teaching positions in secondary schools.

Training of elementary school teachers was the function of the Normal School. Merger with the Manoa campus had been recommended by the 1920 federal survey

Construction of the Manoa campus almost stopped during the Great Depression in the 1930s. Exceptions were projects for which the Federal Emergency Relief Administration provided the manpower: Varney Circle (1934), showing the old Farrington Hall in the background, and Andrews Outdoor Theatre (1935), for a half century the campus venue for convocations and other large gatherings.

Library congestion had been relieved for a time by the construction of George Hall in 1925. A balcony facing the Quadrangle was a favorite location, as for these women students ranged in the campus dress of the early 1930s.

The 1936 aerial view of the campus shows the Quadrangle in left-center complete except for Crawford Hall. Across University Avenue to the far left is Wist Hall. Klum Gym, Andrews Outdoor Theatre, and a few other buildings still make no substantial encroachment on the agricultural fields and farm facilities on the right (Diamond Head direction) area of the campus.

report and then by the Prosser study of 1929. Normal School principal Benjamin O. Wist opposed the idea until, frustrated because he could not get degree-granting authority, he compromised by politicking to retain some control over the teacher-preparation program. The 1931 legislature merged the two schools, creating a Teachers College under the "jurisdiction and management" of the regents but requiring the University to "obtain, as far as possible, the approval of the department of public instruction" on curricular matters. Property of the Normal School, including its new building across from the UH campus (the present Wist Hall) was transferred to the University. Normal School faculty members were appointed to the UH for a year; Wist was named dean of Teachers College—TC, as it was soon referred to.[19]

The merger came just as the University was experiencing the severe budget cuts already described and the new college took much of the blow. President Crawford announced that, while a proposed limit on the size of the overall student body had been rejected, in "Teachers College a more or less rigid limit to enrollment is being fixed in order that we may adjust supply to demand in this profession, which right now is suffering locally from a surfeit of candidates for jobs which do not exist."[20] The college budget was cut 60 percent and its faculty by half.

Wist accepted enrollment quotas determined by the anticipated needs of the public schools. Hubert Everly, a TC student in the 1930s and later dean of education, says that the college kept its quotas strictly: "If they had a quota of 60, . . . number 61 was transferred to Arts and Sciences."[21] Limits on enrollment enabled Wist to require higher academic standards for admission than those of the other two UH colleges. TC students who received poor grades in their first two years were denied further enrollment. Many transferred to Arts and Sciences or Applied Science, enabling Professor Bruce E. White later to claim that the "net result is that the quality of Teachers College students at the University of Hawaii is superior to that of those in the other colleges."[22]

RECOVERY

By the close of the 1930s the worst of the Great Depression was behind; consequently things were again looking up at the Manoa campus. Enrollment regained and surpassed its 1931 level, in 1940 approaching three thousand. By then about one-fifth of territorial high school graduates annually entered UH as freshmen, along with a score or more from Punahou and other local private schools and another score or two from the mainland and abroad.

Manoa students continued to be sustained by employment programs developed during the Depression. Approximately one of five had a campus job, mostly under the federal National Youth Act, which paid up to $15 a month to undergraduates for work in the library, assisting in laboratories, delivering campus mail, and the like.

Territorial scholarships exempting students from the $100 annual tuition fee helped another score or two each year to make their way through college. A few were assisted by a growing but still small number of privately endowed scholarship funds: one for students of Chinese ancestry; the Prince Fushimi fund for Japanese students; the Daughters of the American Revolution scholarships, to be given "if possible to a girl of Revolutionary or early American ancestry."

The academic staff grew modestly. Each spring President Crawford made a recruiting trip to San Francisco and New York, where he interviewed candidates selected by the University departments and research and service units. By 1940 the faculty had gained stalwarts who would serve for many years, including Bruce White, a future dean of Teachers College, and others commemorated by the campus buildings now bearing their names: philosopher Charles Moore; historians Ralph Kuykendall and Shunzo Sakamaki; engineer W. J. ("Jasper") Holmes.

The largest growth was in the English Department, which in addition to its traditional function of helping students to write, was made responsible for improving their speech. Charles E. Bouslog, recruited as a scholar of literature, found that half of the courses he was assigned were in speech improvement—displacing the local pidgin spoken by many students with standard American English.

In this endeavor, the University joined the territorial Department of Public Instruction, which over the preceding fifteen years had established a system of linguistically segregated schools. Students who qualified could enter an English Standard school (such as Roosevelt, the public high school closest to the Manoa campus) while others went to schools where pidgin might be acceptable. By the end of the 1930s, UH had assumed responsibility for ensuring that its baccalaureates could speak properly. Professor Bouslog recalls: "A board sat to examine all candidates for graduation who had not passed, or been excused from, a speech class. One could be sent back. . . ."

Efforts at dialect correction at Manoa were redoubled after a survey, ordered by a committee chaired by Joseph R. Farrington, found that only 14 percent of freshmen applying to the University in 1939 and 1940 had "typical American speech."[23] A concentrated attack on atypical speech was to continue until the 1960s, when the state Department of Public Instruction assumed that responsibility.

Programs begun during the lean years of the Depression gained support and momentum. The curriculum in nursing, started experimentally after an appeal in 1932 for UH to train public-health nurses, gained a secure place in Manoa's program. Training in social work, initiated in 1936 for the staffs of local agencies, in 1940 was offered as a year's course of graduate study, laying the way for a School of Social Work in 1942.

Improving economic conditions also helped foster the ambitious plan of English professor Gregg M. Sinclair to establish within the University a center for Asian philosophy and literature that would commingle scholarship from both sides of the Pacific Ocean. Garnering support on and off campus, Sinclair in 1936 persuaded the administration and regents to create an Oriental Institute. Dean William H. George endorsed Sinclair's vision—"It is confidently expected that the Institute will be a potent force for international understanding and peace in the Pacific."[24] Financial backing gathered by Sinclair in the next four years made the vision seem attainable. In 1940 the program to establish UH as a leading center for Asian studies seemed assured, but the approach of war in the Pacific abruptly aborted the institute. Its reincarnation as the East-West Center was not to occur until Hawaii became a state, years after Sinclair had retired from the presidency of the University.

CRAWFORD LEAVES

The long and constructive presidency of David Crawford, spanning fourteen turbulent years between the approach of the Great Depression and the attack on Pearl Harbor, ended unhappily for him. The root causes of his forced resignation late in 1941, carefully unaddressed in the minutes of the Board of Regents, were revealed only by a legislative investigation.

The roster of the board was mostly new, following enactment of a territorial statute that increased its number from eight to nine but dropped the president from membership. Its minutes reveal an increasing involvement in matters in which it had formerly merely concurred with actions of the administration, notably in faculty appointments and setting budget priorities. Crawford complained that members of his staff and faculty were being summoned by regents to discuss complaints that should have come to him for action. Whether this behavior reflected disenchantment with Crawford's judgment, or a feeling that the growing University needed a different leadership, or merely a greater inclination of the board to interfere with administrative action is uncertain, but a pattern was set of rejecting or deferring action on his recommendations.

When Samuel Northrup Castle joined the Board in May 1941, its rift with the president quickly became a chasm. Castle, member of a prominent and wealthy *kamaaina* family, brought with him a source of reports on campus matters through his close relationship with chemistry professor Leonora Bilger. (He lived with Mrs. Bilger and her husband Earl, also a member of the Chemistry Department.) The new regent criticized Crawford's administration, leading to the suggestion that Castle provide the board with a bill of particulars against the president. Minutes of their June 25 meeting record one accusation—deceitfulness.

> In the short time I have been a member of this board I have been impressed by one thing. . . . Statements are repeatedly made by the Executive Officer which are

> not factual. The board *acts* on the basis of the statements made. [He then gave several examples concerning actions on personnel and budgetary matters.]

Board minutes record Crawford's rebuttal, but no action was then taken.

Castle quickly gained positions of influence, as secretary of the board (who set its agenda and edited its minutes) and as Finance Committee chair. When Crawford presented his budget proposal for the next fiscal year, that committee made substantial changes. His proposal for new appointments was tabled by the Finance Committee. When Crawford requested approval for his annual recruiting trip, on Castle's motion the request was deferred for discussion in executive session.

Minutes of the board do not report on that closed meeting in September 1941, but the record of its next open meeting, on October 2, noted that "President Crawford withdrew after presenting to the Board a letter stating that he would not be available for reappointment next year." Crawford's letter of resignation said in part: "I have contemplated for several years resigning after fifteen years. I have made this decision with no sense of having failed in my duties."

The *Honolulu Star-Bulletin* responded to the announcement of Crawford's severance with a front-page story and a leading editorial (October 8 and 9, 1941).

> IT NEEDS VENTILATION . . . For months it has been no particular secret that a minority of the present board of regents was sharply critical of his regime. That minority has become a majority with sufficient suddenness to require explanation.

An explanation was shortly sought by the territorial legislature. Acting on the motion of Senator Joseph R. Farrington (son of Wallace R. Farrington and himself a former editor of the Honolulu Star-Bulletin), the Senate called the parties to testify behind closed doors, which were readily penetrated by reporters. First, Crawford spoke, "without bitterness . . . or attacks on personalities on the Board of Regents."[25] When, however, the testimony of regents Keppeler and Castle was taken by Crawford as a personal attack, he struck back in a long statement to the Senate on regental interference:

> I have objected to their inquisitional and unfriendly attitude in questioning individual staff members. . . . [T]he decline in morale was greatly accelerated when S. N. Castle came upon the scene, for it appears that this introduced an additional source of fear on the part of those staff members who are *persona non grata* to that fellow faculty member [read Professor Leonora Bilger] with whom he appears to be on especially friendly terms. . . . Mr. Castle is as unfit to be a member of the governing board as the father or other close relative of any faculty member would be.[26]

Since the legislative session was then ending, the investigation was referred by the Senate to an interim holdover committee, which was to function in 1942. Before that committee could meet, however, war had canceled its agenda. Crawford was granted a paid leave of absence to sustain him while he looked for another post. On December 5, 1941, he left Honolulu on the last peacetime sailing of the *Lurline,* not to return to the campus until 1957, when he received an honorary doctorate as the University celebrated its fiftieth anniversary.

The regents named Dean Arthur Keller as acting president while a search for a new executive officer was made by a committee it would appoint. Keller, faced by a board that had increasingly involved itself in the management of the University, asked about his scope of authority to make decisions. When in doubt, he was advised, seek the counsel of a regent. A broader history resolved Keller's uncertainty when wartime martial law took over major decision making for the entire Territory of Hawaii, including its university.

WARTIME

Bombs and antiaircraft shells during the attack of December 7, 1941, fell no closer than a mile from the Manoa campus, but nevertheless the University was profoundly affected by World War II. The instructional program immediately stopped, not to be resumed for two months. The Manoa ROTC unit was ordered into active duty. Quickly, as martial law was declared, the Army came to supervise the digging of bomb shelters on the campus and to commandeer facilities it required.

Sometimes, in the haste of emergency, the wrong things were taken. Bruce White, then associate professor in Teachers College, recalled that on December 8 an Army sergeant, surveying the Castle Memorial Preschool—which was later used by Punahou School after its own campus was taken over by the military—noticed on the lanai of the new building a quantity of plumbing fixtures, still in their boxes. Overriding protests, he had them carted away as necessary for the war effort. After the boxes were opened and found to contain flush toilets and wash basins of kindergarten size, they reappeared on the lanai.

On December 11, Acting President Keller received a letter from Lieutenant Colonel Theodore Wyman stating that the Corps of Engineers would take over Crawford Hall, Gartley, Hemenway, and Atherton, as well as Teachers College. Hemenway Hall was designated as a shelter for people evacuated from their homes by the bombing attack of December 7 and others that might follow. When few evacuees showed up, Hemenway was used for a variety of purposes, including operation of the U.S. Armed Forces Institute, which provided correspondence courses to servicemen in the Pacific theatre of operations throughout the war. Offices and laboratories of the Physics Department were used to train Army radio technicians. In Farrington Hall, the noted Shakespearean actor Maurice Evans, now a captain, trained Army theatre personnel for the hundreds of shows they would present at military bases in the next four years. Company B of the Hawaii Territorial Guard took over Klum gym.

By the time classes reopened on February 11, 1942, about half of the student body and faculty had left to enter war work or military service. Faculty members in military reserve units, such as Assistant Professor of Engineering W. J. Holmes, had already been called up in the months preceding Pearl Harbor, but now most of the anthropology and geography faculty went into the service of the national government. English Department members were tapped, under the direction of Willard Wilson, to censor the civilian mail that had been accumulating in storage since December 7. Four physicists were assigned to the radio technician program. Painter Ben Norris left the Art Department to prepare camouflage at Pearl Harbor. Specialists in agriculture led a campaign to set up Victory Gardens to supplement the Islands' food supply. Other faculty members took leave to serve in military intelligence, civilian defense, the Corps of Engineers, the Federal Bureau of Investigation, the Red Cross, and other agencies.

Most profoundly affected by the war were cadets of the ROTC unit, most of them nisei, second-generation Japanese Americans. Radio announcements on December 7 had called them to arms. Their first order was to watch for enemy paratroopers who might be on ridges bordering the campus. That same day the military governor converted the corps into the Hawaii Territorial Guard (HTG). For two months it remained on duty defending buildings or areas on Oahu selected by the armed forces command, becoming the only ROTC unit in the nation to serve actively in World War II.

On January 19, 1942, all HTG volunteers of Japanese ancestry were discharged by the military without notice or explanation. Their draft status became 4C: enemy alien. Recovering from the shock, they organized to petition the military governor, offering their service to the nation in wartime. The offer was accepted by creating the Varsity Victory Volunteers, a military labor unit under the U.S. Army Corps of Engineers. Ultimately 132 students joined the unit, including 98 who had already registered for the second semester of 1941–1942. The Volunteers were assigned construction duty—stringing barbed wire along beaches, building warehouses, fixing bridges and roads on the Waianae range of western Oahu, blasting rock in the quarry at that range's Kolekole Pass, and the like—until eventually they were accepted into a special all-nisei Army unit, the 100th Infantry Battalion (Separate), later joined with the 442nd Regimental Combat Team, also all-nisei. From this group of once-and-future UH students was to come much of the postwar political leadership of the Islands.

The students who did return to class in February 1942 found that many courses had been deleted for lack of instructors; graduate programs were especially curtailed. No cancellations were made, however, of classes that had been politically unacceptable during the previous war. Unlike the school's reaction in 1917, when the teaching of German was dropped for ten years, during World War II courses in German continued to be offered, along with several in Japanese language and literature. The sole possible basis for charges of disloyalty by members of the faculty had been removed in June 1941, when the regents accepted the resignation of an assistant professor of

The University at World War II

Thomas P. Gill

Thomas P. Gill

The University of Hawai'i in 1940–1941 was the only one accessible to most of us. Some of the "monied class"—usually graduates of Punahou—went on to important mainland universities, such as Stanford, Harvard, or Yale. Public school graduates—from Roosevelt, McKinley, Farrington, the rural and outside Island schools—came to Manoa, which was "it." This made an interesting mix. The English Standard high schools, of which Roosevelt was the largest, produced students somewhat more adept in speaking, reading, and writing English. Their selective admission policies and ability to draw students islandwide encouraged this result. Other public high schools drew from more restricted districts, but in some respects their graduates who went on to UH often seemed more highly motivated. Their ethnic background was heavily Japanese and Chinese; their skills were less focused on language, political science, and history and more on mathematics and hard science.

Most of the students and some of the faculty came out of an almost feudal plantation economy, then still struggling out of the nation's worst depression. The goal of most students was to succeed in their only chance for higher education; for non-haoles, the most promising professional career open was teaching. On campus there was an unspoken awareness that the University was funded by the plantation economy and largely dependent on its political and social superstructure.

This was a university, therefore, with many talented professors serving a generally attentive student body, but also with an administration which had to look over its shoulder at the powers that were, careful not to make too many "waves."

Perceptions and expectations were compounded further in 1940–1941 by the gathering clouds of war in Asia and the devastation of Europe by the Nazis. America's entrance into that war, requiring the drafting of young men of college age, became more likely. Stir this unease, uncertainty, and some racial resentment into the churning energy and general optimism of youth and you get a feeling of the mood of the campus just before the war.

Impressions linger, even after a half-century. They are not always accurate, and may reflect the attitude of the person who carries the memory, but they may show a little about the University at that turning point in history. One quirkish memory is of a course I never took—but heard in part. It was a course in economic principles, taught for many years by the same professor, for which "crib notes" were widely available. The professor had a loud voice, easily heard by students sitting outside the classroom on the Quadrangle lawn. The lecture followed the crib notes, seemingly word for word. Where the notes were underlined to mark a key phrase, the voice grew louder; where they were doubly underlined, the voice doubled in volume. Many found it easier to sit on the

(continued)

(continued)

lawn, listening to and reading the notes while relaxing, than to sit in class.

It may have been this experience that made me skeptical of economics as a "science." If its principles were so clear and certain, I asked myself, how did we get into the stupid depression where we almost lost our house and where many poorer families, whose children would never go to the University, were struggling to grow corn and sweet potatoes on the slopes of Ualakaa on the western rim of Manoa Valley?

Another course I never took was taught by Klaus Mehnert, a history professor. His students went to his classes and apparently enjoyed them. But Mehnert, reportedly a German citizen, was perhaps suspected of siding with the Nazis then sweeping across Europe and North Africa. The University administration wanted to fire him. Being president of the freshman class, I was approached by some of my "constituency" to protest on his behalf. We addressed a petition to the administration, stating that the students liked good teachers, and Mehnert was certainly one, so why should the he be given the "boot" because of his citizenship?

Mehnert was "booted" in the summer of 1941. I read, long after the war, that he had gone to Shanghai and joined the foreign colony there. He was apparently designated by the German government—read "Nazis"—to be their public relations man—read "propagandist"—in the Far East. I don't know how true that aftermath is, but it makes a story with a twist of the times.

I took a freshman course in political science from Paul Bachman, who later had his name engraved in the concrete of the administration building at Manoa. It was a good course, simplistic, but broad in coverage. Sometime in the spring of 1941, issues of the war in Europe came up in class. He raised a number of questions about possible American involvement, asking for our comment. Being, like many others at the time, a bit of an isolationist, I contributed the deep thought that if we were going to kill our young people it would be better to let them fertilize our own soil, instead of the sands of North Africa. Professor Bachman was patient and, I think, understanding. After class he took the time to talk about the dilemma with me—individually. Before the end of that year we learned that not only does history fail to reveal its alternatives, it also doesn't give you many choices.

There were other "wars" at the University before December 7. I had some connection with the drama section and Doc Wyman, who helped our freshman class to present one-act plays in Farrington Hall. Doc attracted many students, male and female, to work both on stage and backstage, introducing them to the theatre both artistically and practically. Some years earlier, I was told, he had a run-in with chemistry professor Leonora "Ma" Bilger, who then served as dean of women. Strict and conservative, as dean she had issued an edict that "girls" (read "women") were to wear dresses on campus, not slacks.

Wyman had a problem with this because much stage work was done by coeds, some of it aloft on ladders. Doc reacted typically. He chose an appropriate day, had the women stagehands don their fluffiest dresses and climb up all the step-

(continued)

(continued)

ladders he could find and pretend to work on a stage set. He then called the dean and asked her to come over to Farrington Hall to see how things were going. She did and he took her backstage to "view the scenery." There is no record of what was said, but to the dismay of the males who were interested in the art of the theatre, the "girls" were returned to their slacks.

This is not to put down Leonora Bilger; she was a tough and rigorous teacher of chemistry. She held her exams in a spacious auditorium, seating test-takers in alternate rows, several seats apart. No notes were allowed. Reportedly, she checked shirt sleeves and palms for any formulas students may have inked in for crucial reference. You had better learn the difference between H_2O and H_2SO_4, and it was easier to study than cheat.

Which leads, by memory, not logic, to ROTC, then a required course for freshmen (not women) and sophomores. Having evaded ROTC in high school, I found no escape at the University. We got to practice such things as "right shoulder arms" and "parade rest." There was a lot of marching around—"close-order drill," it was called—which had more to do with highly polished shoes and well-creased pants than with warfare. However, we got to use that venerable weapon, the bolt-action Springfield '30. The '30 was good for ROTC drill because the bolt made a precise clacking sound when you pulled it open on command. The rifles were kept clean and neatly stacked in the "Rotcy" shack near the old gym. We never got to fire them, for good reason, as we soon discovered.

Most of us paid little attention to this ROTC course, both compulsory and boring. On the first Sunday of December 1941, however, the war lit in our laps. The UH ROTC unit was "mobilized" into the Hawaii Territorial Guard and was told to assemble at once at the ROTC building to gather our weapons. It was then told that there was no ammunition for the rifles—which made no difference, since there weren't any firing pins either. While the command struggled to correct this problem, we got to stand around and watch some buildings in the nearby neighborhood of Moiliili—where some of the students lived—burn when hit by antiaircraft shells that fell to earth before they exploded.

While watching the start of our war from the edge of University Avenue, a report came that parachutists had landed on or near St. Louis Heights, and we were supposed to react. The only working weapon was a .22 caliber target rifle kept locked in a closet in the ROTC building. The regular Army sergeant assigned to our unit grabbed this gun and, with several confused volunteers, sprinted up what is now Dole Street toward the heights. Fortunately, it was just a false alarm, and in an hour or so they all returned with no harm done.

A few nights later, our unit was assigned to guard various public buildings, including Iolani Palace. Firing pins had been found and installed; ammunition was issued. As might be expected on an island still fearing a return attack and invasion, there was nervous shooting at noises and shadows by recruits just learning how to handle a rifle. The palace and smaller buildings around its grounds, as well as the windows of some private showrooms in

(continued)

(continued)

the area, received some "war damage." It is possible that an accidental midnight barrage in the entry to Washington Place helped assure Governor Poindexter inside that he had acted wisely in concurring with the imposition of martial law!

So, what was the University before the war changed it, Hawaii, and the world? It was probably pretty good in tropical agriculture and in the engineering relating to running sugar plantations. From Hawaii Hall you could look across the fields of green, flourishing crops cultivated by the College of Agriculture and be impressed. Teachers College (TC) was a good and productive school, providing a professional opening for many skilled non-haole students who could not expect to get jobs with the Big Five companies—other than in the fields, the mills, or behind store counters. The teaching profession commanded respect and paid a living salary. Nevertheless, some classmates who had entered TC in 1940–1941 and then went off to war changed their minds when they came back and went into less-admired professions—such as the law.

However, the University at that time was circumscribed in the liberal arts. It was not meant to produce "wave makers" or to train professionals who could challenge the existing system, politically or economically. This was obvious to many of us, and certainly to those who finished college after the war on the mainland and then became involved in Hawaii's political revolution of the 1950s.

history who had shown, or was suspected of having, sympathy with the Nazi government.

The ROTC program had been suspended, but uniforms at Manoa made it resemble a military school. In addition to the few hundred servicemen stationed on campus, as the threat of invasion faded after the pivotal American naval victory off Midway in June 1942, an increasing number of military personnel came from Pearl Harbor, Hickam Air Field, and other local bases to begin college courses, which they might continue by correspondence when overseas. New courses were added: chemical warfare, first aid, economics of warfare, the history of the warring nations, nutrition, and so forth.

Everyone on campus, as throughout Oahu, was required to carry a gas mask and to take cover in air raid shelters when the sirens shrieked, as they did occasionally. There were no night classes because of the blackout, but the pace of instruction was stepped up to accelerate progress toward degrees. For the same purpose, the summer sessions of 1942 and later years were extended to six weeks. At the end of August, the largest summer session in the history of the University concluded. The members of the graduating class of 1942 who were still present in Honolulu marched into Andrews Outdoor Theatre in black caps and gowns, with khaki gas masks slung over

Security rules severely limited photography during World War II, when the Manoa campus was largely diverted to wartime uses under martial law. One image remained, the air raid shelter behind Hawaii Hall.

Cadets in the UH ROTC were affected by the military's ban on enlisting Americans of Japanese ancestry. Many AJA students formed the Varsity Victory Volunteers and worked on Oahu defense projects under Army command before being formed into the famed 442nd Regimental Combat Team.

An architectural legacy of the war was the placement around the campus of scores of Army barracks, latrines, a field hospital, and more for conversion into such facilities as classrooms, faculty offices and housing, a bandroom, a snack bar, and this dormitory: "Men's Housing Barracks."

their shoulders. The degree of bachelor of arts and science was awarded posthumously to James Malcolm Toplian, who had been killed in the attack on Pearl Harbor. After the graduates recited the Pledge of Allegiance in unison, an Army colonel delivered the commencement address.

A modicum of calm having been regained on the campus, the presidential search committee created by the regents shortly before the attack on Pearl Harbor took up its mission to find a successor to Crawford. Wartime restrictions barred a national search, for how could mainland candidates be interviewed, and why would any be attracted to a school in a war zone operating under the constraints of martial law? Fortunately for the regents and its search committee, their task was made easy by the presence on campus of an obvious choice. Gregg Manners Sinclair, professor of English, had gained prominence since joining the faculty in 1928. His initiative in forming the Oriental Institute had shown him to have a vision of the University as a cultural force in the Pacific that gained him respect on campus and downtown. With the institute forced to close by the war, he was available. A tall, imposing man, his ability to socialize—an aspect considered by presidential search committees—was enhanced by his young wife, Marjorie Putnam Sinclair, who was to develop as a poet and novelist during his long presidency.

Sinclair assumed office at the beginning of the fiscal year, July 1, 1942, allowing Keller to resume his post as dean of the College of Applied Science. The regents eased matters for the new president by adopting a statement of responsibilities for themselves that proscribed intrusion into the administration of the University in matters such as faculty appointments.[27]

As the war was pushed westward across the Pacific, the campus slowly regained normalcy. Restrictions, such as the wartime freeze on salaries, were eased after February 8, 1943, when the military governor relinquished authority over many civilian functions, including education. Dropping extra wartime duties gave administrators and faculty the time to deal with the academic problems of the University.

A major concern was that the faculty of each college—Arts and Sciences, Applied Science, Teachers College—took their teaching responsibility to be directed to their own curricula and students. The English faculty in Arts and Sciences did not necessarily relish teaching classes in composition for students in engineering, and mathematicians in Applied Science may not have regarded the teaching of students in Teachers College as being as important as their classes for engineers. Sinclair appointed a faculty committee to study the problem. The committee produced a reorganization plan, approved unanimously by the Faculty Senate and then adopted by the regents. To better integrate the instructional program, departments were made subject to the direction of the University as a whole, rather than to the individual colleges. A dean of faculties was appointed, to be responsible for coordinating the work of the academic departments, which by 1943 numbered twenty-two, offering courses in thirty-six subject areas.[28] The simplicity of administering a small school was dropping away.

At this same time, the legislature reconstituted the Board of Regents to require a member from each of the counties of Hawaii, Maui, and Kauai, plus eight others, including the UH president and the superintendent of the territorial Department of Public Instruction. At least one regent had to be a graduate of the University. The new board continued to respect the policy announced by its predecessors to stay out of the details of University administration.

Recruitment, plus the gradual return of people on emergency leave, brought the instructional faculty from its low point of seventy-seven in 1944 to ninety-five in 1945. Courses, from anthropology to zoology, that had been discontinued for lack of staff were restored. Classrooms and laboratories taken for military use were again available for teaching and research.

Student enrollment, both of civilians and military personnel, rose in the last year of the war even faster than faculty and course offerings. Of some thirty-five hundred individuals enrolled for course credit in the year ending June 1945, approximately half were members of the armed forces. Another thousand took noncredit courses. The

University had established an educational connection with the military services that was to continue long after the war, providing instruction at military bases on Oahu, for military units in occupied and postwar Japan, for sailors aboard far-ranging nuclear submarines.

In 1945, Sinclair had a survey made of the postwar needs of the University. It found that with existing buildings and equipment the campus could accommodate approximately twenty-two hundred full-time students. With the prospect of about three thousand enrolling, the regents asked the territorial legislature to provide funds for the construction of a chemistry building, an administration building, six dormitories, and a center for the home economics program. These were not to come until after 1951, but the legislature in 1945 did endorse a ten-year building program for the Manoa campus and appropriated funds to buy 111 more acres adjacent to the campus, space needed for postwar expansion. What no planner envisioned was how large that expansion would be.

2

BECOMING A STATEWIDE SYSTEM: 1947–1968

THE UNIVERSITY EMERGED from World War II with a disheveled campus, a depleted faculty, and the promise of better times to come. As in colleges across the nation, the invigorating force was to be a tide of students returning from the war. The GI Bill of Rights offered veterans unprecedented financial support—covering tuition ($50 a semester), books, and supplies, plus enough cash for a frugal student life—and thus provided the University with a speedily enlarged student body. By September 1947 enrollment on the Manoa campus had surpassed its prewar level, rising to three thousand students, a third of them veterans. These were among the GI-generation of students judged (in a *Fortune* magazine survey of the class of '49) to be "the best . . . the most . . . mature . . . the most responsible . . . group of college students in history." Many of those coming to Manoa had served in the 442nd Regimental Combat Team and the 100th Infantry Battalion. They were Americans of Japanese ancestry, made confident by their widely praised heroism under fire, ambitious for advancement following their acceptance by a white-dominated community as loyal, valued Americans. They, and other GIs who had served in the Pacific and in Asia, were to provide much of the political leadership that ended that domination.

The provincial quality of the campus was irreversibly changed by the vets. Before the war, only a rare and privileged student had experienced the world outside Hawaii. Now most campus gatherings would include men, and often a woman or two, who had experienced the mainland, Italy and France, occupied Japan, or islands across the Pacific.

THE CAMPUS VILLAGE

Returning students found much the same physical campus they had left. The quadrangle of low-rise classroom buildings extended from University Avenue to Varney

Circle. From there to Manoa Stream was the domain of the College of Agriculture—fields of rippling forage grass, barns, poultry yards, pig pens, and laboratories. Across University Avenue students and faculty of the College of Education did much of their academic work, fraternizing with the rest of the campus at the cafeteria and in the library.

The visible reminders of the war were a bomb shelter behind Hawaii Hall and surplus Army buildings—olive-drab, wooden, barracks-type, termite-prone—set around the campus. Money was not available for new construction, so war-weary structures were dragged in from military bases on Oahu to serve as temporary classrooms, office buildings, library annex, snack bar, and men's dormitories. "Temporary" proved to be a euphemism. The freshmen of 1947 found many of those structures still in place when they returned for reunions two decades later. A few "tempos" are still to be seen in the shadows of higher buildings.

A score of these old Army structures provided new faculty members with housing, in short supply for all in Honolulu and particularly for the staff of a university then paying annual salaries averaging about $4,000. The "tempos" were hauled to a corner of the grass fields of the College of Agriculture at the far end of the campus. Wallboard divided the interiors into small apartments, not very private but affordable. More conventional housing, prefabricated cottages of a style then provided by the Olokele Plantation of Kauai for its field hands, made another small neighborhood in "Chicken Corners," convenient to the source of eggs and milk, which faculty families were privileged to buy from the College farm. More of these cottages were hurriedly assembled in the area near Manoa Stream, now the site of the East-West Center. College livestock and faculty children learned to coexist.

The campus was a village for these faculty families. Many of their children attended the College of Education's Laboratory School. Entertainment was at hand: three tennis courts, plays at the lecture hall–theatre called Farrington, concerts by the Music Department, bridge and book club sessions of the Women's Campus Club—which also staged a Christmas party and an Easter egg hunt for faculty children. The cafeteria and snack bar were inexpensive, as well as convenient. So was the barber shop. One had to go off campus only for groceries, liquor, movies, church—and books, for the tiny book store offered little but texts and writing materials. Families socialized on campus, helping each other with baby-sitting, car repair, adaptation to Island ways. Most faculty members knew each other by first name.

The noon hour brought hundreds of students, faculty, and staff to the cafeteria in Hemenway Hall. There Elsie Boatman genially managed an operation that provided excellent food, including superlative home-made pastries, at prices her clientele could afford. Mrs. Boatman's cakes and pies were also featured at the faculty receptions of the early 1950s. Each semester, faculty couples were shuttled by bus up to the mansion on Makiki Heights (now a contemporary art museum) of Philip Spalding, long-term head of the Board of Regents and of the Hawaiian Electric Company, for a splendid tea in a resplendent setting. The bus then returned them to their campus housing and the realities of faculty life.

Dress standards for male faculty members and staff became less formal and decidedly more comfortable. Through World War II, tailored shirts and ties and even coats were expected in classroom and office on a campus that knew not of air-conditioning. In 1946, after an ordeal in the humid heat of registration week, four professors took action for liberation. Political scientist Allan Saunders, historian Arthur Marder, anthropologist Leonard Mason, and economist Ralph Hoeber called their coterie the Faculty Wearers of Aloha Shirts.

Aloha shirts were then rarely seen on adults with any pretension to formal correctness—except, of course, tourists. The UH administration closed its eyes to the rebellion until it attracted the attention of Honolulu newspapers, which in late 1947 printed letters complaining that faculty members were to be seen on campus "with colorful shirttails flying." President Sinclair sent a memorandum to Saunders, stating that "a great number of people have spoken to me of the informality of your dress, and have stated that a professor in the University should present a dignified appearance at least on all official occasions." The cause of sartorial conservatism, however, was forever lost. After Sinclair's memo was publicized, many faculty members who had never worn an aloha shirt began to teach in that costume of defiance. Manoa soon became a campus on which aloha shirts were conservative attire. The administration abandoned any thought of setting dress standards, except for the summer session catalog admonition to mainland students that swimsuits on campus were not in good taste.

A SERVICE UNIVERSITY

From earliest years, the legislature found the University a convenient home for agencies it wished to keep out of the mainstream of politics, because there was some link in their work to campus scholarship, or simply because it could think of no better place to put a new program. A Psychological and Psychopathic Clinic thus had been placed on the campus in 1921 to determine which members of the community should be committed to the Waimano Home for the feeble-minded. Stanley D. Porteus, its first director, also devised tests from which he formulated a theory of racial differences in intelligence, which at the time was generally accepted by scholars and by members of the community who knew of the results. In later decades, however, his methodology and conclusions came under attack (see chapter 3).

About the same time, the Honolulu Aquarium, established in 1904 at the Waikiki end of the Honolulu trolley car system that ran a line into Manoa Valley near campus, was made a responsibility of the University. With the later development of UH research in marine biology, the aquarium became a valued facility, but in the intervening decades the Waikiki tourist attraction was almost as functionally detached from the University as it was physically distant. The regents' continuing concern was that administration of the aquarium enlarged a UH budget already regarded by legislators as excessive.

In 1947 the legislature directed the War Records Depository, created on campus to preserve documents relating to Hawaii's wartime experiences, to prepare a history of the territory's role in World War II. This being done by Professor Thomas D. Murphy, President Sinclair was able to report a rare quick ending to a public agency: "Having accomplished the purposes for which it was intended, the War Records Depository disbanded on June 30, 1949." Its documents went into the University library.

The Legislative Reference Bureau (LRB) was also a wartime addition, placed in the University to shelter it from partisan political influence. The bureau had been created in 1944 to assist the legislature, which had few professional aides, in its work of lawmaking. Quartered in the old library (renamed George Hall in 1956), its collection of governmental materials was conveniently close to the main book collections. During legislative sessions, the small staff—whose researchers usually had split appointments with the Political Science or Economics departments—moved their war-surplus furniture to one of the "tempos" that encrusted Iolani Palace, the territorial capitol. The LRB drafted hundreds of statutory measures and scores of research reports for each session until 1972, when it was severed from the University and put under the state legislative branch.

Of course the largest service organization predated the University itself. Agricultural specialists had been offering advice to farmers before the College of Hawaii opened its doors. Agricultural extension programs of the College began in 1914, and by 1947 the staff of the Cooperative Extension Service was overcrowding old Gilmore Hall—on the site of the present Art Building—the center of a network of service programs reaching throughout the territory (see chapter 8).

THE STUDENTS' CAMPUS

For most students in the years between World War II and the Korean War, the Manoa campus was a daytime place. The library, cafeteria, and snack bar all closed early. Most lived at home and worked off-campus; they rode the bus to class, or walked. Bicycles were not common, and the rackety moped was yet to come. The sole parking lot occupied the land on which Sinclair Library now stands.

It was a quiet campus. Lights and voices after sunset were largely limited to Hemenway Hall and to Atherton House, the YMCA building across University Avenue, which served not only as a dormitory for off-island students, but as a clubhouse. For many coeds, ethnic sororities were the center of campus social life. Each spring,

Looking Back at Manoa

Tomi K. Knaefler

Tomi K. Knaefler

I am one of the University's "forever" students. Over the years, I've enriched my life with courses ranging from religion to poetry to painting. My addiction began in the fall of 1947 when I first stepped onto the Manoa campus, fresh out of McKinley High School. The University was then a small school—a fraction of what it is today in size and scope. The enrollment in 1947 was 3,837, compared with the 1995 total of more than 50,000 for all the campuses, including 20,000 at Manoa. But for me, just three years out of the tiny plantation village of Pahoa on the Big Island, being a freshman at UH was like entering a new universe.

For one thing, I felt mature, even though there was not a shred of supporting evidence. One of the first things that made me feel so grown-up was being called not Tomi but Miss Kaizawa by the professors. No one had ever called me that before. I loved my courses, even the required ones (except foreign language). Then there were the plays, lectures, debates, art shows, and concerts that so inspired me.

And most important, there was the large number of World War II veterans who flooded the University just as they did campuses across the nation, courtesy of the GI Bill. No one loved the swarm of vets more than the coeds, myself included. Dating them always felt so special. With their return, the UH enrollment doubled and tripled to hit a record five thousand by 1950. The ratio of men to women was three to two. It was wonderful having the attention of these interesting "older" men who energized the student body, the faculty, and the administration with a raw, restless spirit.

When I first started at UH, my high school friends and I timidly stuck together. Like most local teenagers of that era, we had no access to a car so we either got a ride to the campus with a friend's older brother or sister, or we took the bus that stopped right across from Atherton House, as it does today. We bunched together before classes and during our tuna sandwich lunches under a shade tree in the Quad to exchange survival notes and to moan over the mountain of homework. We kept up with our reading, using colored pencils (before highlighter markers) to underline the important data likely to appear in exams. We huddled over lecture and reading notes before quizzes and fretted frightfully over grades.

That says what a diligent student I was —at least for the first semester. But something happened to change all that. Just before finals, I lost my world history notes. In a panic, I went to *Ka Leo,* the student newspaper, to place an emergency ad with editor Margaret Chinen. Her face lit up when I gave her my name. "Oh, you're Stanley's sister. He told me you wanted to be a reporter and asked me to be on the lookout for you." My older

(continued)

(continued)

brother had been her faculty advisor for the Farrington High School newspaper. Margaret urged me to join her staff. "You'll have fun." I did; I did. That was the beginning of the end of my classroom diligence. Very soon, most of my energy went into the paper.

Ka Leo (The Voice) was then housed in one of the many faded green World War II Army shacks on campus, some remnants of martial law when the University gave up buildings for military use. This shack sat in front of Hemenway Hall in a dusty parking lot just off University Avenue, where Sinclair Library now stands. It had no windows, just a strip of screening on two sides through which the wind, rain, and dust blew. When it wasn't blowing, we sweltered. But for a dozen or so of us, this was home.

Ka Leo was my first, last, and in-between stop every day. I loved getting my assignments, gathering data, interviewing, struggling with the stories, and finally seeing them in print each Tuesday and Friday. Two nights a week we worked on deadline. The long nights always started with a quick dinner at the campus cafeteria or at Raymond Senaga's College Inn at Dole Street and University Avenue. The restaurant was the home of the fresh papaya-pineapple fruit cocktail, miso soup, or sashimi appetizer that came with your hamburger steak—for less than a dollar. Inside were frescos of Island foods painted by Jean Charlot, in exchange for meals for himself and family.

At the *Ka Leo* office, sometimes we could hear dance bands playing in the nearby student union as we typed away on our manual Underwoods. Paul Kokubun, our associate editor, who later became a Family Court judge, was the only one with a car (a war surplus jeep). So we all had to wait until every story was dummied and every headline written before we could head home well after midnight. A year later, when I had my own tiny office as the managing editor, I requisitioned a bed for naps on deadline nights. When Mary Lou McPherson, executive secretary of ASUH, saw a crew carting the bed across the campus toward the newspaper office, she rushed over and put her foot down: "Absolutely not."

I quickly picked up the mannerisms of being "Miss Reporter." Gosh, did I ever feel big-time smoking those long Pall Mall cigarettes and drinking excessive cups of wicked black coffee out of paper cups at the old snack bar, a shack that squatted between the Engineering Quad and Hemenway Hall. This was a gathering spot to chat or heatedly discuss the writings of Sartre, Kafka, and Camus as introduced in philosopher Harold McCarthy's spellbinding lectures.

What made me feel truly a part of the inner circle was being invited to join beer parties at the dim, smoke-filled interior of Charley's Tavern, across from the Star Market on Beretania Street. Another popular watering hole was Kuhio Grill, on King Street about where the 7-Eleven gas pumps now stand. The grill was old and faded, but owner Mark Miyashiro ("Miya-san") adorned it with paintings and sculpture done by "starving" art students, who are among Hawaii's leading artists today: Tadashi Sato, Satoru Abe, Bumpei Akaji, and Tetsuo Ochikubo. While an allergy to alcohol kept me from being a guzzler, I

(continued)

(continued)

loved going to the beer parties to nibble at the feast of pupu brought to the formica table—chopped steak with green peppers, crispy chicken, sashimi, hot buttered corn. And all the while the beer-inspired discussions flowed on topics ranging from Zen, *Ka Palapala* beauty queens, and Salinger's *Catcher in the Rye* to the new long-play records or Kinsey's study of male sexual behavior, ho-hum today but then a shocker. Another shock was hearing about homosexuality, a hush-hush subject in those days when "gay" meant, well, gay.

Of course, along with the big-picture issues were the myriad of campus-centered headlines. In 1947, the university's Hilo Center was established; Claude Horan introduced ceramics to UH and inspired waves of talented potters, like Toshiko Takaezu, Harue McVay, Isami Enomoto, and Henry Takemoto; the University of Hawai'i Press published its first book, Ralph Kuykendall's *Hawaiian Kingdom;* and students lost a life-long friend with the death of Charles Reed Hemenway, whose door was opened to everyone with these words: "If you should ever need my help. . . ."

Looking back, clearly the biggest part of my university experience was getting to know people—my classmates, fellow staffers, and those with whom I worked on stories. A large percentage were veterans. Some, such as my second editor, Dan Katz, were mainland vets who had seen Hawaii en route to the Pacific War and made good their vow to return. (Katz was later a police reporter with the *Honolulu Star-Bulletin.*) The majority, however, were Hawaii veterans, particularly the much-hailed Japanese-American heroes of the 442nd Regimental Combat Team and the 100th Infantry Battalion.

Curiously, I don't recall any big to-do about the vets after a welcome-back dance in 1946. Those I knew didn't talk about the war, as if they wanted to forget and go on with their lives. It wasn't until years later that I learned during an interview with 442nd vet Katsugo Miho what a tough time men had with their reentry. Restless, unable to settle down, he spent months playing pool and drinking beer with other vets. Finally, he returned to college. He found that setting goals and taking an active part in student politics helped him to adjust, but it took a good year before he could buckle down and study. Miho went on to law school and served as a legislator and later as a Family Court judge.

I could tell who the vets were only because they seemed more mature. There was the occasional vet with a highly visible mark, like a seeing-eye dog, or a black glove over his prosthetic right hand, in the case of now-U.S. Senator Dan Inouye. Like Inouye, the vets I knew were quite serious. They seemed to have a clear direction. They walked and talked purposefully. They even laughed and drank beer purposefully. They had their sights on high-powered careers in law, government, or business. Because the vets studied hard and made top grades, other students used to refer to them as DARs—Damn Average Raisers.

The vet leadership, in concert with other student leaders, asserted themselves on various issues, like pushing for better conditions at Vets Housing, getting greater student representation on the Board of Athletic Control, successfully protesting

(continued)

(continued)

the exclusive use of a room in the student union by faculty wives, and pressing for Hawaiian statehood. For veterans of Asian descent, particularly the Japanese Americans, campus politics proved to be a practice ground for their battle with the established order to gain opportunities long denied them and their families. It was from this group of UH veterans that most of the Democratic Party's young lions emerged in 1954 to end the long Republican hold on the legislature and radically change the course of local history.

But life on campus wasn't all heavy. Evening dances, for instance, returned to the campus with live bands playing tunes like "Tenderly" and "Some Enchanted Evening," with fussy evening gowns, the ballroom filled with the perfume of flower leis. Romance was in the very air. Star athlete Richard Mamiya, now a prominent heart surgeon, and Hazel Ikenaga were a campus item, as were Eichi Oki, a champion debater now an attorney, and Nobuko Shimazu. Another blooming romance was that of the late Judge Barry Rubin and Winona Ellis, future head of the state's Department of Social Services.

For those who liked glamour, the postwar campus had beauty queens galore. The big event was the *Ka Palapala* beauty contest to choose seven "ethnic queens"—Chinese, Hawaiian, Japanese, Korean, Filipino, Caucasian, and Cosmopolitan. There were also queens for Homecoming, various sports events, and ROTC parades. The abundance moved history professor Arthur Marder to quip that if a woman graduated from this university without being a queen of something, she had reason to feel pretty bad.

Equally plentiful on campus were clubs—professional clubs, ethnic clubs, sports and social clubs, and even one called Hui Wiki Wiki to "promote school spirit." And, just as today, sports thrived during the postwar years. Among the big guns in football and basketball were Ed "Hot Dog" Loui, Harry "Clown" Kahuanui, Richard Mamiya, Johnny Dang, and Sol Kaulukukui. The latter also starred in baseball, along with Henry Tominaga and Saburo Takayesu. Tommy Kaulukukui coached both the baseball and football teams. Swimming coach Soichi Sakamoto gained widespread attention with winners like Charlie Oda, Bill Smith, Jr., Halo Hirose, and Keo Nakama.

Those, then, were my days—the early post–World War II era at UH. What most grabbed me in my campus experience was being a reporter. It legitimized my constant curiosity, gave it a shape and discipline that enabled me to build a lifetime career—while having the time of my life.

their nominees competed at a Hemenway Hall gala for selection as *Ka Palapala* beauty queens.

Uniforms were conspicuous. Physically fit males were required to take two years of on-campus Army ROTC training and were offered two more years for those wanting to become commissioned officers. In 1949, an Air Force ROTC program was added. Women were not then eligible for the training, but pretty coeds served as "sponsors" of ROTC units at parades and dances.

Students with political ambitions ran for class offices and positions of leadership in the Associated Students of the University of Hawai'i (ASUH) and Associated Women Students (AWS). As early as 1946, the ASUH conducted a national letter-writing campaign advocating statehood, while *Ka Leo,* the student newspaper, advanced the cause on campus. Two years later, student delegates to a mock convention drafted a "model" state constitution. Some provisions of the students' model, including an article establishing the University as a constitutional entity with legal title to its property, anticipated those later incorporated in the actual state constitution. That document was drafted in 1950 by a popularly elected assembly whose members included an active Manoa dean (Harold S. Roberts of Business Administration) and a retired dean (Benjamin Wist of Teachers College). Several alumni also served as delegates, including Hiram L. Fong (later one of Hawaii's first U.S. senators) and D. Hebden Porteus, a long-term member of the Hawaii legislature, both of them leading Republicans.

POSTWAR EXPANSION

Downtown, in both the business community and the territorial government, support gradually developed for having the University respond to the needs of an increasingly urban community for more and better-trained professionals in fields other than agriculture, engineering, and teaching. In 1948 the School of Social Work launched a master's program, thereby creating a wider career path for students, especially women. The campus had offered social work courses as early as 1922, but a professional school had not come into being until 1940.

The School of Nursing, another profession then readily accessible to women, was established in 1951 when the legislature appropriated the round sum of $25,000 as start-up financing. Courses in nursing had been given at Manoa since 1932, serving students of the primary training agency in the territory, the Queen's Hospital School of Nursing. During World War II a bachelor's program in public-health nursing and hospital supervision had been started on the campus. However, the medical profession, in Hawaii as across the nation, resisted creating a broad professional schooling for nurses. The critical question raised by some doctors in the community, according to Edith Yashike, longtime secretary to the school's director, was "Will they carry bedpans?"

The director herself, Virginia A. Jones, worked assiduously and successfully to gain the respect of physicians for the work of the school. In 1966 the program at Queen's Hospital was merged with UH's. Under this collaboration, students took their academic work on campus and their clinical experience at Queen's. St. Francis

Student Vets and the Quest for Statehood

Ralph Toyota

Ralph Toyota

When President Gregg Sinclair greeted the 1946 freshman class, he noted that it was the largest in the University's history. About a thousand war veterans had returned to campus to resume their educations. Aided by the GI Bill, which paid for their tuition, books, and supplies, plus a monthly stipend, the veterans—mature and serious about their educational goals and prospective careers—set a new tone for the student body.

Aside from complaints about the limited housing on campus and about the administration of some details of the GI Bill, the veterans melded easily into campus life. The quadrangle with Hawaii Hall at its base was the academic heart of the campus, but student life centered on Hemenway Hall with its cafeteria, bookstore, mail room, and offices of the Associated Students of the University of Hawai'i (ASUH).

Mauka of Hemenway was a large shade tree, where the "under-the-tree-gang" stationed itself like a reviewing body to check out the coeds as they walked to and from class. It would have been difficult to foresee that Hawaii's future leaders would be coming from this motley gang, but they did, among them Supreme Court Justices Yoshimi Hayashi, Ed Nakamura, and Herman Lum; Judges Ed Honda, Frank Takao, and Ken Saruwatari; educators Shiro Amioka and Dick Kosaki; legislators Dan Inouye, Seiichi ("Shadow") Hirai, Shigeto Kanemoto, and Alvin Shim.

In an unprecedented show of campus purpose and solidarity, the vets joined with enthusiastic younger students to complete the lower wing of Hemenway Hall. With the cooperation of faculty and staff, they organized a carnival to raise the necessary funds, courageously promising the regents to raise $85,000—a prodigious sum! More than $100,000 worth of tickets were sold before the carnival opened. The final gross was $128,000, and the promised $85,000 was used to complete Hemenway.

The cause of statehood for Hawaii commanded sustained interest. Student vets, along with a majority of the territory's population, were strongly pro-statehood. Despite a disappointing lack of action in the U.S. Congress, campus involvement in promoting statehood mounted to a feverish pitch, as if statehood could be gained at any moment if only we tried hard enough. I became chairman of the ASUH Statehood Committee in March 1946 and promptly got involved in a flurry of activity: *Ka Leo* printed a statehood issue, proclaiming "Statehood Week"; Misao Oyama won a letter-writing contest on "Hawaii's Case for Statehood"; a committee headed by Tom McCabe and Mary Matsumoto produced a statehood brochure that included Oyama's letter and artwork by Jackson Morisawa. The brochure was sent to all mainland colleges, asking students for their support in promoting statehood for Hawaii.

(continued)

(continued)

In January 1948, ASUH Statehood Chairman Patsy Takemoto (Mink) met in Honolulu with U.S. Senator Guy Cordon of Oregon. On April 9 she wrote an impassioned letter on statehood that was printed in *Ka Leo*, and the newspaper proclaimed that "Statehood Still Lives." Student leaders spoke at meetings on statehood around town. The statehood bill remained bottled up in committee. It was painful to learn in May 1948 that a move to report the bill out to the full Senate had failed. Nevertheless, the ASUH pursued its dream in such ways as it could. We held a series of forums—the first led by former territorial delegate to Congress Samuel Wilder King on "What is a Good Constitution?" We supplied an answer by holding a mock convention that spring at which student delegates drafted a complete model constitution for the coming state of Hawaii.

Success on this issue that burned on the Manoa campus during my undergraduate years was only attained in 1959. By that time, the statehood advocates of the ASUH were well launched into their careers, and a new generation of students was gathering at Hemenway Hall.

Hospital graduated its last class that same year, leaving the University with sole responsibility for nursing education in the state.

A College of Business Administration was established in 1949, with Harold S. Roberts as dean. An initially modest list of courses soon grew into expanded curricula for undergraduates, and then for students seeking a master's degree in an increasing number of fields—accounting, finance, real estate, industrial relations, marketing, and more to come. Roberts also created an Industrial Relations Center within the college to study means, other than shutdowns such as the bitter waterfront strike Hawaii had endured in 1949, for resolving labor disputes.

For the most part, immediate postwar expansion remained focused on the needs of Hawaii. There was, however, a resurgence of activity in international fields in which the University was later to gain distinction—Pacific and Asian studies. Organized interest in the Pacific and Asia dated back to 1932, when Professor Gregg Sinclair had created a School of Pacific and Oriental Affairs, but the attack on Pearl Harbor had put an end to the program. In 1950, President Sinclair appointed a faculty committee to investigate how area programs could best be established. (Chapters 4, 5, and 6 trace the development of studies about Hawaii, other Pacific Islands, and Asia.)

Generally, the campus grew modestly. By the mid-1950s total UH employment exceeded 800, though in terms of full-time positions the faculty still numbered fewer than 500. Sparingly, the legislature voted funds to serve the increasing body of students. Bachman Hall (completed in 1949) for a short time held the entire staff of a modestly sized administration.

The first postwar classroom structure, the chemistry building (later Bilger Hall), in 1951 was thrust into the UH farm lands beyond Varney Circle. It had been planned for a site on University Avenue, adjacent to the Quadrangle, but that place was claimed for a new library. Red-bricked Sinclair Library (1955) replaced old George Hall, which had narrowly accommodated the Philosophy Department, the Oriental Institute, and the Legislative Reference Bureau alongside a growing, if always inadequate, collection of books and journals.

Some attention was paid to ornamentation of the architecturally spare Manoa campus. Jean Charlot, an internationally noted artist, was invited to come to Hawaii in 1949 to create the fresco murals ("Relation of Man and Nature in Old Hawaii" and "Commencement") that enrich the two-story interior entry of Bachman Hall. The graduating classes of 1949 to 1952 commissioned the frescoes as their gift to the University. Charlot's students, working without compensation, created the frescoes of Bilger Hall between 1951 and 1955. Later, after the 1967 legislature enacted a law earmarking for artwork one percent of state appropriations for building construction, sculptures began to appear on campus, notably the bright-orange steel "Gate of Hope" in front of Holmes Hall and "To the Nth Power"—often taken to be a representation of Yapese stone money—in front of the Business Administration Building.

For the most part, however, it was nature that graced the campus, where, as a report of the federal Office of Education observed: "Neither university administrative personnel nor the Board of Regents has control of the construction of university facilities." Rather, it was the central government of Hawaii that controlled project planning, employment of architects, and letting of building contracts.[1] The product was a succession of buildings that seldom evoked admiration and sometimes did not work. More recently a veteran journalist put it bluntly: "I have long looked at the buildings of the campus as an example, indeed a virtual metaphor, for what's gone wrong with development in much of Honolulu—a monument to poor planning and pork-barrel politics."[2]

Happily, the collection of exotic plants imported by Professor Rock during the early years of the campus, augmented by the palms, shower trees, teak, tekoma, breadfruit, kukui, banyan, tamarind, bo, and hundreds of other trees placed around the campus in the following decades, raised a green canopy around and above the architecture. Unhappily, the erecting of new buildings brought botanical destruction as the three hundred acres of the campus were pressed into use. A cycle began: beautiful trees were planted, to be cut down to make room for structures, which required more trees for embellishment.

Mid-century brought an expansion of program sites. Part of Coconut Island in Kaneohe Bay was acquired in 1951 for the program in marine zoology, the first academic field in which the University attained national prominence. An expanse of tropical botany in Manoa Valley far above the campus was added to the University's land in 1953 when the Hawaii Sugar Planters' Association deeded its arboretum to the Board of Regents. Named after Harold Lyon, its first director, the arboretum comprised 124 acres of botanical garden, rich in specimens of tropical and semitropical flora. The terms of the gift, which limited its use to research and education in botany, placed the arboretum beyond any notion of using any part of it as space for other programs of the University.

Such space was acquired in 1953 by the purchase from the Bishop Estate of the seventy-eight-acre quarry area below Dole Street. Quarry land immediately provided the site for a new Klum Gymnasium and a new Cooke Field for outdoor athletics, as well as land for much future construction.

THE RED MENACE

A ceremonial opening planned for the new chemistry building brought to the campus the ideological storms of the Cold War. Biochemist Linus Pauling, Nobel laureate and a political liberal, was invited to grace the dedication of the building in March 1951. Then the administration learned that a California legislative committee had denounced him as sympathetic to the "Red Menace." The regents, sensitized by anti-Communist investigations then underway in Hawaii, quickly canceled the dedication ceremony. Pauling nevertheless came to Honolulu to meet with several faculty members and to provide the local press with unflattering opinions of the regents and the administration.

Anticommunism was in full cry, both on campus, where the regents prohibited the distribution of pamphlets by the ILWU, and downtown, where soon after the Pauling controversy the territorial legislature by statute required all public employees to take a loyalty oath. Some 190 faculty members vainly petitioned the governor to veto the measure. A student employee of the University Press, Trixie Tanaka, refused to sign the oath and was fired. A few years later, Beatrice Krauss, invited to teach botany, also refused to sign but did teach—without pay.

The loyalty oath, combined with a drastic budget cut by the 1951 legislature, stimulated a hitherto generally apolitical faculty to consider membership in a union of public employees. The presidents of the two largest associations—the Hawaii Education Association (HEA) and the Hawaii Government Employees Association (HGEA) —appeared before a special meeting of faculty and staff to make their case. Although the HEA, with a membership of public school teachers, seemed to have the greater appeal, the HGEA made a more vigorous statement against witch hunts and issued a stronger invitation to join. Consequently, many UH faculty members signed up with the HGEA and relatively few with the HEA. Both organizations, however, offered their lobbying efforts to improve the level of salaries on the campus, modest considering the high cost of living in Hawaii. The way was set for faculty unionization after 1970.

A LIMITED GROWTH SETS THE STAGE

Gregg Sinclair continued his long presidency to 1955. Throughout his term of thirteen years, he sought a larger international role for the University, expressing the ambition, endemic in Hawaii, to serve as a Pacific crossroads. A step toward that goal was the convening of a series of East-West Philosophers' Conferences, which brought to the campus an array of prominent academicians from Asia and the continental United States in 1939, 1949, and 1959. A sprinkling of foreign students registered for courses (thirty in 1951, fifty-eight by 1954) helped foster the dream of becoming an international university.

Budget constraints and the disappointment of statehood repeatedly deferred in the U.S. Senate continued to frustrate campus ambitions for a larger international role. However, more of the graduate studies necessary to attract students from overseas were established. Between 1953 and 1955 the Regents approved new Ph.D. programs in botany, chemistry, entomology, genetics, soil science, and marine biology. Further, a linguistic base more capable of serving broad areas of scholarship than the few foreign languages previously offered was laid down in the mid-1950s. To the list of Chinese, Japanese, Hawaiian, French, German, Spanish, and Latin were added Korean, Hindi, Greek, Italian, and Indonesian. Instruction in Portuguese, originally introduced in 1938 by direction of the territorial legislature but dropped after World War II for lack of student enrollment, was revived.

The program also included Russian. During the early postwar period, shaped in so many ways by the Cold War, Russian studies at Manoa gained limited attention. The Soviet Union and its doings were perceived as centered in Moscow, half the world distant from Hawaii. Nevertheless, from 1947 Professor John White taught the history of Russia in Asia, and from 1952 Professor Ella Wiswell offered courses in Russian language and literature, courses that gained increased student interest and national funding following the launching of Sputnik in 1957.

For learning any foreign language, a new electronic technology was available. In 1955 Professor Dorothy Aspinwall, chair of the European Languages Department, received a grant to study teaching methods at mainland universities. The result of her investigation was the creation in 1956 of the first language laboratory at UH, a unit of thirty-nine semi-soundproof booths in George Hall. Language teachers made their own tapes, as they were doing at other innovative campuses across the nation, until textbook publishers realized what a lucrative new market was there. Making tapes—two or three per week for each level of each language—was onerous. The recording booth, a glass cage in a corner of the lab, was ventilated only by a louvered window. Many a tape, Dr. Aspinwall reported, had a background of bird song and lawn-mowing.

Tapes gave students the equivalent of a hundred minutes of private language

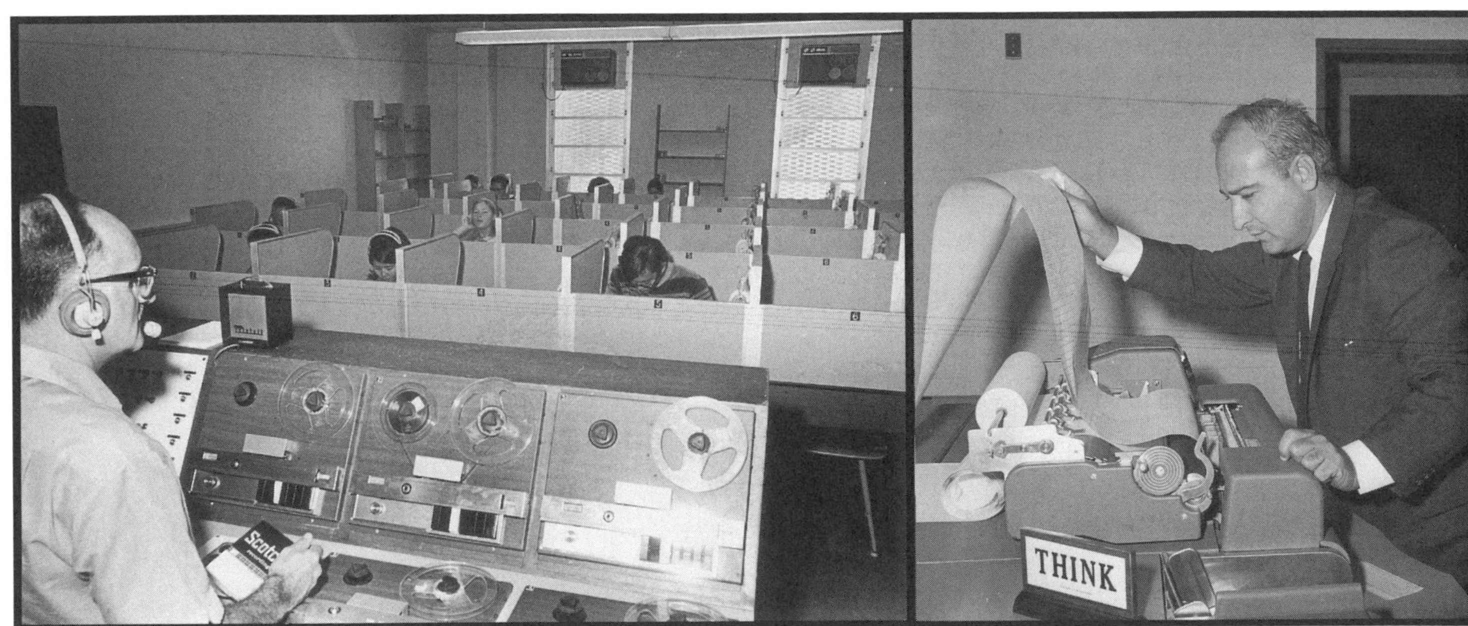

The electronic age came to the campus in mid-century. The first language laboratory, shown here with lab director Jean Theuma, opened in 1956. The first computer, an IBM of the early 1960s captioned with the corporation's slogan, is demonstrated by mathematics professor Christopher Gregory.

tutoring each week, and when Webster Hall was opened in 1961 space was provided for a larger, more sophisticated lab. Newer electronic equipment was installed when the lab moved into Moore Hall in 1970. By that time a wide range of Asian languages was being offered—Hindi, Sanskrit, Indonesian, Tagalog, Thai, Vietnamese, Cambodian—in addition to the staples, Chinese, Korean, and Japanese.

Japanese was a special case. Before World War II the numerous private Japanese language schools in Hawaii had prepared generations of students—not exclusively students of Japanese ancestry—with a competence in the language. After the attack on Pearl Harbor, the schools were closed and their teachers sent to "relocation" camps on the mainland. Only a few reopened after the war. It took several years, as the territorial government sought to achieve statehood by demonstrating the Americanism of its people, for the study of Japanese to escape its wartime image. UH regularly offered Japanese language courses, but enrollment had not been large. However, with two years of credit in a foreign language required for a bachelor of arts degree, the demand for Japanese began to boom. Class enrollment increased by two-thirds between

1955 and 1957. The courses were especially popular among students of Japanese ancestry for various reasons, perhaps including the prospect of an easy A for those who already had a head start.

"A THREAT TO THE UNIVERSITY"

More buildings and more classroom equipment were to come, but in the mid-1950s a succession of tight budgets left an ugly mark on the campus. "Jasper" Holmes, longtime dean of engineering and then dean of administration, reported that the University had the lowest physical plant investment per student of all land-grant colleges, and it looked it.

> The situation is actually worse than statistics can depict. The campus is cluttered up with temporary shacks. The maintenance personnel are at a minimum. The average floor space per janitor is 14,000 square feet, and each general laborer performing gardening work has an average of six acres of grass and shrubbery to care for.[3]

An inspection team from the Western Association of Schools and Colleges, which accredits campuses in the western states and Hawaii, was even more critical. Its 1955 report warned that "an accredited university cannot continue to operate on such meager territorial appropriations." It found that the average cost of operation at Manoa ($550 per student) was the lowest of eighteen western colleges of comparable size and program. Among the sixty-nine land-grant schools, only three—all colleges for Blacks in the South—received smaller legislative appropriations than the $417 per student allotted to the University. No other land-grant college had a student-faculty ratio as high as Manoa's.

The *Honolulu Star-Bulletin* quickly reacted to the report, which threatened the University with loss of accreditation unless budget support improved within the next five years. The newspaper summarized the school's ragged financial history, voicing concern and an appreciation seldom expressed as strongly on its editorial pages since the days when Wallace Rider Farrington was publisher.

> A THREAT TO THE UNIVERSITY. The University was born in a struggle. Many doubters said it wasn't necessary. Its early years were years of constant effort to survive, either indifference or actual hostility—hostility based on the theory that Hawaii didn't need an expanding public college.
>
> The University has earned its way by its products—the men and women it has turned out and its varied services to Hawaii and to the Pacific. Now the Territory must be ready to provide the physical plant and the teaching staff required to hold the accreditation that is the national mark of scholastic achievement.[4]

But adequate appropriations were hard to get in a slow-growing economy. Statehood and prosperity were still around the corner, not discernible in the mid-century fiscal gloom. It was generally a time of caution for administrators on the Manoa campus. Sinclair had provided a vision for the University, to become the academic meeting place of Eastern and Western scholarship. The pursuit of that vision had to await better times.

SINCLAIR'S SUCCESSORS

Dr. Paul S. Bachman was the obvious successor when President Sinclair ended his thirteen-year tenure in 1955. Bachman had a long career at Manoa, coming to the campus in 1927 to become the first chairman of the Political Science Department. Identified by Sinclair as a tough-minded administrator, he had served as dean of faculties and then as vice-president, carrying much of the responsibility for lobbying for appropriations and then trying to live within them.

Curricular expansion continued to be limited by tight budgets, even as the Manoa student enrollment in 1955 edged past five thousand. Plans for new programs were generally put on hold. An exception was the University's Extension Division, largely self-supporting from tuition fees paid by night students at Manoa as well as at a Downtown Center and on military bases where courses were offered. By 1956 it had grown so steadily—with an enrollment of credit students approximately equal to the number in regular daytime classes—that it was elevated to the status of the College of General Studies (eventually, after a succession of name changes, the College of Continuing Education and Community Service).

Among its other advantages, the college provided a flexible and inexpensive place for academic innovation, particularly for new courses that the regular departments were not prepared to offer. In this way a large variety of subjects—Korean and Tagalog, hotel management and the economics of Hawaii, architecture and library science, to name a random few—first found their way into the curriculum. If a course did not draw enough fees to pay its instructor, however, it was canceled, so many a scheduled innovation never came to life.

In 1957 the new college was given administrative responsibility for daytime and evening unclassified students not registered in any degree program. The next year Dean Edmund Spellacy reported:

> There has been a measurable increase in the number of unclassified students who frequent the campus during the day . . . somewhat over five hundred. Two years ago [Willard] Wilson referred to these students as the "shorn lambs." Regrettably, they remain shorn for, being non-degree candidates, no counselling system is available to them. . . . It is hoped that in some fashion not yet determined it will be possible to render them the assistance that they so badly need.

(Four decades later the problem remained. Academic counseling was generally available but typically not much sought by the college's diverse population of "shorn lambs.")

Budgetary prospects improved, and Bachman's administration was beginning to raise its sights, starting plans for the building boom that was to come in the next decade, when the new president suddenly died in January 1957. Bachman's death sent the regents into a protracted national search for a successor, while Willard Wilson served as acting president. During the interregnum, Wilson presented in his 1957–1958 report to the government and people of Hawaii a wide-lens view of their university:

> The University of Hawaii is in many respects the Territory of Hawaii in miniature. We conduct many of the same intricate and complicated operations, we share many of the same interests and aspirations, we shoulder many of the same burdens in an attempt to build a better world. We administer a library, an art gallery, a radio station, and theatres that present a wide variety of musical, dramatic, and informative programs. We maintain buildings, roads, a police force, and a Civil Defense organization. We are bankers, book publishers, hostlers, and restaurateurs. We are florists, horticulturalists and farmers, stockmen, dairymen, and poultry raisers. We pack fruit, train troops, and test materials. We practice clinical and preventative medicine and conduct social work and counseling services. We are weavers, potters, and painters. We administer kindergartens and primary and secondary schools. We operate business machines, laboratories, fishing boats—even an aquarium.
>
> But all these complex operations are only the necessary accompaniments of our basic role: that of providing the advantages of higher education to the people of the Territory. Thus in essence the University is a vibrant, dynamic, living laboratory devoted to the single purpose of producing broad-gauged, well-informed, and productive citizens.

Inventively, perhaps fanned by the winds of change, the regents appointed a faculty committee to aid them in the search for a president. They then ignored the advice of the professors and surprised them by choosing Dr. Laurence Snyder, an internationally honored geneticist and a gifted teacher whose only administrative work had been as dean of the graduate school of the University of Oklahoma. He took office in 1958.

Snyder was a congenial and modest president, qualities appropriate for the late 1950s, when the University began to find it easier to persuade the Hawaii government to appropriate more funds. A new generation of Democratic legislators, many of them UH alumni and war veterans, in 1954 had ended the Republican control of the territorial Senate and House which dated from the beginning of the century. These new legislators put expansion of educational opportunities high on their agenda and voted for tax increases to pay the bill, over the veto of the appointive Republican governor.

The University responded to the opportunity with an array of proposals for expansion. The result, as Snyder later termed it, was a campus "explosion." During his five-year tenure the number of students, of courses, of degree programs, and the size of the annual appropriation approximately doubled. The explosion, however, was most obvious on the ground, as building construction on an unprecedented scale sought to accommodate the growing student body and faculty. In five years thirty-seven new buildings went up at Manoa.

The entire expanse beyond Varney Circle, hitherto the domain of Tropical Agriculture, was opened for development, and the campus assumed its present shape and eclectic style of architecture. Abandoned was the neoclassic symmetry of the old quadrangle on the western side of Hawaii Hall; the architectural future of the campus was to be the pursuit of variety—unfortunately not always with the attainment of beauty or even utility in building design.

Planners doomed Farrington Hall, the old campus theatre, with its resident colonies of termites. Bulldozed were the fields of Napier grass that had fed the livestock of the "Farm," now pastured and studied at Waialee on Oahu's north shore and at other rural acreage acquired for the College of Tropical Agriculture. All farm buildings, most of the wartime barracks, and the faculty plantation houses disappeared. In their place arose an engineering building (Keller Hall), a physical science building, a zoology building (Edmondson Hall), a biomedical sciences building (later named Snyder Hall), the Hawaii Institute of Geophysics building, Webster and Spalding Halls (for classrooms, administrative offices, and the nursing and dental hygiene programs).

At the far edge of the campus the buildings of the East-West Center soon were to line the near bank of Manoa Stream. Along Dole Street there appeared more dormitories (Frear Hall for women students, Johnson Hall for men), the Music Building and its auditorium. Across University Avenue arose the plainly named University School Multipurpose Building and also an annex to Wist Hall. Down in the quarry (euphemized as the Lower or Makai Campus) development started with a new gymnasium and associated athletic facilities. Planners noted that the quarry was a "final collecting point" for campus storm water runoff—no surprise to the people who parked there during a heavy rain.

This noisy, dust-spewing spate of construction more than doubled the number of university structures. The number of classrooms, laboratories, and offices increased even more since many of the new buildings rose above the tree line, which had hitherto generally defined the height of campus construction. Construction costs for the Geophysics Building, Edmundson Hall, and later the structures of the East-West Center came from the Hawaii government and from federal grants. One building, however, was a private gift. The new music building at the corner of Dole and University Avenues, on plots where generations of farmers had raised flowers and vegetables, lacked a recital hall. Happily, the Mae Zenke Orvis Auditorium was added in

1961, the gift of financier Arthur Orvis to honor his wife, once associated with the New York Metropolitan Opera Company.

Changes in the programs and organization of the campus matched the building boom of Snyder's presidency. The College of Applied Science, formed in 1921, was divided into a College of Engineering and a School of Nursing. Twenty-six new academic departments were created, almost doubling their number. New graduate curricula were offered in agronomy, geology, electrical engineering, genetics, French, and music, among others. In 1958 Psychology became the first department outside Marine Zoology and Tropical Agriculture to offer a doctorate. By 1961 the number of Ph.D. programs had increased to sixteen.

Snyder questioned the name of Teachers College, since it also prepared school administrators and counselors; in 1959 it was changed to College of Education. Dean Everly ended the policy of limiting enrollment to the anticipated needs of the public schools and admitted all qualified applicants. One result was the opening of opportunity for more young people of Japanese ancestry. For them, teaching remained the shortest route to a profession and an escape from the plantation and the cannery.

The College of Business Administration, under the deanship of Michael Wermel, in 1961 created a Department of Hotel Management and Tourism to offer a bachelor's degree. It expanded with the visitor industry in Hawaii. By 1966, under the direction of Edward Barnet, the department had grown to become a School of Travel Industry Management, the first such in the Pacific area.

Teaching and research in medicine also began modestly. In 1962 a Department of Public Health was created under the chairmanship of Dr. Richard K. C. Lee, who had been the last health director of the territory. Working with small funds and great tactical skill, Lee gathered support, finessing initial opposition within the local medical profession. In two years the program had become the School of Public Health, with Lee as its first dean. The seed was planted that would produce a medical school.

Departments across the campus, stimulated by a resurgence of interest in international studies, added more instruction dealing with the Pacific and Asia. Economics, for example, had offered undergraduate courses and seminars in the economic history of China and Japan as far back as 1933, but these were discontinued when their teacher, James Shoemaker, retired in 1949. Discontinuance of such courses was in keeping with that time. Bitter recrimination about how China had been "lost" to the United States fed the social pathology called McCarthyism, which made politically dangerous any scholarly discussion of Communist nations. Academic interests, in Hawaii as elsewhere across the nation, shifted to areas safer and more accessible to research than East Asia. Courses on the national economies of East and Southeast Asia were not again offered until the late 1950s when, throughout the College of Arts and Sciences, instruction and research on Asia began to grow.

At mid-century the University had resumed its pattern of growth. The campus center was still the Quadrangle, augmented by the dining-recreational facilities of Hemenway Hall (center of the aerial photograph), but expansion in all directions was about to begin. This 1949 view shows Bachman Hall, the administration building, under construction at the lower right along Dole Street. Sinclair Library would soon follow to the left of Hemenway Hall. War surplus "tempos" were still grouped around the Manoa campus, from the long band building of Teachers College in the lower left to the string of student dorms and faculty "apartments" in the upper right. The farm of the College of Tropical Agriculture was shrinking rapidly.

Graduation exercises and other convocations usually filled Andrews Outdoor Theatre (facing page, bottom) undaunted by the showers that might on any day drift, or sweep, down Manoa Valley. The alternative to carrying on in the rain was postponement, for no structure on the campus yet accommodated more than a few hundred people.

The range of student activities was wide—represented by the UH marching band, organized by Norman Rian in 1946, and the annual *Ka Palapala* ethnic beauty queen contest. The news desk of *Ka Leo* trained generations of journalists, such as the couple in the foreground of a 1947 dance at Hemenway Hall—in freshman beanie, future editor Dan Katz and reporter Tomi K. Knaefler.

THE STUDENT BODY EXAMINED

The University's enrollment grew steadily after 1953, as a college education increasingly became the expectation of young people in Hawaii, and with its expansion the campus population became more diverse. A team from the U.S. Office of Education analyzed the student body in 1962. It found that males and females were about equal in number. Just over half of those enrolled in degree programs were of Japanese ancestry (versus 32 percent of the state population at large); 22 percent were Caucasians (versus 32 percent); 14 percent were Chinese (versus 6 percent). Students identifying themselves as Hawaiians constituted slightly more than 1 percent of the student body (versus 19 percent of the state's population).

By and large, students came from middle-class families whose annual income (at $7,700) averaged well above the state norm. Approximately half reported that their fathers were in professional, managerial, proprietary, or "skilled" occupations. Only about one-fifth said their fathers' jobs were unskilled, "semi-skilled," or in agriculture. Over half (55 percent) lived at home; only 6 percent stayed in campus dormitories. A large percentage of women had room-and-board jobs in town, typically requiring them to baby-sit or do housework for ten hours a week.

More than a fourth of Manoa students reported that they were the first members of their family to attend college. In many cases, older siblings and parents provided financial support. (More limited data for the Hilo campus indicated that about half of its students were first-of-family.) About two-thirds of the Manoa students said they were Christians; one-seventh were Buddhists; 1 percent were Jewish.

Most came from public high schools on Oahu, though a fifth were graduates of mainland or foreign institutions. Applying a standard test of academic achievement, the team found that "the scholastic ability of freshmen who enroll at the University is comparable to those entering similar institutions in other states."[5]

The Manoa faculty and deans noticed that pidgin English was no longer the problem it had been thought to be in prewar years. Instead, the English Department concentrated on writing in Freshman Composition, required of all undergraduate degree candidates except those few who passed a test to exempt them. Special writing courses were devised for engineering and business students. Dean Holmes noted that while engineering students were impatient with the requirement, graduates with some years of experience in their field told him they wished they had more training in effective writing.

Foreign students (soon to be augmented by the creation of the East-West Center) presented more difficult linguistic problems. The College of Arts and Sciences developed a program for Teaching of English as a Second Language (TESL) and even MATESL, a master's in teaching the subject. The College of Education, which asserted that it "owned" the "teaching of teachers," lost the competition for jurisdiction over the new field.

By 1963 the enrollment at Manoa reached ten thousand, double the number in regular credit programs when President Sinclair had left office in 1955. More than a thousand of them came from the mainland United States or abroad. The University had attained a critical mass for recognition as something much more than a cow college with attendant teacher training.

RELATIONS WITH ALUMNI

In its lengthy report, *The University of Hawaii and Higher Education in Hawaii,* the 1962 survey team from the federal Office of Education considered the alumni, as well as the students then enrolled:

> The record of university relationship with its organized alumni is one of long misunderstanding and tension. The major complaint from the alumni is that they have, for the most part, been ignored by the administration. . . . The administration . . . on the other hand, points to the record of chief concern of the alumni in matters only secondarily related to the primary purposes of the institution. This is shown in the standing interest of the alumni in intercollegiate athletics. . . . The chief concern of the organized alumni for intercollegiate athletics and the stadium causes university officials to hesitate in seeking counsel from this group on the formulation or implementation of major policies.

The report might have mentioned that a strong focus on intercollegiate sports was scarcely uncommon among American universities—in fact, it would have been noteworthy if alumni groups acted otherwise, as in expressing strong interest in the academic programs. The situation in Manoa, however, was exacerbated by two things. One was "the Stadium" issue—whether the old ball park on King Street, in which the regents and the ASUH held shares, should be replaced and with what kind of facility. That issue was resolved when the state government erected the large Aloha Stadium far leeward of the campus.

Less tractable was the fact that the alumni association was served by a secretary unsatisfactory to the administration. For a decade she successfully resisted the efforts of UH presidents to remove her from the office she occupied, strategically located at the entrance to administrative headquarters in Bachman Hall. More than thirty years were to pass before an Alumni Affairs Office was created.

IMPACT OF STATEHOOD

The surge of activity during President Snyder's administration was but a prelude to the University's expansion into a statewide system following his retirement in 1963. The catalyst for growth was Hawaii's attainment of statehood in 1959. With statehood, and coincidentally the advent of jet air travel, Hawaii seemed to move a thousand miles closer to the mainland, to become more visible, easier to visit, more attractive for residence, work, and investment. The Island economy boomed and local government revenues swelled, helping sustain the University in a decade of enlargement and improvement.

There was a critical change in the political setting. As a state, Hawaii elected its governor. Surprisingly—for Democratic control over the legislature remained firm—in 1959 Republican William Quinn was voted into office. Equally surprising, he replaced the incumbent regents with a group, mostly corporate executives like their predecessors, but men more appreciative of the University's potential and less apprehensive of its cost. Herbert C. Cornuelle of the Dole Pineapple Company was selected as chairman of the board, which now strongly encouraged the University to plan for its development.

Encouragement from the governor's office warmed further after 1962, when John A. Burns was elected to the first of three terms as chief executive. Burns, a key figure in the history of Hawaii and of its public university, apparently brought ambivalent feelings to his relationship with the school where he had enrolled as a freshman in 1930 (while working on the night desk of the *Honolulu Star-Bulletin*) but dropped out in the first semester. Even when serving as Hawaii's last territorial delegate to Congress, and then as governor, Burns could be defensive about lacking a college education.

Nevertheless, he saw in the University an institution that would help fulfill his dream of raising the people of Hawaii—and particularly those of Japanese ancestry, whose endurance and bravery in World War II he so admired, and who so strongly supported him in the Democratic Party—to a better life. To this end, the governor advocated a broadened educational program, offering more career opportunities to local people.

He also favored attracting mainland and foreign students to bring greater variety and sophistication to the student body. Twice Burns vetoed legislative bills imposing higher tuition fees on nonresident students. His political biographer explained this rare exercise of his veto power as due to a "visionary utopian strain in Burns which saw Hawaii as an education for all of America,"[6] an education that mainlanders could experience on the campuses at Manoa and Hilo.

Statehood brought with it seats in each house of Congress. These votes helped obtain a $2,250,000 grant in lieu of the support given in land endowments to state land-grant colleges under the federal Morrill Act of 1862. Federal funds were also appropriated to complete construction of the Hawaii Institute of Geophysics, the University's first highly sophisticated research facility.

THE EAST-WEST CENTER

The most dramatic consequence to the University of statehood was the creation of the East-West Center, financed by an initial appropriation of $10 million.[7] It began with a speech by Lyndon B. Johnson, Senate majority leader, on April 16, 1959, a month after the Hawaii statehood bill had passed Congress with his support. Discussing the need to foster understanding among nations, Johnson asked, perhaps rhetorically, why there should not be established in Hawaii an international institute where intellectuals of East and West could meet to exchange ideas. Reports of the speech first came to Honolulu radio stations, at one of which John Stalker, professor of history, was preparing his regular commentary on political events. Joined by political science professor Norman Meller, who chaired the Faculty Senate, Stalker urged President Snyder to respond at once to Johnson's suggestion.

A rapid and substantive response was possible because just two months earlier art professor Murray Turnbull, then acting dean of the College of Arts and Sciences, had sent Meller a proposal for the "establishment of an International College of Cultural Affairs" to serve students and visiting academicians from around the world. Snyder, though intrigued by the bold idea, was constrained by budgetary directives requiring the University to carry on "present services at present levels." With the prospect of federal funding, however, Snyder appointed a faculty committee, including Turnbull, Meller, and Stalker, plus Professors Charles Bouslog, Arthur Kirkpatrick, Robert Martin, and Morton Rosenberg, to flesh out a proposal for creating an international college. By February 1960, more than sixty UH faculty members were working zealously at detailing the programs and organization of the proposed center. The State Department, directed by Congress to consider the feasibility of the idea, sent a study group to Hawaii and then expressed cautious support.

Calls and cables to Johnson revealed a difference in concept between Washington and Manoa. Johnson had in mind a facility that would bring Asians to Hawaii to be taught in their own languages, returning home imbued with "the American way of life." He seemed to expect the teaching of medicine, agriculture, and other technologies in which the United States was advanced. The UH faculty planners had in mind cultural interchange, in which Americans would learn as well as teach.

What emerged from the stratagems of Johnson in the Senate was an amendment to the Mutual Security Act of 1960, authorizing the State Department to establish in Hawaii a Center for Cultural and Technical Interchange between East and West. On October 31, 1960, President Eisenhower signed an appropriation act that included approximately $10 million to finance the center's first year of operation, most of it for buildings. Hawaii's legislature had already appropriated $800,000 to help pay for planning. Turnbull, who had continued to head the organizational effort, became the

The abiding ambition of UH to serve as the international university of the Pacific was first put in programmatic terms in the mid-1930s by Professor Gregg M. Sinclair, shown with professors Shao Chang Lee, Wing-Tsit Chan, and Tadao Kunimoto.

World War II terminated the Oriental Institute that Sinclair had organized, but after the war the University, which he then headed, continued to pursue that ambition. The chance came in 1960 with the establishment of the federally financed Center for Cultural and Technical Interchange Between East and West—briefly, the East-West Center. Groundbreaking in 1961 for the first of its buildings on the eastern edge of the campus was the ceremonial work of Vice-President Lyndon Johnson (far right), Governor William Quinn (far left), and U.S. Senators Hiram Fong and Oren Long.

Examining blueprints for building construction are dark-suited Alexander Spoehr, first chancellor of the Center, and Professor Murray Turnbull, interim director, who led its creation.

acting director. By May 9, 1961, the program was ready for a ground-breaking ceremony at which Johnson, by then vice-president under John F. Kennedy, delivered a dedication address and received an honorary degree from the University.

In January 1962, Turnbull handed direction of the center to its first chancellor, Dr. Alexander Spoehr, an eminent anthropologist who headed the Bishop Museum. Thanks to the energetic work of the center's pioneers, more than two hundred persons from around the Pacific, Asia, and the United States were already enrolled under grants, and twenty-six had been added to the UH faculty to help the center's programs, together with eighty-four administrators and support staff of the center itself. Buildings designed by the renowned architectural firm of I. M. Pei were under construction along Manoa Stream, at the far end of the campus previously used to sustain the farm animals of the College of Tropical Agriculture and then to house faculty members. Jefferson Hall, for administrative offices and food services, went up on the bank of the stream, along with Hale Manoa, a dormitory for grantees, Lincoln Hall to house visiting scholars and trainees, and a laboratory/classroom building.

Across the new East-West Road arose the impressive mass of a theatre, later named after John F. Kennedy. The center's administrators had thought the building would be used as its auditorium, but Professor Earle Ernst, who managed the Department of Drama and Theatre with a strong hand, easily prevailed in a tug-of-war for control, for he held the keys to the building as well as the greater determination. A few years later, the federal government signed over the theatre to the University in exchange for campus lands occupied by the center, including the site of John A. Burns Hall, its administrative headquarters.

For several years the East-West Center functioned as an integral part of the University, even though a national board of governors reviewed its operation and an appropriation through the State Department provided most of its funds. Grantees generally took their courses and earned advanced degrees from the University. Many faculty members held split appointments with the center, an arrangement that helped build up the learning resources used by the entire campus.

Rather quickly, however, a polarization began that ended in separation and divorce. The national board increasingly exercised its authority; the center increasingly recruited its own researchers rather than utilizing UH faculty members. Competition was symbolized in a midnight raid by center staffers who carried off much of the Asian collection from the University library to the East-West Center. (The books were later returned after Hamilton Library was completed.) East-West Road became more a line of separation than of linkage between the two institutions. Finally, in 1975, by agreement between the federal and state governments, the center was formally severed from the University. Mutual assistance continued, particularly through joint faculty appointments, but essentially the two institutions went their separate ways.

Looking back at its history, Turnbull found that the fate of the East-West Center was largely determined by the decision of Lyndon Johnson at its creation concerning its place in the matrix of government.

> [T]he fatal blow to the Center came with the positioning of it within the aegis of the Department of State. That Department necessarily and rightly is charged with responsibilities of shaping, explaining, and conducting American foreign policy —this is diametrically opposite to the non-aggrandizing objectives that we sought to invest in the heart and foundations of the Center, whose aim was not to serve a particular point of view of a particular people, but to serve all in the interests of one another.[8]

Even after their divorce, the center continued to foster the University's development as an international institution. Grantees from Asia and the Pacific seeking advanced degrees at Manoa added to the demand for graduate programs in a widening variety of fields—in the social sciences, business administration, the arts, languages and literature, etc.—that might not have been justified, or would have been created only much later. Furthermore, the departments offering these courses were able to recruit and retain scholars specializing in Pacific and Asian studies, many of them shared with the research institutes of the East-West Center.

Other international connections continued to be made by the University. On Hawaii there was a training center for Peace Corps volunteers going to island states in the western Pacific. College of Education faculty served under University contracts with Pakistan, Thailand, and Laos, instructing farmers, technicians, and teachers, until the spreading effects of the Vietnam War brought these overseas ventures to a close.

At retirement in 1963 Snyder could look back at a presidency capped by three years of hectic growth in programs and construction. What he singled out with particular pleasure among the creations of his administration was not a building, however, but a space between buildings. In 1961–1962 a pedestrian mall, generously broad at his urging, was laid out from Varney Circle to East-West Road. Its canopy of wide-reaching monkeypod trees served to soften the harsh lines of structures along the mall, screening the architectural mediocrity in the eastern half of the expanded campus.

But Snyder could not claim victory in a quixotic attempt to remove UH from intercollegiate football competition. Acting on the recommendation of a faculty committee on athletics, he ordered the game discontinued, and during the 1961 season he prevailed; for the first time since World War II there was no football team at Manoa. By 1962, however, Snyder was a lame-duck president, in his last year of service. Even as he left office, the Rainbow Warriors were again scheduled to play mainland college teams, which they did with discouraging results. The question of what to do about football was left to the next administration.

From the early 1960s the University increasingly took on programs reaching across the Pacific. Peace Corps volunteers were trained for their work in Asia by UH staff on the island of Hawaii, as in this planting exercise in Waipio Valley.

In 1969 professors John Bystrom (center), Katase Nose (left), and Paul Yuen developed a program using a surplus satellite to connect Pacific island countries for medical advice, emergency management, education, and the like. Called PEACESAT, the system grew to link twenty-two island nations—including Tonga, whose earth station is shown at its testing.

THE TIME OF HAMILTON

To find a successor to President Snyder capable of guiding the University in the growth that obviously lay ahead, the new Board of Regents undertook a national search. This time—the only such instance in UH history—the regents under Chairman Herbert Cornuelle heeded the advice of faculty members on its search committee. Those Manoa professors used their connections in the national academic network to get confidential information on each of a score of promising candidates winnowed from a long list of nominees. To the regents they recommended two experienced administrators of state universities: Fred Harrington, vice-president of Wisconsin, and Thomas H. Hamilton, president of the multicampus State University of New York. After several interviews, the board offered the post to Harrington. He agreed, but then asked to be released when the president of Wisconsin suddenly died and he was selected to replace him. The regents then turned to Hamilton, who in August 1962 accepted the offer to become the seventh president of the University. Holder of a doctorate from the University of Chicago, Hamilton assumed a formal membership in the Political Science Department, an affiliation that proved ironic at the bitter end of his presidency.

Even before taking office at the beginning of 1963, the new president excited the admiration of the regents, of Governor Burns, and of legislative leaders. Briefed on the tight financial position, Hamilton volunteered to take a 10 percent cut in his annual salary of $33,000. That saving was miniscule in a University budget of $20 million, but it sent a clear message of fiscal restraint to the campus.

Providentially, an official residence, long sought by the University for its presidents, was soon provided. The family of Frank C. Atherton gave the University their fourteen-room residence atop College Hill, near, but not too near, the Manoa campus. Money previously appropriated for a residence was used to renovate the old house. Months went by, however, as the paperwork outpaced the job of reconstruction. A few days before Christmas, the new president summoned the contractors and subcontractors on the job for a conference. Willard Wilson, then observing the campus from his post as corporate secretary of the University, recorded Hamilton's words:

> Gentlemen, I want you to know that in a fairly active administrative life I have had the responsibility at one time or another for millions of dollars worth of construction and remodeling. In all that experience I would like you to know that I have never encountered so much difficulty and incompetence in meeting deadlines adequately as I have encountered on this $100,000 job. I have here on my desk a complete set of specifications, that were originally about one inch thick. As you see now, they are very much thicker than that because I have attached a paper clip and a piece of paper with the description at each place where in the job you have departed from the specifications. I am going to go through these one by one, point them out, and if you have any questions I will answer them

> then. I suggest, however, that there is only one answer to this—that you make this job good if you do not wish this whole miserable performance—which you will recall is being done with State money and not mine—exposed to the public. Now we shall proceed.

And proceed they did, to the satisfaction of the Hamiltons and of the thousands of guests entertained in the presidential residence after 1963.

Hamilton's inaugural speech addressed the "special nature of a university," the duality of its purpose of at once preserving and challenging the beliefs of the society it serves.

> The community desiring excellence in its higher learning must know a great deal about the special nature of a university. A university is the most perplexing, frustrating, difficult, and wonderful social institution devised by man. And it is all of these things because it exists for paradoxical ends. . . . A university is established by a society to insure that the values to which that social order subscribes are perpetuated; there is, in effect, an orthodoxy at stake. And yet, in its rarer moments society also acknowledges that it is equally important to examine and, indeed, to modify that orthodoxy. Thus the university is mandated to question the value system which it is also supposed to preserve. Problems inevitably arise, however, from the fact that the whole society does not uniformly subscribe to both these ends. There are always some to whom it appears that the university ought to be preserving instead of questioning. And to others the reverse is true. This is why universities are so often misunderstood by the society which sustains them. This is why a public university is not like any other agency of government and cannot be so regarded if it is to achieve the excellence of its nature. . . .

Hamilton's own fate was to prove his insight, caught as he eventually was between the political orthodoxy of the community, as expressed in a general support of America's military intervention in Vietnam, and the opposition to the war expressed on campus.

The new president formed his administration in a new way. His predecessors had generally looked to the faculty, or others in the community, to head up the colleges, institutes, and bureaus of the campus. Hamilton did group about him in the central administration campus veterans (Kenneth Lau and Richard Kosaki as special assistants, Robert Hiatt as academic vice-president, Richard Takasaki as administrative vice-president, Willard Wilson as corporate secretary, Robert Kamins as dean for academic development), but college deans were recruited from around the nation. Todd Furniss came from Ohio State University to head the College of Arts and Sciences, John Shupe from Kansas State for Engineering, Schuyler Hoslett from Dun & Bradstreet for the College of Business Administration, Wytze Gorter from UCLA as dean of the Graduate School. A pattern was set: deans under Hamilton were generally selected after a national search. An infusion of new administrators strengthened the linkage of this island university to institutions of higher learning on the mainland.

Hamilton had come at a favorable time. A month after his inauguration, a voluminous report on higher education in Hawaii by the federal Department of Health, Education and Welfare (HEW) recommended that the University become a statewide system, formed of community colleges, the Hilo campus, and the Manoa campus as center for upper-division and graduate studies and research.

Proud in its dignity as a state in the Union, riding the crest of a local economy growing at a phenomenal annual rate of 7 percent, with Governor Burns pledged to support higher education, the Hawaii government readily responded to these recommendations and other expansionary plans offered by Hamilton. Witty and persuasive, he established a rapport with government and community leaders that stimulated appropriations and grants. Between 1963 and 1968 the annual operating expenditures of the University increased from $28 million to $63 million. A statewide university system was formed; its aggregate enrollment expanded from about ten thousand to more than twenty thousand students.

Hamilton brought with him useful experience gained as head of New York State's multicampus university. As he had found essential in Albany, in Honolulu he established good working relationships with the governor and with key legislators. Dealing with the governor was not difficult since Burns was ambitious for UH, strongly supportive of its rising ambition to be a first-class university. In the governor's view (as he told Kenneth Lau) to be first-class, three components were necessary: a medical school, a law school, and a football team that could compete with mainland schools at the Division 1 level.

Hamilton responded that a University administration could take the initiative on the professional schools, but a nationally competitive football team was a goal for which the governor's leadership was essential. Such a team must be recruited in competition with mainland colleges; athletic scholarships had to be provided. Perhaps a winning program would eventually generate box-office receipts sufficient to pay the scholarships, the coaches, and other costs, but in the meantime the UH budget could not cover them. If the governor were to appoint a committee of moneyed sports fans, however, they might raise the necessary funds. Burns agreed, and so was founded Koa Anuenue (Rainbow Warriors), the support group that has helped finance UH intercollegiate sports.

The law school was not to come in Hamilton's time, but the prenatal development of a medical school had already begun with the Pacific Biomedical Research Center, gathering talent from Microbiology and the new departments of Genetics, Biochemistry and Biophysics, Physiology, and Pharmacology. In 1967, with funds provided by the U.S. Public Health Service and mainland foundations as well as the Hawaii legislature, a two-year medical school opened under Windsor C. Cutting, an eminent pharmacologist and former dean of Stanford's medical school.

Fear of the budgetary consequences if a two-year program became four—as Cutting intended from the first—generated opposition on campus and in the legislature. Hamilton, however, defused much of the concern. In the recollection of Hiatt: "Tom Hamilton told the legislature that as long as he was president there would not be a four-year school. At that time we were confident we would not have to go to four years, and I think we got legislative support due to Hamilton's pledge." A full-fledged four-year medical school was to come, but not in Cutting's lifetime or during Hamilton's tenure.[9]

Action came easier to Hamilton's administration than it had to his immediate predecessors. One cause was a relaxation of the tight oversight exercised by the state government. Another was the intimacy of the University, its staff and faculty members, with the state government—a relationship that paid off when funds were readily available. As the HEW report had noted, state administrators and legislators, working only a few miles from the campus, had involved themselves in ways not intended by the Hawaii Revised Statutes, to the detriment of good management.

> The Legislature in Hawaii enters into matters that quite clearly should be the prerogative and the responsibility of the Regents of the University and the university staff. This is true of the legislators as individuals, to a surprising degree, as members of legislative committees and as a total group.[10]

Not that legislative intrusion was necessarily resented by faculty members and administrators lobbying for their programs. One department chairman, considering the campus-capitol connection, observed: "There has been interference . . . if it can be called interference . . . both ways. In the past, the result has been good for the University. Now the University is coming of age. It is time to let the baby go."[11]

Interaction between campus and legislators was more complex than the visiting hew team or most faculty members realized. Hubert Everly, longtime dean of the Col-lege of Education, after his retirement told an interviewer how he had garnered support for laboratory schools, including a new high school, to train teachers.

> INTERVIEWER: How did you sell the idea of a lab school? Were you questioned at all, "Why isn't the DPI [territorial Department of Public Instruction] doing this?"
> EVERLY: That was the attitude of the University, yes. This is why they wouldn't support it. But we didn't ask for their support. I . . . allied myself . . . with the educational establishment, the DOE [state Department of Education], and with the legislature, and with the teachers' union. Those were the allies of the College of Education. The teachers' union, after all, was composed primarily of my graduates. The DOE is composed primarily of my graduates. . . . And the legislature, many of them are graduates, some of the College itself, but certainly of the University. And they also respond well to the need for public education, particularly when the Democrats came into power . . . so that we found a ready audience and a willing supporter of things out of the College of Education which had not been

> approved by the university itself. . . . [T]hat's how the lab school . . . and the University High School was put together. . . .
>
> It wasn't long before we were under political pressure and pressure from regents to get their children into our school. So it became, then—well, it was a political asset rather than a liability. . . . I recall once the chairman of the House finance committee was giving me a bad time with my budget. . . . [H]e said: "Goddamn you Everly! I tried to get my kid in your lab school and you wouldn't take him." And he says, "Now I'm chairman of the House finance committee and you're going to pay." I said, "Goddamn it. How did I know you were going to become chairman of the House finance committee?" He looked at me and he laughed, "Goddamn it, you're right! Okay."[12]

It took time for legislators to gain enough confidence to grant the UH administration control over appropriated funds, but in 1966 the chairman of the Senate Committee on Ways and Means, Nadao Yoshinaga, said that the University now had "full flexibility, authority, and accountability" in the expenditure of its funds.

Accountability, there certainly was. The state adopted an elaboration in fiscal management made fashionable by the Department of Defense during the Vietnam War called the Program-Planning-Budgeting System, or PPBS for short. During testimony on the University's budget, Senator Yoshinaga asked Hamilton if the UH was operating under PPBS. "Yes, sir," he replied, "Richard [Takasaki] here handles the PP and I do the BS."[13] Hamilton was making a point, for he recognized that PPBS was based on physical measurements of an agency's achievement, such as the body count of those killed by a military unit. It was a mode of accountability ill-suited to the intangibles of a university, teaching and research. The UH modified version, Takasaki noted, was informally called the Planning and Budgeting Linking and Unification Method (PABLUM).

The scope of political involvement increased when the University suddenly expanded from the school at Manoa plus a Hilo branch to a system of higher education with campuses on each major island. In 1965 the vocational schools of the Department of Public Instruction became part of a network of community colleges under the Board of Regents. With systemwide enrollment projected to reach fifty thousand students in a decade, new community colleges were erected in former sugar cane fields beyond Pearl City and at the State Hospital in windward Oahu. There was talk of creating a new upper-division campus to serve the rapidly growing population of west Oahu.

The electronic reach from Manoa also became statewide. In April 1966, an educational television station began operations, broadcasting to the schools in the afternoon, to the general public on weeknights. KHET, based across University Avenue next to the College of Education, started with a federal grant of $178,000 plus modest state funds. By 1972 it was an independent public television system, beamed to all the Hawaiian islands. The University later also provided a first home for public radio in Hawaii. KHPR began broadcasting from Manoa in 1981. In its formative years, the studio was in one of the "temporary" wooden cottages shoehorned around campus—latterly in the recesses of the Lower Campus. The station, independent of the University, moved off the campus in 1987. KTUH, a low-wattage, student-operated station, continued to broadcast from Hemenway Hall, the old student center.

STIMULATING AND HANDLING GROWTH

The pressure was on and the ambition present to expand the work of the University in two directions: horizontally, to reach out to many more undergraduate students around the state; vertically, to create the research and graduate programs necessary to establish UH as a respected "first-class" university. Hamilton early realized that an explicit plan was needed to bring coherence to the University's development. He called on Vice-President Robert Hiatt, who appointed a small task force of faculty and administrators under Dean Robert Kamins, which in 1963–1964 worked intensively in consultation with the many units of the campus to produce Academic Development Plan I. For the first time, the goals of the university and means of attaining them were set down in print, program by program, for both the Manoa and Hilo campuses.

Federal and state funding sources were impressed by this evidence of planning, especially as presented by an explainer of intentions and achievements as persuasive as Hamilton. Academic Development Plan II followed in 1968, with more data on more programs, now expanded to include articulation of the community colleges within the new UH system. Plan II emphasized the responsibility of the University to keep abreast in its teaching with technological change and international linkages.

> The freshman of 1975 came into this world at about the same time as atomic energy, jet flight, space exploration, electronic computers, and commercial television. He will graduate from a University located in a state only three hours by supersonic jet from New York, Tokyo or Melbourne. He may find a job at the Hawaii terminal of an international satellite-linked computer network, in the statewide mass transportation system, or in an underwater mining plant off Kauai. . . .

This vision of the future may have been somewhat blurred in detail, but it challenged traditional instructional programs to respond to a world changing at a bewilderingly rapid rate. Response to the challenge was most evident in the research component of the University. An organizational arrangement to make Manoa a campus increasingly productive in research and graduate studies was needed. The traditional academic departments—such as botany, zoology, physics, and chemistry—had concentrated on teaching, leaving research to the individual initiative of faculty members. Some different arrangement, joining the separate disciplines, was needed to foster more intense, more sustained, and better coordinated research programs of the kind that could attract grants.

That arrangement was the research institute (described by Robert Hiatt in chapter 11). A $3 million grant from the National Science Foundation for the construction in 1963 of the Hawaii Institute of Geophysics Building marked a turning point. By its success in research, in attracting researchers, and in garnering federal funds, the HIG provided an organizational model for the succession of research institutes and centers that followed, including those in astronomy, biomedical and cancer research, gerontology, marine biology, natural energy, marine and atmospheric research, social sciences, and water resources.

Graduate degree programs, many of them linked with the research institutes, also multiplied, stimulated by a continued rise in research funds, primarily from the federal government. In the fiscal year 1960–1961 the University had received slightly under $2 million in extramural grants. Ten years later it was given more than $12 million. Over the decade, the number of fields offering graduate degrees rose from forty-three to ninety-seven, including twenty-eight new master's degrees and twenty-six doctorates.

As for undergraduate studies, funds were not abundant, but faculty initiative was. An array of new or experimental programs were devised. One, widely chosen by students seeking an alternative to the standard courses for meeting a science requirement, was an interdisciplinary option in general science. Created in 1957, it flourished through the 1960s. More broadly, the Honors Program offered special classes and advising to undergraduates with grade-point averages high enough to qualify. In Liberal Studies they could devise their own "major," with an emphasis on tutorials and directed reading. Other innovative programs for undergraduates were planned in the encouraging environment of Hamilton's administration, to be tried out—some to continue, others not—under the next president.

The classroom experience of some undergraduates changed in other, less satisfactory ways. More and more frequently graduate assistants instructed introductory courses. Some were excellent, despite the demands of their own studies. Others were less proficient and students complained. Dependence on graduate assistants was a side effect of increasing emphasis on research, with a consequential lessened emphasis on teaching lower-division courses. By the old dispensation, most faculty members had taught four courses each semester, and some, for example Harold McCarthy in philosophy and Carleton Green in English, taught with uncommon zest and devotion, leaving them little time for or interest in research publishable in scholarly journals.

The concentration on research prevailed, however, and set a new compact between faculty and administration. From the mid-1960s, as professors were recruited with greater attention to their publication lists and research grants, the departments adjusted to the changed agenda of the campus. Teaching loads were reduced to three courses for most faculty members, and fewer for those with well-funded research projects. "Publish or perish," the watchword of the time in academe, was not a great exaggeration. Hawaii followed the same path, attracted by the same goal of eminence in research, as other universities across the nation.

Nationally known scholars were recruited, and more national and international conferences were held on the campus, all assisted by a rising tide of federal grants. The state government became even more supportive when UH reported that it had come within range of the most prestigious universities in the value of federal grants received. By 1967 it had moved from obscurity on this chart of success to forty-second place among the two thousand and more institutions of higher learning in America. Judged at least by that measure of academic recognition, UH was no longer a small urban college but a major research university.

Downtown Honolulu acknowledged the achievement by sponsoring chairs for distinguished scholars, funded by corporations to pay salaries above the norm for other professors. At the start of 1966, Hamilton was able to report that four named chairs had been filled: Nobel Prize winner Georg von Bekesy to a chair in sensory sciences supported by the Hawaiian Telephone Company; Henry Stommel to the *Honolulu Advertiser*'s Captain Cook chair in oceanography; Edward Shaw to the Alexander & Baldwin/Matson Navigation Company chair in economics; while Pulitzer Prize–winning biographer Leon Edel occupied the Citizen's Chair earlier provided by the Hawaii legislature and utilized by the English Department.

With the expansion of teaching and research departments, the secretariat of the University also broke into new ground. In earlier times, a full-time secretary was the prestigious prerogative of senior officers, down to deans and directors. In the 1960s, first the largest departments, such as English, then the middle-sized, and at last all departments rated secretaries. These women, mostly of Japanese or Chinese ancestry, as a group highly capable and hard-working, provided administrative continuity and human connection on the campus as deans, directors, and chairmen came and went. For example, in his 1975 history of the College of Engineering, Dean Holmes reported:

> It is noteworthy that since World War II, through all the changes or organization and personnel, there have been only two secretaries of the College, Matsue Miyamoto succeeding Hazel Hee when the Administrative Vice President's office was organized. Between them these two secretaries have been acquainted with about ninety-five percent of all the engineering graduates since engineering education began in Hawaii.

Across the campus, similar tales were told of the administrative continuity—of knowing how things were done, what the precedents were, what reports had to be made, how to shortcut bureaucratic pathways—provided by the civil-service secretaries. The accounts survive, however, only as anecdotes since universities no more celebrate in print the roles of their secretaries than armies celebrate the essential work of their master sergeants.[14]

More programs, faculty, staff, and students needed more buildings. At Manoa, in short order there arose Kuykendall Hall for the large English Department, the Hawaii Institute of Geophysics building, dormitories, graduate library, student health center, multipurpose education building, a Thai pavilion, a Japanese garden and tea ceremony house as well as the theatre and other major buildings on the East-West Center end of the campus and more. *Time Magazine* observed that the University had become "an empire on which the cement never sets."

Expanding research programs at Manoa of the 1960s continued to demand more space. Further up in the valley, the University acquired sixty acres to be used by agricultural science programs, an astronomy institute, and also the University of Hawai'i Press. A facility for marine biology at Coconut Island in Kaneohe Bay was developed, and research facilities for the Pacific Biomedical Center and an ocean engineering laboratory were started at Kewalo Basin in Honolulu. The oceanography program by 1966 was operating four research vessels in the Pacific, home-ported in Honolulu. On campus, the new Institute for Astronomy began planning for the powerful telescopes that were to rise atop Mauna Kea on the Big Island. Federal grants supported these and other programs, maintaining the University's place among the nation's research centers.

New professional and vocational programs filled the buildings and demanded even more room. A School of Public Health (1964) and Pacific Biomedical Research Center were soon followed by the experimental two-year School of Medicine already noted. The new Travel Industry Management program in the College of Business Administration was accompanied by a curriculum in real estate to supply experts for the other rapidly growing market within the Island economy. The College of Education added programs granting the Ph.D. and (later in 1974) the Ed.D.

The new graduate library (later named after Hamilton) was scaled to hold 677,000 volumes, compared with the 500,000 capacity of Sinclair Library, which continued to serve undergraduates. Unlike Sinclair, the graduate library was air-conditioned, not merely for the comfort of its patrons and staff, but to protect books from the ravages of tropical temperatures and destructive molds. To administer it came Ralph Shaw, dean of the Library School at Rutgers, succeeding Carl Stroven, who in his long tenure had managed the growth of the library from a facility essentially for undergraduates to one that also served the more varied and expensive needs of a research university.

Shaw, "an eminent, toughminded efficiency expert intimately familiar with all aspects of library operations,"[15] revamped operations while expanding the collection closer to the standard for a university of excellence. In his four years of service, annual acquisitions rose fivefold, nearing one hundred thousand volumes. Working at a prodigious rate, Shaw also organized and initiated a Graduate School of Library Studies, with a focus on serving in the Asia-Pacific area as well as in the United States.

A growing student body—about nine thousand in 1962–1963, more than sixteen thousand in 1967–1968—brought greater diversity to the campus. Students from the mainland and abroad, some recruited by the East-West Center or by the UH athletic teams, or simply attracted by varied academic programs and low tuition, helped change the look of the place. Saris and Afro hair-dos became commonplace; Samoan lava-lavas and Nehru jackets no longer seemed exotic; shorts became shorter; and "go-aheads" became standard footwear.

More than attire changed. The ethnic mix continued to shift, reducing the statistical dominance of Japanese and Caucasians in the student body. The percentage of students of Hawaiian and Filipino ancestry, however, continued to grow only slowly. Among the faculty there were more women and more non-Caucasians, but still fewer than 1 percent were identified as Hawaiian or Filipino. The lag in recruiting non-Caucasians other than Japanese and Chinese set the stage for affirmative action programs in the 1970s to attract more "minority" faculty members and students.

The increasing population of faculty, staff, and students needed more space on campus for their persons and their vehicles—now cycles and mopeds, as well as cars. The old quarry below Dole Street was pressed into more intensive use. Cooke Field, long the school's outdoor athletic facility, was moved down into the "lower campus" near Klum Gym. The Duke Kahanamoku Pool was completed between 1963 and 1968, delayed by problems of design, construction, and dealing with the water accumulated in the quarry shell after heavy rains. Planning began for a parking structure to relieve the congested lots in the "upper campus" and for dormitories along the border of the of the quarry.

All the construction, however, did not adequately cope with the rising tide of campus population. More old barracks were hauled onto campus to serve a variety of needs. One near Hemenway Hall became a no-frills snack bar, where faculty, staff, and students could talk together and sometimes to each other. Thrifty tea drinkers pinned their wet tea bags to a clothes line strung within the building for such repeated use.

Improvisation was needed to provide classroom space, such as scheduling Saturday and night classes on campus and morning lectures in the Varsity Theater, the movie house near King Street. For a decade, beginning in 1966, undergraduates walked, biked, drove, or hitchhiked past the Founders' Gate, the Rainbow Inn on the corner of Dole Street, and down the long slope of University Avenue to the Varsity. There they heard some of the best lecturers on the faculty, among them young histo-

The 1960s were a race between campus building and student enrollment, in which buildings always lagged. The 1969 aerial photograph shows a campus that has converted its farmland to construction sites and parking lots, except for the lawn in front of the administration building (lower right) and Andrews Outdoor Theatre behind it.

Before each semester, long lines of students waited to register in the humidity of Klum Gym.

For almost ten years, students walked (or rode or hitchhiked) down University Avenue to attend classes held at the Varsity Theatre, for lack of large lecture halls on campus. Hemenway Hall, still the campus center, bulged with students and faculty members. Those willing to accept self-service around picnic tables gathered at the Snack Bar, one of the World War II "tempos" that still remained.

rian Gavan Daws, artist Duane Preble, biologists Albert Bernatowicz, Alison Kay, and Jan Newhouse.

There, too, some students joined in a peaceful demonstration, protesting the inability of the University to teach them on their own campus. Bernatowicz argued that the Varsity had some decided advantages over campus lecture halls: it was air-conditioned and had good acoustics. The protesters probably did not include the many who bought hot-dog, popcorn, and coffee breakfasts at the lobby snack bar, or those whose girl friends joined them in the dark confines of the movie house.

Conformity and tradition were challenged. The academic calendar, unchanged in a half-century, was recast in 1968 to start before Labor Day and to give a month's break—over Christmas and New Year's—between semesters. An Interim Session during that break provided time and campus space for displays, discussions, demonstrations, and other events, to which the public was invited without charge. The Interim Session died off in three years, doomed by working against the academic grain and the caution of a later administration. The new calendar remained.

The questing of the time for new ways was represented in extreme form by the work of Toshi Suematsu, self-taught creator of hanging sculptures that expressed mystical relationships of space (between bamboo sticks) and number (represented by lengths of string). Few understood Suematsu or his message, but the fragile webs he wove in front of George Hall, at the Founder's Gate, and down University Avenue at the Church of the Crossroads were admired or tolerated unless they blocked entryways. Suematsu's last project on campus involved stringing his sculpture from the roof of Sinclair Library, at which point the authorities said stop.

Amid all the noise and crowding in of more students and more buildings, the hurley-burley of more programs and more innovations, there was a feeling of accomplishment on campus reflected downtown. An editorial in the *Honolulu Advertiser* of July 24, 1966, expressed that judgment: "The University of Hawaii continues to grow—not only in quantity but, happily, in quality—at a rate so remarkable that it's hard for most of us to keep posted." The challenge, Hamilton said, was to handle growth. "What we have to do is find ways to humanize bigness." Those ways could not be ordered, but only "inculcated by example. And this is the treatment of each person on the campus—student, faculty, administrator, secretary, janitor, even president—with courtesy, with understanding, and with good temper." All too briefly, such was the climate of the campus.

THE END OF AN ERA

Courtesy, understanding, and good temper, however, were soon found to be insufficient. Nineteen sixty-seven was astonishing as the year of student rebellion around the world. In Hawaii, as throughout America, the Vietnam War was bitterly divisive.

Student protests at the University were low-keyed, in keeping with Island style, and only sporadic, but sentiment against the expansion of the military action built up over the mid-1960s as the savagery of the war was nightly pictured on television. One daily expression was the sorrow of the mute protesters—students, faculty, staff, and people from off campus—who at the noon hour silently stood around Varney Circle. Anger was expressed at campus gatherings, notably noontime meetings in Webster Hall classrooms of the Manoa chapter of the Students for a Democratic Society. Countervailing hostility to campus antiwar sentiment grew within community groups that supported the American campaign in Southeast Asia.

The Hamiltonian Age was abruptly ended by the collision of these forces in 1967, culminating in the Oliver Lee case. Lee was an untenured assistant professor in Political Science—the department in which Hamilton held nominal membership. On campus and off, Lee had been speaking out against America's fighting in Vietnam. Politically conservative groups in the community protested his protests, and they criticized the University for allowing him to make what they deemed seditious statements. Hamilton in 1966 had defended Lee's right to challenge America's actions, responding publicly to a letter from an organization called "We the Women." He wrote: "No university, if it is true to its nature, can or should try to avoid the controversial, because it is the controversial that at any given moment is of prime importance to the society as a whole."[16]

A year later, however, controversy tested Hamilton and his administration to the limit. A front-page article in the *Honolulu Star-Bulletin* of June 1, 1967, quoted a mimeographed manifesto received from the Student Partisan Alliance, a campus organization with about fifteen members. The handout called for a grotesque "military infiltration program" in which draftees would destroy U.S. weapons, "eliminate" their officers during combat, learn military secrets and leak them to prostitutes, and so forth. Alliance leaders hastily withdrew the manifesto, but front-page coverage in both Honolulu dailies continued when it became known that the advisor to the student group was Oliver Lee, who had helped the students duplicate the statement on his department's mimeograph machine. Lee made no denial, justifying his action on the grounds that the students had no other ready means of publication. He said he had warned them of possible legal consequences, but otherwise had not tried to dissuade them; he was their advisor, not a censor.

Lee's critics were outraged. Robert Adelman, president of the Waikiki Lions Club, announced that unless the University barred the award of tenure to Lee the Lions would march up University Avenue, carrying American and Hawaiian flags, to the campus. Hamilton said that if they came he would be in his Bachman Hall office. The Associated Students of the University of Hawai'i met in emergency session and resolved "not to condone" the advice of the Alliance to draftees. They took no stand on Lee's role or his fitness for tenure.

It so happened that Lee and the UH administration were in the middle of the long and complex process to decide if tenure was to be granted. Only a few days earlier, Lee had received a letter from his college dean, stating that on the recommendation of the senior Political Science faculty (voting four to two) the administration intended to grant him tenure after the next academic year if he continued to perform satisfactorily. The newspaper stories on the Student Partisan Alliance threw this decision-making process into reverse. A hasty reconsideration by the dean, approved by Hamilton, resulted in a new letter to Lee on June 5 revoking the prospect of tenure. Neither the Political Science Department nor any other faculty group was consulted.

The reversal, also reported on page one of the Honolulu daily newspapers, brought applause from prowar groups, including the Waikiki Lions, who canceled their threatened march. Adelman called Hamilton's decision the "greatest thing since statehood." The about-face, however, affronted many faculty members, concerned that the careful mode of making tenure decisions established by the American Association of University Professors (AAUP) and hitherto respected by the University had been abandoned. The chairman of the Political Science Department said that Lee had been refused tenure because of his political beliefs, violating the principle of academic freedom.

During the summer of 1967 the paper fight raged on. Editorials demanded Lee's ouster. He appealed to the Board of Regents. A petition signed by about a thousand faculty and staff members asked that the tenure decision be held open while a thorough investigation was made. The regents told Lee to take his appeal to the Manoa Faculty Senate, which put the case before a special hearing committee.

As the fall semester began, word of how the closed committee meetings were going was eagerly sought but seldom obtained. Reporters watched vigilantly, as did the national office of the AAUP and the local chapter of the American Civil Liberties Union. The chairman of the Faculty Senate hearing committee broke silence only to define the issue: "whether the administration had reasonable cause to revoke its letter of intent to grant tenure." A state deputy attorney general sat in to assist the committee; two faculty members served as Lee's counsel.

On June 28 the regents met and rejected Lee's appeal; more petitions and letters followed. The hearing committee of the Faculty Senate at last revealed its unanimous finding three days before Christmas: the administration and regents did not have reasonable cause to discharge Lee and had failed to follow due process required by University rules. Hamilton immediately announced his resignation, saying "it is time for someone to stand up for academic responsibility, and I do so now."

Expressions of shock and dismay filled the campus, the editorial pages, the six-o'clock news. The next day, Christmas Eve, the Executive Committee of the Faculty Senate met in emergency session to urge Hamilton not to resign. The day after Christmas about half of the faculty filled Kennedy Theatre while two hundred more stood outside. They adopted resolutions urging Hamilton to stay. So did a letter signed by fifty-seven clergymen. So did the regents, who expressed "full confidence" in him and affirmed that due process would be followed in seeing the Lee case to its conclusion.

Hamilton refused to reconsider, saying that to go back on his decision would appear to be "showboating," and he didn't like showboating. He then left on a previously scheduled visit to Fiji, where he had been named to the governing board of the new University of the South Pacific. While he was gone, the governor, legislators, community groups, newspaper editors, union leaders, churchmen, the ASUH, and various faculty groups asked Hamilton to stay on. On his return to Honolulu in early January, 1968, he received these pleas with thanks but turned them down.

Hamilton's presidency was finished, though not the upheaval on campus generated by the long war in Vietnam. He continued to occupy his office in Bachman Hall as the spring semester of 1968 began, preparing for his exit from academic life. The war in Vietnam escalated, and with it protests against the military draft. A series of "teach-ins" on the war, which linked protest to the ousting of Oliver Lee, were held in Bilger Hall auditorium. Student turnout was not large, since it was already May and final examinations were approaching.

Then the event that on mainland campuses had already marked wartime protests happened in Hawaii. In the late afternoon of May 20 a considerable number of students—estimates varied from 150 to 200—trooped up the stairs of the administration building. On the second floor they sat in the offices of Hamilton and his staff, overflowing them to occupy the passageways, stairways, and the small fire escape landings of the building. Hamilton received from Linda Delaney, president of ASUH, and other student leaders their demands that the University follow academic due process in reopening the Lee case. Hamilton offered cigarettes, but said he could not force the regents to change their minds. He then left Bachman Hall, never to return.

The students settled in. They passed the hat for money to buy take-in dinners. Undergraduate Ellie Chong tuned up her guitar for a nighttime sing-along. Administrators who had remained in their offices held long conversations with their uninvited guests, longer than some had experienced in their entire teaching careers. Voices were animated but not angry. Guitar music and a small country music band hired by the administration provided a party background.

By nightfall of the second day of the sit-in, Delaney and other student leaders were talking with Vice-President Robert Hiatt—who had assumed executive responsibility—and the other administrators who were negotiating for the students to leave. Delaney said that their purpose had been accomplished in dramatizing support, if not for Lee individually, then for academic due process. In fact, a wide variety of student opinion, some more concerned with protesting against the war, was expressed in the sit-in. Delaney spoke for the ASUH.

Presidential assistant Kenneth Lau and Associate Dean for Academic Develop-

The decade of the 1960s began rather quietly, as represented by the peaceful stroll of students past old Gilmore Hall (now the site of the Art Building). Escalation of the agonizing conflict in Vietnam, however, shattered the peace of the campus. In May 1968 students occupied Bachman Hall to protest the decision not to grant tenure to a faculty member who had served as advisor to an antiwar group. Students bannered the building as "Liberation Hall," as reporters and the police looked on. The occupation was without violence.

A column of male students marched across the campus behind the American flag in counter-demonstration, supporting America's intervention in the war. Pro and con, students met to debate the war and the tenure decision—vigorously but nonviolently.

ment Robert Potter helped work out an agreement: if police had to be called to regain control of Bachman Hall, the students would be given ample warning so that those who wished to avoid arrest could leave with dignity; Delaney would ask her followers to go peacefully, having achieved their purpose. Agreement reached, administrators and students went back to their desks and stairways to wait for a peaceful end to the occupation.

It did not work. Communication with and among the Honolulu police force was confused. After midnight, without the agreed-upon notice, police cars began pulling up in nearby parking lots. Delaney, decrying double-cross, left Bachman Hall with scores of other students just before the police entered. Some 160 others, including Oliver Lee and a few other faculty members, remained to be arrested. Potter, weeping with frustration at the mix-up, went along to help post bail.

Thomas H. Hamilton joined in celebrating the retirement in 1969 of Willard Wilson, whose career spanning four decades with the University included service in each academic rank and at every senior administrative level.

The next day, May 23, the regents met again on the case of Oliver Lee. They voted to offer him a contract for the ensuing academic year, 1968–1969, with the understanding that it would be his last. Tenure was denied. (It was to come quietly in 1970.)

Bachman Hall remained decked with a huge banner proclaiming it "Liberation Hall." The demonstration continued in the open courtyard, where scores of students camped through the first week of June. Each day they sang and heard talks by student leaders, faculty members, and a variety of people from off-campus. Not all were supportive: Art Rutledge, portly head of the local Teamsters' Union, told them they were acting foolishly and should get back to their classes. A counter-demonstration of students, almost all male and led by engineering and physical education majors, paraded through the campus with American flags.

The protest was limited to the Manoa campus, and even there most students who could escape the blare of the protesters' bull-horns paid little heed. Final examinations were about to begin and the libraries were full. After a week, the camp-in dwindled; in ten days it was gone. Damage to Bachman Hall from the entire demonstration was limited to one broken glass louvre, for which apology was made and compensation offered. The regular academic year ended and most students dispersed.

The Oliver Lee case was an abrupt turning point in the history of the University. Its Golden Age was over. Not only was a charismatic president lost. Gone also was a feeling of abiding confidence and institutional well-being among faculty and staff. And weakened was the trust of the state government that the UH administration was master of its house, to be trusted with increased funds and reduced scrutiny. No successor president in the twentieth century was to experience the easy good times—the buoyancy, the admiration, the favorable press, the respectful legislature, the ready appropriations—that Tom Hamilton had enjoyed for five years. Support for the further growth of the University, crucial as it might be to a rapidly developing state, was not to come easily.

3

EXPERIENCING MATURITY: 1969–1995

WHEN THE REGENTS accepted Thomas Hamilton's resignation in May 1968, Vice-President for Academic Affairs Robert Hiatt was named acting president. Student protests on a number of campus issues continued, notably on course requirements for graduation and the lack of student housing, but in a lower key. Committed to academic freedom and freedom of speech, Hiatt was open to students and faculty who raised questions about the University as well as about larger social issues. In a statement quoted in the *Honolulu Advertiser,* he defended those rights but opposed unlawful actions.

> As a university we certainly recognize the right of people to dispute or question any facet of their society, including the university society, and to engage in dissent and protest actions against things they feel are wrong. As university officials, we would certainly want to extend this right to the student community with respect to the activities and policies of the University of Hawaii. We also . . . expect the concerned persons . . . to present any issues for discussion in an orderly fashion —not by any mob action or anything of that sort.[1]

A group of students came to his office to protest requiring certain courses for graduation. One of them began using strong profanity to abuse Hiatt, who quietly said to him, "If you say that one more time, out you go." The student remained but modified his speech.

The faculty generally expected Hiatt to be named president, as he had been an effective "executive officer" while Hamilton concentrated on building community and legislative support. Hiatt had been instrumental in establishing the research institutes and in securing federal funds to support them. But he was not a player in the local political system and bore the handicap of having been the administration's chief negotiator during the 1968 student sit-in. Although neither the sit-in nor its outcome had been due to any fault on Hiatt's part, some of the adverse community reaction had attached to him.

When it became apparent that he would not be named president, Hiatt resigned to become the first director of the Research Corporation of the University of Hawai'i, an agency established to employ staff for research projects without going through the state's civil service system and to administer grants, thus avoiding the skimming off of a sizable percentage in "overhead" charges by the state government.

Vice-President for Business Affairs Richard Takasaki served as acting president during the search for a new president. Student demonstrations continued. After a day-long sit-in at the East-West Center, Takasaki issued a statement similar to Hiatt's:

> I wish to reiterate the position of the University of Hawaii that an atmosphere of freedom of expression is essential to the educational process. We will continue to respect and protect the right of honest protest and orderly dissent, but will not tolerate action which violates the freedom of others or impedes the essential functions of the University.

Hiatt and Takasaki each tried to mend fences with the community but in their brief tenures were able to restore little of the public support that had been lost.

The role of the Board of Regents changed during this interim period. Under Hamilton, it had left most administrative decisions to the president and his staff. Formal meetings were brief, having followed an off-the-record closed session in which the president had presented the agenda with his recommendations for action. Regents' questions already addressed, the official meeting was mostly undebated approval of items on the agenda. With Oliver Lee's 1968 appeal of his tenure denial, however, the board found itself involved with the kind of personnel decision it had previously only "rubber-stamped." A critical precedent was set, expanded on when the board's Personnel Committee began to review the dossiers of faculty members recommended for tenure or promotion. Where the board had previously limited its concern to personnel policies, it now began to decide on individual cases.

The mentality of the board had also changed. During Hamilton's tenure, it had been dominated by leading businessmen who recognized the division of authority between a board of directors and its appointed administrators. Under their leadership, the board's main function had been to select and support the president. Many regents of the 1970s, however, saw their role as similar to that of legislators, and they began to exercise in detail their formal powers, intruding further and further into university administration. Board committees overseeing budget, academic matters, and student affairs found themselves directly confronted by students and faculty over specific issues. The campus community began to see regents as antagonists. Board meetings were often stormy, with delegations making demands and leveling accusations. At one meeting, students railed against graduation requirements while faculty members defended them, both accusing the regents of failing to understand the role of a university. The profanity and vituperation of students testifying shocked the regents but did not deter them from deciding academic matters that had traditionally been the responsibility of the faculty. The absence of a president increasingly induced board interference in what should have been the routine administration of the campus.

The Department of American Studies invited Harlan Cleveland, U. S. ambassador to NATO, to give a lecture on May 7, 1968. A student in the audience asked if he had come to talk about the presidency. Cleveland admitted he had met with the Board of Regents; they had no comment. He and Graduate Dean Wytze Gorter, the other candidate openly discussed, each informed the regents that he would not accept appointment as long as the Oliver Lee controversy remained unresolved.

That resolution took time. On April 12, 1969, the board by a vote of five to two reinstated Lee as an assistant professor without tenure and on probation. Three days later, Acting President Takasaki informed Lee that he would receive tenure after a year's probation. The action not only cleared the way to appoint a president, it also avoided censure by the American Association of University Professors.

CLEVELAND TAKES OFFICE

On April 26, 1969, the regents named Harlan Cleveland president. He brought limited experience in institutions of higher education, never having completed a graduate degree or served as a faculty member. His only work in university administration had been as dean of the Maxwell Graduate School for Citizenship and Public Affairs at Syracuse University from 1956 to 1961. His larger experience was in diplomacy and as editor of *The Reporter,* a magazine of political commentary.

In announcing Cleveland's appointment, Regent Robert Cushing said that 120 nominations had been reviewed with an advisory group including the Faculty Senate executive committee, the president of the Associated Students of the University of Hawai'i, and the head of the Graduate Student Organization. However, Cleveland was not the choice of the Manoa faculty, who generally favored Gorter. Cleveland took office September 2, with some faculty members and students already sounding hostile. Jim Smith, president of the Students for a Democratic Society, called Cleveland an "apologist for U.S. imperialism."[2]

Cleveland began by blowing the whistle. Presented with Academic Development Plan II, produced by a committee of faculty, administrators, and students, polished by English Professor Emeritus Alfons Korn, and already accepted by the Board of Regents, Cleveland had it shelved, complaining of its "turgid prose." Directing his staff to produce a new statement, Cleveland published in January 1970 his "Prospectus for the Seventies." Unlike the Academic Development Plan, which was quite specific about growth and priorities, the "Prospectus" was largely generalities based upon ADP II.

Cleveland termed his administrative style "creative ambiguity," perhaps a carry-over from his diplomatic days, but perhaps also, as critics alleged, as a way of distancing himself from executive decisions. He created the position of chancellor of the Manoa campus, with Richard Takasaki as acting chancellor, and put the Hilo campus and Hawai'i Community College under an umbrella organization with Paul Miwa as its chancellor. Richard Kosaki, vice-president for community colleges, was given the new title of University vice-president, and Harold Masumoto was named director of community colleges services.

Cleveland issued guidelines so ambiguous that administrators could not be sure of his support when they acted. If one made a decision about which another complained to Cleveland, the administrator was likely to find the decision vetoed without explanation.

Manoa faculty members were no less frustrated. When his reorganization plans were questioned by the Manoa Faculty Senate, chairperson Ruth Iams confessed she could not get answers from the president. "I am not able to get through the diplomatic finesse and I don't know who is. Cleveland believes in ambiguity and practices it." Vice-chairperson Anna Keppel added that she too had tried without success. "The president makes the issue that the administrative charts do not pertain to governance at all."[3]

Worse, Cleveland antagonized legislators. Under Hamilton, testifying before committees was generally handled by Hiatt, Takasaki, and the college deans, who knew first-hand the specifics of budget items. Cleveland himself testified, sometimes with unhappy results. When, for example, legislators pointed out that funds provided for undergraduate counseling and reducing class size had been diverted to graduate programs, he lectured them as if they were the newcomers. Not surprisingly, the *Star-Bulletin* reported that Senator Francis Wong "blasted the University administration" in a speech, charging that "The real problem at the University is . . . the lack of planning."[4]

Ironically, although aloof and priding himself as an "institution builder," Cleveland was most successful as a moderator of student protest. After America's bombing of Cambodia, he announced that on October 15, 1969, afternoon classes at Manoa and Hilo would be canceled to permit campuswide discussions on ending the war. Although many students stayed home that day, some of the gatherings at Manoa were well-attended and aroused lively discussion. Speaking to a large assembly in Hemenway Hall, Cleveland forthrightly opposed the war. The text of his speech was printed in the *Honolulu Advertiser.* A line from it was uncharacteristically personal:

> To the extent that it is considerations of "face" that are holding us back from larger military withdrawals or from political initiatives we might take for peace

> in Vietnam, I have to say in this particular situation, the "face" of my country is not worth the life of my son.[5]

The day ended with a march by some 550 students and faculty from Manoa to the state capitol, where they joined with 150 Leeward Community College students, who had walked all the way from their campus, and a smaller group from Kapi'olani Community College.

At that time a faculty-student committee was examining the policy of allowing twenty course credits of ROTC toward graduation. The issue was deeply divisive; but on the same day as his Hemenway Hall speech, Cleveland told a Manoa Faculty Senate meeting that ROTC should remain.

> Until we can put together an international peacekeeping arrangement that dependably keeps us out of future wars, the education of officers for the U.S. Armed Services will be one of the options open to young Americans who enter college. . . . On a free and open campus, I don't see how we can deny a student the widest possible choices of what he wants to do with his life and help him find the kinds of education that best fit him for what he wants to do.

He thus defended recruitment on campus by the armed forces and also upheld Defense Department research by faculty and students as "an obligation to protect each individual's freedom to do the research he wants."[6]

Demonstrators occupied the Air Force ROTC buildings for six days in April 1970. Again, unlike demonstrations of that period at several mainland institutions, no violence occurred, no one was injured. Property damage was minor. (The following February, however, a campus ROTC building was burned down. Outsiders were charged with arson.)

In May 1970, the Manoa student government (ASUH) called for a week-long strike to protest the Vietnam War and America's bombing of Cambodia. The Leeward Community College student and faculty senates both voted to set aside May 11–16 as "a special week for consideration of U.S. involvement in Southeast Asia." Cleveland directed that no one be failed or given a lower grade for being on strike, since students "have the right to absent themselves on a matter of conscience."[7] Some three thousand attended a rally in Andrews Outdoor Theatre. Class attendance at Manoa dropped markedly for several days.

Disgruntled students in that springtime created a "tent city" on the lawn outside Bachman Hall. This time the issue was housing: about half of Manoa's eighteen thousand students lived at home; others queued up for 1,441 dormitory beds or settled into private accommodations, frequently substandard and overpriced. The protest forced acknowledgment of the need: Cleveland authorized leasing rooms in two Waikiki hotels to serve as temporary housing. The legislature in turn appropriated funds to build fifteen hundred more dormitory spaces by 1973.

Cleveland described his approach with student protestors as "engaging them in relentless conversation." Kenneth Lau, who filled numerous roles in the UH administration, wrote, "On more than one occasion, meetings which started out with angry statements by students ended an hour or two later with the students drifting away quietly after calm and lengthy discussion by Cleveland."[8]

Unity, or Independence for Hilo?

An important change during Cleveland's administration was creating the University of Hawai'i at Hilo (UHH). Big Island legislators, long wanting to convert the Hilo campus into a four-year, degree-granting institution, had blocked the transfer of the Hawaii Technical School to the UH system when the other technical schools became community colleges in 1965. However, after the regents added an upper-division curriculum to the Hilo campus in 1969 and named it Hilo College, the legislature authorized transferring the technical school to the University as Hawai'i Community College.

Hoping to draw on his connections in the federal government, Cleveland proposed to convert the University's Peace Corps Training Center on the Big Island into a Center for Cross-Cultural Training and Research and put it, Hilo College, Hawai'i Community College, and other university activities on Hawaii under a University of Hawai'i at Hilo umbrella administered by a chancellor, a new position authorized by the Board of Regents in January 1970.

Such arrangements did little to satisfy those who claimed that UHH and the community colleges would remain stepchildren until they had their own governing boards. Bills to that effect were periodically rejected by the legislature. Similarly, over the years there were recurring proposals to move the College of Tropical Agriculture and Human Resources (CTAHR) from Manoa to Hilo. As much of the CTAHR program in agriculture is at the graduate level, its faculty argued successfully that its research requires a greater institutional infrastructure than an undergraduate UHH could provide, an argument reminiscent of Wallace Farrington's 1907 report to the legislature explaining why the College of Hawaii should be in Honolulu. Once more the Hilo faculty and its supporters felt that their school had lost a battle to the larger campus.

Selective Excellence

Academic Development Plans I and II had both advanced the criterion of "selective excellence" for choosing the teaching and research programs to receive strong financial support. In a few areas, the choices were easy. Hawaii is obviously an excellent place to study the ocean, its floor and biota. Except for Puerto Rico, UH is the only land-grant college with opportunities to study tropical agriculture. No other place in the nation has a conveniently located, dependably active volcano or a site equaling the peak of Mauna Kea for astronomical observation.

Outside the natural sciences, however, finding a basis for favored program development required greater inventiveness or special circumstances. In the field of Asian drama, the Manoa campus was able to draw on an interest of students and community that went back to its early years. The same was true for teaching and research in Asian languages and in Hawaiian. The training of teachers had been done in Hawaii for almost a century. Intercollegiate athletics had long received strong support in the absence of professional teams in Hawaii.

Other programs had to find their own justification for claiming "selective excellence." Two examples illustrate the growth that continued during Cleveland's administration, despite the administrative confusion. Of old, the Economics Department had been interested in the national economies of Asia, modestly expressed in the limited course offerings of what had been a small faculty. The establishment of the East-West Center, with a major focus on economic development and a steady stream of grantees seeking advanced degrees in that field, presented an opportunity for developing a program in international economics with joint faculty appointments to the center and the department. Even after the center was formally separated from the University, more than half of all graduate students in economics still held grants from the center.

The East-West Center connection stimulated the growth of professional relationships between the department and economic agencies and universities in Asia. Increasingly, UH economists held consultancies or other affiliations with the Asian Development Bank, the Association of Southeast Asian Nations, the World Bank, and United Nations agencies serving the Pacific area. Professors Harry Oshima, Fred Hung, Seiji Naya, James Mak, and others became familiar figures in collaborative research on the region. Faculty exchanges with universities in the Philippines, Thailand, Korea, Japan, and China expanded the network linking the Manoa campus with the rapidly growing economies of East Asia. As UH graduates in economics returned home to take positions with Asian governments or universities, a second generation of connection was formed.

Conversely, the physics program was nurtured by mainland connections, especially with California. That linkage had existed from 1923, when Paul Kirkpatrick, the University's first full-time physicist, was recruited from Berkeley, which also supplied Willard Eller, who chaired the UH department from 1931 to 1957, and Stanley Ballard, who conducted most of the limited research undertaken here in the prewar period. However, the development of a substantial research program is traceable to the recruitment in 1955 of Kenichi Watanabe, who had earned his doctorate at the California Institute of Technology after two years as an undergraduate in physics at Manoa. He in turn brought from Cal Tech Vincent Peterson, a rising specialist in nuclear physics, and John R. Holmes, the retiring chairman of Physics at the University of Southern California, both with extensive research experience. The new faculty came with or obtained federal grants to support research, as in particle physics and nuclear physics, utilizing facilities in California, such as the proton synchroton at

Berkeley, the Lawrence Berkeley Laboratory, and Stanford's linear accelerator. After 1970, Hawaii and Berkeley physicists regularly collaborated in neutrino research at the Fermi Lab accelerator.

After Watanabe died suddenly of a heart attack in 1969, a new building, named after him, provided quarters for an expanded department, since 1964 named Physics and Astronomy. During the 1970s, international research collaboration was developed through the neutrino research of the UH high-energy physics group. By 1992, when Peterson retired as leader of the Hawaii group, a project involving Japanese, German, and Swiss collaborators sought to detect ultrahigh-energy neutrinos from star systems and other astrophysical sources, using instrumented regions of the deep ocean as both target and detector.

Medical and Law Schools

While the growth of most academic programs continued to be incremental and slow, it was sudden for the two professional schools earlier identified by Governor Burns as essential to a first-class university. In 1973 the two-year medical school was extended to four years despite strong opposition from some in the local medical profession and from some Manoa faculty members, who foresaw that the cost of a medical school would lessen budgetary support for other programs. Opponents of the expansion maintained that the argument advanced to create the existing program was still true: its graduates could readily find places to complete their training in mainland medical schools, which regularly experienced heavy dropouts after the first two years. Further, some faculty members suspected that the medical school expansion was intended as much to honor Governor Burns as to meet an urgent social need. Indeed, it was subsequently named the John A. Burns School of Medicine. By the mid-1980s the school was well established and respected, utilizing community hospitals for clinical training and thus avoiding the large additional cost of building and running a teaching hospital.

In 1989 the school began to phase in an innovative replacement for the traditional curriculum—using a preponderance of lecture time in the first years—it had originally adopted to assure acceptance, particularly by the accreditation authorities. A new problem-based, self-directed approach to learning in the first years had students meet in small groups, each with a faculty tutor, to analyze problems encountered in their observation of patients or in their study. Also innovatively, integrated programs for health care in community centers on Oahu brought student practitioners from Medicine to work in concert with students from the Schools of Social Work, Nursing, and Public Health.

A professional program for training lawyers came soon after the medical program. As early as the mid-1960s, Hawaii Supreme Court Justice William S. Richardson had proposed creating a law school at Manoa, but as he admitted in a 1966 letter to the law dean at the University of Maine, "My proposal has received approval, objection, and indifference from the legal community here."[9] Support came from attorneys who saw in the creation of a local law school opportunity for continued legal education, for more convenient recruitment of new members by their firms, and —for some—the chance to teach as adjunct professors. Opposition came from practitioners concerned about competition for clients, even while recognizing that in the legal profession supply stimulates demand: for every plaintiff's case there has to be a defense.

Manoa faculty opposition to the medical school as a costly enterprise that must come at the expense of existing programs was as nothing compared to their outrage at the suggestion of a law school. Against their argument that there already were enough lawyers in Hawaii, Regent Wallace Fujiyama put the case for equal access to higher education. "I can afford to send my sons to the best law schools in the nation, but how can the kid from Nanakuli afford to choose to be a lawyer if we don't have a law school in Hawaii?"[10]

In 1971 the legislature enacted a statute creating a school of law at Manoa, which opened in 1973 with fifty students—all but one having a strong Hawaii connection, including John Waihee, later to be governor. The first classes met in wooden "tempos" aligned along the lower campus road in the quarry. The American Bar Association, giving provisional approval to the instructional program in February 1974, warned that full accreditation would require the provision of adequate quarters for classrooms, offices, and library. The legislature, lobbied by Richardson and Fujiyama, appropriated the necessary funds. Two handsome low-rise buildings on Dole Street overlooking the Lower Campus were completed by 1983, and the school received full accreditation.

To a cautiously innovative curriculum, which included such courses as legal ethics and decision making other than through litigation, the law school gradually added instruction responsive to its time and place. These included courses on the law affecting the elderly, feminist legal theory, environmental and hazardous-waste law, and native Hawaiian rights. In 1992, at the suggestion of its students, the school adopted a requirement that each student volunteer at least sixty hours of unpaid legal service prior to graduation.

Contrary to its policy of not naming a building or school after a living person, the Board of Regents named the latest professional school after its earliest and strongest advocate, William S. Richardson, by then retired from the judiciary and serving as a trustee of the Bishop Estate.

Enrollments Rise, Budgets Lag

Even as these expansions were occurring, they had to be fitted into constricted funding. In the budget rounds of 1973, the state government ordered UH to trim 14 percent from its request. With a budget made up predominantly of salaries, the only way to make such a reduction was to eliminate positions. In June the University notified 160 tenured faculty members that their contracts would expire on June 30, 1974, raising a great outcry from students and the community. Governor Burns agreed to release additional funds, and Cleveland promised savings from "drastic measures to reduce costs, increase productivity, adjust teaching loads and class sizes, and review and re-order program priorities." In rescinding the notifications, Cleveland said losing the "best of our young scientists and scholars . . . would be a major erosion of the quality of education we can provide for residents of Hawaii."[11]

The financial crisis was compounded by enrollments whose projections far exceeded the capacity of the Manoa campus, even if the community colleges served most freshmen and sophomores. Hamilton's administration had considered creating a second major campus, but took no action. In a feature newspaper article, Cleveland showed the need to spread the growing student body around the University system. In 1969, the enrollment at Manoa had been 18,474, with 864 at Hilo and 8,584 in the community colleges, for a total of 27,922. He predicted that in 1976 the figures would be 23,000 at Manoa, 2,500 at Hilo, 21,000 in the community colleges, and 3,500 on a new campus.[12]

Those estimates proved reasonably good, except for the new campus, whose creation was caught up in political controversy. Burns wanted it to be at Waimea, Hawaii, in a rural setting and as a way of stimulating economic development of the Big Island. Educators argued that a major campus needed a supporting social and physical infrastructure that the Big Island lacked. Large landowners on Oahu offered tracts for the campus, expecting it to occasion rezoning of agricultural land for the profitable construction of residential and commercial centers. Political and commercial pressure concerning the University as a user of real property was always present and rarely subtle. Cleveland commented that the Hawaiian vocabulary could be shortened if the word for "land" was also used to mean "politics." When the legislature decided to place the second campus in west Oahu, where the population was growing most rapidly, it began as an upper-division college.

The Board of Regents accepted Cleveland's policy statement for the "Controlled Growth of the University of Hawaii," setting fifty thousand as the maximum for all campuses in 1976. Out-of-state students would comprise no more than 20 percent at Manoa and no more than 10 percent at Hilo. This limitation on nonresidents was linked with a legislative mandate to maintain a tuition differential between local and out-of-state students, negating the earlier policy of encouraging newcomers on the grounds that they provided socialization and a learning resource for local students with limited opportunity to travel.

Unionization

During Cleveland's presidency unionization became a source of controversy, one that subtly but profoundly changed relationships between the faculty and the administration while allying those who taught on the Manoa and Hilo campuses with those at the community colleges. The underlying issue was the political process by which the level of campus salaries was determined. In earlier times, administration and faculty had generally worked in concert to seek legislative approval of salary levels high enough to satisfy present faculty members and attract new ones in the national market. While the University was relatively small and administrative posts were commonly filled from the ranks of the faculty, this unity of action remained easy.

Until 1956, the faculty had little voice in the governance of the University. At the annual meeting of the faculty, "President Sinclair did all the talking, and after committee reports, of which there were almost none, he adjourned the meeting."[13] In 1956, the regents approved a charter for a Faculty Senate, which included the president as chairman, all chief administrative officers, all tenured professors and associate professors, plus forty members elected from the ranks of the assistant professors and instructors. It was defined as "the policy-recommending body of the University faculty." In 1962 a new charter changed the Senate into an elective body of seventy-five members, representing each rank and each college at Manoa. Except for the president, administrative officers were excluded. This charter gave faculty members a strong voice in working closely with the administration until the very end of Hamilton's presidency.

Divisiveness arose, however, from a 1968 amendment to the state constitution that authorized public employees to organize for collective bargaining and from a 1969 statute that defined thirteen bargaining units within the state service. Unit 7 included the faculty of the entire UH system. The other bargaining units ratified their choice of agents without much debate, but the development of a faculty union was contentious. Many faculty members, particularly at Manoa, considered a union inappropriate for their profession and threatening to the Faculty Senate. Others, including many at the community colleges, countered that, if unrepresented, faculty members would be at a disadvantage against unionized groups when seeking legislation affecting salaries or other employee benefits. An additional factor was a distrust of Cleveland and the Board of Regents, a "them versus us" attitude that had replaced the mutual confidence of the 1960s.

A survey in 1971 by the Industrial Relations Center of the College of Business Administration found sharp differences in faculty attitudes toward collective bargaining. On the Manoa campus, just under half of those responding agreed that they needed a union, and slightly over half at Hilo, while two-thirds of those in the community colleges favored unionization. More significantly, only 12 percent of them all felt that the administration adequately represented the faculty in dealing with the governor and the legislature.

Responding to a petition for an election to choose a bargaining agent, the Hawaii Public Employment Relations Board (HPERB) in July 1971 identified five choices which would be on the ballot: the Hawaii Federation of College Teachers (HFCT), an affiliate of the American Federation of Teachers; the Alliance between the local chapter of the American Association of University Professors (AAUP) and a newly formed UH Faculty Association; the College and University Professional Association (CUPA), an affiliate of the National Education Association (NEA); the Hawaii Government Employees Association (HGEA); and "no representation."

In the first election, held in October 1972, 1,955 of 2,523 eligible faculty cast valid ballots. None of the four competing units commanded as much as 30 percent of the votes cast; "No representation" got 15 percent. Shortly before the run-off election, held November 20–21, CUPA combined with HFCT and defeated the Alliance 995 to 805. The Manoa faculty preferred the Alliance, 672 to 549, but Hilo and the community colleges gave HFCT a decisive edge, 435 to 114.

The first round of collective bargaining—with the combined University system faculty represented by its new agent and the administration by a governor-appointed bargaining team—was conducted under the cloud of a perceived threat from the state legislature. At its session early in 1972, the Senate had resolved that the University should develop criteria for awarding academic tenure and undertake "periodic review of the performance of tenured faculty members."[14] This was taken by the faculty as rejecting the long-established system of "peer review" at department and college levels of a faculty member's qualifications to attain and hold tenure. Coincidentally, a national study of faculty salaries showed that those at UH had dropped significantly relative to other state universities. The HFCT bargained for salary increases at the risk of endangering peer evaluation and tenure. An angry faculty, especially those on the Manoa campus, rejected the proposed contract by a ratio of five to one in November 1973.

Another amalgamation of competing unions then brought together the AAUP, generally preferred on the Manoa and Hilo campuses, and the NEA, favored by the community college faculties. The unit thus created, called the University of Hawai'i Professional Assembly (UHPA), was elected and certified as the exclusive bargaining agent for the faculty. In 1975, it won a favorable contract, which the faculty ratified.

A bridge had been crossed. No longer were faculty and administration joined in representing the University's budget needs to the governor and legislature. Henceforward, in setting salaries and other conditions of faculty service, the UH administration was seated at the bargaining table with the state's negotiators, across from representatives of the faculty union. A mechanism for institutional conflict was in place. In good years, when state funds were more readily available, negotiations were relatively smooth. When money was tight, however, they could be rough, foreshadowing faculty strike calls in November 1983, when the UH campuses were shut down for two days, and January 1997, when a strike was narrowly averted.

Academic Innovations

A number of academic experiments planned in the late Hamilton years came into being, with varying degrees of support, under Cleveland. Among them were the Survival Plus program and New College, innovations within the College of Arts and Sciences. New College, housed in an old residence off University Avenue, began in the fall of 1970. The ninety freshmen and sixty-five juniors enrolled had a major role in its governance, which academically conservative members of the Manoa faculty thought mistaken. The first two years of study were in prescribed interdisciplinary surveys, but beyond the sophomore year students were to choose courses so as to permit each to complete a "major creative work." Some of Manoa's brightest teachers persuaded their departments to lend them to the experiment; student enthusiasm was high.

Budget cuts in the departments, however, and new interests of the participating faculty, led to an abrupt reduction of talent. Replacements were temporary lecturers, and when history professor Richard L. Rapson, who had conceived the idea and was its first director, went on sabbatical leave, the students voted to hire two faculty members denied tenure in regular departments—one of them, Joan Abramson, to direct New College. Abramson was passed over by the English Department in 1972 because she did not have a Ph.D. However, a member of the department personnel committee was recorded as saying that they did not need to give her tenure because as a faculty wife she would always be available for teaching. In long litigation with the UH administration, charging gender discrimination, she was unsuccessful. (Her account was published in 1975 as *The Invisible Woman.*)

The College of Survival Plus, a brainchild of Professors Arnold Schwartz and James Linn, organized the first two years' requirements around six "ecological and social crises"—for example, war, depletion, and famine—with the expectation that these would form the nucleus of the student's subsequent major. Although it attracted lively faculty and students, like New College, it suffered from "creative faculty burnout," wherein the founders, having "done that," returned to their original departments. Students were enthusiastic about individual courses, but the Curriculum Committee of Arts and Sciences found little evidence of adherence to the "core requirements" in English, mathematics, and sciences.

In the spring of 1973, the faculty Curriculum Committee of Arts and Sciences issued a critical report on New College but recommended an additional three years of probation. Dean David Contois and Manoa Chancellor Wytze Gorter concurred, but Academic Vice-President Stuart M. Brown vetoed the recommendation. New College's budget for 1973–1974 had been only $90,000, a small sum for teaching 270 students. Although the students protested strongly to the regents, on August 9, 1973, the board voted to end both New College and Survival Plus.

Arthur Goodfriend, commissioned by Cleveland to do a study of the life and death of New College, wrote its epitaph:

> From birth . . . New College was on a collision course with traditional faculty, with competing departments and provisional programs, and with all those

> who . . . are . . . addicted to conventional assumptions and approaches. Inevitably, with students behind the wheel, unlicensed, uninsured and impetuous, riding on the left side of the road, their vision impaired, . . . New College crashed into Bachman Hall [the administration building] and the Board of Regents. New College was killed.[15]

Three innovations did take hold: the liberal studies major, the Freshman Seminar Program, and ethnic studies. Professor Robert Clopton guided liberal studies students in designing individualized courses of study, freeing them from the constraints of prescribed majors. This established a format for subsequent baccalaureate programs in such areas as women's studies, Russian studies, marine studies, and dental hygiene.

Brainchild of psychology professor Abe Arkoff, the Freshman Seminar Program (FSP) began in 1971. Housed in the basement of Johnson Hall dormitory, FSP offered undergraduates basic courses led by advanced students under the general supervision of a faculty member. The program allowed students to take active part in classes of ten, receiving constant peer stimulation and support. The advanced students leading the sections gained leadership skills and greater mastery over their subject by teaching it. In its first semester, FSP offered seven courses for a total of forty-two sections. In the next two decades, more than twenty departments offered basic courses through the FSP in up to sixty sections a semester.

CLEVELAND RESIGNS

By 1973, the Manoa faculty had developed a discernible hostility toward Cleveland and his administrative style. The *Faculty Handbook,* approved by the Board of Regents, had been regarded across the campus as an authoritative statement of procedure for faculty and administration alike. It specified that the president was to consult with the faculty on academic programs, budget, and personnel practices and to forward to the regents any proposals by the Faculty Senate. Cleveland ignored this rule.

In March 1973, a Faculty Senate task force appointed to study the problem called for an investigation by the legislative auditor and a censure of the administration for its failure to comply with Board of Regents policies. The report complained that faculty proposals "were spending years on the president's desk without submission" to the board or response from the administration. It noted that although UH had been directed to make heavy cuts in its expenditures, the administration was budgeted for sizable increases. Central administration and the Office of Business Affairs had already grown from 106 positions in 1967–1968 to 184 in 1971–1972, and their cost had more than doubled, despite the fact that many of their functions had been shifted to the chancellors of Manoa and Hilo and to the vice-president for community colleges. The report concluded that

> The present administration has imported many high-cost administrators whose experience in state universities is virtually nil. . . . They know little about higher education, less about state universities, and nothing about the special problems of higher education in Hawaii. As a result, while a few administration spokesmen receive the publicity and salaries and create general ineffectiveness at the top, the real work [of managing the University] is done by staff workers whose authority and responsibility have never been clearly defined by a confused central administration.[16]

The Faculty Senate unanimously accepted the report in April 1973 and expressed "strong objections" to Vice-President Brown's statements to the Senate Higher Education Committee regarding review of tenured faculty. "Neither in these remarks nor in other matters does he speak for the faculty."[17] Shortly thereafter, Brown resigned and returned to Cornell.

It was not only with the faculty that Cleveland had trouble. At a Board of Regents meeting on March 8, 1973, Regent Charles Ota made an emotional attack on Cleveland, charging him with being "financially irresponsible."

> We have a monster with no head. We don't have leadership at the top. I don't think [Cleveland] has credibility with the Governor, with the Senate Ways and Means Committee, with the House Finance Committee.[18]

The next day, Regent Clarence Chang told the newspapers that if Cleveland did not resign, he should be fired.[19] The regents soon decided that Cleveland had to go but allowed him to complete five years of service so that his state retirement benefits would be vested. Cleveland announced his resignation on December 6, 1973, to be effective in the fall.

WHAT SCOPE FOR THE BOARD OF REGENTS?

In 1974 the Manoa campus was thrown into confusion by the sudden resignation of Chancellor Wytze Gorter. Early that year, two regents had negotiated directly with football coach Larry Price, extending his contract from two to five years. Although not members of the faculty, coaches hold staff appointments, which also originate at the department, college, or campus level. The regents' action overrode the recommendation of Gorter and the objection of Regent Herbert M. Richards, who cast the only negative vote. In his letter of resignation Gorter wrote that, while the action was "certainly a prerogative of the board," it had "administrative implications that I cannot accept. . . . It critically weakens the ability of the administration to do its job."[20] Three other Manoa administrators also resigned, and several others announced they were considering doing so.

The Manoa Faculty Senate supported Gorter. Its executive committee met with Board of Regents chairperson Harriet Mizuguchi and its most outspoken member,

Wallace Fujiyama, one of the regents who had negotiated Price's contract. The senate asked the board to establish clearly defined roles in the governance of the university.

This faculty-regent discord tied into the selection of a successor to Cleveland. In 1973 the regents had appointed a new vice-president for business affairs, Fujio Matsuda, known generally as "Fudge." Born in Honolulu, a graduate of McKinley High School, Matsuda had studied engineering at UH before enlisting in the 442nd Regimental Combat Team in 1942. In 1946 he returned for a year and then transferred to Rose Polytechnic Institute for a degree in civil engineering. After completing a doctorate at M.I.T., he served as a researcher there for two years and another year at the University of Illinois. He taught in the UH Engineering Department from 1955 to 1962, leaving to become director of transportation under Governor Burns.

When Cleveland announced his resignation, five local candidates were immediately proposed: Matsuda, Gorter, Richard Takasaki, Kenneth Lau, and Richard Kosaki. It was soon clear that Matsuda was the regents' choice, despite contrary faculty sentiment on all campuses. The faculty's growing mistrust of the state's leaders heightened their belief that Matsuda's appointment was politically motivated. Further, antipathy to the Board of Regents and administration was transferred to Matsuda. On the other hand, there was strong faculty support for Kosaki, a nationally recognized scholar of higher education and a well-seasoned political scientist, known and respected by legislators, but clearly a political decision had been made.

During the summer of 1974, the Manoa Faculty Senate Executive Committee continued to argue that a presidential appointment should not be made until the Board of Regents had defined its own role in university governance. Faculty Senate officers Norman Meller and Robert Potter were summoned to meet with Mizuguchi and Fujiyama. The regents were prepared to announce the appointment of Matsuda as president and wanted to know what faculty reaction would be. The two professors promised a boycott of Matsuda's inauguration unless the regents first defined the governance roles of the board, the administration, the faculty, and the students along lines recommended by the American Association of University Professors. Meller and Fujiyama discussed the regents' involvement with faculty appointments, and in particular Fujiyama's public statements about hiring "locals" in preference to candidates from outside Hawaii. Meller warned that if the regents named Matsuda without clarifying the governance roles, the faculty would consider the president was "nothing but a stooge." Meller then repeated that message to Matsuda, who said he would be no stooge but "his own man."[21]

THE PRESIDENCY OF FUJIO MATSUDA

On July 25, 1974, the regents announced Matsuda's appointment, at the same time issuing a two-page paper spelling out the roles of governance. Before accepting the post, Matsuda got the regents' assurance that "the University president is the chief executive officer and not the Board of Regents" and told the press that there was a "clear understanding that the board makes policy and I administer."[22] A crisis had been averted.

Matsuda presided over a difficult period of adjustment. Manoa enrollments leveled off and then fell for several years, while those at the community colleges and UH-Hilo continued to grow. Support from the legislature, strong under Hamilton, had eroded under Cleveland. Appropriations were reduced, and Governor Ariyoshi—successor to Burns, but without his zeal for the school—annually withheld portions of University funding. Matsuda fought a continuing battle to preserve what he could, quietly using his longtime political ties to protect the UH budget and restore legislative confidence.

However precarious other funds might be, money for construction continued. Buildings sprouted like mushrooms, but not overnight. Each construction job seemed to last an eternity, making campuses so noisy that it was often impossible to hold classes in some buildings. Campus growth was especially marked at Honolulu, Kaua'i, Maui, and Kapi'olani Community Colleges and at UH-Hilo.

At Manoa remaining green spaces and parking lots were covered with new structures. "Temporary" buildings moved onto campus from military bases in 1946 were finally replaced with "permanent" buildings, and some older "permanent" structures were demolished to provide space for new ones. Despite a sit-in led by ethnobotanist Beatrice Krauss, old Gilmore Hall was demolished to make room for the Art Building, but a famous baobob tree nearby was preserved. The old swimming pool was removed to allow space for the Campus Center Building. Termite-ridden Farrington Hall was demolished in 1975 for a parking lot, on which a student services building was constructed in 1994. Several new dormitories changed the Manoa campus from what had been almost entirely a commuter campus to a more conventional college. The first women's dorm, Hale Aloha, built in 1922 and quickly outgrown, had housed the School of Nursing and later the first offices of the East-West Center. Demolished to make room for the College of Business Administration, its name was given to the cylindrical tower dormitories on the quarry rim.

Architects with little sense of Hawaii's climate or geology, but with the blessing of the State's Department of Accounting and General Services (DAGS), paid only perfunctory attention to faculty suggestions or warnings. A recent example had been the Business Administration Building, built in 1971 on a hillside watered by a natural spring. Because construction bids had all exceeded the sum appropriated, DAGS reduced the plans by one floor, cut back on ground preparation, substituted concrete blocks for poured concrete walls, and eliminated such "luxuries" as carpeting and sound-deadening wall hangings. To no one's astonishment, the building leaked in rainstorms, classroom reverberations made lectures difficult to hear, and—in seeming response to a curse that philosopher Harold McCarthy had put upon the structure for its destruction of a beautiful site—the complex of seven units began slowly sliding down hill. The courtyard was rebuilt twice; F-tower was declared unsafe and torn down in 1980.

Even naming the building had been controversial. Those familiar with the College of Business Administration knew that the late Professor Harold S. Roberts had led its development as organizer and first dean; they surmised that the new building would be named after him. When it was left unnamed, the conclusion widely drawn on campus was that opposition of the International Longshoremen's and Warehousemen's Union was the barrier. Roberts had offended the ILWU during the bitter waterfront strike of 1949 when the fact-finding board he chaired recommended a wage increase that fell short of the union's expectations. Subsequently, he had disappointed the ILWU when arbitrating industrial disputes. Although the union's membership and political influence had declined markedly, it was still sufficient to block this expected honor to Roberts, who had died in 1970. The University administration did allow his widow to place his ashes in the ground on which the building would arise.

Controversy now arose over naming the social science building for pioneer psychology professor Stanley Porteus, who had served on the faculty from 1922 to 1948, long before his death in 1972. The internationally known Porteus Maze Test had become the tool for deriving his theory of intelligence, which attributed racial and gender differences to genetic inheritance and led to his conclusion that Caucasians were generally superior to other races. Arguing that Porteus was racist, a group of faculty and students, led by Professors Robert Cahill and Danny Steinberg, in 1974 protested naming the building after him. Psychology professor Ronald Johnson charged that the objectors ignored the historical setting of Porteus' work in a period when academic studies of interracial differences were in their infancy. The name remained.

While much new construction was under way through the mid-century decades, routine campus maintenance was postponed because of budget constraints, just as Dean Holmes had reported during Sinclair's presidency. An accreditation team estimated that the Manoa campus needed approximately $90 million to $100 million in repairs and maintenance and that parking and student housing were "deficient."

Energy and Marine Research

Increased external funding, on the other hand, sustained continued growth in the scope and variety of the University's research activities. In 1972 a multidisciplinary team of Manoa faculty undertook to search the island of Hawaii for a geothermal source that could support the generation of electricity. Geologists located a hot spot in Puna among ancient volcanic flows; engineers worked out the technology for tapping steam generated by the magma far below the surface and using it to drive turbines; an economist estimated likely costs and benefits; a lawyer pondered the owner-

A building boom that began in the 1960s and continued through the 1980s filled the Manoa campus, from the pagoda-like Biomedical Science Building at its *mauka* extremity to the dormitory towers erected in the old quarry (the "lower" or "makai" campus). An aerial view taken in 1987 shows the close array.

McCarthy Mall along the eastern end of the campus, under its canopy of shower trees, provided shaded space and the Korean Studies Center some distinction of architectural style.

ship of such steam, whether with the state or the land owner. Steam was found in 1974 and, during a time of skyrocketing oil prices, also funds to install a generating plant. About five megawatts of power were developed, enough to supply a village, but the experimental well was noisy and smelly. Downwind residents complained of respiratory problems and sacrilege to Pele. Wiser, if not necessarily chastened, the professors withdrew to their labs. Further geothermal development became a concern for private enterprise, slackening as world oil prices declined.

Nevertheless, the legislature established the Hawaii Natural Energy Institute in 1974 to focus on research, development, and demonstration of technology, such as that for generating electricity by using the temperature difference between deep offshore waters and the near-shore shallows at the laboratories in North Kona on the Big Island. In that same year, UH, along with the University of Michigan and Louisiana State University, became a Sea Grant institution, receiving half of the $2.8 million allotted by the U.S. Department of Commerce for marine-related research. Even as state financial support faltered, that of federal agencies continued to rise.

Affiliating the Alumni

During Matsuda's administration the University disassociated itself from the sixty-two-year-old UH Alumni Association. In 1977, the Manoa ASUH called for reorganizing the association, charging that its longtime executive secretary was not fulfilling her duties. UH presidents had long tried to remove her. Action finally came after a committee studying the alumni association reported in 1982 that fewer than two thousand of more than one hundred thousand Manoa graduates belonged and little effort was made to secure members. In July 1984 the administration announced that since negotiations had shown reorganization to be impossible "without a public fight," it no longer recognized the UHAA.

Because of the UHAA's failure to raise funds, the regents had established the University of Hawai'i Foundation (UHF) in 1955. In the 1970s the UHF began to develop lists of graduates from all the UH campuses. It could establish records for fewer than half of the institution's estimated two hundred thousand former students, many of whom were in their prime earning years or possibly considering bequests in their wills. Less than half a million dollars had come from alumni. Only 4 percent of them contributed, compared with an average of 16 percent for all American public universities.

Under executive director Don Mair, the UHF succeeded in raising funds from the community at large as well as from alumni. From just over a million dollars in 1976–1977, contributions grew to almost eight million in 1988–1989, still a small proportion of the $400 million UH budget.

To further stimulate affiliation, the Board of Regents in 1988 created an Alumni Affairs Association, a "systemwide umbrella," authorizing individual campuses and colleges to establish their own alumni groups to raise funds and otherwise engage their graduates. More than thirty college, campus, and regional alumni associations came into operation, including the original UHAA and the Beijing UH Alumni Association.

More Administration Problems

Matsuda appointed Durward Long chancellor of Manoa in 1979. Long, who had been vice-president for academic affairs since 1975, considered his academic specialization to be the administration of higher education. In meetings with deans and with the Manoa Faculty Senate, he talked about decentralizing the Manoa administration but himself repeatedly made decisions that should have been made by deans or department chairs. Worse were the protracted delays before reaching those decisions. Soon deans openly opposed Long, followed shortly by the Manoa Faculty Senate. Hostility grew until he was removed from office in September 1981. Shortly thereafter he left Hawaii.

The Manoa Faculty Senate continued to object to the layers of administration through which curricular proposals and personnel actions had to pass, complaining that they created a situation in which no one could be held accountable for decisions made—or not made. Proposals languished for months as papers were shuffled back and forth, with deans and directors unable to find the sticking points. A Faculty Senate task force examined the problem and submitted a report which the Manoa Senate adopted in January 1983. It called for "dismantling the central administration" and giving more authority to the Manoa chancellor. An alternative proposal was to return to the pre-Cleveland organization in which the president was also the chief executive officer of the Manoa campus. Faculty senates of the other campuses generally disagreed with the latter idea, fearing that it would result in favoritism toward Manoa. While the report brought no immediate changes, the controversy may have influenced Matsuda's decision to retire in 1984.

THE PRESIDENCY OF ALBERT SIMONE

Albert J. Simone, vice-president for academic affairs under Matsuda, served as acting president while a national search was conducted for a new president. Prior to coming to UH in 1983, Simone had been dean of the College of Business Administration at the University of Cincinnati. He was an active candidate for the presidency but was informed that the Board of Regents had decided on another.

The appointment of Cecil Mackey, outgoing president of Michigan State University, was announced by the board on January 4, 1985. His negotiated remuneration, including a base salary of $80,000 plus $28,000 from the University of Hawai'i Foundation, as well as a house, life insurance, and other benefits, far exceeded the $95,000 ceiling set by the legislature. It was asked to enact a law permitting the University to use UHF funds to meet his demands, but the bill failed to pass. Thereupon Mackey announced that he would not come to Hawaii, pointing to state interference with the constitutional authority of the regents and the UH administration. The regents then named Albert Simone president. Simone, whose academic field was decision making, chose to serve as both UH president and chancellor of Manoa, in effect implementing the 1983 Faculty Senate report on administration.

The 1985 accreditation report of the Western Association of Schools and Colleges (WASC) once more highlighted outside interference. It criticized state officials for not giving the University the authority it "deserved" and admonished the faculty for undermining the administration by lobbying with the legislature. The report recommended that UH "pursue obtaining acceptance and respect for the 1978 constitutional amendment granting exclusive jurisdiction to the Board of Regents over the internal organization and management of the university." It went on to add: "If necessary, this may necessitate legal action."[23]

The accrediting agency warned Governor Ariyoshi that Hawaii had until the following May to show that progress was being made in upholding the constitutional provision or the University would be put on probation.[24] Ariyoshi responded to the threatened loss of accreditation by curbing the role of the Departments of Accounting and General Services and Budget and Finance and other state agencies in their oversight of the University.

Testifying before the legislature in January 1986, Simone predicted that the Manoa campus would lose accreditation if it failed to grant the University greater independence. A bill passed, giving UH more fiscal autonomy. The state had been taking a large percentage of federal and other grants to offset the overhead involved in the state's management of those funds. The reform law, by limiting the percentage withheld, increased the amount of research funds available. The 1991 accreditation report praised the University for obtaining a greater measure of control over its operations.

New Programs and Clusters; Old Question of Emphasis

The profusion of research and instructional programs in the sciences, humanities, and social sciences on the Manoa campus stimulated departmental amalgamation during Simone's administration. Growth in Pacific and Asian programs led in July 1987 to the creation of the School of Hawaiian, Asian, and Pacific Studies, placing under one dean nearly three hundred Manoa faculty members with Asian and Pacific expertise. In 1988, the School of Ocean and Earth Science and Technology (SOEST) was established, incorporating geology, geophysics, meteorology, oceanography, and ocean engineering plus the Institutes of Geology and Marine Biology and the Natural Energy Institute. The Sea Grant and Space Grant College programs, the Undersea Research Laboratory, the Center for Volcanology, the Joint Institute for Marine and Atmospheric Research, and the Aquarium were included as well. In 1992 SOEST had 170 faculty and more than 500 staff members.

An annual $150,000 grant from the National Aeronautics and Space Administration (NASA) made UH one of only twenty-one universities with "space grants" and one of four that received land, sea, and space grants. (The other three were M.I.T. and the universities of Washington and California.) The land, sea, and space grants stimulated research and education leading to more external research and training grants, bringing millions of dollars to the state.

The Spark M. Matsunaga Institute for Peace was established in 1985 in memory of the late U.S. senator. Focusing on research and education on the problems of peace and war, especially in the Asia-Pacific area, it added to the UH curriculum a certificate program exceptional among American universities.

Although most of these new units offered undergraduate courses, much of their work was concerned with graduate studies and research. The 1990 WASC report criticized the University for putting "less emphasis than wise" on undergraduate education while building up research programs and for neglecting academic advising.[25] In reply, Simone pointed out that average class size (twenty-four) and student-faculty ratio were low compared with other schools. He admitted that undergraduate advising had "faltered" and said the campus would add more academic advisors.

The Computer Age Begins

The computer, hitherto largely limited to engineering and scientific research laboratories, became increasingly prevalent in the University system from the mid-1980s. The appointment of John Haak as librarian in 1983 saw a push to fully automate the catalog and processing functions of the UH libraries. By 1986 the catalog of the Manoa collections, grown to two million volumes, went online to the public; access through a modem to a network of mainland libraries was also provided.

Contemporaneously, the complex task of student registration, so long achieved by waiting in slow lines during the late-summer heat, was also computerized, culminating with registration by telephone or computer. Computer labs came to be installed around the campus for student use. By the 1990s courses on computer theory and application, which had started out in electrical engineering, had spread to virtually every program. "Teleducation," enabling students on the other islands to interact with professors and resident students on the Manoa campus, was being prepared by the School of Library and Information Studies. Proposals for more ambitious programs in computer-based learning were soon to come.

Social Issues and Actions

Sexual harassment and its prevention became a subject of controversy during the Simone years. Like other schools across the nation, UH struggled to develop a policy and procedure that would protect students and staff and yet not imperil the personal relationships inherent in a teaching program. In 1990, a University-wide task force developed a policy that forbade all intimate relationships between faculty members and their students. Some critics argued that the policy was an invasion of privacy. Others objected that it did not go far enough in defining forms of harassment. Mie Watanabe, the affirmative action officer, reported that sanctions against harassers had ranged from reprimands, to suspension without pay, to the required resignation of one nonfaculty staff member.

A few days prior to the 1990 WASC accreditation inspection, Simone announced that UH would seek funds to help hire more members of minority groups and more women for faculty and graduate assistant positions. According to Simone, 27 percent of the Manoa faculty were women, compared to a national average of 21 percent at public research universities, while 29 percent were of ethnic minorities, compared to the national average of 10 percent.

The 1990 WASC report expanded on the race and gender analysis. It said that the UH "may be the most ethnically diverse public university in the nation," showing that 31 percent of its students were of Japanese ancestry, 24 percent Caucasian, 11 percent Chinese, 7 percent Filipino, and 6 percent Hawaiian. It found, however, that Filipinos and Hawaiians continued to be underrepresented among students, faculty, and upper-level staff. Acknowledging that efforts had been made to recruit and retain members of these ethnic groups, the report said that "more needs to be done." Noting that only about a fourth of the faculty and of those in executive and management positions were women, it recommended developing "a clearly stated policy on affirmative action along with a central office that monitors affirmative action processes."[26]

Inevitably the campus participated in the recriminations that accompanied the rising debates of the time on ethnic awareness and Hawaiian sovereignty. Philosophy student Joey Carter sent a letter to *Ka Leo* in November 1990 complaining of "anti-haole prejudice," saying that Hawaiians should not blame all white people for injustices suffered in the past. Professor Haunani-Kay Trask, director of the Center for Hawaiian Studies, replied that Carter should go back to the mainland, saying that "Hawaiians would certainly benefit from one less *haole* in our land." The Philosophy Department asked the Faculty Senate to censure Trask for "intimidating" a student. She in turn broadened the controversy to include sexual harassment on campus, white domination in Hawaii and on the UH faculty, the rights of native Hawaiians to self-determination and reparations, and the return of lands lost in the 1898 annexation. Its Committee on Professional Matters reported to the Faculty Senate that Trask's comments were inappropriate because she headed a teaching department and her words had been directed at a student. Trask replied that she had never met Carter and the fact that he was a student was irrelevant. The senate refused to investigate the matter, affirming her academic freedom to speak her mind.

The issue boiled along for some weeks, generating many letters in *Ka Leo* and the local newspapers. Simone ordered an investigation, which Trask called an attempt to intimidate her and the Hawaiian community. The exchange of charges and countercharges continued for the remainder of the 1990–1991 academic year.

Simone Leaves

Simone resigned in late 1991 to become president of the Rochester Institute of Technology. Interviewed in July 1992, he summarized the accomplishments of his eight years as president, including forty new academic programs, expanded student counseling, and involving official student advocates in the university administration. Research grants had reached $120 million a year, four times the average of a decade earlier. Increased emphasis had been given to teaching, and senior professors taught more of the undergraduate classes. The ratio of students to faculty was among the lowest in the nation—eleven to one, the same as at Stanford.

Vice-President for Academic Affairs Paul C. Yuen served as acting president during a lengthy national search for Simone's successor. The early 1990s was no easy time for an interim administration. Enrollment, outside the Manoa campus, continued to rise, while a devastating series of budget cuts began. Problems of collective bargaining, affirmative action, dealing with alleged sexual harassment, and other difficult issues plagued Bachman Hall. The rivalry within Simone's administration—detailed by Professor David Yount in *Who Runs the University?*—did not slacken during the interregnum. Yuen, one of those considered for the presidency, was not eager for the post.

KENNETH MORTIMER'S PRESIDENCY BEGINS

The regents selected Kenneth P. Mortimer, the head of Western Washington University and previously vice-president and vice-provost at Pennsylvania State University, where he directed the Center for the Study of Higher Education from 1976 to 1981. Dr. Mortimer was installed as the eleventh president of the University of Hawai'i and as chancellor of the Manoa campus on September 15, 1993. Dr. Yuen, after serving for a year as interim senior vice-president for academic affairs, returned to his longtime position as dean of engineering.

The new administration and the reconstituted Board of Regents faced a recurrent problem. For the fifth time in the University's history, policy decisions were dominated by an imperative need to cut expenditures—a crisis not as sudden as Governor Pinkham's order to slash territorial appropriations in 1915, not as deep as in the Great Depression, but more arresting by far than the lean years of the early 1950s and 1970s.

The Hawaii economy, and therefore its tax base, had been shrunk by a decline in tourism following the Gulf War of 1991 and by the virtual disappearance of its old staples, sugar and pineapple production. On taking office in 1995, Governor Benjamin J. Cayetano felt obliged to avoid a budget deficit by reducing state expenditures drastically—tax increases being ruled out by the political temper of the time. Cayetano, the first governor in thirty-three years who had not studied at UH, was not predisposed to shelter the University from the general cuts: its share for the 1995–1996 fiscal year was more than $7 million.

The University administration responded in familiar ways, by freezing staff size, cutting purchases of library books and journals, restricting out-of-state travel, and by deferring building repair and campus maintenance. Smaller teaching faculties required a cut in the classes offered. The resulting distress first brought reaction on April 28, 1995, by some two hundred—estimates vary—faculty members and students who brought to the central administration their protest at the scheduled deletion of fourteen classes of the Hawaiian language. Like the last incursion of Bachman Hall, almost thirty years earlier in the time of the Vietnam War, the protesters came peacefully but shouldered their way past security guards to occupy the building. They were met at the stairs by Vice-President Joyce Tsunoda, the senior administrator present, and Vice-President Thomas Gething. They invited representatives of the group to Tsunoda's office; and, after receiving her assurance that the classes would be offered because teaching Hawaiian was a "UH priority," the whole party joined hands in the building's foyer to sing "Hawaii Aloha." A student-faculty protest against planned reductions in Hawaiian classes at the Hilo campus was similarly peaceful and successful.[27]

Apprehension became general in July, when President Mortimer announced that the University, along with other state agencies, had been ordered by the governor to reduce by 10 percent the expenditure of funds already appropriated. For UH, that meant an additional loss of $31 million, bringing the University's appropriated funds down from approximately $350 million in 1994 to $280 million in 1996. Mortimer told an open forum on the Manoa campus: "I cannot take a $31 million cut with no impact on quality. That's just impossible."[28]

By the time the new academic year began in late August, speculation about forced reductions in programs obsessed all of the University's constituencies—students, faculty, staff, administrators. Not only were the number of courses, instructors, teaching and lab assistants, librarians, book collections, advisors, computer facilities, and all the other components of a large university threatened, entire programs were said to be in jeopardy. Honolulu newspapers reported that the administration was even considering closing or "privatizing" the professional schools that Governor Burns had deemed essential for a first-class university—medicine and law.

When Mortimer told a meeting of the Manoa faculty on October 18 how he proposed to address the budget crisis, the students of the entire UH system found their interests directly affected. Standards of admission to Manoa were to be raised and remedial courses there discontinued, the growth in graduate programs checked, and tuition fees raised, as much as 75 percent—on all campuses.

The level of protest increased and focused on the governor. On Halloween Day, a long column of students and faculty members marched from the Manoa campus to the state capitol, where they joined protesters from the community colleges. After speeches by their leaders, Governor Cayetano attempted to talk to the thousands of people crowded on the lawn of the capitol. He was rebuffed by jeers, obscenities, and flying objects (thrown by "a handful of hecklers" gathered near the podium, it was reported).[29]

The governor accepted an invitation to attend a special meeting of the regents a few days later and there heard apologies for the indignities he had suffered and an appeal for support of the University. Cayetano replied that the University community failed to appreciate either the seriousness of the fiscal crisis or the degree to which other state agencies were required to make sacrifices. UH would have to act decisively to tailor its programs to the limited money available. Was the law school really necessary? Shouldn't the University's admission standards, including those of the community colleges, be raised? This of course would reduce the number of students, the number of faculty members required, the number of classrooms and buildings.[30]

No action was taken on the suggested demise of the law school, but the administration had already addressed the question of admission standards, though in a way different from Cayetano's. In his meeting with the Manoa faculty on October 18, Mortimer, in a long speech, "Focus on Quality," had stipulated that the Manoa campus, a research university providing the only graduate and professional training offered within the UH system, had to raise its standards by limiting admission of undergraduates to applicants who could show a "superior high school record" or completion of an associate of arts degree. Remedial courses at Manoa must be limited. The open-door admission policy of the community colleges, however, would be continued so that the University, "as a *system,* [would] continue to provide *access* to all citizens of the state who can benefit from the postsecondary experience." The community colleges were the appropriate providers of most remedial education in reading, writing, and mathematics.

As for the Manoa campus, "we simply cannot afford to continue the growth of graduate programs at the rate of the 1980s." (As Mortimer spoke, the campus was offering eighty-seven master's and fifty-nine doctor's degrees, plus graduate work in seven professional schools.) Resources to support the school's "drive to prominence in research" would have to be channeled into a "relatively limited number of areas" where the University could claim national and international distinction.

In turn, he claimed to be reducing administrative overhead. "We have too many deans and directors and we are too fragmented for a campus of 20,000 students." Five areas were under close review: the schools of Public Health and of Library and

The 1990s saw the physical completion of the Manoa campus. New buildings included a Special Events Arena, which at last accommodated commencements—such as the 1994 winter granting of advanced degrees shown here—as well as basketball and volleyball games. A new Student Services Building (1995) at Varney Circle ended the slow, hot drudgery of registration by providing for course selection by telephone and computer.

Financial crises again struck the University after 1995, when state appropriations were drastically cut. Following discussions at the several UH campuses on Oahu, represented by this faculty teach-in on Bachman lawn (October 9), on Halloween columns of students converged at the State Capitol to protest the cuts, calling on the governor to save UH and them.

Information Studies, the Graduate Division, the College of Continuing Education and Community Service, and the Office of Research Administration. In the meantime, as people retired and short-term contracts expired, a freeze on new appointments continued to shrink the size of the faculty and constrict the number and variety of classes offered.

Even during a mounting fiscal crisis, however, the momentum of projects conceived in earlier and easier years carried forward building construction, an economy-stimulating activity of which the governor approved. At Manoa, the old Quadrangle was completed with the construction of an Architecture Building along University Avenue, styled in approximate harmony with the grandfather it faced, Hawaii Hall. The architecturally distinctive Center for Hawaiian Studies on Dole Street neared completion. At Windward Community College, a science building went up, the first structure built for that made-over campus since its creation in 1972. Plans were readied for expanding other community colleges and UH at Hilo. The state government moved, finally, to provide a site for West O'ahu College by a land exchange (see chapter 19).

An Electronic Campus?

By the mid-1990s the University had turned to cyberspace as a medium to serve students of community colleges on the Neighbor Islands. A new University center expanded programs wherein Manoa faculty members used interactive television for courses to students on Maui and Kauai. These, combined with live courses offered by visiting West Oahu faculty, would enable community college students to earn bachelors' and certain masters' degrees. Already the Maui Community College Skybridge system provided classes by interactive television teaching to students on Lanai and Molokai, while Leeward Community College had a learning facility at a shopping center on western Oahu where students could see, hear, and respond to televised lectures given on the college campus. Several courses were broadcast on cable, available to anyone with access to a television set. Other community colleges were following suit.

Governor Cayetano, however, wanted the University to go much further in computer-based higher education. He announced in November 1996 that Hawaii would commit $100,000 as its share of seed money for a "virtual university" being formed by thirteen western states, in which UH would participate. The Western Governors University, as it was provisionally named, was conceived as an electronic "campus" —a computer network of course instruction by which students in each of the states could see and hear lectures presented at the other member schools. President Mortimer was to represent Hawaii in planning the operation.

The potential scope of instruction beamed from universities and colleges in a dozen mainland states to students in Hawaii, its variety and low cost, gained the respectful attention of more than the governor. In a time of fiscal pain the prospect of teaching through cyberspace offered possible relief from the enduring pressure for more courses, more instructors and staff, and more buildings on real campuses built on costly land.

But there were critics. A member of the Higher Education Coordinating Board for Texas, which initially did not join the Western Governors University, wrote that while computer and television networks could enrich college instruction when used "appropriately," the "kind of virtual university envisioned by the Western governors seems likely to produce only virtual learning."[31] Skeptics predicted that, at worst, the technology of teaching at a distance would produce a sophisticated correspondence school, offering more courses to more people, but mechanically, devoid of the oversight and counseling needed for effective teaching. Cyberspace instruction would be used primarily for community colleges, widening the gap between the teaching offered their students and what was presented live on the university campus. So the argument began, in Hawaii and across the nation, with governors, legislators, and university administrators generally ranged as proponents and faculty associations speaking out skeptically or in opposition. It promised to continue for some time to come.

Thus, as the millennium neared its close, the University of Hawai'i was again being reshaped by the converging forces of technological change, monetary needs, and political pressures. As during each of its recurring financial crises, UH was being forced to find new ways of fulfilling the duty imposed on it when, almost ninety years earlier, the territorial statute creating the school obliged it to offer "thorough instruction" with a standard "equal to that given and required in similar universities on the mainland of the United States." How acceptable standards were to be achieved with reduced support from the state government was by no means evident. All that seemed clear was that the University would spend the closing years of its first century as it had spent the opening years, dealing with rapid and unpredictable change, but now functioning as a major element in the economy and politics of Hawaii.

PART II

MANOA COLLEGES AND PROGRAMS

Development of teaching and research on the campus at Manoa occurred differentially in its several colleges, many departments, and array of programs, the telling of which would overwhelm this volume. A sampling of these individual histories gives a sense of the initiatives taken, the problems encountered, and the achievements experienced by the collective enterprise of the campus.

4

THE HAWAIIAN LANGUAGE AND HAWAIIAN STUDIES

Rubellite K. Johnson

THE UNIVERSITY OF HAWAI‘I may not leap to mind as a guardian of Hawaii's indigenous speech and culture, but that in fact has been its historical role. Only the University's abiding commitment to teach Hawaiian has kept it alive as a disciplined language spoken now by increasing thousands of people in these islands.

At the beginning of this century, when the University was starting up, Hawaiian was alive in Hawaiian-speech communities, still numerous but in decline. There was also a "mixed" linguistic sharing between the native Hawaiian population and those haoles who could speak the language fluently. Indeed, in the last half of the nineteenth century, the kingdom was officially bilingual, with Hawaiian used in the legislature and in the courts of justice. After the overthrow of the monarchy in 1893, English became the standard language of instruction in the schools, but the rapid demise of spoken Hawaiian was not yet foreseen. A critical factor was the decision of the territorial legislature against providing for Hawaiian to be used as the language of instruction in public schools with large enrollments of Hawaiian students.

Another kind of speech was replacing both Hawaiian and English in the everyday discourse of the mass of people. This was "pidgin," or what used to be called "broken English," whose basic structure was Hawaiian with the addition of auxiliary verbs borrowed from other languages, notably Portuguese, and a changing mix of Japanese, Chinese, and English words and phrases. Pure Hawaiian was more and more becoming limited to services in Hawaiian churches.

Educators were well aware of the need for local students to master English in order to succeed in the classroom and in the world of business dominated by Americans. From its founding, the University accepted only English as the language of instruction, except of course in foreign language classes. In its first stage—as a college from 1907 to 1920—the small number of languages offered did not include Hawaiian.

In early 1921, after the territorial legislature had expanded the College of Hawaii to become the University, the Board of Regents was asked in a legislative inquiry to declare its intentions with regard to Hawaiian. The board replied that "it has been a part of the plan of the University of Hawaii to give instruction in the Hawaiian language. . . . The University should become the center for the study of Hawaiian and a strong effort made to preserve the language in its purity."

Frederick W. Beckley, who had served as the last official Hawaiian interpreter in the Supreme Court of the monarchy and had taught Hawaiian history and language at the Territorial Normal School, was engaged as instructor in the Hawaiian language, offering a year's course, Hawaiian 100–101, described in the catalog as "a course for beginners [covering] pronunciation, grammar, vocabulary, reading of easy prose, composition and conversation." A second two-semester course, added in 1923, included the "reading of legends, mele, and more difficult prose, including legal documents. The figurative language. Conversation. 3 credits."

After five years as instructor, Beckley was promoted to the rank of professor in 1926, his last year of service. He was succeeded by Professor John Henry Wise, a former territorial senator, after whom the University's first athletic field was named. Alone, he taught the curriculum in Hawaiian, which by then included elementary, intermediate, and advanced language courses, as well as Hawaiian literature and arts.

The courses offered by Beckley and Wise were broad in scope. For example, Beckley's treatment of syntax addressed not only the rules of Hawaiian but also its historical development within the Polynesian group of Austronesian languages. Another Beckley subject, "Comparison of Hawaiian and European Classics," in today's political climate might be laughed to scorn, notwithstanding that there still may be students who would enjoy Hawaiian translations of Shakespeare's plays or Aesop's fables.

What Beckley and Wise accomplished between 1922 and 1934 (when Wise retired and was succeeded by the Reverend Henry Judd) was to lay the foundation for what eventually became the University's degree program in the Hawaiian language, a curriculum unique in the academic world.

In 1926 a significant change was made in the place of Hawaiian in formal education: the University listed it, along with Latin, Greek, French, German, Spanish, Chinese, and Japanese, as the languages offered from which candidates for the bachelor of arts degree could earn elective credits. By this action, the University gave Hawaiian an academic status equal to that of the traditionally required languages of the Occident and Orient, languages with highly developed literatures. Few then could have realized the importance of the decision to place the indigenous language, rich in oral tradition but not in writings, in the curriculum alongside the classical languages. It was an act of innovation by a new university, a kind of institution usually given to the cautious following of example while establishing its place in academe.

At the same time, the University changed its entrance requirements by adding

Hawaiian to the list of languages accepted for credit. That had more symbolic than practical effect, for Hawaiian was little taught in elementary or high schools—not even at the Kamehameha Schools, where, indeed, students were prohibited from speaking Hawaiian.

With teaching materials in Hawaiian (such as dictionaries and the Lahainaluna textbooks) largely out of print, the teachers at Manoa had to choose from the few religious works then available, or write their own text. Beckley relied on the Hawaiian-English New Testament for his introductory course. Judd wrote a text and a dictionary, collectively called *The Hawaiian Language,* which served his students for many years.

When Judd completed ten years of campus teaching in 1945, he was succeeded by the Reverend Edward Kahale, pastor of Kawaiahao Church. It began to look as if the Congregational ministry had taken over Hawaiian language instruction. The sad truth was that the Hawaiian language was "dying" for lack of speakers in the urban population. The church, where congregations still sang from Hawaiian hymnals, heard sermons in Hawaiian, and conducted their senior classes in Hawaiian, was the last refuge of the spoken language within the cities. Like his predecessors, Kahale saw the need for textbooks for college students, and these he created at three levels, *Elementary, Intermediate,* and *Advanced Hawaiian.*

While Beckley and his successors were establishing Hawaiian language studies, the University, without any plan to do so, was adding teachers and courses that would later lead to another unique program, that in Hawaiian studies. Inevitably, given its location, the University's developing academic departments began offering Hawaii-related courses in the regional context of the Pacific, such as Hawaiian history, taught by Ralph Kuykendall, and Hawaiian geography, by John W. Coulter. Felix Keesing, appointed in 1934 as the University's anthropologist, offered a course on Polynesian culture. Sociologist Romanzo Adams lectured and wrote on race relations in Hawaii. Hawaiian lauhala weaving was offered as a course in the industrial arts curriculum of the School of Agriculture. In Teachers College, the music courses taught by the young Dorothy M. Kahananui included Hawaiian songs. E. S. C. Handy of the Bishop Museum found a niche in the religion curriculum to consider the ethnology of Hawaiian religion as "Nature Worship in Hawaii," dealing with "the religious experiences, mythology, deities and ritual in relation to life and culture in Hawaii and Polynesia." From this he produced the monograph *Polynesian Religion,* which for many years was the only authoritative treatment of a subject touching upon a most sensitive area of heart, mind, and spirit in Polynesia.

Handy's participation was one example of the benefits that the University enjoyed in its affiliation in research with the Bishop Museum, which had begun in the 1920s. Museum staff members, appointed as "affiliate" or "adjunctive" faculty, brought expertise in areas of Polynesian studies that the University was otherwise not staffed to teach. Dr. Peter Buck, the noted ethnologist, regularly taught on the Manoa campus in the 1930s.

This growing aggregation of courses, mostly taught by non-Polynesians, showed a natural line of development for the University, but one of which it was not yet conscious. It is fair to say that while the school's leaders envisioned a future as the center for Pacific studies, their interest was more directed to the cultures of Asia than that of the Islands. In his farewell report in 1941, President David Crawford surveyed achievements during his long term and urged more Oriental studies, but he had no word for the study of Hawaiian language and culture.

The disruption of the campus by World War II stopped the growth of Polynesian studies, although courses in the Hawaiian language were still taught. Postwar expansion of the faculty brought new strength. Samuel H. Elbert was recruited in 1949 to assist Kahale in teaching sections of elementary and intermediate Hawaiian. A professional linguist, Dr. Elbert brought a fluency in Hawaiian, Samoan, and Trukese acquired in the field, as well as an acumen in linguistics that helped give students of Hawaiian a better understanding of its relationship to other languages of the Pacific that had evolved from the Austronesian languages.

The Hawaiian ministers on the faculty, who later included the Reverend Samuel Keala as well as Kahale, attracted Hawaiian students who wanted to train with a "primary language" resource, also Hawaiian. Others, attracted by the scientific skills of a gifted linguist like Elbert, gathered at his open office door, behind which were shoe boxes filled with note cards bearing Hawaiian words translated by Mary Kawena Pukui, Elbert's mentor at the Bishop Museum, with whom he was preparing the authoritative Hawaiian-English dictionary. Elbert also wrote textbooks, *Conversational Hawaiian* and *Spoken Hawaiian,* in which he transformed explanations of Hawaiian grammar and syntax away from the unrelated Latin models of description used by nineteenth-century missionaries. His influence and that of Dorothy Kahananui, who joined the Hawaiian language faculty in the late 1950s, were instrumental in producing a new generation of teachers who ensured that the learning of Hawaiian would continue, even as the pool of primary language speakers, including the Hawaiian ministry, continued to shrink.

Anthropology at Manoa in the 1950s enjoyed an upsurge that laid the basis for further concentration in Hawaiian studies. Two affiliate professors from the Bishop Museum, ethnologist E. S. C. Handy, teaching Customs and Lore of Old Hawaii, and archaeologist Kenneth P. Emory, teaching Hawaiian Culture, brought to their classes the richness of their extensive research. Recruited to the new Department of Anthropology were Professors Leonard Mason, Saul Riesenberg, and Katharine Luomala. Their broad knowledge of island cultures, though not directly focused on this archipelago, brought an expertness about the peoples of the central Pacific that complemented Hawaiian studies.

An assembling of courses dealing with the Pacific being taught in various departments was achieved in 1950 with the formation of the Pacific Islands Program. At that same time—long before programs in ethnic studies became commonplace in American universities—Samuel Elbert bravely proposed creating a curriculum in "Hawaiian Studies." Years passed, however, before a program concentrating on the native people and culture of Hawaii was developed. That occurred in the 1970s, a decade in which this university, like many across the nation, had become receptive to the idea of creating programs of ethnic studies. Elbert's proposal was reintroduced with some modification by his students who had joined him in the newly formed departments of Indo-Pacific Languages and Linguistics. To the instruction in languages, anthropology, and history suggested by Elbert were added courses in travel industry management, musicology, education, ethnobotany, art, marine biology, folklore—and almost anything else bearing the name "Hawaiian."

By thus broadening the participating faculty, a hesitant College of Arts and Sciences was induced to accept the idea. A program in Hawaiian studies was established in 1970. Originally, it was an undergraduate major in arts and sciences, administered by the Liberal Studies Office under its general mandate to help students design courses of study fitted to their individual interests. For this major, "some competence" in the Hawaiian language was required.

Hawaiian Studies did not get its own head until 1979, when Abraham Piianaia, then on the faculty of the Geography Department, assumed direction of the program and taught two courses—Perspectives in Hawaiian Studies and a senior seminar in Hawaiian studies. Initially, he served as director without compensation. Soon, the program became more autonomous and more focused, with its own degree requirements in anthropology, Hawaiian music, history, language, and so forth. By the end of the 1980s, the courses in the Hawaiian language offered in the Department of Indo-Pacific Languages exceeded twenty, covering the works of Hawaiian scholars and Hawaiian poetry, as well as language instruction.

In 1985 Dr. Haunani-Kay Trask transferred from the American Studies Department to Hawaiian Studies, becoming its first full-time faculty member. The placement and direction of the program changed markedly. First, in 1987, it was made a Center for Hawaiian Studies in the newly constituted School of Hawaiian, Asian, and Pacific Studies, with offices in Moore Hall. Under Trask, joined by Dr. Lilikala Kame‘eleihiwa (and later by Kanalu G. T. Young), the center became more assertive about Hawaiian rights as well as the Hawaiian culture, its faculty members playing conspicuous roles in the Hawaiian sovereignty movement of the last two decades.

Course offerings grew to a dozen, ranging from mythology and the genealogy of chiefly lineages to contemporary political issues of concern to Hawaiians. In 1994, construction began of a distinctively designed structure to house the center near

Frederick W. Beckley began the teaching of Hawaiian at the University in 1921, after which it was regularly offered at a time when linguistically correct Hawaiian was fast disappearing from use. Professor Samuel H. Elbert (shown with Aldyth Morris of the University of Hawai'i Press) in 1950 proposed creating a program in Hawaiian studies. Finally established in 1970, the program gained its own distinctive facility in 1996.

Manoa Stream on Dole Street, next to the taro beds cultivated there, emblematic of the Polynesian culture.

Instruction in Hawaiian also flourished at the University of Hawai'i at Hilo. There a master of arts program in Hawaiian language and literature, the first graduate degree in the field to be offered anywhere, was in preparation. Funded in part by the Office of Hawaiian Affairs, it was approved by the Board of Regents in 1996. At the close of the twentieth century, the University had become an important agent in fostering the Hawaiian Renaissance.

5

THE PACIFIC ISLANDS PROGRAM

Norman Meller

ORGANIZED INTEREST in the Pacific at the University of Hawai'i dates from 1932, when the University, with the assistance of the Carnegie Corporation, established a School of Pacific and Oriental Affairs. Initial attention was focused on large Asian nations bordering the Pacific, which then eclipsed island areas within the vast ocean. Nevertheless, out of this slowly evolved what became the nation's premier Pacific Islands program.

After World War II, President Gregg Sinclair appointed a faculty committee to consider the establishment of area-study programs. It identified the Far East and the Pacific Islands as promising regions and, after investigating the resources available, proposed creating a Center of Pacific Island Studies. In 1950 the University approved initiating the Pacific Islands Program (PIP), utilizing courses already being taught in several academic departments. Under the oversight of an advisory committee appointed by Sinclair, graduate students would earn credits toward an area-study master's degree in approved courses relating to the Pacific. As a commentator later said, "the ad hoc nature of PIP's administering committee, and the absence of funds, facilities, and support staff for the program" set a precedent for the next eighteen years.[1]

Typical of the delay experienced in launching a new academic program, which requires dovetailing it into ongoing University procedures and disseminating information to faculty and students, registration did not get under way until 1952. Then, under the leadership of anthropology professor Leonard E. Mason, PIP enrolled its first two students; the first M.A. was awarded in 1956. At that early stage, a grant from the Carnegie Corporation, shared with Yale University and the Bishop Museum, helped provide funds for field work in the Pacific.

The program organized a multidepartmental seminar in 1953 and for almost a decade focused the attention of interested faculty and students from various disciplines on relevant Pacific Island subjects—in history, anthropology, sociology, political science, and the like. This portion of PIP was ultimately abandoned when it failed to fulfill its purpose of developing a distinctive interdisciplinary approach to Pacific Island studies. As in other master's programs, students were then given a choice of writing a thesis or completing a larger number of courses and demonstrating their scholarly aptitude in a research paper. In 1979 a certification program was initiated, enabling students with the requisite training in Pacific Island subjects to have their area of competence certified on their academic records.

Over the years, most students enrolled in the PIP were motivated by academic interests in the Pacific, since the programs were not designed to equip them with marketable skills or prepare them for employment. Nevertheless, in an unpredictable way, individuals completing the program found a variety of applications—for example, in careers in the State Department, as a trustee of the Bishop Estate, as a staff member of the Bishop Museum, as a Hawaiian language teacher, as a program administrator of the Polynesian Cultural Center at Laie, Oahu. The number of students enrolled in the program continued to grow until plateauing at several dozen, with approximately three M.A. degrees being awarded annually.

A focus on the Pacific enriched the University in ways transcending the program itself. Most important was the creation of a strong basis for research by faculty members and students interested in the area. By the end of the 1950s, aided by a grant from the Rockefeller Foundation, attention was turned to systematically building a distinctive Pacific Islands Collection within the University library. A special library committee, with membership overlapping that of PIP's advisory group, was appointed by the president to oversee the expansion. Renee Heyum, a renowned specialist in the area, was recruited as curator with the task of building a Pacific Collection of world preeminence. Before her retirement in 1989, Heyum had achieved that goal.

The focus on Pacific Island cultures established at Manoa spread to other campuses of the UH system. Examples are the Pacific Islands Studies programs developed at Hilo and at Kapiʻolani Community College, as well as a Hawaiian and Polynesian program at Windward Community College.

The Pacific Islands Program itself experienced the reshuffling common to academic programs that reach outside established departments. In 1967 it was transferred to the College of Arts and Sciences, which already sheltered the Asian studies programs. The University administration proposed to combine both into a single international study program in order to facilitate the preparation of federal grant proposals. While supporting its move from the president's office, PIP successfully opposed the merger, fearing its Pacific Islands identity would be blurred by the larger Asian programs already well established. The shift to Arts and Sciences did bring the program its first allocation of office space, so that its affairs no longer had to be conducted out of the departmental quarters of it chairman. The move also furnished the program with its first budget allocation: $500 for student help and office supplies. In the following years additional funding supported a half-time position for the director and secretarial assistance. In 1985, the University began funding a full-time directorship and allocating a number of faculty and support positions to PIP, staffing urgently needed to sustain further development.

Faculty involvement in research concerning the islands of the Pacific continued to grow. A 1968 census of the Manoa faculty revealed that most of the 143 responding had some field research experience in the area. To serve their interest, and also help integrate the University's Pacific activities, the program began publishing a newsletter to inform them of ongoing research and to acquaint them with pertinent developments, such as restrictions on field research imposed by Pacific Island governments.

After many applications to the federal Office of Education, PIP won a grant to support its operation in 1973, followed by annual awards in the next two decades. This federal assistance enabled PIP to train Pacific librarians, offer courses in languages of the Pacific, provide a counselor for Pacific Island students enrolled on the Hilo campus, support faculty travel, and generally encourage Pacific curricular development within the University and in Hawaii's schools. Federal funds were also used to publish a series of working papers, providing an outlet for research papers on the Pacific Islands that were too long for scholarly journals.

In the 1980s a "scam" operation directed against the University fortuitously supported creation of the program's Pacific Islands Monograph Series, which subsequently produced a distinguished set of scholarly publications. It began when PIP asked the University of Hawai'i Foundation for assistance in printing the first monograph of the series. In turn, the foundation referred to the PIP director a Texan who had come with an offer of support to UH. The donor did provide about $38,000 in good money but then triggered a scheme to divert to himself a flow of funds ostensibly going to the foundation. When the truth was discovered, funds that were not legally transferred were returned, ending the Texas connection. Since $38,000 was not enough to launch the series, additional funding was obtained from the University and from private sources. By the mid-1990s a dozen books had been printed, establishing an outlet for scholarly writing long desired to stimulate research on the island communities of the Pacific.

As the quality of the University's Pacific resources became more widely recognized, PIP received assistance from national and international agencies to engage in outreach services relating to the Pacific. An exchange program brought faculty and students from mid-Pacific universities to the Manoa campus, in return for visits by Hawaii scholars. Such recognition also led to financial support from companies doing business in Hawaii, as in the sponsorship of lecture series by which PIP brought Island and Pacific Rim leaders to address local audiences on a range of pertinent subjects.

After a slow start, the Pacific Islands Program was thus identified by the University administration as a potential area of "selective excellence." In 1987 the program was renamed the Center for Pacific Island Studies—the broad title originally proposed almost forty years earlier by the faculty committee that reported to President Sinclair. As the scope of the center's activities continued to grow and as it established a reputation as a reservoir of Pacific scholarship by virtue of faculty expertise and library resources, recognition came that Pacific Island studies at the University of Hawai'i had become preeminent in its field.

6

ASIAN PROGRAMS AND LINKAGES

Robert M. Kamins

FROM ITS EARLY DAYS the University was envisioned as an institution of higher learning that would connect America with Asia. Hawaii's intercontinental position and its multiethnic environment, in which scholars from Asia could find languages, cuisines, and religions familiar to them among the exotica of America-in-Polynesia, argued for developing here a university to span the Pacific. William Kwai Fong Yap's 1919 petition made that connection a chief justification for transforming the College of Hawaii into a university: "Islands located at a point where the civilizations and commerce of the United States, the Orient and the islands of the Pacific meet, are therefore at the strategic point for a University unique in its opportunities."

The next year, a visiting study team from the U. S. Office of Education came to the same conclusion:

> [T]he commission believes that with vision and energy the University of Hawaii can become the University of the Pan-Pacific. Already a commendable movement is well underway, initiated and fostered by far-seeing citizens of Hawaii, looking toward the winning for Hawaii the honor of being designated as the natural meeting place for sessions of joint commission and of scientific, social, and educational groups made up of leaders in their respective lines of the several countries bordering the Pacific. There is every reason for believing that the University of Hawaii, if it were to set about it, could draw upon these countries heavily for its student body, and in turn could come to wield a powerful influence in the development of the races and peoples of such countries. Such a high purpose could well challenge the ambition of any university.[1]

Response to that challenge was at first necessarily modest. In 1921 Tasuku Harada (former president of Doshisha University, his doctorate from Edinburgh) and Shao Chang Lee (graduate of Canton and Peking colleges, doctorate from Columbia) were recruited to serve, respectively, as professors of Japanese and Chinese language and history. Other Orientalists followed; there were always to be Chinese and Japanese scholars on the faculty. From the beginning the library set out to establish a collection in those languages; it multiplied by purchase and gift, notably by the donation of some five thousand volumes of Japanese literature by Gensaku Nakamura of Honolulu.

Students began to come from Asia, first a trickle, by the mid-1920s a dozen, then a score, not only from Japan and China but from Korea, the Philippines, and India as well. Local and mainland students enrolled in the courses offered in the languages, literature, and—minimally at first—the history and culture of Japan and China. In 1928 a Department of Oriental Studies was formed, offering a major to be selected from those courses plus others on the art and government of the two nations. By 1930 UH was ranked by the Institute of Pacific Relations as America's third leading university in Asian studies.

The time was propitious for responding to the challenge presented earlier by the U.S. Office of Education. A series of international conferences held by the Pan-Pacific Union starting in 1920 and then by the Institute of Pacific Relations, which placed its headquarters in Honolulu, drew attention to Hawaii as a meeting place for scholars and national spokesmen.[2] Grants from the Rockefeller Foundation to support research in anthropology and racial differences and from the Carnegie Endowment for International Peace to pay visiting professors in international relations greatly helped the new university to gain support from the local government and community, just beginning to take it seriously as a center of research outside agriculture and the natural sciences.

The Board of Regents in 1931 approved the formation of a School of Pacific and Asian Affairs to function as a special part of the University's 1932 summer session. Professor Charles E. Martin, brought in from the University of Washington to direct a program focused on political and educational problems, assembled a faculty of twenty, drawn from Japan, England, and mainland universities of high repute, augmented by a few leading members of the Manoa faculty. A Carnegie grant helped finance the program. The 1933 session of the school was directed by Gregg M. Sinclair, associate professor of English, who had joined the faculty in 1929 after several years of teaching in Japan. This session, offering courses and seminars on cultural trends across the Pacific, was also well attended by local students and townspeople. During the 1934 session Sinclair was on a sabbatical leave in Asia, gathering ideas, materials, and support for the next and more ambitious attempt of the University to establish itself as a major connection between Occident and Orient.

This was the Oriental Institute, directed by Sinclair, which began operations as a year-round division of UH in 1938. Its faculty, based on the Department of Oriental Studies and enhanced by visiting Carnegie professors and members of other Manoa departments (such as philosopher Charles A. Moore and historians Ralph Kuykendall and Shunzo Sakamaki), presented a wide range of courses, primarily centered on Asia but with some attention to Hawaii and other Pacific Islands. The next year the curriculum was expanded to some fifty courses, and Moore, encouraged by Sinclair, arranged a summer's East-West Philosophers' Conference, attended by a score of philosophers, many distinguished, from around the world. (Resuming after World War II, the conferences continued periodically.)

Campus and community leaders were highly supportive of the institute; the Carnegie grant, other private gifts, and modest legislative appropriations made its future seem assured. Sinclair asked the territory's leading architect, C. W. Dickey, to draw plans, and they were handsome, for an Oriental Institute building. A graduate scholarship program and a series of scholarly publications were initiated; the library organized the collection of Asian materials, already one of the largest in the United States; an *Oriental Institute Journal* began publication.

Then came World War II. While the institute continued to function in the academic year 1940–1941, money failed abruptly as America's involvement in the war became evident. With America's declaration of war, the Oriental Institute disappeared, and the Asian program at Manoa again fell back to the Department of Oriental Studies, plus a few related courses in other departments.

A new start was made in 1948, when Sinclair, now president, invited heads of several eminent universities to attend the fortieth anniversary of the University and to lecture on the future of mankind in the Pacific. He announced that UH, renewing its focus on Asian studies, had formed a Graduate School of Pacific and Asiatic Affairs. It was from this second start, through a series of transformations in title and scope, that the present graduate programs on Asia evolved.[3]

The new initiative, however, was slow to begin, for the 1950s was a decade of budgetary constraint. Annual catalogs of the University made no claim of special competence in Asian studies. A master's degree was offered in Far Eastern studies, but the curriculum was meager: instruction in Chinese, Japanese, and Korean; a scattering of courses in the history, geography, sociology, and philosophic thought of South and Southeast Asia—and then, gradually, a course or two in economics and government, in art, music, and theatre, according to the faculty members available.

The flowering of Oriental studies that Sinclair had envisioned began suddenly, but four years after he had retired. Creation by Congress in 1959 of the East-West Center, following a plan devised by Professor Murray Turnbull with other UH faculty members, financed a major expansion of resources—in library materials, research facilities, offices and dormitories, scholarships, faculty positions—needed to attract and serve a large influx of students, scholars, technicians, and conferees coming to Manoa from East and West. Between 1960 and 1975, when it was removed from the University's administrative control, the center provided some twenty-five thousand scholarships and grants for degree candidates, established scholars, and technical trainees from forty-one Asian and Pacific countries and the United States.[4]

Under the forced growth stimulated by association with the center, Asian studies at Manoa flourished. By 1970 Eastern philosophy had become a major section of an enlarged department; instruction was given in a dozen Asian languages; sixteen courses on Asian art had been added along with a range of graduate seminars on the geography, economies, governments, and social systems of South and Southeast Asia. The History Department offered twenty courses on those areas, as many as the number in American history.

The University had also been developing a reputation for research on the biota of the Pacific, one which established relationships with scientists around and across that ocean. Examples, work in marine aquaculture and entomology, are noted in chapter 12 on the biological sciences. In fact, all the sciences and virtually every other department in the College of Arts and Science experienced a sea change, as more students and scholars arrived from Asia, joined by their American counterparts pursuing Asian studies in one discipline or another.

Professional schools of the Manoa campus also had been making their own connections across the Pacific, many financed by federal grants. In the College of Education, an Office of International Programs recruited faculty members to serve in Southeast Asia. In Laos, for example, they helped teach students, until then without schooling, how to read and type their own language, how to use stoves and other electrical appliances that were then coming into more general use, and how to teach teachers. The School of Medicine established an American-style residency program at Chubu Hospital on Okinawa, designed to induce Okinawan graduates of Japanese medical schools to return to Okinawa to practice there. In collaboration with the School of Public Health, it undertook research and medical service in treating parasitic diseases of Southeast Asia and the Pacific.[5] The law school developed a program of Pacific and Asian legal studies, covering the law affecting trans-Pacific trade, comparative labor law in Asian nations, and modes of dispute resolution practiced there. The international program of the School of Library and Information Studies attracted students from many Asian countries. Cross-cultural courses in social work were augmented by field studies in the Philippines, Hong Kong, and Taiwan. The list goes on and on.

Nevertheless, the chief linkages with Asia were in the humanities and the social sciences. Three decades of expanding Asia-connected teaching, research, and service produced at UH an academic program permeated with Asian content and emphases, especially in languages and literature, theatre and dance, music, art, philosophy and religion, history, geography, and anthropology. The spread of courses on Asia was contagious, as other departments also found ways to join what was obviously becoming a chief thrust of the University. To illustrate the permeation: Psychology developed a course on Asian perspectives on the working of the mind; Urban Planning, a course on design in Asia; Architecture taught Asian Architecture and Culture; the Textiles and Clothing curriculum added Costumes of Asia; Travel Industry Management offered Tourism in Asia; Industrial Relations, Labor Problems in Asia; the law school, Law in China. And so on, throughout the course listing.

A survey of international studies made in 1987 by Professor Roland Fuchs[6] found that virtually every department, institute, and professional school of the Manoa campus was involved in some way with the Orient, either by teaching about Asia, by faculty and student exchanges with Asian universities, or, as in the natural sciences, by participation in internationally collaborative research programs. Within the University system, every campus was teaching at least two major Asian-Pacific languages. For UH-Hilo, whose "mandated mission" was to foster understanding of cultures of the Pacific Basin, that focus was found in half of its forty-four courses dealing with international studies. At the fledgling West O'ahu College, upper-division courses in Asian literature, on Chinese and Japanese culture, and Korean history were among a growing number directed toward East Asia. The community college system offered instruction in Oriental languages, Japanese studies, and Asian art. Four of its six campuses had student exchange programs with schools in Japan. Leeward Community College's theatre regularly presented performing arts companies from Japan, China, and Taiwan.

Throughout the University system, formal institutional connections to Asia multiplied. Fuchs listed approximately fifty exchange agreements with universities and other research or teaching institutions in East Asia, including the former USSR through its Far Eastern Science Center at Kharbarovsk. By 1995 that number had doubled. The agreements were for faculty and student exchanges and research collaboration; their subject matter ranged across the UH curricula. Some were general "sister school" agreements with flexible bounds. En masse, they provided a widening bridge between the University and Asia across which thousands of students and scholars passed.

Supporting the expanding range of Asian scholarship at the University were its library, which over the course of a half century had assembled one of the largest collections of materials from and about Asia to be found in America, and the University of Hawai'i Press, which since the 1970s had became a major publisher of books dealing with Asia and the Pacific Basin.

Proliferation of Asian-related instruction at Manoa prompted new administrative arrangements. First an Asian Studies Program was formed to encompass studies focused on East, Southeast, and South Asia. A unit in Korean studies, established in 1972, was brought in under that curricular umbrella in 1980 when it was expanded and renamed the Center for Asian and Pacific Studies. A program in Philippine studies was added in 1972 and one on the Soviet Union in the Pacific Asian region in 1986. Then a Buddhist Studies Program followed two years later. All of these, along with the Center for Hawaiian Studies and the Pacific Islands studies program, were aggregated into a School of Hawaiian, Asian, and Pacific Studies, organized in 1987 to help focus and coordinate the work of about three hundred faculty members teaching more than five hundred courses related to Asia and the Pacific.

Within the school, the Centers for Japanese and Chinese Studies, matured after decades of experience, with justification claimed a greater breadth and depth in their respective fields than was to be found at any other university outside of Asia. Each center now lists more than two hundred relevant courses offered by Manoa's academic departments. The Center for Southeast Asian Studies, almost as large, was adjudged one of the best in the United States. The newer Center for Korean Studies is exceptional for an American campus; the Center for Philippines Studies and the (renamed) Center for Russia in Asia are unique.

Outside of the humanities and social sciences, the most energetic approaches to teaching about Asia took place within the College of Business Administration. Its initial response to the presence of the East-West Center was simply to place some emphasis on doing business in Asian nations. A concentration began in 1977 when Professor Nae Hoon Paul Chung, with degrees from Chungang University in Seoul and Michigan State University, started a modest summer program with a grand title, the Pacific Asian Management Institute (PAMI). Attracting corporate managers, government officials, teachers, and students from both sides of the Pacific, the institute developed extensive summer sessions focused on East Asian economies, followed by study tours of enterprises in several nations of the area, recently including China and Vietnam.

For persons already in international management or seeking that career path, the college devised innovative programs, first (1990) a Japan-focused "Executive MBA" and then one centered on China. The Japanese program, offered in conjunction with the Japan-America Institute of Management Science (JAIMS, a private institute for intercultural executive development established in Honolulu by a Japanese computer company) offers intensive training in the culture and language of Japan, as well as the customary MBA courses, capped by a three-month internship with a corporation in Japan. The China program draws upon a large number of University faculty members to teach Mandarin and the history and culture of China, along with courses in international business focused on China. Again, an internship in China or other centers of Chinese business in Asia completes the fifteen-month program. At a cost of about $60,000 these executive MBAs are not cheap, but they are distinctive and perhaps unique.

In consequence of the range and depth of its teaching about commerce in Asia, the college was, and continues to be, designated by the U.S. Department of Education as a Center for International Business Education and Research, a recognition that carries federal funding. *Business Week* ranked it the best of any university on Asia-Pacific management issues.

In sum, it may be fairly said that the University has become that institution joining the "commerce and civilizations" of Asia and America prophesied by Yap as well as that bridge of cultural connection with the Orient envisioned by Sinclair. Whether it will also become that "powerful influence" in the development of nations bordering the Pacific, as challenged by the visitors from the U.S. Office of Education in 1920, is a judgment for the next century.

7

THE COLLEGE OF ENGINEERING

Wilfred J. Holmes

ENGINEERING AND AGRICULTURE share the distinction of being the progenitors of all higher education in Hawaii. When the College of Agriculture and Mechanic Arts of the Territory of Hawaii opened its first full academic year in September 1908, four of the five regular students were engineering students, but John Mason Young was the only engineer in a faculty of thirteen. After the school moved its expanding program to the Manoa campus in 1911, Young taught approximately half of all the engineering courses. He served as dean of the College when it had no president and as acting president during the absence of President Arthur L. Dean. In 1920, after the College was reorganized as the University of Hawai'i, Young became president of the Pacific Engineering Company, but he continued to teach part-time until he retired in 1938. For thirty years he taught structural design to all engineering seniors. As president of Pacific Engineering Company, he designed and supervised the construction of some of the early buildings of the University, Miller, Dean, and Crawford Halls. John Mason Young can truly be called the father of engineering education in Hawaii.

Most of the money to operate the College came from federal land-grant college appropriations, only about one-fifth of the income coming from territorial funds. The purposes for which federal money could be expended were restricted. Consequently, reasonably adequate funds for engineering instruction, and equipment of the engineering laboratory, were available even when territorial appropriations for buildings and

Adapted from "Engineering Education in Hawaii," written in 1975 by Dean Holmes for the unpublished Hawaii Bicentennial Encyclopedia, with updating based on "A History of Engineering Education at UHM 1907–1992," supplied by the office of Dean Reginald H. F. Young of the College of Engineering.

for liberal studies were stingy. Despite the emphasis of the College of Hawaii on agriculture, the engineering curriculum attracted the most students.

When the College moved to Manoa, provision had to be made to house engineering laboratory equipment, which could not be installed in Hawaii Hall. The Engineering Materials Testing Laboratory was the second permanent building to be built on the Manoa campus. This single-story concrete building with 3,600 square feet of floor space was built at a total cost to the territory of $8,146. Still standing and in use, it probably represents the territory's best bargain in public buildings.

The most important piece of equipment in the engineering testing laboratory was a 150,000-pound Reihle Universal Testing Machine, purchased secondhand for $800. Placed in the Engineering Materials Laboratory, it not only served its nominal function of demonstrating to engineering students the behavior of materials under stress but also provided facilities for testing much of the construction material of Hawaii, including the concrete for Pearl Harbor dry dock. It was an object of general interest and curiosity.

In the beginning, curricula in mechanical, electrical, and civil engineering were offered, an ambitious program for a faculty of two professors. This caused little difficulty because the program of the first two years was common to all three curricula and consisted largely of mathematics and general studies. Professor J. S. Donaghho taught all the math courses. The only engineering courses in the common curriculum of freshman and sophomore years were drafting and surveying. Woodworking, forge, and machine shops were also required until John McTaggart, the shop instructor, died in 1918, after which shop work was no longer required. At that time it was also decided that the expense of equipment for laboratories in mechanical and electrical engineering was not warranted by the limited student demand, and the offering in engineering was more realistically limited to civil engineering.

Four degrees were awarded in the first graduating class in 1912—one in engineering, one in agriculture, and two in general science. The following year, the total enrollment of the College was twenty-four regular students, of which ten were in engineering, four were in agriculture, one in home economics, and nine in general science. (There were also 104 "special" students, not working toward degrees.) In the eight graduating classes of the College before it became the University in 1920, a total of only nine engineering degrees were awarded.

Under these conditions, junior and senior engineering classes were very small—fortunately. As it was, Arthur Keller taught ten different engineering courses in a year, and Young carried an equally heavy teaching load. Both were also heavily involved in extracurricular work. Keller served on the territorial Board of Health, on the Honolulu planning commission, on a board that designed a sewer system for the city—and played on the 1911 College football team.

World War I created many problems for the College. The Student Army Training

Corps (SATC) was more popular than the draft, and College enrollment increased by 50 percent to sixty-eight regular students. Part of the engineering testing laboratory was turned into an SATC mess hall. Nevertheless, Young, helped by temporary appointments of local engineers, managed to carry on, graduating one engineer each war year.

In 1920, when Keller returned from the war, the College had become the University of Hawai'i and he the first dean of its College of Applied Science, which was responsible for curricula in engineering, agriculture, home economics, and sugar technology.

Between World Wars I and II, the University steadily increased in stature. By 1940 it enrolled more than two thousand regular students, exceeding the most optimistic projections. Engineering participated in this growth but not proportionately. In 1936 fourteen engineering degrees were awarded, but University graduating classes between the two wars averaged only about seven engineers. There were six on the engineering faculty during the 1930s, but the engineering and mathematics departments were combined and most engineers doubled in brass. The normal full-time teaching load was fifteen or sixteen semester hours. Russell Brinker, a young instructor, taught mechanical drawing, surveying, and mathematics. W. J. Holmes, also an instructor, who joined the faculty in 1936 at an advanced annual salary of $2,400, taught a mixed bag: physics; electrical, mechanical, and civil engineering; and mathematics, varying each semester as the need arose.

Before World War II, no woman had remained in the engineering curriculum long enough to obtain junior status. Had any female met the entrance requirements for admission to the informal fellowship of the upper-division engineering students, who owned the Engineering Quadrangle, a most embarrassing situation would have been created. Keller had designed the four new buildings of the Engineering Quadrangle for maximum space utilization and economy, with no corridors, closets, or plumbing. The only toilet at hand was partially concealed from public view in the storeroom of the engineering materials laboratory. It was not until 1939, when the Home Economics Building (Miller Hall) was built adjacent to the engineers' domain, that the situation was alleviated.

The bombs that fell on Pearl Harbor disrupted the University. For nearly two months it ceased to function as a teaching institution. When it opened again, Keller was acting president, in addition to his other duties. Half the student body and a large share of the faculty had been drained off by the war effort. In 1942, however, fourteen degrees in civil engineering were awarded. Two years earlier, the foresighted Keller had initiated a program of evening classes in naval architecture, taught by Pearl Harbor naval architects to senior engineering students and recent graduates. The design section of Pearl Harbor Navy Yard eagerly absorbed the graduates of the program, but the engineering department rapidly declined until there were only two engineers on the University faculty and only one degree in engineering was awarded in 1946.

In 1947 Keller retired and Holmes, who had returned from wartime naval service, became the second dean of the College of Applied Science. Agriculture split off and became the fourth University college, leaving Applied Science with curricula in engineering, nursing, and medical technology.

The University had been crowded by two thousand students in prewar years. When Congress passed the GI Bill, providing educational benefits for veterans, it was apparent that double the number of students would soon be clamoring for admission. It was difficult for many to realize that the days of the little cow college under the rainbow at the foot of Manoa Valley were over. A few old-timers wanted to restrict enrollment, particularly the engineering enrollment, until adequate faculty and facilities could be provided. Fortunately that view did not prevail. In the best land-grant college tradition, the University determined that the generation that fought the war should not be denied equal educational opportunity, even if classes had to be held under the trees. It did not come to that, but for a while the facilities were minimal and the faculty overworked and underpaid.

Joseph F. Kunesh joined the staff, first as University engineer and then, for four years, as dean of the College of Applied Science. He acquired an entire surplus Army field hospital for the University and transported about ninety barracks-type wooden buildings to the campus. He set them up in any available open space, to be converted into offices, classrooms, workshops, a cafeteria, and faculty housing units. This made it possible to more than double enrollment. It was confidently expected that within ten years these shacks could all be torn down and replaced by proper permanent buildings. In this, the year of our Lord 1975, some of them are still in service where Kunesh placed them.

Mae Nakatani, the first woman to earn an engineering degree from the University of Hawai'i, graduated in 1950. She and her fifty-two male classmates constituted the largest class in engineering up to that time. On October 1, 1951, the civil engineering curriculum was accredited by the Engineers' Council for Professional Development. In a period of only four years, the University graduated as many engineers as it had in the previous forty years. Moreover, what had been regarded as a peak of engineering graduates turned out to be a brief plateau before the trend turned upward again. A limit was imposed on freshman engineering enrollment, but fortunately this was short-lived. Statehood, jet air travel, a new engineering faculty of bright young men, and national accreditation of the engineering curriculum broke down inherent insularity, and engineering education in Hawaii became an integral part of engineering education in the United States. Some Hawaii engineering graduates went to mainland colleges for postgraduate work. Mainland organizations sent recruiters to Hawaii to hire graduating seniors, and what had threatened to be a surplus of engineers quickly turned into a shortage.

Increasing engineering enrollment made it desirable to broaden the engineering program. In 1953 the Hawaiian Electric and the Westinghouse Electric companies donated equipment for a heat power laboratory. This made it possible to increase course offerings in the mechanical engineering field and enabled the University to offer a curriculum in general engineering in addition to civil engineering. Further expansion of the program had to be deferred because of very limited University budgets.

Administrative changes in mid-century affected the engineering program. When President Sinclair retired in 1955, Wilfred Holmes became administrative vice-president. In 1958 the School of Nursing achieved college status. When nursing and medical technology left the bed and board of the College of Applied Science only engineering remained. The name was then changed to the College of Engineering. William M. Wachter became its first dean in 1959. About six months later, Wachter took over the administrative vice-presidency, and Holmes became dean of engineering.

Meanwhile, in step with changes in curricula in mainland universities, a gradual change was taking place in civil engineering. More engineering science courses were included, at the expense of precalculus mathematics, surveying, and some of the electrical and mechanical engineering courses previously required. A master's degree in engineering, with professional experience and a professional engineer's license, had been considered adequate qualification for a faculty appointment, but higher academic qualifications now became desirable.

Dr. Shigeo Okubo was the first member of the engineering faculty with a doctor's degree, followed by Fujio Matsuda, Stephen Lau, Arthur Chiu, Mateo Go, and others until about half of the faculty had doctor's degrees in their fields. The faculty was also enriched by a system of visiting professors. President Sinclair had obtained a generous grant from the Carnegie Foundation for a succession of distinguished visiting professors, and engineering received its fair share.

The year Hawaii became a state (1959) was a banner year in the development of the college. Keller Hall, a classroom and faculty office building for engineering and mathematics, was completed, freeing space in the old Engineering Quadrangle for electrical engineering laboratories. It thus became possible to offer a curriculum in electrical engineering, a development too long deferred by lack of space and funds. Under the direction of Ralph Partridge and then Paul Yuen, the electrical engineering curriculum developed rapidly. In 1961 the first group of fifteen electrical engineers graduated. A curriculum in mechanical engineering was first offered in 1960, and in 1963 the first group of three mechanical engineers received degrees.

Until then, organized research and graduate instruction had been neglected due to the urgent need to concentrate on the development of undergraduate programs.

Master's degree programs in civil engineering and in electrical engineering were established by the University in 1963. A Hawaii Engineering Experiment Station was authorized in 1962 with Fujio Matsuda as its director. Before the program could get off the ground, however, Governor Burns requested his services to head the state Department of Transportation. As it was expected that Matsuda would return in two years, the Experiment Station remained a paper organization. Matsuda remained away for ten years, to return as the first UH alumnus and the first engineer president of the University.

In 1965 Holmes retired as dean and was succeeded by Dr. John Shupe. The University was growing rapidly. That year, its expenditures (including the East-West Center) were more than $32 million. Its buildings were valued at more than $30 million. Expenditures for the College of Engineering were over $500,000 while 118 engineering degrees were awarded. Shupe had arrived just in time to take over the reins as the college began its most interesting period of development.

In 1972 the college moved out of its ancient home in the Young Engineering Quadrangle in the crowded center of the campus and into a new building named after Dean Holmes, also vacating most of Keller Hall. Reorganization eliminated the Department of General Engineering, its faculty transferred among the civil, electrical, and mechanical engineering departments. At the instigation of the General Contractors' Association, which provided initial funding, a curriculum in construction engineering was added, helping meet the demand for building which had swelled after Hawaii became a state.

The major research project of the 1970s was the Additive Links On-line Hawaii Area (ALOHA) Systems Network, undertaken by a group led by electrical engineering Professor Norman Abramson. It developed a new form of communication architecture that provides multiple access for transmitters on a common digital channel. The Department of Electrical Engineering and the Information Sciences Program designed a radio-linked computer network to connect the several campuses of the University, enabling them to share their computer resources. Funded by IBM, the Nippon Electric Company, the National Science Foundation, and the National Aeronautics and Space Administration, the project attracted the attention of researchers internationally. By the 1990s, various forms of ALOHA channels were the most popular protocol used in some one hundred thousand VSAT (Very Small Aperture Terminal) networks around the world.

Computer automation for the college began in 1982 with its first general computer lab, equipped with IBM personal computers. Over the next decade, more powerful hardware was installed at work stations, providing students with access to the college's main computer systems, enabling them to do class assignments and projects electronically and giving them a flavor of applications encountered in professional practice.

The study and improvement of tropical agriculture, the central purpose of the College of Hawaii, used most of the Manoa campus and required experiment stations across the Territory, such as this vegetable planting on Maui. From 1914 Frederick G. Krauss, photographed near the end of his long career with the College and University, led the extension service in Hawaii, demonstrating better cultivation methods to agricultural producers. Contemporary research is represented by genetically engineered papaya (1996).

The other specialty of the College of Hawaii was engineering. Professor John Mason Young (standing left) posed with his class (sometime in the 1920s) and with the pride of the engineering program, the Reihle Universal Testing Machine, used to test the strength of construction materials. Contemporary electrical engineering is represented by students posed in a laboratory around the apparatus for developing sensors used for medical diagnostics.

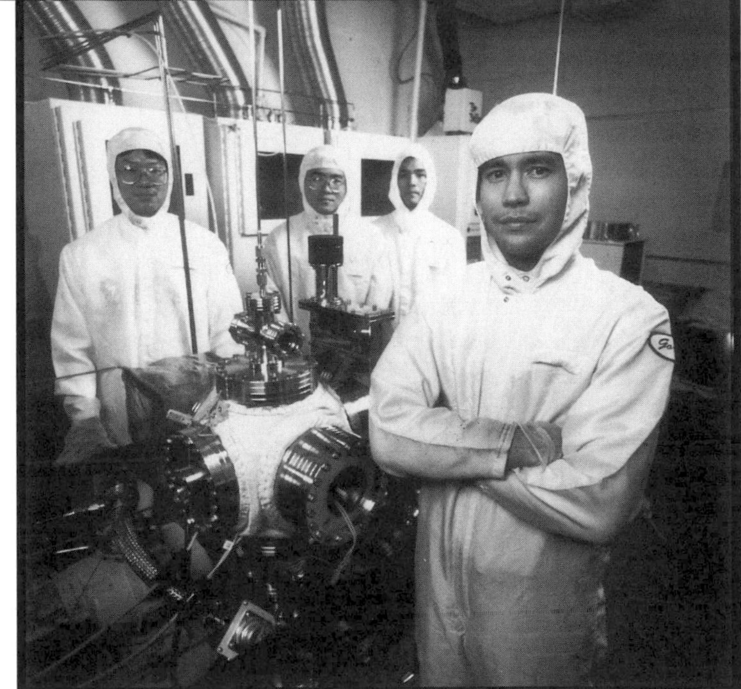

In 1989 three college programs—the Ocean Engineering Department, the Water Resources Research Center, and the Hawaii Natural Energy Institute—were assimilated into the newly formed School of Ocean and Earth Sciences Technology. The school also linked the work of other relevant disciplines, including geology, geophysics, meteorology, and oceanography.

Doctoral programs of the college were expanded: a Ph.D. in mechanical engineering was offered in 1985 and one in civil engineering in 1992. By the 1992 commencement, the college over its eight decades of service had awarded almost seven thousand degrees—5,913 bachelor's, 924 master's, and 76 doctorates.

In 1991, the University signed an agreement with Kanazawa Institute of Japan (KIT), Japan's largest technological institution of higher learning, providing for faculty and academic exchange. The program allows for collaboration in research of particular potential in the fields of robotics and electronic and computer-aided devices, where the college and KIT have common research interests.

8

THE COLLEGE OF TROPICAL AGRICULTURE AND HUMAN RESOURCES

Wallace C. Mitchell

The College of Tropical Agriculture and Human Resources (CTAHR) has origins predating those of the University. It was shaped by federal legislation that profoundly affected agricultural research and the spread of higher education throughout the United States.

The Hatch Act of 1887 authorized establishing agricultural experiment stations across the nation. At the turn of the century, the Department of Agriculture asked Dr. W. C. Stubbs, director of the Louisiana station, to determine the need for one in the new Territory of Hawaii. He visited the Islands and reported to Congress in 1901. Recognizing that the Hawaiian Sugar Planters' Association (HSPA) already had a research station serving its dominant industry, he recommended that a new experiment station in Hawaii concentrate on other production, such as fruits and vegetables, rice, coffee, livestock, and dairying.

Consequently, the Hawaii Agricultural Experiment Station (HAES) was established in 1901 as an agency of the Department of Agriculture, independent of local institutions. It remained so, though with increasing cooperation with the scientists of Hawaii's new College of Agriculture and Mechanic Arts, until 1938, when it became the agricultural research arm of UH.

The Cooperative Extension Service (CES), established by the federal Smith-Lever Act of 1914 to provide practical demonstration of better cultivation methods and otherwise to advance the welfare of farm families, was from the beginning administered within Hawaii's new college, although Hawaii received no funds under the act until 1928.

The teaching function of CTAHR also derives from federal law, the Morrill Acts of 1862 and 1890. As a territory Hawaii was ineligible for the land grants made to states under the Civil War statute, but it could receive federal appropriations for a college "to teach such branches of learning as are related to agriculture and the mechanic arts," under the Second Morrill Act. By establishing its college in 1907, Hawaii joined the national land-grant college network.

Over the decades, the UH agricultural program repeatedly modified its structure, seeking best to organize its functions of teaching, research, and demonstration. When the new College opened in 1908, it offered instruction in agriculture. When it became the University of Hawai'i in 1920, agricultural courses were placed in the new College of Applied Science, where they remained until a Graduate School of Tropical Agriculture was created in 1931. In 1947 the extension service and experiment station, along with the formal instructional program, were all joined into a College of Agriculture. Further integration was sought in 1978 by merging research and extension functions into one institute within the newly renamed College of Tropical Agriculture and Human Resources.

Integration has been the mode of development, but each of the College's three functions has its own history in the Islands. They merit separate telling.

RESEARCH

While the Hawaii Agricultural Experiment Station was not completely incorporated into the College of Agriculture until 1938, the college had long worked with scientists of the federal agency on problems of diversified agriculture. The station and the college had their start in a period when there was being sought for Hawaii, and particularly for native Hawaiians, some means of opening up an independent life on the land. The early territorial government had tried to follow the homesteading experience of the continental United States, with little success. Then the federal Hawaiian Homes Commission Act of 1920 set aside approximately two hundred thousand acres of land for settlement by persons of 50 percent or more Hawaiian ancestry, and some of that land was suitable for cultivation—given enough water. But, for those homesteaders and other cultivators who wished to supply the market, what could be grown advantageously and how? The emerging national network of agricultural research and demonstration facilities based at continental land-grant colleges provided few relevant answers for tropical agriculture. Farms were established to demonstrate new crops and new cultivation methods for Hawaii.

The HAES demonstration farms, when incorporated into the College of Agriculture, made it a territorywide enterprise. Over the first half of the century, when the rest of the University was essentially limited to its Manoa campus and an extension at Hilo, the College of Agriculture was operating on all major islands of Hawaii. An inevitable consequence was the involvement of the college in the hopes and politics of each county.

The search for crops and cultivation methods to sustain a diversified agriculture was broad and determined. Early attention was focused on breeding rice varieties from Japan. Agronomists researched the feasibility of producing grains, grasses and forage crops, rice, corn, Irish potatoes, sorghum, and cotton.

These are a few examples of the experimental demonstration work undertaken. Over the years, joint projects between HAES and University agricultural scientists covered a wide range of crops, as well as dairy and meat production, tobacco, coffee, honey bees, silkworms, rubber, and many others, all experiments undertaken to lessen Hawaii's reliance on food imports and export of sugar and pineapple. As President David Crawford later summed up the effort (*Hawaii's Crop Parade,* 1937), diversification did not fail initially to win great success "for lack of trying." During the first two decades of experiment and demonstration work, more than 150 plants were worked on for either export or local markets. Most never reached commercial production, but some experiments, patiently pursued over many years, yielded important results for growers in Hawaii and other tropical areas of the world.

Chief among the successes were macadamia nuts and papayas. The macadamia was early evaluated for development. Trial plantings were made in 1915 on the HAES substation at Makawao, Maui; problems such as thick shells and small kernels were studied. Trees bearing nuts with desirable qualities were then selected for propagation. In 1928, Ralph H. Moltzau, a horticulture technician, was the first to successfully graft macadamia trees. J. C. Ripperton and colleagues in research conducted after 1931 demonstrated the greater suitability of "smooth shell" nuts for processing, and selective cloning of trees established the strain exclusively used in commercial plantings. This work was vital to developing Hawaii's macadamia nut industry, leading to its first exports in 1933. In 1948, horticulturalist William Storey introduced five varieties for commercial planting. Subsequently, seven more varieties, all selected and named by University researchers, supplied almost all macadamia nuts grown commercially worldwide.

Research on papayas produced another export commodity. In 1938, Storey published the first report on the genetic basis of sex inheritance in papayas. His findings eliminated reliance on pollination by male plants since self-pollinating hermaphrodite plants alone could be grown in commercial plantings. Vapor-heat disinfestation of papayas was developed in 1939 as treatment for fruit fly infestation and for stem-end-rot control to meet quarantine regulations, permitting shipping of the fruit to the mainland.

Defense against the tephritid fruit flies had early become an abiding concern of

HAES scientists. About 1895 the melon fly had been accidentally introduced from Asia but caused little concern because Hawaii was not then exporting fruits and vegetables. The response was different, however, when the Mediterranean fruit fly, introduced from Australia, was reported in Hawaii in 1910. A mainland quarantine barred the import of papayas, mangos, and avocados grown in the territory, motivating researchers to devise fruit fly controls.

This effort presented the young college with its first test of academic freedom. Local farmers, denying the seriousness of the infestation, deplored public display of the work on fruit fly biology and control undertaken by Henry H. P. Severin, professor of entomology. Responding to pressure, the Board of Regents directed Severin to restrict his medfly research and withhold his findings. He refused and was fired in 1912. Severin moved to the University of California, where he published his data on the medfly problem in Hawaii. Ironically, it was California that obtained the quarantine against Island fruits.

Several new forage crops were tested. Napier grass was added to the list of pasture grasses and, its value established, soon became a major feed source for Hawaii's expanding livestock population. The dairy industry was threatened with calamity when Napier grass was virtually wiped out by disease, but HAES researchers developed forage grass varieties resistant to the disease, saving the industry.

With America's entry into World War I in 1917, a perceived national food emergency led to a plan to cultivate vegetables on military bases. Locally, HAES supplied seeds, plants, and advice to the military, and assisted and encouraged Hawaii's citizens to produce their own vegetables in "emergency war gardens." After the war, the demonstration and extension services continued to advise homemakers on the selection and preparation of food, but a Department of Human Nutrition was not established until 1929.

During the 1920s, functions of the College of Agriculture and HAES became increasingly integrated. Amalgamation was made official in 1929, when agricultural extension activities were transferred to the college. However, a complete transition of HAES into the University system did not take place until 1938, when their personnel and facilities were pooled.

Willis T. Pope, for whom the Pope Laboratory is named, was hired as horticulturist in 1921. His appointment turned the research program toward improving horticultural management practices throughout the territory. Research was conducted on macadamia, pistachio, coconut, mulberry, lychee, poha, carob, guava, and tamarind. Experiments were also continued on starch production from edible canna, tree fern, cassava, sweet potato, Irish potato, and banana.

Hawaii's major plantation industries, sugar and pineapple, generally went their own way in research but increasingly relied on the college to train young technicians for their fields and production facilities. The Hawaiian Pineapple Canners Association in 1924 created the Pineapple Research Institute (PRI) experiment station to study production problems. Researchers at the long-established HSPA experiment station concentrated on sugar cane problems. Producers in smaller industries, such as banana, rice, and starch-producing crops, remained dependent upon research at HAES.

The college expanded its research and demonstration capacity as funds permitted. Two specialists, one in human nutrition, Carey D. Miller, and one in poultry, Charles M. Bice, were added to the HAES staff. Harold A. Wadsworth, an irrigation engineer and soil physicist, and Louis A. Henke, an animal husbandry researcher, were hired in 1932. The budget of the experiment station increased even during the long Depression, from $15,000 in 1930 to $101,000 in 1936. With greater funding, the range of research widened to include evaluation of locally produced feeds for swine, poultry, and livestock. Nutritional values of avocado, opihi, and a variety of Japanese foods were determined.

A maritime strike in 1937, blocking imports for three months, showed the importance of producing more foodstuffs locally. The college studied the food supply in terms of "what might occur during a Pacific war" and to "identify vulnerable spots in the economic structure, from the viewpoint of self-sufficiency." The discussion, coming just two years before World War II and summarized in HAES Bulletin 29, was soon to be in great demand.

The University was closed for two months following the Pearl Harbor attack on December 7, 1941, and functioned on a wartime basis until 1945. Faculty and experiment station staff worked on potable water analyses, censorship, fingerprinting, guard and police duty. The staff was seriously depleted as members went off to war or to more lucrative defense employment. Those remaining worked to alleviate emergency problems of food production. Special projects, such as the preservation of blood plasma, were undertaken. Nutritionists provided service to the Red Cross and to the armed forces, helping stimulate a rapid expansion of garden plots. Staff members made recommendations on parasite and insect control and on cultivating plants used for camouflage.

Local food production received increased attention because Hawaii was in the war zone. Many important economic tropical crops, such as rubber, sisal, ramie, quinine, tung oil, coconut oil, castor oil, rotenone, and cassava starch, were of interest because imports of these materials had been reduced or cut off. Hawaii became an important source for several of these crops.

In 1944, research showed the effectiveness of a new insecticide, dichloro-diphenyl-trichloroethane (DDT), in checking insect infestation of vegetables and fruit. No one envisioned its accumulation in body fat and the detrimental effects on organisms in the food chain. The high cost of imported livestock feed led to using sugar cane and pineapple by-products. Chopped pineapple tops were found to be a good substitute for alfalfa, reducing imports and improving Hawaii's trade balance. Thirty years later, however, pesticide residues in pineapple chop were shown to have created health problems.

In the decades following World War II, sugar and pineapple output began to decline in the face of competition from areas with substantially lower costs of production. The plantations, hitherto largely independent in their research and development programs, turned to the HAES and the CES to find new uses for lands taken out of plantation production.

Plant physiologists studied the influence of various factors on the growth of sugar cane and developed a system for predicting yields on large plantations. An innovative method of optimizing the irrigation and fertilization of sugar cane, known as crop logging, was devised by Harry Clements and his associates; with further refinement, it was adopted by the industry. In 1948, HSPA gave the college $100,000 to build and equip an Agriculture Engineering Institute.

The battle against fruit flies was resumed after the mango or oriental fruit fly, which infests more than three hundred species of fruits and vegetables, was discovered on Oahu in 1946. To protect worried growers in California, quarantines were again placed on all known fruit fly host crops coming from Hawaii. Entomologists from the USDA Bureau of Entomology and Plant Quarantine, the University of California Agricultural Experiment Station, the Territorial Board of Agriculture and Forestry, PRI, HSPA, and HAES all pooled their resources in an attempt to solve the problem. The territorial legislature in 1950 funded construction of a food-processing laboratory. A laboratory was built on the Manoa campus which used an experimental gamma irradiation unit (cobalt 60) to disinfest foodstuffs. Irradiation of fruit fly hosts, such as papayas and mangos, controlled eggs and larvae, extending the shelf life of produce.

Under the direction of D. Elmo Hardy, the University became a center of tephritid fruit fly studies. He became interested in the vinegar flies of the family Drosophilidae. This family, by far the largest group of animals in Hawaii, here presents one of the most rapid evolutions of insects to be found anywhere in the world, making them ideal for studying the processes of speciation and evolution. Hardy gathered an international group of scientists to study these unique insects, their research forming the basis of the Hawaii Evolutionary Biology Program.

Expansion of the college's network of research stations accelerated as funds became available. During 1958–1960 an animal research station was developed at Waialee, Oahu, for the Departments of Animal Science, Poultry Science, and Parasitology. A branch research station was established on Kauai and a demonstration farm on Molokai during the next biennium.

Conducting agricultural research that impacted on the political concerns of local government enlivened the work of college administrators. County representatives might seek to influence appointments of college personnel stationed on their island.

After testifying before the Hawaii legislature about the college budget, a representative from Kauai asked me why I didn't fire Mr. X and replace him with someone the representative preferred. "So-and-so is a snake," he said. "You know what I do with snakes? I kill them." "Know what I do with snakes?" I replied. " I put them in the corn crib to control rats." Mr. X stayed on the job.

Demands of Hawaii County elected officials that the college be transferred from Oahu to the Big Island began early and continue to this day. This the University has steadfastly resisted.

The range of college research continued to expand during the 1960s. The biology, ecology, and control of subterranean termites were studied after methods for rearing and handling them were developed; a new fumigant, sulfuryl fluoride, held promise for controlling drywood termites. Nutritionists evaluated many oriental foods, such as kampyo, kiri kambu, nori, kanten, fie, and kimchi. Soluble crystals of passion fruit, mango, guava, and papaya made by a vacuum-puff freeze-drying process were found to produce the base of a delicious, and profitable, drink.

In the 1970s, HAES research projects concentrated on safeguarding the environment, developing new energy sources and conserving energy, drip irrigation, aquaculture, and insect and plant disease control. Several fruit and vegetable cultivars were developed and released to growers and home gardeners.

In the 1970s and 1980s, the college redoubled its efforts to aid diversified agriculture, as with the decline of sugar and pineapple more plantations became subdivisions, hotels, golf courses, and shopping centers. Research helped floriculture to flourish. New technologies were developed for ornamentals, including orchids, protea, anthuriums, and foliage plants, as well as guava, feed grains, and forage crops. Propagation of orchids and anthuriums by tissue culture was proved successful. New selections of macadamia nuts, sweet potatoes, pangola grass, tomatoes, guavas, and several ornamentals were released to producers.

The closing years of the Experiment Station's first century brought new forms of old problems as well as new challenges. Further research on treating papayas and avocados showed methyl bromide or ethylene dibromide fumigation to be effective in fruit-fly control, but Environmental Protection Agency (EPA) regulations banned their use, so acceptable technologies had to be developed to satisfy quarantine regulations. Holding avocados at 45°F for five days was to be found effective in killing fruit fly eggs. Vapor-heat treatments for papaya were fine-tuned for export shipments.

As the public became increasingly concerned about the use of pesticides, the college implemented integrated pest management programs developed by its researchers. Reducing the number of pesticide applications and the amounts of pesticide used in vegetable, fruit, nut, and turfgrass management programs cut undesirable side effects and reduced the cost of pest control.

Of particular concern was finding new ways of checking subterranean termites, the pest most devastating to Hawaii's homes. Control had required soil treatments with residual chemicals and structure fumigation. When chlordane, aldrin, dieldrin, and other organic long-lasting chemicals were banned by the EPA, effective alternative means had to be found. Dr. Minoru Tamashiro's laboratory studied the biology and ecology of the pests and found that rock granules ranging from 1.7 mm to 2.4 mm in size were too large for worker termites to move and that interparticle spaces were too small for termites to move between them. A layer of the Basaltic Termite Barrier beneath house slabs protects wooden structures from subterranean termites without the use of pesticides.

In summary, during its first century of operation, the research of HAES in many respects aided the course of agricultural development in Hawaii. Crops such as macadamia nuts, avocados, papayas, proteas, anthuriums, foliage, and other ornamentals developed by research became important products. Increasing yields with new varieties and production methods helped cut unit costs—benefiting producers and consumers alike.

EXTENSION

Prior to the establishment of the College of Hawaii—and long before the territory began to receive funds to support agricultural extension work under the Smith-Lever Act in 1928—researchers were in the field offering advice to the farm population. Extension programs were first established in Hawaii in 1914 with the appointment of agronomist Frederick G. Krauss as superintendent of extension at the federal Hawaii Agricultural Experiment Station. In that same year, noncredit extension courses under the direction of Vaughan MacCaughey began at the College, designed to serve people unable to attend regular classes. In this way, many citizens around the territory gained access to the new college.

Much of the extension work customarily done by mainland land-grant colleges was initially carried out in Hawaii by the HAES, HSPA, and the territorial Boards of Health and of Agriculture. Instruction was offered in many ways, ranging from mobile libraries to correspondence and night-school courses. In 1908, for example, twenty-six evening classes provided instruction on soils, entomology, fertilizers, botany, poultry raising, agronomy, plant breeding, forestry, and horticulture. Short courses for teachers were presented at the college on Monday afternoons. Much of the teaching was done as public service by the college staff. Six farmers' co-ops established by the HAES in 1913 also provided agricultural education to their members.

During World War I, the visibility of extension and HAES researchers increased as Hawaii began to seek greater agricultural diversification. The University responded to sugar planters, who needed more trained people, by establishing an extension program in sugar technology. By 1925, short extension courses in poultry raising and horticulture were being offered, as well as correspondence courses and lectures for Neighbor Islanders. Free seeds, produced on the HAES farms, were given to people in exchange for reports on the results of their experimental plantings.

In 1929 the Cooperative Extension Service became a division of the University. In February CES received its first Smith-Lever grant of $48,000, conditioned on the territory's contributing an additional $18,000 per year. Nine months later the stock market crashed and a national depression followed. Some sugar and pineapple lands fell idle. The need to diversify agriculture, long advocated by extension faculty, finally found wide acceptance as plantations turned to the CES for ideas. Several crops were recommended, but the response in diversifying production during the 1930s was limited.

The attack on Pearl Harbor quickly put the extension staff into emergency operation. Agents were swamped with telephone calls from scared clientele, many not understanding English, needing reassurance and guidance. Response was immediate. The Wahiawa office opened a shelter for residents fearing a second attack, and all offices were fully functional the next day.

Extension personnel realized that Hawaii's food supply was precarious, despite more than forty thousand home/farm visits made in 1940 to emphasize preparedness. The Islands produced less than half of the food consumed, and a huge influx of military personnel limited the civilian supply of fruits and vegetables. Agents worked diligently on programs to create "Victory Gardens" for the home and plantation, to improve nutrition, and to increase poultry, cattle, and swine production. Extension personnel took on additional responsibilities, such as issuing permits to buy tires and insecticides and inspecting consignments of fruits and vegetables for the military. An important duty was interpreting the military governor's edicts to non-English-speaking residents on ventilating blacked-out rooms, conserving food, and complying with evacuation orders.

After the war, the CES again had to shift gears, now assisting its clientele in adjusting to shortages, strikes, skyrocketing prices, and mainland competition. Agents taught farm families to budget, make do, substitute, and compete. Emphasis on diversification continued along with the development of entrepreneurial skills. Orchid growers and lei sellers were organized to promote quality control and improve marketing programs.

In 1950, extension specialists were placed in the appropriate academic departments of the college to improve cooperation with researchers. The Cooperative Extension Service had ten offices throughout the territory, demonstrating improved farm and home practices through extension clubs of adults and 4-H clubs for youth. Expanded home demonstration programs informed clientele on nutrition, home management, and clothing.

During the 1950s, extension staff increasingly assisted in planning for changing agricultural conditions. Agents helped in the development of farm lands, introducing new crops and identifying new markets. Reduction of the rural population and the growth of farm organizations stimulated closer ties among agricultural agencies. In 1955 CES programs reached more than forty-five hundred urban and thirteen hundred farm families and trained 360 leaders for clubs that had four thousand members. UH extension clubs made up the largest women's organization in the territory.

In 1963 a reorganization was initiated to bring the college, HAES, and the Extension Service together under centralized control, although it took several years to complete the process. By 1979 the extension service and the experiment station were united into the Hawaii Institute of Tropical Agriculture and Human Resources (HITAHR), facilitating cooperation between researchers and extension personnel.

In the last two decades extension programs have focused on assisting rural and urban people to improve their life in a changing society. A Family Community Leadership Program has trained individuals to lead and participate in public affairs. In workshops and institutes, participants gained skills in communication, conflict resolution, and developing methods of community improvement. The 4-H program was increasingly directed to urban youth. A Master Gardener Program was started in 1982 to provide research-based horticulture training to gardeners who in return volunteer to promote gardening skills in their communities. With more than 160,000 gardeners in Hawaii, the program provides an increasing number with know-how developed by college researchers.

The community nutrition education program, active for more than twenty years, teaches low-income homemakers how to feed their families economically and better, taking into account ethnic preferences in food and its preparation.

At its centenary, the CES had developed a range of services in the spirit of the Smith-Lever Act, providing at least one extension office in each county. Information is available to anyone requesting it; most publications are free. Its outreach program, adapting to changing modes of communication, provides research-based advice in person, by fax, by mail, in newspaper articles, and in radio and television programs. Computer networking shares expertise throughout the world.

INSTRUCTION

The 1908 prospectus of the Hawaii College of Agriculture and Mechanic Arts offered instruction in four fields: agriculture, household economics, science, and engineering. General horticulture, entomology, use of insecticides and fungicides, tropical fruit culture, pomology, vegetable and ornamental gardening, floriculture, and forestry were specialties in the four-year course of study.

Mainland temperate-zone agriculture curricula were then well founded on knowledge but tropical agriculture was largely unstudied and instructors had to create much of their subject matter through experimentation and observation. Personnel from HSPA, the territorial Board of Agriculture and Forestry, Bishop Museum, and the Pineapple Research Institute were called upon to lecture on their specialties. By 1910 requirements for advanced study were developed. A master of science degree in agriculture required a bachelor's degree plus a year's residence or two years of graduate work elsewhere. Candidates had to meet thesis requirements and pass required examinations.

At commencement in June 1914, Alfred Warren received the school's first M.S. degree, awarded in entomology. His thesis was on the food habits of Hawaiian dragonflies. Warren's research showed the importance of their predatory habits of feeding on mosquitoes and flies. Reprints of this pioneer work are still in demand.

When the College of Hawaii became the University of Hawai'i in 1920, it was divided into two colleges, Applied Science and Arts and Sciences. Curricula in Applied Science included agriculture, sugar technology, home economics, engineering, and general science. To the home economics curriculum a course in household sanitation was added, covering ventilation, heating, drainage, plumbing, lighting, home furnishing, and pest control.

Growth came slowly. In 1923, the total enrollment in the College of Applied Science was twelve seniors, twenty-five juniors, thirty-two sophomores, and sixty-two freshmen. To attract more students, courses on the fruits of Hawaii, soils, crops, sugar and pineapple production, animal and poultry husbandry, feeds, forestry, horticulture, irrigation, and farm management were all added. Instruction in home economics, grouped into two curricula, art and design and household science, also presented a widened range of choices. Art and design offered freehand drawing; history of architecture, sculpture and painting; ceramic design and porcelain decoration; textiles and elementary garment making; dressmaking and design; millinery, needlework, and advanced dress making. Household science added courses in food preparation and nutrition, food economics, and household management.

In 1931 the Graduate School of Tropical Agriculture was established to facilitate research and graduate training in branches of science relating to tropical agriculture. Dr. Royal N. Chapman of the Pineapple Research Institute was appointed dean of the school.

The first doctor of philosophy degree conferred by the University was presented in 1933 to John Sydney Phillips. His dissertation, directed by Dr. Walter Carter of PRI, was "The Biology, Distribution and Control of Ants in Hawaiian Pineapple Fields." Carter reported that Phillips, already an established scholar, was so incensed at being required to take written examinations in his field that he answered in rhyming verse. Upon graduation he was employed on a coconut plantation in the Solomon Islands.

President Crawford reviewed the instructional programs in agriculture in 1939.

In addition to the doctoral program, a master of science program was available, with majors in nutrition, soil science, sugar technology, entomology, and general agriculture. A bachelor of science curriculum offered majors in general agriculture, sugar technology, and home economics. Crawford observed that many students in agriculture were from the city, with no opportunity to work on a farm. Summer jobs on farms or experiment stations were thereafter arranged by the college as part of its instructional program.

World War II reduced the college staff by a third. Agriculture students were mostly able-bodied men who entered defense work immediately. Women students in home economics remained in class in larger numbers, many supplementing their classroom work with Red Cross and other volunteer activities. Along with the rest of the campus, the college did not return to its usual functions until 1946.

The postwar college offered six bachelor's programs: tropical agricultural production; agricultural science; vocational agriculture; general home economics; institution management; and dietetics and vocational home economics teaching. Graduate programs for the master's degree were in plant science and soil science. A doctoral degree was still available only in entomology.

In 1947 enrollment in agriculture rose from 84 to 139 and in home economics from 109 to 139, and it appeared that the college was geared for expansion. However, cuts in appropriations in 1950 forced a retrenchment in course offerings. Summer sessions were self-supporting and continued to offer four home economics courses, adjusted each year to meet students' needs. The 1950 offerings give some indication of what was then in demand: trends in clothing construction, methods in nutrition for health, a laboratory for home management, and a seminar in family life. The home management course required four or five students to live as a group for six weeks with supervised practical training in food preparation, time and money management, human relationships, and methods in teaching home care for the sick.

Agricultural economics was added to the curriculum in 1952. A general agricultural training program in crop production was designed for students planning to enter diversified farming. Nevertheless, college enrollment, following the national trend for agriculture education, continued to drop. A survey of 1948–1955 graduates of the school revealed that, excluding graduate students, 47 percent were teaching agriculture, 34 percent were employed in private industry or government, 14 percent had college positions, while only 5 percent farmed.

In 1960 the college was again renamed, becoming the College of Tropical Agriculture. Its instructional programs, increasingly designed for professionals in agriculture and home economics, now offered three curricula in agriculture—technology, economics, and science—each with several options. Home economics presented five options: general home economics; clothing and design; institutional management; home economics education; and nutrition.

Human development options in home economics became popular in the mid-1960s. Faculty members in the program reviewed their curriculum and shaped it to prepare students for professional careers in enhancing the well-being of individuals, families, and the community. Courses concentrated on child-rearing, group leadership, community resources and family relationships were offered in a Human Resource Development Program. In the next decade, the enrollment in human resources classes exceeded that in agricultural courses.

In 1971–1972 an option of pre–veterinary medicine was added to agriculture. Students took prescribed courses and worked in an animal clinic to gain the experience required by mainland schools offering degrees in veterinary medicine.

The present name, College of Tropical Agriculture and Human Resources, was approved by the regents in January 1978, and the college moved into the new Gilmore Hall. Interdisciplinary instructional programs were developed to meet student needs. For example, the curricula leading to advanced degrees in plant pathology were now offered jointly with the Department of Botany in the College of Arts and Sciences.

Over the past decade, undergraduate programs were restructured in recognition of the pervasive fact that graduates would face problems whose solution require a team approach. They must gain competence with computers in working out answers to the unpredictable challenges of modern agricultural industries. Four options in agricultural technology—general agriculture, animal technology, horticultural technology, and mechanized agricultural production—were developed to meet the needs of industry. Other curricula were in agricultural science, agricultural and resource economics, food science and human nutrition, and human resources.

As the twentieth century neared its close, the college anticipated that the next century would bring more of what it had experienced from its origin: changing needs of the agricultural enterprises and families it was created to serve and fluctuating fiscal support for responding to those demands. Indeed, the past is prologue.

9

ARTS AND SCIENCES AFTER STATEHOOD

Deane E. Neubauer

The College of Arts and Sciences was established at the founding of the University in 1920, when the College of Hawaii was expanded from a technical school, concentrating on the training of engineers and agricultural specialists, to a broader institution of learning that—in the words of the statute that created the University—would also provide "thorough instruction" in the "physical, natural, economic, political and social sciences, language, literature, history, philosophy. . . ."

With that mandate, Arts and Sciences immediately became the principal part of the instructional force of the Manoa campus, larger by far than the other college, Applied Sciences, in which were combined the vocational curricula. Its predominance continued even after Teachers College was joined to the University in 1931. As new training programs for nurses, social workers, librarians, and other vocations were added, they also were served by Arts and Sciences. It provided the instruction in English, mathematics, history, and the physical and social sciences, which were required as a broad foundation of understanding—variously called "general" or "liberal" education—for all students seeking a bachelor's degree. This "service" function for the other colleges, plus its responsibility for teaching its own students, required Arts and Sciences to employ well over half of the entire instructional faculty, as it offered approximately two-thirds of all the courses given at the Manoa campus.

Similarly, except for the work of the College of Tropical Agriculture and its experiment station, most research at the University was carried on by faculty members in the College of Arts and Sciences. During the formative decades, research activities were limited by the concentration of energies and funds on what was perceived as the chief responsibility of the University, the education of its students, most of whom were undergraduates.

This pattern and understanding of mission began to change in the 1950s with the establishment of facilities for organized research institutes. In the next decades, aided by increasing federal grants, the research institutes—in marine biology, geophysics, ocean sciences, social science, biomedical studies, astronomy, for example—came to dominate research. The growth of the institutes, coupled with the establishment of the East-West Center and then a medical school and a law school, transformed the University and the position of the College of Arts and Sciences within it.

Doctoral programs, embellished with facilities and opportunities for research, proliferated. Graduate enrollment soared and with it the necessity of devoting more instructional time to graduate courses. As at other universities across the nation, faculty members turned to the production of research publications, increasingly essential for attaining tenure and promotion. Graduate assistants took over much of the teaching of sections in lower-division courses.

The shift of emphasis to research, graduate studies, and professional schools raised troubled voices in Arts and Sciences. Allan Saunders, dean of the college in the early 1960s, had warned that the teaching of undergraduates, the primary responsibility of his college, was being neglected. As a consequence, the college was understaffed and underfunded. His successors repeated the warning. The ensuing debate on this proposition, based on conflicting assumptions as to the relative importance of the several roles of a late-twentieth-century "multiversity" in Hawaii, underlay the budget wars that were to come in the 1970s and beyond.

The history of the college following statehood can be cast as three distinct phases. The first, sharing the general expansion of the University in the 1960s, saw departments grow and new ones form, together offering a widening variety of graduate studies. The second phase, starting in 1972, was shaped by the first of the recurring budget crises to UH and its largest college that would endure in the closing decades of the century. As the first phase was one of growth, the second was characterized by constraint, consolidation, and in some areas decline. The third phase, overlapping and growing out of the second, was marked by the reorganization of Arts and Sciences into four subunits and its renaming as the College*s* of Arts and Sciences.

PHASE ONE: EXPANDING THE COLLEGE

The 1960s began with a college staff that could still meet in a good-sized auditorium —275.5 full-time equivalent (FTE) faculty. The college ended the decade with more than a thousand such positions. Reports prepared by the University for periodic visits of its accreditation agency, the Western Association of Schools and Colleges (WASC), documented the growth. In 1959 the college served seventeen hundred students, mostly undergraduates; it offered six doctoral programs. By 1965 ten more departments had developed Ph.D. programs, and a dozen new master's programs were available. By 1970 another nine doctoral degrees and three master's had been approved. The creation of new undergraduate degree programs, while not as remarkable, was significant in expanding the reach of the college curriculum.

Growth was fueled in a self-reinforcing cycle of recruitment and budgetary support. As the mission of the college broadened and student enrollment soared, more faculty and staff were added; as new faculty members came aboard, Arts and Sciences and its many departments were infused with an expectation of continued expansion then prevalent in universities across the nation. Responding to the siren's call to create a "quality university" (later transmuted to a "world-class university" under President Albert Simone), the administration regularly appeared at the legislature to request program expansion.

The legislature was accommodating. The college budget was $2.5 million at the start of the 1960s and almost $7 million in the last year of that decade. Budget growth was paralleled in student enrollment. During the period 1965–1970 the lower-division workload of the college, defined as the number of student-hours taught, increased by a third, while upper-division instruction grew by 42 percent. The graduate teaching workload doubled; the number of courses offered increased by more than 11 percent between 1968 and 1969 alone. During the last five years of the 1960s, Arts and Sciences offered 72 percent of all classroom instruction at Manoa, provided half of all master's degrees and four-fifths of all doctorates.

Like any organization experiencing such rapid growth, the college found it difficult to work within its existing form. Dean Todd Furniss in the mid-1960s pondered how to reorganize, a question that would challenge his successors into the 1980s. With the college apparently destined to expand in the number and size of its departments, how much and how many could a single dean effectively oversee? Already, the college was an amalgam of some forty units (not all yet full-fledged departments) and even when aided by two assistant deans—one in charge of curriculum, the other student affairs—its chief administrator was overloaded.

Rapid expansion brought other growing pains. A mounting enrollment of local students raised concerns that many freshmen were insufficiently prepared for college-level work, requiring remedial training in English and mathematics. In 1964, Willard Wilson had written to the executive director of WASC that "the perennial problem of the special importance of good written and spoken English is again to the fore" at the University. How could the college address this concern of the entire campus?

Coping with its problems, the college continued to be the predominant part of UH, holding most of the faculty and teaching most of the courses, both undergraduate and graduate, at Manoa. It was linked to the research institutes and to the East-West Center by many joint appointments of its faculty members. Much of the curricular innovation of the time—such as interdisciplinary programs (notably in Asian studies), the Honors Program, Liberal Studies, New College, the Freshman Seminar, and Survival Plus—depended upon the departments and faculty members of Arts and Sciences.

Spirit and morale were high. A relatively young, largely new faculty saw itself as hard-working and creative. The future looked bright as the college anticipated new challenges in the 1970s.

PHASE TWO: CONTRACTING THE COLLEGE

The challenges came, but they turned out to be far different from those experienced in the glowing years just behind. Rapid expansion came to a sudden halt with the budget crisis of 1972. A sharp drop-off in expected state revenues brought a severe reduction in the University's appropriation. As the largest unit, Arts and Sciences was the largest target for retrenchment.

The next three years saw a rising, eventually rancorous debate within the college over the reason for the financial cutback. Relationships between the college and its former friends in the state government, especially the legislature, had deteriorated. The crux of the issue for many within the college was that in some important ways the budget crisis was "not real." By this they meant that the estimates of future revenue receipts, on which the state depended in making budget decisions, seemed unrealistically pessimistic. When that turned out to be true, a sense of betrayal arose that would become a part of the common culture of the college in the 1970s and 1980s, affecting attitudes of faculty and staff toward the governor and legislature.

The cuts impacted on the college severely. The University was directed to reduce its 1972–1973 budget by 15 percent. As this was particularized during legislative hearings, the Manoa campus was required to cut its faculty by 157 full-time equivalent positions—over two-thirds to come from Arts and Sciences. Dean David Contois sought to shift more of the retrenchment to other units, which he felt were not contributing their fair share, notably the research institutes. Able to raise external funds, they were perceived by legislators as a "good investment" of state money, a selling-point that the college lacked. Contois by determined argument won back a dozen positions, but the cut was still deep.

Contraction of the college was dramatized by the fate of its innovative programs. The fledgling New College, Survival Plus, and the Freshman Seminar had been moved into Arts and Sciences in 1972, just in time to center the college in the battle over their survival. During that academic year, each program was thoroughly examined by a college committee, its reviews then forwarded by Contois to Chancellor Wytze Gorter with positive recommendations. Within a month, word on the campus had it that the regents were going to terminate all three programs. Lobbying of President Harlan Cleveland and the regents by advocates of the programs, including their students and faculty members as well as other supportive faculty and interested community members, was intense. In August 1973, after lengthy debate in its Committee on Academic Affairs, the regents voted to end New College and Survival Plus immediately, while continuing the Freshman Seminar. For many in Arts and Sciences this seemed a blow against innovation and expansion of curricular choices, in short, against the values of the last decade. The savings from the two small programs abolished was trivial within the UH budget, but the symbolic damage was large.

In the new year, Chancellor Gorter was still keeping up the good fight on behalf of the college and its doomed innovations, only to be lectured by President Cleveland:

> Given the nature of the faculty committee report on some of the innovative programs—that is, the evidence and findings of the faculty could just as well have led to a recommendation to terminate the programs—the Regents' action was consistent both with good practice and with the role prescribed by academic tradition for the Regents in such matters.[1]

The sense of frustration during this period of contraction was well communicated at a somewhat later date by Dean Contois in a required self-evaluation of his performance in 1977. (Contois' memos were savored on the campus as the measure of the man: candid, humorous, and biting.) His long response to then Chancellor Douglas Yamamura, dated June 3, 1977, took the form of a football coach's report on the last season.

> One of the significant events in the annals of the A & S Paupers that occurred this year concerned one of our specialty squads—the Department of Architecture. At some point during this season . . . it could be said that the squad was out of the locker room and back on the field. (And if true, a real goal was scored.) But, dammit, a hell of a lot of people, in addition to myself, have been trying to shape up that outfit for at least five years! And the process has involved a good deal of work in all of the areas you list—A.1 through A.10. Faculty relationships? I'd rather forget most of 'em. Research? Yeah, a bit . . . but mostly for my own edification in order to develop a game plan. Student relationships? Delegation after delegation with few cheer leaders among 'em. Community service and relationships? I've serviced more booster clubs than any four whores on Fort Street. . . .
>
> [M]ention should be made of at least a few of our not inconsiderable losses, broken plays, etc. in which this player was involved. . . . The worst disaster occurred off the field. The team will lose 20 players at the end of the season as a result, in part, of decisions by the league's commissioner. It wouldn't be so bad if they were members of our taxi squad. But when they include such sterling performers as Anderson, Brown, Chang, Covell, Denney, Kamins, Levi, McDonald, McCarthy, Meller, Naughton and White, this franchise is in deep trouble. And the damage is not about to be repaired by the recruitment of a few feckless rookies at a dollar a pound. We'll be in no bowl game next season, that's for sure.
>
> In conclusion . . . this season has not been a smashing success in terms of the performance of your player-manager. In recent years I've come to settle for a

> .500 season, but this one will end far short of that. Perhaps the legs have gone and the scouts (WASC) are right. "Administrative and fiscal capability [of the College of Arts and Sciences] for coping with these problems seems to diminish each year."

PHASE THREE: REORGANIZING THE COLLEGE

The reorganization of Arts and Sciences has a long and tortured history. Realization of the need for restructuring the college emerged during the growth period of the 1960s. The sheer size of Arts and Sciences relative to the other colleges argued for some kind of devolution into smaller administrative units.

One proposal that came close to implementation was to create a new undergraduate unit to be called Manoa College. It would have been divided into several divisions —such as Biological Sciences, Social Sciences, and Humanities—each headed by a dean, thus giving sharper focus to undergraduate programs, it was argued, creating academic units to which students could more readily identify. Manoa College seemed close to creation in late 1971, when candidates for the positions of divisional deans were interviewed. By 1972, however, reorganization plans were shelved as the college struggled to deal with budgetary cutbacks.

But the issues that had provoked reorganization remained. One was the span of control exercisable by its dean. Contois believed that a college with more than forty reporting units and a faculty larger than a thousand could not be properly managed by one person. A related issue was more directly political. Contois called it the "voices in the choir" problem, meaning that when Manoa's academic council met it consisted of himself, representing more than half of the faculty of the campus, and eight other deans representing the much smaller professional schools. He felt that the voice of arts and sciences was often lost in the discussion of academic planning and operation. This imbalance of representation cost the college both in the allocation of resources and in the broader conversation over the academic direction of the campus. Reorganization into smaller units, each headed by a dean, would bring more college voices into the councils of administration deliberation.

Another attempt at reorganization occurred in the mid-1970s, again largely stimulated by Contois. The proposal called for the devolution of the college into six or seven divisions, each containing five or six academic departments. The plan was approved by the administration, now under President Fujio Matsuda, which was then pondering the reorganization of the entire University, including the creation of a new campus in west Oahu that would offer a liberal arts curriculum.

The ensuing divisive debate, which ultimately reached the legislature, convinced Contois that reorganization of his college was not about to happen. In the self-evaluation letter to Chancellor Yamamura quoted above, he wrote:

> As a final example drawn from our other numerous routs, there's that old plan for league reorganization. . . . The year can be said to mark its interment. But after four years of life and a funeral that has lasted as long, it's probably only proper.

A third attempt to reorganize the college took place following the appointment of Durward Long as Manoa chancellor. Long had come to the University in 1977 as vice-president for academic affairs and became chancellor following the untimely death of Douglas Yamamura. This pitted him directly in opposition to Contois.

They did not like each other for a variety of reasons, but that in itself was not a barrier to working together. Rather, each saw something quite different to be gained in reorganizing the college. Publicly, Contois continued to press for reorganization as a vehicle for more effective management. Privately, he also sought more "voices in the choir" in support of liberal arts education in competition with the professional schools. In his view, the focus of those schools put them in direct contact with professional support groups in the community—such as doctors and lawyers—for whom they trained practitioners and from whom they could garner assistance, both political and financial.

Arts and Sciences, by contrast, had the broadest mission in the University, including general education as well as the specialized instruction of its many departments. Its primary goal was to imbue students with a sense of the world, inculcating in them attitudes conducive to good citizenship and a richer life experience. These traditional values had rhetorical appeal to broad constituencies, including the legislature, but somehow at the time of making crucial budgetary decisions they tended to lose out to the more focused interests of the professional schools. After some fifteen years of this experience, Contois was convinced that the creation of administrative units within his college was a necessary counterweight in the continuing contest over relative academic importance.

Long was at first tepid toward reorganization. He had come to the campus with an agenda focused around himself as an "activist" administrator. As academic vice-president, he viewed Manoa and its chancellor as totally in thrall to the "old guard," those long in service on the campus and consequently "overrepresented" in faculty governance and administrative positions. Further, he suspected that at the margin this group put Manoa's interests above "the University's," with little regard for the legitimate authority of the central administration. And if Manoa regarded itself as superior to the other campuses, at Manoa the College of Arts and Sciences tended to the same superiority complex relative to the other colleges and schools. Long seemed to believe that he had come to deliver the University from what he perceived as the old guard coterie and its influence, centered in Arts and Sciences.

One of his first moves was to change the authority for appointing department chairmen from the college deans to his office and to reduce their terms from three years to one. The obvious effect was to weaken the ties between chairmen and deans by making department heads accountable to Long. Given that most professional schools had strong deans and relatively weak chairs, the chairmen in Arts and Sciences saw this change as directed against the power of their dean. They sent a memorandum to Long resolving that the normal term be continued at three years, as provided in the Faculty Handbook approved by the Board of Regents. For the moment, college reorganization was again stalled.

It resumed again on the initiative of the Arts and Sciences Faculty Senate in 1980. Over objections that splitting the college would balkanize it into small units with little contact, the senate created a committee to recommend a course of action on reorganization. After the entire college faculty voted against another proposal of Chancellor Long, their senate in May approved a reorganization into four units, as recommended by its committee. These units, after some modification of names, became the current colleges—Arts and Humanities; Languages, Linguistics and Literature; Natural Sciences; and Social Sciences—together constituting the Colleges of Arts and Sciences.

After review by Long and President Matsuda, the plan went to the regents for approval in December 1980. The regents named four "deans designate" to supervise the four new units, while Contois was redesignated as acting provost of the composite group. Full board approval did not come until the end of 1984.

Throughout those four years, debate went on between the reconstituted college and the central administration over the identity of the new units. Long wanted them to be called "divisions," a term resisted in Arts and Sciences as symbolizing their separation. Finally, it was agreed to call them "colleges" and to form a coordinating council of their respective deans, one of whom would chair the group on an annual rotation.

Against the preferences of the chancellor's and president's offices, associate deans were established to provide academic coordination among the four units and to oversee academic services for their students. In these ways it was hoped to keep alive the traditional liberal arts experience, institutionalized within the coordinated curriculum of the four colleges.

The struggle to control Arts and Sciences and its new colleges peaked in 1982–1983 with the return of the budget crisis and another cut in the college allocation proposed by the UH budget office. Contois was still serving as acting provost but was now housed within the office of Chancellor Long. Proximity did not improve their relationship. When in 1983 President Matsuda requested an evaluation of the chancellor, Contois expressed a complete lack of confidence. Shortly thereafter Long left the campus on administrative leave, not to return. The office of chancellor was recombined with the presidency in the next administration.

THE AFTERMATH OF REORGANIZATION

In subsequent years, especially during the administration of President Simone (1984–1992), the new Colleges of Arts and Sciences continued in the pattern of hard negotiation to which Arts and Sciences had become accustomed in seeking a more equitable distribution of funds. Even after a decade or more of experience with four deans to represent the colleges, it is difficult to validate Contois' stratagem of gaining more "voices in the choir."

An example illustrates the ambiguity of the evidence. Shortly after assuming office, Simone was startled to learn that he had virtually no discretionary funds available to meet unexpected needs for the ensuing year. That was remedied by assigning funds budgeted that year to cover costs of inflation. By the time that Arts and Sciences —ever in dispute with the UH Budget Office—learned that money might be available for the next academic year, most of the discretionary fund had already been spoken for. On this evidence it seems to have made little difference whether Arts and Sciences had one voice or five.

In the intervening years, the four deans continued to meet with the president to seek greater support. They continued to argue that the proportion of all teaching performed in Arts and Sciences substantially exceeds that of the rest of the campus, a contribution to the overall educational mission of the University not adequately recognized in budget allocations. The legacy of the budget cuts of 1972–1974 lived on.

Within the colleges, debate over identity also continued. In conversation, the current associate dean for academic affairs, Ronald E. Cambra, lamented the absence within the four constituent units of a sense of collective purpose—much as the early opponents of reorganization had predicted. In his view, balkanization had already occurred. Richard A. Dubanoski, recent dean of the Colleges of Arts and Sciences, promoted an effort to create a coherent identity. Named "college focus," it sought to develop programs of instruction and research across Arts and Sciences.

It may be that this quest for identity is misdirected. From the years leading to statehood to the time of its reorganization, the focus of the college was largely affected by the personality of its deans and some of its more illustrious faculty members. In a small college, these luminaries stood out, magnified by their proximity. As the college grew in size and organizational complexity, it became more difficult to see it as a whole. In this sense, the personality of the dean became more critical. From Allan Saunders to Todd Furniss to David Contois, a sense of definition of the growing college was given by the person heading it. Even after reorganization, Contois as provost remained for many the "real dean" of the college, the voice of its purpose and aspirations. With his death in 1988, the college lost a symbolic center that could not be replaced by an administrative group, such as the Council of Arts and Sciences Deans, however capable its individual members.

10

THE UNDERGRADUATE HONORS PROGRAMS

James R. Linn

IN THE 1930s a faculty committee allowed talented undergraduates to substitute for their major a two-year course of independent study culminating in the award of "Special Honors," but for the next two decades the honors degree depended solely upon grade-point average. By the mid-1950s, however, faculty members at Manoa, like those across the country, had become disturbed by the neglect of our most promising students. In 1957 Provost Willard Wilson convened two committees of faculty and administrators, the first of which proposed a lower-division program of Selected Studies, and the other an Honors Program for juniors and seniors. Professor Judson Ihrig (who served 1958–1964 and again from 1986) coordinated both. The first group of approximately twenty freshmen began Selected Studies in 1958. Two years later, nearly fifty juniors were admitted to the Honors Program, and in 1962 fifteen students from eleven academic departments formed its first graduating class.

In 1957 the Rockefeller and the Carnegie Foundations underwrote the establishment of an Interuniversity Committee on the Superior Student (ICSS) to sponsor regional conferences and especially to issue a periodic advisory newsletter describing problems and variations in honors programs nationally. Thanks to the pooled wisdom of our campus committees and the ICSS newsletters and the energy of Dr. Ihrig, the programs had attained their permanent shape by the time he resigned in 1964.

Selected Studies provided small discussion-centered classes of fifteen to twenty-five students in many of the courses required in the core curriculum. Instead of attending lectures with one hundred or four hundred others, Honors students who enrolled in History 161A, for example, would discuss major events on the basis of their study of original texts and partisan arguments presented in their source books. Admission to the program was by invitation to high school students whose grades or recommendations were high. They were given individual academic advising—an advantage too often precluded by other demands on the time of faculty volunteers—and so the core of the program lay in the small "A-sections." Although some of these were subsidized by the program, the majority were furnished by the departments that participated.

Faculty members welcomed the challenge of working with talented students and the chance to experiment in teaching, while their departments gained some promising majors. Moreover, many an experimental A-section, like Economics 120 or English 105, developed into the department's standard offering. There were problems: if too few selected studies students registered, an A-section might be filled with the remnants of general registration, to the frustration of all. Again, some teachers regarded the A-section as a pool of potential majors for their department. Generally, however, over the years student evaluations were highly favorable; and, perhaps as significant, those who took the most A-sections made the highest grades.

Separation of the two programs was intentional. Although a good case can be made in its favor (and often was), the concept of an integrated four-years Honors College was resisted. Among several reasons, including a cultural suspicion of elitism in students and faculty alike, perhaps the most compelling was that a four-year commitment would divert too much emphasis to a rigorous initial screening. Far better, it was thought, to admit all the potentially capable and allow them a graceful exit.

Components of the Honors Program had varied success. One, a comprehensive exam for all its students, was soon abandoned. Another, the college or departmental program, flourished here and there on the campus. The English Department, for example, maintained a highly successful program of tutorials, thesis defense, and individual career counseling and support. During the 1960s the College of Education established A-sections in each required "core" course and for practice teaching; indeed, at one time, Honors students could do their practice teaching abroad. Departments like Psychology and programs like Biological Sciences experienced periods of ebb and flow, but in most departments a supplemental honors program was short-lived. The chief problem apparently was not a failure of funds or faculty interest, but rather a break in continuity: inspired and perhaps assisted by a lively group of Honors seniors, a department would create a challenging program—only to abandon it because of a dearth of exceptional juniors in the next few years.

For the past thirty-odd years, then, Honors degrees have been recommended by the Honors Council on the basis of high grades and the successful completion of two other requirements—one of which, the Colloquium, may have been unique to this university. At some time during their last two years candidates must take two semesters of this interdisciplinary discussion course, wherein a dozen students from different majors meet weekly to analyze a significant problem, theme, book, or—in the early years—a talk by a prominent member of the community. Each section is led by a volunteer from the faculty or community; for years the chief executive of the Kahala

Hilton Hotel led discussions of "Tourism: For Better or Worse?" In the mid-1960s, under the course chairmanship of Professor of Religion Friederich Seifert, many groups were led by specially trained students. From the beginning, the Colloquium demanded analytical papers as well as participation in discussion. To protect those less verbal, it became one of the pioneers of pass-fail grading.

The final requirement, and the most visible, is the senior honors thesis. Under the guidance of a faculty member of their choice, students spend a year producing a work that falls somewhere between a master's thesis and a conventional term paper. They may have explored research methods in a junior-year Honors course, but most learned by doing. Students in the arts offer recitals, exhibitions, or performances, appending a short paper demonstrating the critical analysis underlying their thesis offering. Periodic comparison with similar mainland programs showed the standard of theses at Manoa to be remarkably high. They usually won the research prizes offered on this campus, and many have been published in revised form in scholarly journals, particularly in the natural and social sciences. In 1971 Paul Bienfang read part of his thesis at a Rome convention of the UN Food and Agriculture Organization. Michelle Cruse Skinner published her collection of short stories as *Balikbayan: A Filipino Homecoming* in 1988; and the theses of Diane Nosse on "Community Power Structure" (1967) and Cynthia Okazaki on "Land Use Policy" (1978) exerted considerable influence upon state and county government in Hawaii.

With the appointment of Hubert Frings in 1964 as their second coordinator, the programs took on an additional focus. While continuing to labor for increased enrollment, more A-sections, and some semblance of a budget, Frings began to develop what he called "nuclear courses"—interdisciplinary surveys taught by faculty teams. He hoped eventually to present at least four such courses, which together might form the core of lower-division general education requirements. Accordingly, he and the Political Science Department sponsored "Man in Society," to be team-taught by American Studies Professor Floyd Matson and others from the social sciences. Shortly after that, General Science created "Science and Ideas," and a survey course in the arts was under development. By the time he resigned in 1966, Frings had given the Honors Programs a new dimension and, perhaps inadvertently, an extra mission.

His successor, James Linn (who served 1966–1986) was the first to enjoy the luxury of a full-time assignment, a sterling full-time secretary, a furnished reading room in the penthouse of Sinclair Library, and a renewed allocation of seven teaching positions. While valued, the positions were inadequate to staff Colloquium sections and Nuclear Courses for a student enrollment that had grown to 144 in Honors and 375 in Selected Studies. Moreover, he saw the interdisciplinary courses less as the basis of an honors curriculum than as stimulating learning experiences for students generally.

In the ferment of the time over Freedom Marches and the War on Poverty, "relevance" and "innovation" in education had become national catchwords. They were reflected on the Manoa campus, where the Honors office became the administrative home, and often the generator, of an astonishing variety of experimental courses and programs, all of them open to any qualified student. The 1970 UH catalog listed thirty-three courses in Special and Interdisciplinary Studies, ranging from Sex-Roles to Legal Reasoning. Paralleling a statewide Conference on the Year 2000, in 1970 the Manoa faculty offered a constellation of six "Hawaii 2000" courses united by a common colloquium. In the following year, Honors designed Survival-Plus, a program attempting to link most of a student's undergraduate studies to an examination of six ecological crises.

Liberal Studies, under Emeritus Professor of Education Robert Clopton, from 1968 assisted students to devise their own majors, in the process providing them with much more academic advising than most undergraduates had available to them. It also supervised a semester abroad experience and provided the apparatus for developing new degree programs in women's studies, Hawaiian studies, marine studies, and the New College. New College was designed by historian Richard Rapson and his students in a section of the Honors Colloquium, while ethnic studies arose from a 1970 committee proposed and chaired by the Honors director.

Perhaps the most extreme example of this outreach, and one of the most successful, was a unit jointly designed by Honors and Honolulu's Model Cities Program. College Opportunities brought to the campus thirty high school dropouts, most from ethnic minorities underrepresented in the University's student body. It gave them a summer of intensive preparation for college, housed, tutored, and advised them—and demonstrated that two-thirds of them could complete their first-year work (indeed, one made the dean's list). Like other experimental programs, College Opportunities was "spun off" as soon as it could stand alone. Since 1970 it has admitted more than fifteen hundred potential "losers," of whom a fourth proceeded to graduation from this university alone.

Enrollment in Honors and Selected Studies by 1970 had grown significantly, to 325 and 709 respectively. Approximately twenty departments were offering A-sections and sixty-three faculty members were acting as advisers. For several years in a row the president of ASUH had been an Honors student, and others were active in campus and community affairs. Seventy-six early admissions students from high school in that year took some one hundred University classes, and four-fifths of them gained at least a B average. Twenty-seven students were on exchange at mainland universities; another twelve were legislative interns. With a position count of seven, the Honors office was generating more student credit-hours than all but the largest colleges of the Manoa campus. It was a heady time, and the downfall was steep and sudden.

Although Honors had employed as part-time lecturers a few locally prominent critics of the Vietnam War, the draft, or the ROTC program, neither the programs nor its students were conspicuous in the campus sit-ins and other protests of the period.

But in the spring of 1971, ASUH, the student government, hired one of Ralph Nader's Raiders to lead an offshoot of the Honors Colloquium. With a group of activists, Honors students and otherwise, Davitt McAteer published a sensational pamphlet that implied that Hawaii's environmental problems—such as pollution of the ocean off Waikiki—were in fact urgent crises concealed by bureaucratic self-interest. "Downtown" was outraged. Honors was accused of gross negligence for providing an academic platform for such a man, and the legislature mandated the transfer of Honors to the College of Arts and Sciences. By notable coincidence, it also mandated the expansion of the medical school and creation of a law school at Manoa—to be funded in large part by "trimming the fat" from established colleges. Arts and Sciences, which provided most of the A-sections and Colloquium leaders, was especially hard hit.

In the years of drought that followed, even the most enthusiastic departments became loath to supply Honors courses when their own were threatened. The program's budget was slashed; worse, its currency was frozen. Formerly a department could combine a quarter- or half-position from Honors with a fraction swapped from somewhere else and thereby staff a couple of A-sections or an interdisciplinary studies course. Now, however, in the struggle to mold the Manoa campus, the Hilo campus, and the community colleges into a "system," each faculty position was given a fixed bureaucratic identity, so that a loan could rarely be recovered without firing the incumbent. Like other small departments, Honors became locked into the status quo. In the three years from 1972–1973 to 1975–1976 its enrollment declined by a third.

Perhaps bleakest of all, the social environment, which had generally supported innovation in education, changed its field of concern. Special programs for the gifted underachiever were increasingly confined to high schools, particularly private schools. At the university level, attention shifted to aiding those newly perceived as disadvantaged: women, ethnic minorities, the physically handicapped, the marginal student.

As the century neared its close, it appeared that Honors might yet fall victim to political correctness. But whether they emerge in new form, or are left to await the next swing of the pedagogic pendulum, the Undergraduate Honors Programs had already compiled a distinguished record. They have stimulated countless students and faculty members, not only within the programs themselves but in the "spin-off" courses and innovative programs as well. Honors graduates are notable among the new leaders of Hawaii—in the professions, in academe, and in community affairs. The record makes the case for the proposition that improving the education of the gifted and motivated is a most effective way of improving education for all.

11

ORGANIZED RESEARCH UNITS

Robert W. Hiatt (as told to Robert Potter)

MARINE LABORATORIES

When Bruce White retired as graduate dean in 1954, President Gregg Sinclair asked me to serve and added the title of director of research. Prior to that time, in 1948, the Hawaii Marine Laboratory, the first major research unit on the campus, had been organized as a budget entity. We had no particular physical facility. It was just people like me in zoology and botany working in the marine area. We composed a little group. The quarter-time reduction in teaching load we were granted for research was allotted to that budget. We had almost nothing to buy equipment with. We operated mostly through our academic departments.

In 1951 the marine laboratory on Coconut Island was established. Previously, we had an organization but no facility. We obtained an Army surplus target-towing launch as a research vessel. It was forty-six feet long and well outfitted, had a good-sized deck and a good engine. That boat was berthed in Kaneohe Bay at a shoreside pier. Edwin Pauley, his brother, and a couple of others bought Coconut Island about that time. It had eighteen acres and excellent boat facilities. I called on Mr. Pauley and told him what a nice place Coconut Island would be to dock our boat. He said, "We have a lot of other facilities here. Could you use anything else on the Island?" I said, "I'm sure we could."

We walked around the island to inspect potential facilities. Chris Holmes, a previous owner, had developed a lot of saltwater tanks and kept fish and even porpoises in large ponds dredged in the surrounding reef. During World War II, the Army had built some wooden barracks along the edge of the island. Pauley said, "If you want to fix up those buildings and those aquaria and ponds, you may use them."

Pauley asked me to bring Gregg Sinclair over there one day to have lunch with the Pauley family. Pauley said he wanted the University to use the facilities and agreed to give us $10,000 to help put them back in shape. Ten thousand dollars at that time was quite a bit of money because we did all the work "in-house." Our University shop people as well as faculty went over and did it.

About this time, the director of the Rockefeller Foundation happened to visit the University, and I invited him to go to the island. As we walked around, I told him what research we were doing, how we were trying to get a seawater system built so we could operate a regular marine laboratory, not only for our own faculty but also for visiting researchers who wanted to work on coral reefs. At that time no marine laboratories were available for that research. He became interested in the prospect and gave us another $10,000. So with $20,000, plus what we could pry out of the University, we built a new water system, remodeled the buildings into laboratories, built a new dock so we could bring our boat right alongside, and put all the aquaria and ponds in order. We got two more launches from military surplus to ferry people from the shore. The University bought a couple of cars to transport staff between campus and the boat landing. That's how we started the Hawaii Marine Laboratory.

Our main laboratory building was visited by two U.S. presidents. After Harry Truman left office, he spent six weeks at Coconut Island as Pauley's guest. Every day Truman would walk around the island, a good constitutional walk. Every day he'd stop in at the lab. He got to know all the people by name and learned what research they were doing. Every day he'd want to know the progress they'd made.

Lyndon Johnson was at a governors' conference in Hawaii in 1960, and Pauley invited the governors to the island for a barbecue. Johnson walked around and came into the lab office where our secretary, Laura Ing, was working. He was wearing a khaki outfit, looking like a farmer. He said, "Young lady, can I use your telephone?" She looked at him and asked, "Do you work here?" He said, "I'm the vice-president of the United States."

That lab burned in 1961, destroying research records, including mine. I appealed then to the National Science Foundation (NSF) for assistance in building a new lab. By that time, we had an impressive list of publications and had hosted many visiting researchers. Because of Pauley we had an arrangement with the University of California for its faculty to use the laboratory. The NSF was quite impressed with what we were able to do with very little support and gave us $350,000 for a new building. It was completed in 1964.

The Enewetak laboratory was developed earlier as an outgrowth of the Bikini atomic bomb operations. In 1946, I had been invited to go to Bikini along with several others to do a preliminary study of the reef. We also did a survey there after the bomb blast to get some idea of what had happened to the reef. During that survey we made a trip to Enewetak. The Atomic Energy Commission (AEC) wondered if researchers could use some of the extensive Enewetak facilities in between bomb tests, which were scheduled for about every eighteen months. Of course we said yes.

We had fantastic support facilities because the atomic bomb tests were a very large operation. We quickly sketched out a laboratory building that we'd like to have built, with ponds and fish tanks and the like. The AEC accomplished this for us very soon. They made me director of what we named the Enewetak Marine Biological Laboratory (EMBL). It was only for visiting researchers, with no permanent staff. Dr. Donald Strasburg, one of my students, went with me early on, and we made an extensive study of the reef fishes and their ecology. Other than that, I was at EMBL for only short periods to see that the lab was operating well.

The University had an AEC grant of about $25,000 to operate EMBL, enough to pay for special equipment and supplies. No one was paid to go there. It proved to be a nice arrangement to work on a mid-Pacific reef, more productive than the Hawaiian reefs because it's located in warmer waters closer to the Indo-Pacific faunal center. For example, in Hawaii we have about fifty species of coral; at Enewetak, there are about two hundred.

The marine laboratory developments impressed President Sinclair. When he gave me the title of director of research he said, "Now I want you to do for several other areas of the campus what you have done for the marine laboratory." That was quite a mandate.

GEOPHYSICS AND ASTRONOMY

The first thing I tackled was a geophysical institute. Again we organized an entity in the budget with the staff already on hand. Jack Naughton in chemistry was doing research on something having to do with geophysics. Don Sherman was doing the same in soil science. Several in the Geology Department fit the category. We induced Ken Watanabe to return from the University of Illinois, where he was doing research on the upper atmosphere. We brought Colin Ramage from New Zealand to start a meteorological program. Thus, we organized a group of faculty into a geophysical institute, essentially only on paper, but an entity in the University budget which provided quarter-time reduction for research.

Just before we got into our act, the Institute of Geophysics at the University of Alaska had been developed, getting a million dollars from Congress. At that time (1958–1959), Jack Burns was Hawaii's delegate to Congress. On a trip to Washington, I talked with Jack about starting a geophysical institute and mentioned that we had several geophysical faculty on the campus already. Since Alaska had gotten an appropriation for their institute, I thought it would be nice if we could get similar help to build ours. Jack did the essential work of getting a bill into the congressional hopper. When Hawaii became a state, I got Senator Oren Long to introduce a bill in the Senate for the Institute of Geophysics Building in Hawaii. The congressional committee that heard the bill sent the request to the National Science Foundation, thinking it was the proper agency to handle it. We prepared a proposal for NSF, and it responded by sending a group of high-level scientists from various disciplines to investigate. They talked to our concerned faculty. A Hawaii National Guard plane flew us around Mauna Kea, where we already had a weather station, so they could see where we wanted to put an observatory. Through the International Geophysical Year (1957–1958), we had received money from NSF to put a solar observatory atop Haleakala. The foundation realized we were already in business and serious about a geophysical institute.

The committee reported favorably to NSF, which granted us $3,000,000—the largest single grant it had made up to that time. We employed architects to design the building and got it under way in 1963.

The next question was getting a director for the institute. One person who had come to campus to attend a Pacific Science Congress in 1962 was George Woollard, head of geophysics at the University of Wisconsin. I talked with him then about this possibility, and he seemed interested but didn't give me any indication that he would take the position. I wrote to him and requested another talk. So I visited him in Madison. George had four of his own children and then adopted five Euro-Asians. He had decided that Madison wasn't the best place in the world to raise those kids, but Hawaii would be perfect. That's how we got Woollard to be the first director of the Hawaii Institute of Geophysics (HIG). He was instrumental in building it into a very successful operation and one of the major things that people know about the University of Hawai'i.

When HIG was started, we knew we had the world's best observatory sites on Haleakala and Mauna Kea. The Institute for Astronomy originated in HIG. Physics professor Walt Steiger, in cooperation with the International Geophysical Year, was instrumental in establishing the observatory on Haleakala for observing the corona of the sun.

We had great trouble getting the top of Haleakala reserved for the coronograph observatory because the Air Force wanted to put a radar station there, which would have rendered Haleakala useless for astronomy of any type. At a meeting in Governor Burns' office, I explained that Haleakala and Mauna Kea were the two best sites in the world for astronomical observations. John Felix was then the governor's assistant, so Burns turned to him and said, "Why don't you go to your office with the adjutant general and Dr. Hiatt and see if you can work this difficulty out." We did so, and I said, "By the time your radar picks up a missile coming in, it's going to be too late. You're fighting the last war, not the next one." The adjutant general didn't like that, but he had to admit they could detect a missile only six minutes away. The upshot was that the Air Force backed off from its claim to Haleakala.

We recruited John Jefferies from Australia to organize astronomy at the University. John very much wanted to put an observatory on Mauna Kea. To do this, we had to get state land at the summit. We met with Governor Burns again, explaining what it would mean to the scientific world if we could have the top of that mountain reserved from all other interference. There are no cities nearby and thus no lights to bother astronomers. The governor conceded that this was possible. We asked that an area 2,000 feet down from the summit and around the mountain be saved for scientific work. The legislature subsequently approved that, after assuring the sheep hunters they could still hunt there. Our dream of what was going to be at the summit of Mauna Kea is up there now. It's the main astronomical center of the world, with several major observatories.

MEDICAL SCHOOL

In the late 1960s, there was a move afoot in medical education to build two-year medical schools. The fact behind this concept was that during the first two years medical school classes were crowded, but in the last two, the clinical years, students worked in different spaces, off campus. The idea of the two-year school was to feed more students into that clinical period. Several such schools had already been started. The NSF along with the National Institutes of Health convened a meeting in Washington on the two-year-school concept, and I attended. I decided that the best way to get started was to create a two-year school of basic medical sciences. We could capitalize on the faculty we already had by building a research institute to bolster the idea. It was thus that we conceived the idea of the Pacific Biomedical Research Center (PBRC).

I went to the Stanford Medical School and recruited Dr. Terry Rogers to head the PBRC. Then I prepared a proposal to the NSF for money to build the PBRC and get it moving. The foundation provided $350,000 for constructing the building at Kewalo Basin in Honolulu. The fundamental idea was that basic research on marine organisms could be utilized for better understanding of biochemistry and cellular biology, which were becoming important research fields. The PBRC fit right into this circumstance because one of the best organisms for research was the sea urchin, whose eggs are plentiful and large and can be handled in the laboratory better than mammalian eggs, for example. We recruited a couple of cell biologists and brought back one of my former students, Newton Morton, in human population genetics. Thus we had a basis for a health-related, medically oriented institute.

Following the establishment of PBRC, we organized a School of Basic Medical Sciences, over the strong objection of many legislators and members of the medical profession. We sold Governor Burns on the idea, and he helped to get this concept through the legislature. We obtained an appropriation, and I recruited Dr. Windsor

Cutting, who had been dean of Stanford Medical School, to be dean of our School of Basic Medical Sciences. He wasn't here long before he had started turning it into a four-year medical school. The strange thing is that the objection that we had from the medical fraternity quickly turned into a very positive attitude as soon as the four-year school was established. The physicians all wanted to become adjunct professors! The ones that had opposed it wanted to belong to the school, and they finally became part of it, in one way or another. In retrospect, the medical school seems to have succeeded very well.

SOCIAL SCIENCES

The Social Science Research Institute was outside of my field. I was involved only in the know-how to get it started. Already established was the Romanzo Adams Laboratory in sociology and a psychological research center in operation on the Manoa campus. Both were very small entities, but a number of faculty in history, political science, and sociology were interested in doing social research that related especially to the Pacific area and to Asia. Anthropologist William Lebra had an intense interest in getting something started. I worked with him, and the Social Science Research Center was established in 1961. No physical plant was involved. It functioned primarily as a budgetary organization that secured funds for the faculty who participated in it.

The lesson of the history of organized research units at the University of Hawai'i is clear. First must come the idea and then an entity in the budget must be established with whatever resources are at hand. Funds, buildings, and expanded research programs can follow.

12

THE BIOLOGICAL SCIENCES

E. Alison Kay

THE HAWAIIAN ISLANDS have been recognized since the late eighteenth century as unique in natural history. The archipelago is the most isolated group of islands on earth; new islands are periodically generated by volcanic activity, providing new habitats for colonization; and they possess an array of animals and plants found nowhere else in the world. This remarkable island biota played a major role in the development of the natural sciences at the University from its founding in 1907 as the College of Agriculture and Mechanic Arts to its present status as a major research university.

The form the biological sciences would take was prophesied in November 1906 at a meeting of the Social Science Association in Honolulu, when William T. Brigham, first director of the Bishop Museum, described his vision of a teaching and research institution in Hawaii: a college for the study of general biology, a marine biological station, a zoological garden and aviary, and a botanical garden. At the association's December meeting, William Alanson Bryan, curator of ornithology at the Bishop Museum, proposed yet another facility, "a scientific institution for the study of Oceanography with a headquarters in Honolulu," and researchers who would study, group by group, the islands of the Pacific. This idea was even more daring than Brigham's for it would place Hawaii firmly in the field of scientific research in the Pacific. The visions of Brigham and Bryan for research and teaching in Hawaii were fulfilled as the elements of their plans evolved over the years to compose the framework for the biological sciences at the University today.

THE EARLY YEARS: 1907–1942

The first classes in the biological sciences, botany and physiology, were taught by Willis T. Pope, professor of botany and horticulture and acting dean. In the College prospectus, he established that course work in the biological sciences should be based in Hawaii, noting that for botany "the Territory of Hawaii, particularly Honolulu and vicinity, furnish us with a great field for this important and interesting subject." In that first September session of 1908, three courses each in botany and zoology were taught, three by Pope and two by Bryan, who by then had been appointed professor of zoology. A third course in zoology, one in entomology, was taught in a series of lectures by Jacob Kotinsky.

Those first courses were structured around two themes: "to foster and propagate teaching and investigations that pertain to the agriculture of the tropics," that is, applied science, and "in accordance . . . with the environment. The Tropics present a great many problems of inquiry and research . . . oft-times the theories and practices of the Temperate Zone do not apply fully . . . to the Tropics . . . therefore . . . the College should engage in all lines of research and investigation that will promote those lines of instruction . . . ," that is, pure science.[1] Pope distinguished between the two themes in his description of how botany would be taught: "as a pure science" and "as a science forming the foundation of Agriculture."[2]

Botany

The challenge of an amalgam of the practical with pure science was met in botany by Vaughan MacCaughey, appointed assistant professor of botany and horticulture in 1910. His first report stressed that "the primary function of the department is *training*." His agenda encompassed the unique flora of the Islands; the Hawaiian legacy of an intensive system of crop production ("Much of this old knowledge could be profitably revived"); and the necessity of adapting to local conditions fruits of commercial importance, such as pineapples and avocados.[3] In three years, the original three courses in botany multiplied to eight, including one in bacteriology, and a ninth course provided opportunities for research. MacCaughey, dividing his time between botany and horticulture, published an array of papers on Hawaiian flora. His descriptions of the vegetation of Manoa Valley, of lava flows, and of the coastal strand are still important today.

Botany as a "pure science" was also supported by the appointment of Joseph F. Rock to the Botany Department in 1911. The Austrian-born Rock brought to the College the herbarium that he had assembled between 1908 and 1911 as botanical collector and assistant with the territorial Division of Forestry. The herbarium, described as "the most complete collection in the world of the indigenous flora of Hawaii,"[4] was to serve as the centerpiece for training in plant classification. Rock's interest in tropical plants extended beyond the herbarium and courses in systematic botany, as is evident in a 1913 listing of the College's needs where he advocated establishing "upon these grounds a Botanical Garden where all the plants of the tropics suitable to this elevation, climate and soil could be grown." He eventually developed two acres of the campus as a botanic garden, planted with more than five hundred different species from Hawaii, Asia, Indonesia, and the Americas.[5] Many of them were collected by Rock during a sabbatical leave—the first taken by a member of the new college—which he had to cut short when notified that the federal funds on which the College heavily depended would not cover his salary while on leave. Rock remained on the botany faculty until 1919, publishing more than fifty papers and books on Hawaiian plants.

Zoology

Elements of both practical and pure science are also visible in zoology under the leadership of William A. Bryan. To the initial three courses (entomology, invertebrate and vertebrate zoology) a course in oceanography and one in ichthyology were added during the next two years. Bryan needed a marine laboratory to teach these courses satisfactorily and as early as 1910 began his plea for a facility associated with an aquarium "where the breeding habits and the problems pertaining to fish culture could be adequately studied." He based his argument on the College's mandate to support diversification:

> A great deal has been said . . . regarding the diversification of industries and the conservation of our natural resources. The establishment of a Marine Biological Laboratory as a branch of the Department of Zoology would be one means of accomplishing these objects. Everyone is familiar with the present scarcity of edible fish existing in our waters, and we are also familiar with the high prices . . . there are no adequate regulations regarding the kind and size of fish that may be taken . . . , or the seasons when they should be left undisturbed for breeding . . . these are paramount questions if our fish supply is to be adequately maintained.[6]

Bryan's request for a laboratory caught the attention of a townsman, who offered to build a seaside laboratory for the College at Waikiki. Plans were prepared, but opposition to the site caused the offer to be withdrawn. Bryan persisted: "We are spending in Hawaii large sums annually in agricultural experimentation; . . . consider the possibilities of marine development . . . mullet growing. . . . The pearl oyster . . . and sponges could probably be grown here on a commercial scale. . . ."[7]

In 1916 he secured "temporary quarters on Pier 6 for the equipment of a small laboratory in Honolulu . . . [which] no way lessens the demand for the establishment of a properly located and thoroughly equipped marine biological laboratory."[8] In 1919 he made yet another plea and suggested that at least one trained biologist begin to investigate the life histories of reef and bottom fish, lobsters and crabs, and the introduction of shellfish. That year the Charles M. Cooke Estate offered $10,000 to create a laboratory, provided that the aquarium was put under the College.

Another service that Bryan suggested Zoology could render under the College's mandate to support agriculture was to advise the territorial government on the introduction of insectivorous birds. The introduction of these birds had "long been a pressing problem," and it was essential that "no mistake be made and no bird set at liberty until its food habits in its natural habitat and in Hawaii were known."[9] The College, Bryan said, "stood ready to undertake the task."

Pure science was also included in Bryan's zoology curriculum. In a departmental description, courses were "arranged to take advantage of the wealth of illustrative and research material available in the Island fauna. . . . The Islands have already furnished rich material . . . widely used by philosophical zoologists in their attempts to explain the great fundamental problems of evolution. . . ." The "rich material" to which he referred included references to Hawaiian plants, shells, and birds in several texts on evolution which had appeared following publication of Darwin's *The Origin of Species*. In 1916 Bryan added a final course to his offerings in zoology, titled "Evolution and Animal Life."

Entomology

Entomology was among the first courses taught in the new College. Majors in entomology received the first bachelor's degrees; eventually the first master of science degree was for a thesis in entomology, and the first Ph.D. degree also was for a dissertation in that field. Entomology courses were closely allied with the agricultural mission of the College as a land-grant institution.

Henry P. Severin was the first professor in entomology, initially teaching six students. He was succeeded by Professors James Illingworth (1912–1919) and David Crawford (1919–1926). It was in Crawford's time that entomology courses were listed with zoology. When Crawford became president of the University in 1927, E. H. Bryan, who had received his bachelor's degree in entomology the previous year, taught all four courses in the field.

THE YEARS BETWEEN: EDMONDSON AND ST. JOHN

Two towering figures in the biological sciences represent the epitome of teaching and research at the University, Charles Edmondson in zoology and Harold St. John in botany. Each gained national recognition. Edmondson pioneered work in the growth of corals, the productivity of coral reefs, and fouling organisms. St. John was the key figure in the Pacific linking modern systematics with the nineteenth century.

Edmondson came to Hawaii in 1920 with a joint appointment: as professor of zoology and director of the Marine Biology Laboratory of the newly constituted University and as zoologist at the Bishop Museum. He arrived as the Cooke Laboratory was being built seaward of the aquarium, two months before the first Pacific Science Congress convened in Honolulu and three years before the *Tanager* and

Whippoorwill expeditions sailed into the Pacific. He would participate in all three ventures.

Edmondson's first concern, however, seems to have been the zoology curriculum. His impact was immediate and profound. The courses taught by Bryan were consolidated as General Zoology, Comparative Anatomy of Vertebrates, and Systematic Zoology, thereby providing both depth and scope. Histology and bionomics (the relations of organisms to their environment) were then introduced. In 1922 mammalian anatomy and Edmondson's own subject, marine ecology, became part of the curriculum. Bryan's physiology course was transferred to the Zoology Department in 1929; seven courses in entomology from the College of Applied Science were incorporated in 1930; parasitology became a departmental course in 1937.

With courses came additional staff. Jens Mathias Ostergaard, employed first in Honolulu as a streetcar conductor, became so proficient in Edmondson's classes that he was appointed assistant in zoology in 1922, becoming the first of more than twenty assistants, instructors, and professors who were to serve in the department during Edmondson's tenure. Among the assistants was Spencer W. Tinker, appointed a teaching fellow in 1932, subsequently the second director of the aquarium (1940–1973), and author of several books on Hawaiian fishes, shells, sharks, and rays.

Edmondson reigned supreme in the Cooke Marine Biology Laboratory. In a paper at the First Pacific Science Congress in August 1920, he announced the opening of the laboratory, inviting members of the congress to use it, and expressed his hope that it would "stimulate interest in biology in our own students and encourage some . . . to continue in research." In the laboratory he taught by example, exploring the shallow waters of the reef off Waikiki, pioneering studies on corals, regeneration in starfishes, and crustaceans, and painstakingly documenting the habits and habitats of reef animals.

Edmondson's breadth of interest in marine biology was expressed over the years in myriad papers on corals, shipworms *(Teredo)*, crustaceans, starfish, and fouling organisms. He participated in expeditions to Johnston, Wake, and the Line Islands and ventured on his own farther into the Pacific, all of which provided him with material for papers on distribution and relationships of Hawaiian fauna. He published the now classic *Reef and Shore Fauna of Hawaii*,[10] one of the first texts on tropical marine animals.

Between 1919, when MacCaughey and Rock left the University, and 1929, the Botany Department was chaired by Herbert F. Bergman, a physiologist with interests in commercial plants, such as pineapple and papaya. During his tenure, there was little change in the curriculum that MacCaughey had introduced. Rock's herbarium was under the care of Otto Degener, appointed instructor in botany in 1925. Although Degener did not remain at the University long, his research on Hawaiian plants was a major contribution to the understanding of the unique Hawaiian flora.

Harold St. John was appointed professor of botany in 1929, coming to Hawaii from Washington State College. He taught at Manoa for twenty-nine years, retiring as senior professor in 1958. St. John was twice chairman of the Botany Department, 1929–1940 and again 1943–1954. He began his tenure, as had Edmondson, by restructuring the curriculum and increasing the staff. In 1929 under Bergman and a single instructor, eleven courses were offered. In 1930 St. John, Assistant Professor Earle Christopherson, and an assistant taught twenty-one courses, including those that were to be St. John's hallmark: systematic botany of the flowering plants and taxonomy. He later added a course in taxonomy and exploration and also taught the history of science as a survey course.

On his arrival in Hawaii, St. John, like Edmondson, immediately plunged into research in the Pacific, and the first of what were to be more than three hundred papers on Hawaiian and Pacific plants appeared in 1931. He participated in the Mangarevan Expedition of 1934, sailing with Kenneth Emory, C. M. Cooke, Jr., and E. C. Zimmerman of the Bishop Museum into the far reaches of southeastern Polynesia, returning with "the richest collections ever made in . . . plants in Polynesia."[11] Following World War II he led the University into Pacific research as a member of a committee appointed by the National Research Council, studying flora on islands throughout Micronesia and Polynesia. After retiring from the University, St. John continued his work on plant classification at the Bishop Museum until his ninety-ninth birthday.

THE SCIENTIFIC WORLD DISCOVERS THE PACIFIC

Edmondson retired in 1942 when the University was absorbed in World War II. Christopher Hamre, professor of zoology and entomology, who succeeded him as chairman of Zoology, and St. John in Botany had to contend with the impact of the war, as more than half of the students and faculty members left for war work or service. Despite the war, a few faculty appointments were made that were to be important for the University's future in the biological sciences. Assistant Professors A. H. Banner and Robert W. Hiatt came to the department in 1943 and 1944 respectively. Botanists and zoologists turned their attention to the war effort, joining in research directed at increasing local fish production and exploiting oceanic fisheries.

The impact of the war in the Pacific was decisive. The botany and zoology of Bryan and MacCaughey had been relevant to what was then the key element in Hawaii's economy—agriculture—and their research was focused on Hawaii. Edmondson and St. John, on the other hand, looked outward into the Pacific, Edmondson studying the relationships of the Hawaiian marine fauna to that of other areas of the Pacific, St. John having "profound influence on the development of botany in the Pacific Basin."[12] At the end of the war, many botanists and zoologists at the University were figuratively thrown into the Pacific Ocean.

By 1945 it was clear that the United States would be deeply involved with the Pacific islands formerly mandated to Japan. Discussion in the National Research Council, at which St. John represented the University's biological sciences, led to creation of the Pacific Science Board (with six divisions that included Plant Sciences and Zoological Sciences) and establishing a scientific research base station and documentation center in Hawaii. The interest of the American government in the Pacific was twofold: first, given its new responsibility for the mandated islands, it had to achieve a better understanding of all aspects of island life; second, to maintain weapons superiority, it had to support a program of atomic testing, which even then was being set up in the northern Marshall Islands.

Of the forty-five scientists involved in Pacific Island projects during the first ten years of the Pacific Science Board, twelve were associated with the University. Their work led them to the Marshall Islands, the Carolines, the Gilberts (now Kiribati), and the Tuamotus, as well as the Marianas. Hiatt's wartime studies of Hawaiian fishponds evolved into extensive research on reef ecology, resulting in a seminal paper (with then graduate student D. W. Strasburg) on the feeding habits of the fishes of Enewetak. Hiatt also worked with Sidney J. Townsley on radioactive uptake in food chains, a subject important to the atomic bomb testing program. Banner studied the alpheid shrimp of virtually every Pacific island group and innovatively researched the causes of ciguatera fish poisoning; Maxwell S. Doty and his students investigated intricacies of coral reef productivity; Ernst Reese worked on the behavior of hermit and coconut crabs at Enewetak; and St. John and his students studied the pandanus and atoll plants throughout the Pacific. In the period 1956–1975, eighty-nine UH graduate students in the biological sciences worked in the central Pacific, reporting their research in theses, dissertations, and subsequent publications.

Zoology faculty and staff members also administered the federal research program in the Pacific, and when a marine laboratory was constructed at Enewetak in 1954, Hiatt, then chairman of the Zoology Department, was appointed its first director. A series of University faculty members succeeded him.

EXPANSION

The decades 1950–1990 were a time of rapid expansion and changes in the biological sciences at the University. Staff and students increased tenfold, and millions of dollars from the Atomic Energy Commission, National Institutes of Health, National Science Foundation, Office of Naval Research, and local government agencies supported scientific research in Hawaii. A Ph.D. program in genetics, now divorced from botany, was approved in 1951, and doctoral programs in zoology and in what is now called botanical sciences were established. New buildings provided better facilities and also spatial separation on the campus: Zoology moved into Edmondson Hall in 1962, Botany into St. John Plant Science Laboratory in 1971.

The development of specialization within the traditional disciplines reshaped the curriculum. The first moves had actually occurred in 1942, when bacteriology courses, which had been taught in Botany, were incorporated in a Department of Bacteriology (renamed Microbiology in 1959). In 1960 entomology courses offered under the rubric of zoology and entomology were transferred to a Department of Entomology in the College of Tropical Agriculture; and during the 1960s in botany itself, physiology and pathology were housed in separate departments in Agriculture, but remained conjoined with botany in a graduate field of botanical sciences. In 1965 an undergraduate Biology Program was jointly initiated by the Departments of Botany, Microbiology, and Zoology.

Marine biology, a major focus in both Botany and Zoology, was the center of much of the action. Although it was already clearly recognizable as a curricular entity in the 1920s and 1930s, only during the last half of the century did three major areas of concentration emerge within marine biology (in the broad sense of the term) as disciplines in their own right.

Traditional marine biology, focused on ecology, behavior, and systematics, was accommodated in the Marine Biology Laboratory until 1974. But the laboratory itself had been changing. In 1952 the *University Bulletin* described it as a "Marine Laboratory with Branches at Waikiki and Coconut Island." Its new status was the result of a 1950 agreement giving the University a lease to part of the island in Kaneohe Bay. The laboratory, in 1951 renamed the Hawaii Institute of Marine Biology and divorced from Zoology, developed teaching laboratories and research facilities at Coconut Island.

At the Waikiki laboratory, facilities were increasingly utilized for other aspects of marine biology which focus on developmental, cellular, and molecular biology. For this work, a modern marine biological laboratory, the Kewalo Marine Laboratory of the Pacific Biomedical Research Center, was opened in 1972 at the mouth of the Kewalo small-boat harbor in central Honolulu. It facilitated research on sea-urchin eggs as models for cell division, fertilization, and the like, and on molluscan development, focusing on the cellular and molecular basis of growth, settlement, aging, and other problems.

Another offshoot of marine biology was fisheries biology, developed in the wartime research of Hiatt and others on local and oceanic fisheries. The effort was continued after the war, supported by the U.S. Fish and Wildlife Service, which built a facility adjacent to the Manoa campus. Under the leadership of Albert Tester, a fisheries biologist who joined the Zoology Department in 1948, fisheries biology became a significant component of zoological research. Tester was internationally recognized for his studies of tuna and sharks.

Research on the productivity of ocean waters began in the Botany Department with the appointment of Maxwell S. Doty in 1951. Doty led the way in developing marine biology with pioneer work in productivity and later in marine aquaculture.

Ocean sciences were a strength at UH since the pioneer work of William A. Bryan (upper left), who in 1919 succeeded in getting funds for a research facility at the Waikiki Aquarium (top). Robert W. Hiatt, another creative marine biologist and

persuasive fundraiser, after World War II led the establishment of research laboratories at Coconut Island off Oahu (lower, left) and at Enewetak in the Marshall Islands (above).

Hiatt (below, center) is pictured at the dedication of the Coconut Island research facility in 1966, standing between Professor Vernon E. Brock (left) and Edwin W. Pauley, who had given the site to the University. In 1995 the Pauley Foundation donated $9.6 million to UH to purchase the rest of Coconut Island.

He became known internationally for his work in stimulating development of seaweed farms in Southeast Asia.

Oceanography was recognized as a discipline in the late nineteenth century during the era of great oceanographic expeditions and was increasingly distinguished from marine biology by the 1940s. The 1961–1962 UH catalog noted that although no program in oceanography was listed, several courses were available, including Science of the Sea and Oceanography in Zoology, Biological Productivity of the Sea in Botany, Oceanographic Chemistry in that department, and Marine Geology. The following year these courses were amalgamated in a new Department of Oceanography. Laboratory and oceanographic facilities were provided by the Hawaii Institute of Geophysics, formed in 1959. It and the Oceanography Department are now integrated in the School of Ocean and Earth Science and Technology.

ONE SMALL FLY

Although marine biology seemingly held center stage in the biological sciences at the University for more than forty years, the terrestrial biota was also well served in Botany by MacCaughey, Rock, Degener, St. John, and Raymond Fosberg, a student of St. John. The department was enhanced in 1953 by the donation, at the suggestion of Harold L. Lyon, director emeritus of the Hawaiian Sugar Planters' Association Manoa Arboretum, of that botanic garden to the University, which renamed it the Harold L. Lyon Arboretum.

The major emphasis in entomology was initially in applied science rather than theory. In 1948, however, the first five volumes of *Insects of Hawaii* by Elwood C. Zimmerman were published by the University of Hawai'i Press. Zimmerman, who had been on the faculty of the Department of Zoology and Entomology in 1940–1941, drew attention to the unique insect fauna of Hawaii, noting among others the fruit flies: "Some of the most remarkable of all *Drosophila* are found in Hawaii."[13]

Elmo Hardy, appointed to the Department of Entomology in 1948, had by then collected and was naming what he estimated were at least seven hundred species of *Drosophila*. In 1963, with Wilson Stone of the University of Texas, Hardy gathered geneticists, evolutionists, and other biologists from around the world for a meeting on Hawaiian *Drosophila* at the University. From that summer meeting there developed an interdisciplinary study resulting in the most intensive collection of data ever gathered on the evolution of a single family of animals. More than five hundred investigators—botanists, entomologists, geneticists, molecular biologists, population experts, and even a musician, led by Hardy, Hampton Carson of the Genetics Department, and Kenneth Kaneshiro of Entomology—became involved in studies that resulted in headline stories about Hawaii's "dancing flies" and new theories of evolution.

In the Botany Department, George Gillett and Gerald Carr brought new dimensions to the study of Hawaiian plants with their experimental approaches to the beggar's tick, the silverswords, and their respective relatives. Carr's multifaceted study of chromosomes, morphology, and hybridization of the silversword alliance led him to conclude that the array of three genera and twenty-eight species evolved in Hawaii from the seeds of a single tarweed from Baja California. In 1967 a course in the natural history of the Hawaiian Islands was initiated by botanist Charles Lamoureux and zoologist William A. Gosline, and in 1970 ornithologist Andrew Berger of the Zoology Department introduced courses on the terrestrial biota, and graduate students began studies of Hawaiian birds.

The interdisciplinary *Drosophila* project; evolutionary studies in botany; the new interest in birds in Zoology; the discovery by a graduate student in entomology of a caterpillar that behaves as an ambush predator, feeding on flies in the rain forest—all signaled recognition of the advantages of a multidisciplinary program in which investigators, marine and terrestrial, would benefit from their interaction. There was also a sobering recognition that the unique Hawaiian biota was threatened—by urbanization, predators, pesticides, introduced animals and plants, soil erosion, and the like. From such recognition and concern a program in Evolution, Ecology and Conservation Biology (EECB) evolved, with a faculty of more than thirty, their home bases in Botany, Entomology, Genetics, Geography, Zoology, the College of Tropical Agriculture, the University of Hawai'i at Hilo, and the Bishop Museum.

EECB was not the first interdisciplinary program in the biological sciences at UH, but its success provided guidance for other programs and stimulated several other cooperative ventures, among them graduate programs in cell and neurobiology (Physiology and Zoology) and marine biology (Botany, Oceanography, and Zoology).

VISIONS AS REALITY

The visions of Brigham and Bryan in 1906 became reality as the biological sciences in the College of Hawaii evolved in the University of Hawai'i: the college, the marine biological station, a botanical garden, and a means for exploring the Pacific were all created. Their visions, however, were of facilities. What neither Brigham nor Bryan could have foreseen was that the biological sciences of the early 1900s would be transformed within the century by three revolutions in scientific thought, or that the biological sciences of the College, as the University of Hawai'i, would play major roles in two of those revolutions and be transformed by the third.

The notion that continents move and its evolution as the theory of global plate tectonics took final form in the 1960s, changing our ideas of how islands were formed and of their ages. The theory came about in great part as a result of the scientific exploration of the Pacific in the 1950s and 1960s in which University scientists and their students had engaged.

Darwin's theory of evolution by natural selection also underwent several changes. Led by the work of Hampton Carson of Hawaii's Department of Genetics and of Kenneth Kaneshiro of Entomology in the 1970s and 1980s, using *Drosophila* as their model system for insights into how species evolve, Carson proposed that a new species can arise by random chance, and a "dancing fly" suggested to Kaneshiro that behavior plays a major role in the evolution of new species. The third revolution, the discovery in 1953 of the structure of DNA and its evolution as molecular biology, provided the tools with which the genetic structure of populations can be explored and new ways to look at the classification of animals and plants.

In 1907, when the College of Hawaii was created, the biological sciences were fact-based, relatively easily carved up into courses on vertebrate and invertebrate zoology, cryptogamic and phenogamic botany, and insect morphology. The disciplines —botany, entomology, and zoology—remain today, but they are joined in interdisciplinary specializations by ever-changing bridges of theory and technology.

13

ASTRONOMY

Robert M. Kamins

FROM ITS EARLIEST YEARS, the College of Hawaii offered astronomy as a course of instruction. Among the small faculty, not yet divided into departments, a mathematician or physicist would teach an introductory course with the aid of a small observatory in nearby Kaimuki. A six-inch refractor, bought by public subscription in 1910, had been installed there on a rise near Diamond Head to observe Halley's comet. Both it and a somewhat better telescope moved there from Punahou School were available to faculty of the College/University, but the optics were inadequate for scientific studies. (Struck by lightning, the derelict observatory was finally demolished in 1958.)

After College became University in 1920, mathematician John S. Donaghho taught an introduction to astronomy during his long tenure. When he retired in 1934, the course was dropped, whether from lack of a qualified instructor, the loss of the observatory, or lagging student interest is not clear.

Astronomy at UH had its rebirth after 1953, when Walter R. Steiger joined the Physics Department. His search for research areas in which Hawaii enjoyed a natural advantage yielded the thought that astronomy had that potential. By 1958 he introduced an undergraduate course, but access to research telescopes was a critical barrier to creating a significant astronomy program.

The mountains of Hawaii already intrigued astronomers from far and near. Steiger began to think of their potential for observing the sun. "It became my dream to establish a solar observatory on top of one of the mountains"—Mauna Loa, Mauna Kea, or Haleakala.[1] Encouraged by the director of the High Altitude Observatory in Boulder, Colorado, he began testing the transparency of the skies above Haleakala, then the most accessible of the three sites. The feasibility of a solar observatory on Maui was demonstrated, but no funds were available to build it.

Eventually, those funds came because of the second celestial event that spurred the development of astronomy in Hawaii, the exceptionally high level of sunspot activity that inspired a worldwide network of solar research during the International Geophysical Year of 1957–1958. The Hawaiian Islands, given their location and clear atmosphere, were obviously a prime location for observing the sun as well as for tracking the first earth satellites that would be launched.

Steiger had his dream for Haleakala, and events were conspiring to make it come true. In 1956 Dr. Fred Whipple of the Smithsonian Astrophysical Observatory in Cambridge, Massachusetts had written to Dr. C. E. Kenneth Mees in Honolulu asking if he knew of some way that a satellite tracking station could be built here. Mees, the developer of Kodachrome color film, was well known among astronomers for the creation of special photographic emulsions for astrophotography. Steiger tells what happened:

> Dr. Mees in turn contacted me at the University and he made an offer: if I would undertake the project he would donate some of his Kodak stock to underwrite the cost. I accepted because I could see that Haleakala was the right place for such a tracking station and this would give the University an opportunity to acquire the land and establish a base of operations on Haleakala in preparation for the solar observatory.[2]

The University sold the stock for $15,000, using the money to build a small cement-block building with a sliding roof to house a tracking camera. In due course, eighteen acres atop Haleakala were set aside for UH as a science preserve. The Smithsonian Astrophysical Observatory ultimately provided funds to enlarge the facility and build a dormitory for observers on the mountain. In 1962 the dreamed-of solar observatory was finally built at Haleakala, funded by the National Science Foundation as part of the grant that established an Institute of Geophysics at UH. The facility, named after Mees, soon attracted researchers from around the world and provided the essential base for developing a major astronomical program at the University.

The next forward leap of astronomy research in Hawaii was also the consequence of a natural event, in this case the tsunami that heavily damaged Hilo in May 1960. The devastation weakened the chronically insecure economy of the Big Island, prompting a search for new sources of investment and employment. Mitsuo Akiyama, executive secretary of the Hawaii Island Chamber of Commerce, undertook that mission. In 1963, he began writing to research institutions and universities with strong astronomy programs, inviting their attention to Mauna Loa and Mauna Kea as potential observatory sites. Months went by without a serious reply.

Finally, there came an enthusiastic letter from a major figure in the field, Dr. Gerard Kuiper, former director of the Yerkes and McDonald observatories, discoverer of the fifth moon of Uranus and the second moon of Neptune, and in 1963 the head of the Lunar and Planetary Laboratory at the University of Arizona. A key advisor to the National Aeronautics and Space Administration (NASA), Kuiper had already been involved in getting funding from NASA for site testing at Haleakala. Test results convinced him that the higher altitudes on the Big Island were preferable for observations.

Early in January 1964 Kuiper returned to Hawaii to consider which mountaintop would best serve as the site of a major observatory. He favored Mauna Kea over Mauna Loa because it was less subject to interference by seismic and volcanic activity. The immediate obstacle was access. A road to Puu Poliahu near the summit of Mauna Kea at 13,631 feet would cost money that NASA could not provide—$42,000 as it turned out to be. Kuiper flew to Honolulu and got the assurance of Governor John Burns that funds would be provided. Next he met with University President Thomas Hamilton and Dr. George Woollard, director of the UH Institute of Geophysics, to ensure cooperation between the Universities of Hawai'i and Arizona. By mid-February of 1964 the road was in and work began on a small sight-testing observatory for which Kuiper got a $25,000 grant from NASA.

> That wasn't enough, so he asked Akiyama to find people to help build the dome. Akiyama asked some of his friends to help contractors put up the 12½-foot dome and test telescope. . . . By June 11, 1964, the foundation, dome, and . . . telescope were in place.[3]

At the ceremony to dedicate the observatory site, Kuiper accurately celebrated the event. "This mountain top . . . is probably the best site in the world . . . from which to study the Moon, the Planets, the Stars. It is a jewel! This is the place where the most advanced and powerful observations from this Earth can be made."[4]

Kuiper first proposed a cooperative arrangement between Hawaii and Arizona universities which would move to Mauna Kea a 28-inch telescope from his Lunar and Planetary Laboratory. Then he submitted to NASA a proposal to construct a new 60-inch instrument on Mauna Kea. There was, however, a feeling at NASA that Kuiper was already overcommitted.[5]

NASA asked Harvard to submit a competing plan. The University of Hawai'i then made its own proposal, calling for the construction of an 84-inch telescope to cost $3 million. After some hesitation—perhaps caused by the fact that the local university had yet no department of astronomy—NASA accepted Hawaii's proposal and then in 1965 selected it over Harvard and Arizona. Understandably, Kuiper was furious.

Leading the UH group was John Jefferies, then working at Haleakala while on leave from the Joint Institute for Laboratory Astrophysics in Boulder, Colorado. A theorist specializing in solar spectra who then knew little about the construction of night-time telescopes, Jefferies took over the project with vigor. He brought in expe-

The College of Hawaii's first telescope, six inches in diameter, was mounted in a tiny observatory built on a lava cone in Kaimuki to view Halley's comet in 1910.

By the 1990s a dozen giant telescopes atop Mauna Kea, a complex initiated by the University, built and operated with international participation, had made the site one of the world's premier observation points.

rienced consultants, engineers, and designers, who put together specifications for a telescope patterned after the 84-inch instrument at Kitt Peak, Arizona.

The mirror blank, a disk of fused silica glass, was ordered from Corning Glass Works with the specifications "84 inches diameter, plus 4 inches, minus zero"—wording that reflected the tendency of large mirror blanks to come out of the mold with flaws around the outer edge. In effect, Jefferies was ordering an 88-inch mirror in the hope of getting at least 84 usable inches. He was in luck. He got the full 88. And the "88-inch telescope" it became.[6]

The telescope took four years to build and install on the wind-swept summit of Mauna Kea, where winter blizzards bedeviled workers putting in the concrete construction of the observatory. When the telescope went into operation in 1970 it was the eighth largest in the world. The University had leaped into world prominence as a center for astronomical research.

Jefferies, with great prospects suddenly opened in the skies above the Hawaiian Islands, was persuaded to stay on for what developed into a tenure of nineteen years. He convinced the University and state administration that Hawaii had a great future in astronomy—if the program stood on its own, outside the Hawaii Institute of Geophysics—and in 1967 an Institute for Astronomy was established on the Manoa campus. Jefferies set out to recruit more staff members to join the three solar astronomers already working with him.

Recruitment was not easy at first. "[T]here were many more jobs than applicants in those days. Worse, too many astronomers seemed to think of Hawaii as some kind of never-never land full of palm trees, pineapples, and tourists. They certainly did not see it as a place to live and to do serious astronomy."[7] The institute initially attracted the young and adventuresome. By 1975, however, a handsome new Institute for Astronomy building—spacious, well equipped, and quiet in its Manoa Valley setting several blocks upwind of the crowded campus—was an amenity to be offered in the recruitment of established astronomers.

More important, Mauna Kea's summit, almost twice as high as any other major observatory site, aroused the interest of the international astronomical community. First to come forth with an acceptable proposal was a Canadian and French consortium that lacked adequate access to the larger optical telescopes in the northern hemisphere. In October 1973, the National Research Council of Canada, the Centre National de la Recherche Scientifique, and the University of Hawai'i signed an agreement for the construction and operation of a 144-inch optical/infrared telescope on the mountain. Its cost of $31 million was equally shared by the two international partners, while the University provided the site within the environmentally protected zone established atop Mauna Kea. UH was to bear 10 percent of the operating costs.

The Canada-France-Hawaii Telescope Corporation (CFHT) observatory was completed in 1979. In that same year a 150-inch infrared telescope was installed on the summit by the United Kingdom and a 120-inch instrument, also infrared, by NASA. By 1994 three more telescopes—including the 394-inch Keck I, the largest optical telescope in the world, and the 590-inch James Clerk Maxwell, the largest submillimeter radiotelescope—were in operation on Mauna Kea. In each case, the University was assured observation time, 10 to 15 percent of that available, giving its astronomers a large and varied access to instrumentation at what was rapidly becoming the premier observation site north of the equator. Planned for completion by the close of the century were four more telescopes, including Keck II and the 315-inch Japan National Large Telescope (Subaru).

In August 1994 one of the 24-inch telescopes was removed from Mauna Kea, after two decades of service, to make space for Gemini, a 315-inch telescope to be linked in research with a similar instrument to be placed in Chile. The project was to be funded multinationally, borne by the United States, United Kingdom, Canada, Chile, Argentina, and Brazil.

Mitsuo Akiyama's mission had indeed brought an economic resource to the Big Island. In 1994, the Institute for Astronomy reckoned that the annual operating costs of the nine instruments then in use and of the four additional telescopes planned for Mauna Kea would approach $50 million. The support staff on the summit, in Hilo, and in the nearby town of Waimea, would exceed three hundred persons. That was the economic equivalent of a sugar plantation, and much more likely to continue into the next century.

Mauna Kea plus Haleakala was a strong magnet for astronomers, established as well as aspiring. By 1983, when Jefferies retired, to be succeeded as director by Dr. Donald N. B. Hall, the institute was attracting scientists from Europe and Asia, as well as North America, as visiting colleagues or in other research associations. Over the next decade the staff continued to grow, so that by the mid-1990s the institute's faculty numbered approximately fifty.

The teaching of astronomy continued in the department, now renamed Physics and Astronomy. Larger undergraduate classes met in Watanabe Hall, the campus quarters of the department. Small advanced classes and seminars for the twenty-five to thirty graduate students enrolled in a year were more likely to enjoy the off-campus facilities of the institute.

Postdoctoral researchers in residence in the mid 1990s had doctoral degrees from the Australian National University, the Universities of Florence, Yale, Harvard, Stanford, and Irkutsk. Students came from Chinese, Japanese, British, and Canadian universities, as well as from other American institutions with strong programs in astronomy. Astronomy was a major success in the University's continuing bid for recognition as an international center for advanced research.

14

MUSIC AT MANOA

Dale E. Hall

IN THE EARLY DAYS, music on campus was an extracurricular activity—glee clubs or bands. Leona Crawford directed a men's glee club from 1917 until she became busy with her duties as wife of the president. During 1920–1921 a coed glee club introduced Monday noon hour "songfests" under the leadership of Charles E. King, later a celebrated Hawaiian composer, who as territorial senator had cosponsored the bill creating the University.

A strong U.S. military presence made military bands common in the Islands. An ROTC drum and bugle corps organized during 1923–1924 under a student bandmaster was the forerunner of a wind band of more than twenty players directed by Dewey Robbins, a trombonist with the Hawaii Theatre orchestra and the Honolulu Symphony. It is not surprising, then, that the 1927 UH catalog listed Band as the first music course to be offered for credit. Open to male students, practice sessions were in the locker room of the swimming pool. In the 1930s, a band room was provided in Farrington Hall, the lecture hall/theater.

Paul Saunders, McKinley High band director, conducted the University Band, apparently under the aegis of Military Science, from 1929 to 1935. Saunders, the first of several McKinley directors to move to UH to teach large music ensembles, was later followed by Richard Lum (1960–1985) and UH Orchestra director Henry Miyamura (from 1979). By the time of his retirement, Lum had trained three-fourths of Hawaii 's public school band teachers.

From 1920 through 1933, music courses taken at Punahou School could be credited toward UH graduation. When the Territorial Normal School merged with the University in 1931, Dorothy M. Kahananui, a Normal School teacher from 1924, became the first UH instructor in music. For some years, music courses were taught in Teachers College. Fritz Hart, long-tenured conductor of the Honolulu Symphony

Orchestra, served as the first professor of music from 1937 to 1942. He designed an undergraduate curriculum: history of music, harmony, counterpoint, musical form, and analysis. He also organized the Bach Choir, a mixed chorus of fifty voices drawn from students and the community.

During World War II, Mrs. Kahananui was the only music instructor on campus. The band had played at a football game on December 6, 1941; members took their instruments home after the game and never returned them.

In 1946, among the fifty-five new faculty members arriving at the reviving University was Norman Rian, who helped establish the Music Department. Discouraged at seeing the improvised music rooms of the campus, far inferior to those in Honolulu's high schools, he sent a letter of resignation to President Sinclair, but was persuaded to stay on. Rian served on the music faculty at Manoa until 1968 and then at Leeward Community College until he retired in 1979.

After the war, band was listed as an ROTC activity for cadets who preferred to carry a musical instrument instead of a rifle. Colonel Honnen, professor of military science, acknowledged his responsibility to provide instruments but was unable to find a supply. A local music company salesman told Rian that after the war the Army had stored band instruments on Sand Island. Rian and Honnen located a building stacked to the ceiling with banged-up brass, woodwinds, and drums. It took hours to find twenty-four instruments in playing condition. A band was formed to lead the 7 A.M. ROTC reviews. Group instrumental music was thus revived on the campus.

Rian also fostered choral work, as later did others, such as Robert Hines, who joined the faculty in 1972. This choral tradition complemented Hawaiian choral singing dating back to the mid-nineteenth century. Hawaiian musical culture was further incorporated in the department in 1972, when Dorothy Gillett, daughter of Dorothy Kahananui, established the Hawaiian Chorus, which sings in Hawaiian.

A theatrical connection was made in the late 1940s when, with Earle Ernst as dramatic director, Rian staged University productions that included singers such as Charles K. L. Davis, Helen Noh Lee, Mildred Tolentino, and Shigeru Hotoke, all of whom later had careers in teaching or the performing arts. Assisting in these productions was a new music faculty member, Richard Vine, an effective voice coach. Vine formed the "Go for Broke" Opera Company, named after the 442nd Regiment's rallying cry. Its productions in the early 1950s at the Armed Services YMCA were the forerunners of Hawaii Opera Theater. "Go for Broke" featured many of Vine's students, among whom were James Shigeta and Alvin Ing, who later had distinguished theatrical careers on the national scene.

The Music Department experienced rapid growth in mid-century. Whereas in the late 1940s there were about ten students annually majoring in music and three to five faculty members teaching them, by 1978–1979 there were 272 students and fifty-five faculty, including lecturers who taught applied music. In 1980 enrollment dropped but by 1994 was again rising.

Facilities for teaching and learning were greatly enhanced by the construction of a music complex during 1958–1959 at a cost of $285,000; it included faculty offices, studios, practice rooms, and a large choir rehearsal room. Three years later, the Mae Zenke Orvis Auditorium was opened, given by Dr. Arthur Orvis to honor his wife, a former opera singer.

The University was one of the first in the nation to offer courses in non-Western music. Barbara Smith, who joined the faculty in 1949 as teacher of piano and music theory, became interested in ethnic musics because of her students' diverse cultural backgrounds. After spending a sabbatical gathering materials, she began offering Music of the Far East, the first UH course in ethnic musics. Other courses in Asian and Pacific musics followed. She and Dorothy Gillett devised Pacific and Asian Music in Education, a course first given in the 1959 summer session to acquaint prospective teachers from all over the United States with Pacific and Asian music and dance. Teaching materials were practically nonexistent, so they notated music and dance movement directions, translated song texts, and brought to class performers of Asian musics. In the years that followed, many of these visitors were appointed as lecturers, among them Harry Nakasone, highly honored for his mastery of the Okinawan *sanshin*.

Through the work of Smith and Gillett, UH became a leader among American universities in teaching the musics of Asia and the Pacific and in integrating multiculturalism into teacher preparation. The department cooperated with the East-West Center and worked with the departments of Anthropology, American Studies, and especially Theatre and Dance in presenting authentic stage works of other cultures.

Smith encouraged her students to become performers of the music of Asia and the Pacific, serving as a role model by learning to play the Japanese koto. Another example of the department's "getting inside" the music of another culture was the purchase in 1970 of a Javanese gamelan (percussion ensemble) of twenty-five pieces. Named Kjai Gandrung ("Venerable in Love") and already 110 years old, it had once belonged to the Sultan of Jogjakarta. Javanese musician and ethnomusicologist Hardja Susilo was appointed ensemble director.

While music of other cultures was finding a place on campus, new kinds of Western music were also being heard. Piano teacher Marian Kerr had started the Festival of the Arts of This Century at Punahou School in 1957. When she moved to the University full-time in 1959, the festival came with her. Until her retirement in 1972, it brought renowned composers such as John Cage and Toru Takemitsu to the campus, to perform and hear their works played. The festival was a major showcase for contemporary compositions of America and Asia; altogether, it presented 473 works, 100 of them world premieres, by 234 composers of twenty nationalities.

Professor Dorothy Kahananui, over a career of five decades with the Territorial Normal School, Teachers College, and the Music Department, championed ancient Hawaiian music and conducted a glee club for more than twenty years. She also taught Hawaiian and wrote Hawaiian language textbooks. The Diamond Head wing of the Music Building was named for her, the first Native Hawaiian whose name graces an academic building on the Manoa campus.

The study and practice of the music of Asia was stimulated by the teaching of Professor Barbara Smith (shown playing the koto in the 1950s) and by the acquisition of a gamelan in 1970.

Dances of Asia, presented with increasing frequency after the 1960s, included this courtship dance of Sulu, performed in Kennedy Theatre in 1994.

In the 1960s the department created a small studio for electronic music, where pianist Peter Coraggio and his students produced compositions in the new medium. Armand Russell, Allen Trubitt, and Neil McKay added to the growing reputation of the department through their compositions, many of which were premiered by the Honolulu Symphony Orchestra or in recitals by faculty members, students, and local musicians. Russell, who chaired the department from 1965 to 1972, was instrumental in securing accreditation by the National Association of Schools of Music of the department's curricula and in the construction of the Dorothy Kahananui wing of the Music Complex, completed in 1975.

By 1962–1963, master of arts degrees were established with concentrations in ethnomusicology and musicology, and a master of fine arts in composition and performance, later changed to a master of music. Dance ethnomusicology (1968) and music theory (1970) were added as M.A. fields. In 1992, the regents approved a Ph.D. with an emphasis on ethnomusicology and research in cross-disciplinary areas of music, dance, drama, and Asian and Pacific studies, reinforcing the University's commitment to its role as a bridge between East and West.

15

THEATRE AND DANCE

Robert M. Kamins

THEATRE CAME EARLY to the Manoa campus and flourished. As far back as 1913 performances were staged by Theta Alpha Phi (a drama club), by the College of Hawaii Dramatic Club, or by the College itself. In the mid-1920s, a score of theatrical pieces were shown each year, most of them skits or one-act plays, but by 1927 and 1928 the offerings extended to full productions of Shakespeare and modern plays, such as Barrie's *The Admirable Crichton.* Actors faced their audience in a lecture room in Hawaii Hall, unless a larger house was needed, when the venue shifted to the Hawaii Theatre or Liberty Theatre downtown, to the Mission Memorial Hall near city hall, to McKinley High School, or to the Scottish Rite Auditorium in nearby Makiki.

The construction in 1930 of Farrington Hall at a cost of $30,000 supplied a proper stage, dressing and green rooms, and a seating capacity of about 440. A campus theatre organization was then formed, calling itself the Theatre Guild until, it is said, New York's Theatre Guild objected to this borrowing of its name, and in 1950 the University company became the Theatre Group. It was organized and run by students.

Professor James R. Brandon of the Department of Theatre and Dance has described the early years, long before a department existed:

> Under the umbrella of the University Theatre Group, a season of four plays was performed each year during the 1930s. An original Hawaiian music and dance performance, a Chinese opera, and a Japanese drama—normally a Kabuki play—were studied, rehearsed, and performed in the English language by students of the respective ethnic groups. Their audiences, and greatest appreciators, were parents and friends in the community. . . . [The] fourth [was] a *haole* . . . play . . . acted by Caucasian students.

> Thus began a University-community tradition which is unique in the United States. The University was far ahead of the times in accepting the performing arts of non-white cultures of Asia and the Pacific as valid and *equal* components of world theatre. . . . In retrospect, it was courageous in the 1920s [when student theatre groups began] for community leaders and university administrators of the white-ruled American colony to encourage young people of Asian and Pacific cultures to express their arts via the adopted English-language in drama and theatre.[1]

Advisor to the University Theatre Guild was Arthur E. Wyman, nicknamed "Doc." Wyman came from the New York stage in 1931 as assistant professor of dramatic art. He brought a particular interest in Asian theatre and during a summer visit to Japan gathered scripts for translation by University colleagues. Professionals of the Kabuki theatre living or visiting in Honolulu provided costumes, wigs, properties, and coaching in the technique of Japanese theatre. Under Wyman's direction, students presented Kabuki (along with Chinese and Hawaiian plays) from 1931 to 1941, a series that spanned eleven years. As Brandon reported, the play scheduled for 1942, *Fair Ladies at a Game of Playing Cards (Kaoyo Utagaruta)* never opened. "When the Japanese bombed Pearl Harbor, that was the end of Kabuki at the University for ten years."[2]

The English Department had become the operational center of the Theatre Group. As Wyman prepared to leave Hawaii in 1941, Earle Ernst and then Joel Trapido, bearing doctoral degrees from Cornell, were recruited to join the department. It offered one or two courses in theatre each semester and supported a small production staff. Ernst brought a dedicated interest in Japanese theatre, which the outbreak of World War II stymied until the occupation of Japan, where he was stationed in charge of censorship of the Japanese stage.

When Ernst, now well steeped in the literature and style of Japanese theatre, returned to Manoa he found the theatre program claimed by rival academic departments. It was first transferred from English to the new Speech Department, but soon (December 1950) he and Trapido persuaded the administration to establish a Department of Drama and Theatre, authorized to offer bachelor's and master's degrees. Besides Ernst and Trapido, the faculty consisted of Lucy Bentley—then midway in her long University career—and graduate assistant Edward Langhans—just starting on his. (Forty-five years later, the department included seventeen full-time faculty members, a score of lecturers and another score of graduate and special assistants.) Stage productions were expanded to offer a diverse billing, including *The House of Sugawara*, the first postwar (1951) Kabuki play, necessarily still played in English, but with increased attention to authenticity in staging, performance patterns, and intonation. Casting now ignored ethnicity. It brought together faculty members, actors from the community, and students—such as the diminutive Patsy Takemoto (the future Congresswoman Patsy Mink), who starred in Ferenc Molnar's *The Swan*.

A Great Plays Cycle presented on Farrington's stage a rotating array of classical drama *(Oedipus Rex, Lysistrata, Everyman, Hamlet, King Lear, Tartuffe, Hedda Gabler,* and *The Cherry Orchard),* offered over a four-year period for the liberal education of Manoa students. Tickets were prepaid in their registration fee. The idea of getting undergraduates to see eight masterworks was generally appealing to the faculty as an educational experience unusual, perhaps unique, in American colleges. However, after the cycle had run its course, faculty criticism of the repetition ("oh, *Hamlet* again?") stopped the rotation.

Theatre on campus flourished, but Farrington Hall deteriorated. The roof leaked badly. Termites feasted and in their unpredictable swarming bedeviled stage action, as when a thick column flew down the spotlight's beam to muffle Hamlet's soliloquy. Termite control and roof repair were not successful. The department began making plans for a bigger and better theatre when funds might become available.

Fortune came with the creation of the East-West Center in 1960. Federal funds were appropriated for constructing several buildings for the new center, one identified as an "auditorium." A sympathetic UH administration relabeled it as a "theatre auditorium." The result was a state-of-the-art theatre, seating 630 before its main stage.

Money for the kind of theatre envisaged by the drama faculty was a problem, since federal funding was for construction alone. The $250,000 needed for equipment did not exist. But the department had an ally. "There is a historian [Professor John Stalker] who had acted often in faculty productions who has a friend in the Hawaii State Legislature [Senator Vincent Esposito]. That lawmaker is convinced that the State of Hawaii, not just the federal government, should leave its stamp on some tangible aspect of the East-West Theatre. The equipment money is found. . . ."[3]

The "theatre auditorium" was completed in 1962, leaving the department and the East-West Center to work out how it would be used. Ambitions for use of the structure, easily the most imposing on campus, clashed. The building was part of the East-West Center complex, whose staff envisioned international conferences and other large meetings in the auditorium. However, the Drama Department operated the building and had prepared an ambitious first season—Shakespeare to Brecht, plus Hawaiian, Japanese, Korean, and Indian stagings—to demonstrate what could be done. Their busy schedule readily conflicted with assemblies of the center. Since Ernst held the keys, the advantage was with the department. Memoranda went back and forth until the center's interest dwindled as its program changed to require fewer large meetings. Finally it relinquished all claims, and the structure became unambiguously the University theatre. The federal government was later compensated with a transfer of land on the opposite side of East-West Road as the site for Burns Hall, the center's administrative headquarters.

Drama on the old Farrington Hall stage included *The Swan* (1947), starring Patsy Takemoto (Mink), and a 1953 production of a Kabuki favorite *Benten the Thief (Benten*

Kozo), shown in rehearsal under the critical eye of Professor Earle Ernst. In 1963 *Benten* opened Kennedy Theatre.

The new theatre was to have opened with *Of Thee I Sing,* Gershwin's musical spoof of presidential elections, but only days before its opening in November 1963, President Kennedy was assassinated. Hurriedly, a Kabuki play, *Benten the Thief,* was moved up to be the opener, and the building was named the John Fitzgerald Kennedy Theatre.

The rest of the 1963–1964 season was appropriately East-West, including, among eighteen productions, this international fare: two Kabuki plays; Korean, Indian, and Japanese dance groups; *Hamlet* (without termites); *The Way of the World; Hedda*

Gabler (starring noted actress Viveca Lindfors and historian Stalker); *Cat on a Hot Tin Roof; Caucasian Chalk Circle;* and *Spirit Island,* a Hawaiian play by art professor Jean Charlot. *Of Thee I Sing* was eventually shown in 1964, its cast including UH student Bette Midler, who appeared in several roles during the first two seasons at Kennedy before going off to gain national prominence as an actress and singer.

In its new building, the department's range of instruction and performance rapidly expanded. Transpacific plays, especially Japanese and Chinese, were performed with increasing authenticity in seasons that also presented a wide variety of Western and Hawaiian theatre. Two men with extensive professional experience in western theatre joined the faculty in 1969–1970, Glenn Cannon from New York and Terence Knapp from London. They were recruited under a plan to develop at Kennedy a performing company from which students could learn acting and other theatre skills, an ambition then widespread in American universities. The plan was never executed, as independent theatre groups began to flourish in Honolulu, but the department was enriched to include, over the following decades, a wide range of courses in acting for stage and for television, play writing, directing, set design and lighting, costume and make-up, theatrical dance, and the like, as well as more academic courses in the history and literature of the theatre, East and West. In campus careers spanning the next quarter-century, these two men enlarged the curriculum in Western theatre and theatre technique, while as directors and actors they enriched the acting companies in Hawaii. Cannon was particularly strong in musical theatre, while Knapp was the leading Shakespearean in the state.

Courses in puppetry, offered in the 1960s by Lucy Bentley, were coupled by Tamara Hunt after 1970 with teaching theatre for young people. A degree program in theatre for children, started in 1987, generated productions that annually played to thousands of youngsters.

From these programs came a growing supply of trained artists and technicians for the expanding theatre world of Hawaii. Graduates of the department increasingly staffed productions around the state—as directors, actors, designers, choreographers, stage managers, and so forth—for the Diamond Head Theatre, Manoa Valley Theatre, the U.S. Army's Community Theatre, the Honolulu Theatre for Youth, the Starving Artists Company, the theatres of the community colleges, and the other companies that were formed, some to go dark, most to play on, in the closing decades of the twentieth century.

To provide a stage for local playwrights, under the leadership of Professor Dennis Carroll, members and students of the department in 1971 formed an experimental theatre, Kumu Kahua ("Original Stage"). Its presentations tapped local multiethnic experience, such as those of Americans of Japanese ancestry in Hawaii and in wartime relocation camps, and of Hawaiians in a rapidly changing society. For years Kumu Kahua wandered from one borrowed stage to another. In 1994, an independent organization, though still with strong ties to the department, it gained its own downtown theatre.

At Kennedy, programs on the main stage continued to present a wide range of drama and musical theatre—from Aeschylus to Sondheim—directed by faculty members and enacted mostly by students. Dance and puppetry programs drew upon the art of East and West. The smaller laboratory stage, named after Earle Ernst, came into heavy demand for the production of master's theses. By 1993, Lab Theatre programs of contemporary and experimental pieces were being staged after 10 P.M.

The special attention of the department to the cultures of Asia and the islands of the Pacific continued to grow. A new linkage followed the creation of a dance program in 1966 by Carl Wolz. Wolz (a former East-West Center grantee) provided administrative leadership, choreography, instruction, and direction, as well as being the leading dancer for a time. His program was Western—ballet and modern dance. At the same time, a program of ethnic dances, focused on the dance traditions of Hawaii, Japan, Okinawa, Korea, the Philippines, and other Asian cultures, was developing across campus in the Music Department, alongside its work on the music of transpacific peoples. As early as 1959, Halla Pai Huhm taught Korean dance. The hula, taught by the legendary Iolani Luahine in summer session courses after World War II, became a regular offering in the 1960s. In 1989 the two dance programs were combined, administered in the newly renamed Department of Theatre and Dance, but retaining a dual connection. Student dance concerts are presented not only in Kennedy but also in Orvis Auditorium and in an area of the Music Building that accommodates the large Javanese gamelan orchestra.

The department's specialization in Asian theatre, initiated by students and Wyman, firmly established by Ernst, was deepened by James Brandon, Roger Long, and Elizabeth Wichmann. From the 1970s, plays from Asia, mostly Japanese but also Chinese, Filipino, and Indian, received their first performances in English on the Kennedy stage. Visiting artists came to Manoa with increasing frequency to perform, direct, and teach authentic techniques to student actors, dancers, and stage musicians.

With its long experience in Kabuki, the University program first turned to Japanese theatre. Professionals came to participate in staging Noh, Kyogen, and Kabuki theatre that became a staple of the Manoa stage. UH students began going to Japan for professional training. The *Forty-Seven Samurai,* first presented at UH in 1924 in Masefield's heavily Anglicized adaptation of the revenge play, was brought back to campus in 1978–1979. This time a noted Kabuki actor led a team from Japan that intensively trained student actors and musicians. The production played at Kennedy and then toured fourteen states in spring, 1979.

In 1988–1989 the department presented a year-long program devoted to Noh and Kyogen. Brandon brought in masters of the Japanese stage who trained UH student actors to perform a classic Noh drama, *The Pining Wind,* and two Kyogen plays—

Tricked by a Rhythm and *Buaku the Bold*. The latter were then performed by the UH cast in the National Noh Theatre in Tokyo.

Beijing opera, staged at Manoa as early as 1963 as a master's thesis production, was established in the curriculum in 1981, when graduate assistant Elizabeth Wichmann was appointed to the faculty. Courses in Asian theatre, including Asian acting for Western actors, already well developed for the Japanese stage, were expanded to include the Chinese tradition, especially for the production of opera. Chinese operas in English translation became a regular component of the Kennedy stage. Wichmann directed *The Phoenix Returns to Its Nest* in 1985 and 1986. She then translated and directed *The Jade Hall of Spring*, for which student actors and musicians were trained by master artists from Beijing opera. After its local performances, the production toured in mainland China. By the 1990s, the UH program had developed relationships with Beijing opera companies, the Academy of Chinese Opera, and the Chinese Theatre Artists Association that enabled its graduate students to study in the People's Republic.

Accomplishments in Asian theatre occurred alongside an expanding program in the theatre and dance of the Occident. Kennedy served as the chief stage in Hawaii for Western classics, especially productions of Shakespeare and Greek theatre, as well as a wide range of contemporary plays and dance forms. This exceptional combination of Western and Asian programs created a curriculum and opportunities for performance that attracted students from around the United States and across the Pacific.

16

SUMMER SESSION

Victor N. Kobayashi and Robert E. Potter

UNIVERSITY SUMMER SESSIONS are uniquely American, with roots in three educational movements: the Lyceum lecture and public forum movement begun in 1826; the remarkable Chautauqua movement, which began in 1874 as a summer conference for Sunday school teachers and grew into a major program in adult education; and teachers' summer institutes led by educator Henry Barnard at Hartford, Connecticut, in 1839. These programs spread across the nation and then moved to college campuses, largely unused during the summer. Harvard was the first to start summer programs in 1869. William Rainey Harper, who had been involved in the Chautauqua movement, made summer study an integral part of the University of Chicago academic calendar in 1892. In 1900 Harvard president C. W. Eliot promoted the summer term to accelerate the completion of college in three years.

Summer sessions in Hawaii began before there was thought of a university here. In 1896 Henry Townsend, inspector general of schools, persuaded the Board of Education of the Republic of Hawaii to permit him to hold a three-week summer session for teachers with a guest lecturer to come from the Los Angeles State Normal School, now UCLA. Successful, it was continued until 1899, bringing in such famous educators as Colonel Francis W. Parker, Flora J. Cooke, and John Dewey.

Townsend was too liberal for the conservative leaders of the territorial government, and in 1890 Alatau T. Atkinson, the new superintendent of public instruction, removed him. With Townsend gone, there were no more summer sessions until 1910, when the Department of Public Instruction began holding annual sessions to prepare applicants for the teacher's certificate examinations. These programs, which merely reviewed elementary school subjects, were described by Benjamin Wist, who taught in them, as "cram sessions." When Wist became principal of the Territorial Normal School in 1921, he radically changed the nature of the summer program, "giving teachers in service an opportunity to study the new things in education."

In 1926, Wist inaugurated a summer session for secondary school teachers, prompting the University to offer its own program. The next year the regents authorized President Crawford to plan the first UH summer session on a self-supporting basis, with the tuition fee set at $25, or $15 for those taking only one course. Matson Navigation offered discounts on its liners for teachers coming from the mainland to attend the UH summer session. Under director Thayne M. Livesay, enrollment grew from 236 in 1927 to 1,322 a decade later.

When the Normal School and the University merged in 1931, the UH summer school enrollment almost doubled. In 1938, a three-week "post-session" was added to the usual six-week term, enabling teachers to earn up to nine credits toward a degree, many having become teachers in earlier years when the Normal School had been essentially a secondary school.

Although professional development of in-service teachers remained the main purpose of the summer session through the 1930s, it broadened its scope markedly. The School of Pacific and Oriental Affairs, begun in 1932 as part of the summer session to gather distinguished scholars of Asian studies for seminars on international and race relations, became a regular part of the UH in 1936, when it was transformed into the Oriental Institute under Gregg Sinclair. In 1936 a five-week Seminar-Conference on Education in Pacific Countries was jointly sponsored by Yale University and the UH. From 1932 to 1939, the UH Summer Session hosted Seminar-Conferences on Comparative Philosophy directed by Professor Charles A. Moore, which developed into the internationally known East-West Philosophers' Conferences. Even before World War II dramatized the role of Hawaii in the Pacific, the Summer Session was spotlighting the importance of Asia and its cultures.

During the war, the summer session was extended to twelve weeks "as a war measure in the interest of an acceleration of student progress in degree programs." Students could earn up to fourteen credits. After the war, the summer session grew slowly under the directorship of Dr. Paul S. Bachman, who held that post as one of his many administrative duties. When he became UH president in 1955, history professor Shunzo Sakamaki was named dean of the Summer Session.

Under Sakamaki, the UH Summer Session grew enormously in offerings and enrollment. An effective administrator and vigorous entrepreneur, he developed the program through skillful planning and advertising, for from its beginning the Summer Session was supported only by tuition fees. Promotion of the program on the mainland as well as locally pushed the 1957 enrollment to more than five thousand; in 1960 the eight thousand enrollees included twenty-five hundred from the mainland, representing all states and the District of Columbia. Indeed, self-financing was so successful that in 1956 the territorial government expropriated more than $32,000—a hefty sum at that time—from Summer Session reserve funds to help cover salary raises for state employees.

Sakamaki drew up "an amplified statement of the role of summer session" in 1965, establishing that the Summer Session, although independent of state appropriations, was nevertheless responsible for executing during the summer the broad ongoing responsibilities of the University. These included: maximizing year-round use of UH facilities; helping students to accelerate degree programs; providing directed research opportunities for graduate students; giving school teachers a chance to take courses; bringing outstanding scholars to campus; pioneering with courses new or designed to meet particular community needs; and contributing to the cultural life of the community through public lectures, concerts, recitals, and exhibitions.

Sakamaki excelled in bringing in noted scholars from Asia and the mainland, including Pulitzer Prize winners and Nobel laureates as well as internationally famous professors. His Summer Session bulletins read like a who's who of the artistic and intellectual world of the time: surrealist painter Max Ernst; artists Josef Albers and Dorothea Tanning; art critic Alfred Frankenstein; theatre scholar Mordecai Gorelik; weaver Anni Albers; social scientists Hilda Taba, Robert Havighurst, Gardner Murphy, and Kingsley Davis; semanticist S. I. Hayakawa; mathematician Anatol Rapoport; scientists Edward Teller and Werner von Braun; philosophers D. T. Suzuki, S. Radhakrishnan, Wing-Tsit Chan, Hu Shih, and F. S. C. Northrop; psychologists Lee J. Cronbach and Julian Stanley; education philosophers George Axtelle and Maxine Greene. They attracted not only local students but also large numbers from the mainland as well. The cartoon figure of the coed who came to Hawaii for the beaches and courses in ukulele, hula, and swimming might have existed, but many serious students came to learn from the outstanding faculty Sakamaki assembled each summer.

Since Summer Session courses did not have to go through the long bureaucratic review required of those offered in the regular academic semesters, many new subjects were first introduced in the summer. Some proved so popular that they became part of the year-round curriculum, thus fulfilling Sakamaki's purpose of pioneering new courses. If Sakamaki thought a course might pay for itself, he would authorize it, but many times he accepted a course that he knew could not cover the stipend of its instructor because he believed it was needed for students or the local community. For example, courses in library science were introduced in 1957, leading to the establishment of the Graduate School of Library Studies in 1965.

Between 1964 and 1965 enrollment jumped from 10,882 to 15,508, enabling UH to claim it had the third largest summer enrollment in the nation, smaller only than the Universities of Minnesota and Indiana. For the next several years, the UH summer session continued as one of the three largest in the nation, reaching a peak enrollment of 20,638 in 1968. With mounting enrollments, Sakamaki built up a large reserve fund, which gave him the flexibility to fund more "losing" courses and special programs. He also undertook other projects, such as subsidizing the UH-Hilo summer sessions until 1971 and painting the exteriors of many Manoa buildings before mainland visitors arrived.

So many students were participating in the summer session that, beginning in 1967, the University instituted a commencement program in August to recognize those who had completed their degree programs through the acceleration that Sakamaki had included as a purpose of the summer session.

Sakamaki also introduced summer study-abroad courses, as well as programs for visiting students from Japan and other special international programs and seminars, some of which are now year-round operations of the Summer Session office. In 1970 the first international seminar program was started with the Hakubi Kyoto Kimono School. Since then, a rising number of universities and other institutions abroad have sent their students for UH Summer Session special programs. Most have come from Japan, but groups also have come from Europe, Colombia, Indonesia, Korea, and elsewhere. Some of these programs were held year-round, such as that of the Kobe Women's University, which sent students almost every month to study English and American culture under the auspices of the Summer Session. Some of these international programs developed after Sakamaki's retirement, but his leadership showed the way.

Beginning in 1969, summer enrollments began to decline. One reason was that most teachers had earned their baccalaureate degrees and many their master's degrees and fifth-year certificates, thus reducing the demand by in-service teachers. A more important reason, however, was charging out-of-state students double the tuition charged resident students; this, coupled with the rising cost of living in Hawaii and the rising cost of transportation from the mainland, did much to stem the flood of mainland students. As enrollments declined and fewer courses could pay for the professors' salaries, Sakamaki was forced to reduce offerings, and a cycle of decline set in.

Sakamaki retired in 1972 and died in 1973. For the next three years, professors Douglas Yamamura and Takeshi Moriwaki served as acting deans. History professor Robert Sakai became dean in 1975 and established a noncredit course for students from abroad wanting to improve their English skills. Known as the New Intensive Course in English Program, it became another year-round program of the Summer Session, attracting students of all ages from many countries, but primarily from Japan.

After Sakai retired in 1987, Education professor Victor Kobayashi became dean and started to revitalize the Summer Session in much the same fashion as Sakamaki had done. As did his predecessors, Kobayashi developed international education and other special programs that became continuing offerings, many conducted year-round. Summer Session provided resources to begin the Pacific Peace Seminar and The Pacific Preservation Field School. It greatly expanded the number of cultural events offered, holding a Manoa Film Festival each summer and an annual Film and Video Summer Institute since 1986, with increasing attendance each year.

The Summer Session also sponsored major public service programs with international themes: "Canada: A Pacific Nation" in 1987, "Shanghai Kunju" (1987), "The Grand Kabuki" (1988), "*Bungei Shunju* Comes to Hawaii" (1988), Southeast Asian Studies Summer Institute (1988, 1989), "USSR: A Pacific Neighbor" (1990), "Festival of Indonesia" (1991), "Festival of Korea" (1992), "Poland: Tradition and Transition" (1993). These programs offered free talks by prominent leaders, films, concerts, and art exhibits. Many garnered awards from regional and national associations of summer sessions.

In the mid-1990s, the Summer Session was registering about fifteen thousand students in credit programs plus four thousand in noncredit programs, including the public service programs focused on international areas. About 85 percent of the students in the credit programs were Manoa regular students; visitors came from almost every state of the Union, and a large number came from abroad.

The University in 1969 acquired the historic Pineapple Research Institute buildings, which, with their courtyard garden and lily pond, had in earlier years provided a beauty spot of the campus. One of the buildings was so deteriorated that the University sought to demolish it in 1988, but it was on the Hawaii Register of Historic Sites and advocates opposed its destruction. After years of negotiations with the state, it was restored in 1995 solely with Summer Session funds. Remodeled to provide seminar rooms and a large audio-visual room and to serve as Summer Session headquarters, it was rededicated in April 1996.

From its beginning as a short program with the limited purpose of upgrading teachers, the Summer Session had become an integral, but still self-funded, part of the University of Hawai'i at Mānoa.

17

THE UNIVERSITY OF HAWAI'I PRESS

William Hamilton

ON JULY 1, 1947, President Gregg M. Sinclair wrote to the territorial attorney general: "I feel it is one of the important obligations of a university to publish under its imprint books written by members of its faculty and by others who make valuable contributions to knowledge and understanding . . . work which, while of great value to society, would not ordinarily be undertaken by private enterprise and therefore would not otherwise see the light of day." In response came the attorney general's opinion that establishing a press was within the power of the Board of Regents. The board created the University of Hawai'i Press on September 5, placing its administration under the president.

The start was modest. From Bachman Hall, the new press was run by the Office of Publications and Publicity, whose head, Thomas Nickerson, was to serve half-time as press director. He chaired the first faculty advisory board, which consisted of William W. Davenport, A. Grove Day, Carleton Green, Joseph McGuire, Euphie Shields, and Leonard Tuthill. It was with this personnel, inheriting one academic journal *(Pacific Science),* and with an allocation of $10,515 ($8,046 to be used for *Pacific Science*) that the press began operation.

Its first publication, in January 1948, was a reprint of *The Hawaiian Kingdom* by Ralph Kuykendall. It was an ideal start, showcasing the caliber of scholarship to be expected from the fledgling press. Three other titles received editorial board approval and financial allocations from the regents in 1948: *The Pacific Era,* edited by William Davenport, a collection of speeches celebrating the University's fortieth anniversary; *Insects of Hawaii,* by Elwood C. Zimmerman, which became a standard work; and a history of the Pearl Harbor Navy Yard, which was never published.

During the next four years, more than 250 manuscripts were submitted, most of them by local faculty or scholars residing in Hawaii. Twenty-eight—in history, culture, economics, and science—were selected for publication. Reflecting a conscious geographic focus, sixteen of the first twenty books issued from the press dealt with Hawaii and the Pacific, the other four with Asia.

By 1951 a staff of two and one-half positions was editing, designing, producing, and promoting books and the journal *Philosophy East and West,* the first to carry the press imprint. (*Pacific Science* followed in 1953.) Nickerson found that the number of manuscripts accepted by his board exceeded the staff's capacity to prepare and publish them in a reasonable time period. Requests for new positions were denied in the University's slow-growth period of the 1950s. The backlog grew.

Lack of adequate editorial staff was not the only reason for delays. Territorial law required all materials emanating from local government agencies to be printed in the Islands. Most Hawaii-based printers were set up to print newspapers, advertising materials, and other relatively simple materials—not books. Nonetheless, the press had to solicit local bids and accept the lowest, which often was more than twice that of off-Island printers. For example, *The Pacific Era,* the press' second published title, received a $4,500 local bid and one of $1,800 from the printing operation of Yale University. The press was forced to operate in this wasteful manner until 1961, when the new state legislature passed a law allowing government agencies to use off-Island printing if the bid differential exceeded 5 percent (now 15 percent). This enabled the press to get more for its printing dollar and expand its list of publications.

Another problem was the inability to retain revenue generated from the sale of books and journals. Since all sales income was returned to the territorial treasury, the press had to get funds from the regents for each publication. Many early projects accepted by the editorial board carried the notation, "Subject to the availability of funds." Despite evidence that the press needed its revenues in order to respond to the market, requests for relief were repeatedly rejected, forcing it to operate on this highly restrictive basis for more than twenty years, well after statehood and a rising prosperity had loosened other fiscal constraints.

Nevertheless, the press showed a remarkable consistency in output during its first decade, publishing an average of five books and eight issues of its two journals per year. These set the tone for the kinds of books the press found attractive for its publishing program: Kuykendall's *Hawaiian Kingdom* (eventually comprising three volumes); *Insects of Hawaii* (now fifteen volumes, the most recent published in 1991); *Hawaiian Legends in English,* by Amos P. Leib; *Hawaii's War Years,* by Gwenfread Allen; *Hawaii's People,* by Andrew W. Lind; *Fruits of Hawaii,* by Carey D. Miller; *The Tax System of Hawaii,* by Robert M. Kamins; and *Ambassador in Arms,* by Thomas D. Murphy—all well researched, heavily referenced, and adroitly written. The press had positioned itself as the primary publisher on Hawaii and its people.

The principal publication in the 1950s was the *Hawaiian-English Dictionary* by Mary Kawena Pukui and Samuel Elbert, a collaboration of University and Bishop

Thomas Nickerson, the first director of the University of Hawaiʻi Press, shown meeting with his faculty advisory committee in 1947. Clockwise: Euphie Shields, A. Grove Day, Nickerson, Leonard Tuthill, William Davenport, Carlton Green.

Alphabetizing a dictionary in the days (here mid-1950s) before the computer. Shown working on the Hawaiian dictionary of Mary Kawena Pukui and Samuel H. Elbert in the home of Aldyth Morris (lower left) is a group that also includes Gail Yoshida (standing to left), Elbert (center), and Kenneth Emory (leaning forward). The dictionary, which proved to be a most popular issue of the Press, was published in 1957; there were new editions in each succeeding decade.

Museum scholars. The territorial legislature advanced $20,000 for its production. A scheduled first printing of 2,000 copies was increased to 2,500, since the press chairman did not want to risk having the first run go out of print before the regents approved a reprinting. The decision was a wise one. The book was so popular that the press presold 1,000 copies and returned $15,000 of the territorial loan in the first ten months and the balance midway through the second year of publication.

Throughout the 1950s and 1960s the press continued to expand its offerings, added new journals to its list, and began a modest yet effective marketing campaign on the U.S. mainland. An expanding publishing list that continued to focus on Hawaii and the Pacific, but included many works on Asia, stimulated a demand beyond Hawaii and the West Coast. Marketing, in addition to the other responsibilities associated with a developing press operation, was beginning to overwhelm the director, who was also supposed to handle the University's public relations. In 1962 the regents finally separated the press from the Office of Publications and Publicity, appointing Nickerson as full-time director. The press was established as an academic support unit with departmental status, its director considered the equivalent of an academic dean.

Nickerson's final report summed up the problems that remained: "Inability to retain the returns from sales; . . . Classification of Press personnel under a Civil Service system that offers an inadequate reservoir of candidates; Rules for contracting for printing that are unadaptable to the printing trades." Unfortunately, Nickerson was unable to convince the powers of the press' needs before he retired in 1966. His successor, former managing editor Robert Sparks, inherited the problems but was able to enjoy luxuries that had eluded Nickerson: new quarters for the press and a warehouse (of sorts) to store its inventory. The first warehouse was located in a building on the Manoa campus, off the beaten path but refrigerated because it included space used by a research unit to store cadavers. Warehouse workers did not last. The press moved its offices from Dole Street (originally the Hale Laulima dormitory) to Ward Avenue. The near-town location was inconvenient, but a bar downstairs eased the pain, and the offices were spacious and uncluttered.

The press continued efforts to professionalize its operation. Sparks spent much time educating the University community and the legislature on the value of the press to the University and to the state. He enlisted an accounting firm to review operations and design proper cost-accounting systems and business procedures. A by-product of the study was legislative permission for the press to retain its revenues, thus becoming the last of sixty-eight university presses to become self-financing.

The 1970s can be summed up as the decade in which the press established itself as the leading publisher of Hawaiiana and as a major publisher of books on Asia. In 1970, twenty-three years after the press was established, annual sales passed the hundred thousand dollar mark. Key publications in the decade included several still in print and widely used: *Atlas of Hawaii,* published in 1973 and prepared by the Geography Department; two books by Martha Beckwith, *Hawaiian Mythology* (1970) and *The Kumulipo* (1972); *Shoal of Time: A History of the Hawaiian Islands* (1974), by Gavan Daws; *Volcanoes in the Sea: The Geology of Hawai'i* (1970), by Gordon Macdonald and Agatin Abbott; and several Hawaiian language and linguistics titles by Mary Kawena Pukui and Samuel Elbert. Books on Asia were primarily devoted to Eastern philosophy and language and linguistics. Eliot Deutsch, editor of the journal *Philosophy East and West,* authored four works on comparative philosophy. Linguist Teresita Ramos wrote the first two of her seven books on the Tagalog language: *Tagalog Structures* (1971) and *Tagalog Dictionary* (1971).

In 1971, after considerable debate, the operations of the East-West Center Press and the University of Hawai'i Press were combined. A consultant had noted that pooling the limited resources of the two operations would make one strong press. The East-West Center and the University, agreeing with the recommendation, each provided the new entity with an annual operating subsidy. To express the dual constituency of the merged press, the regents named it the University Press of Hawai'i. The two staffs were combined under the direction of Sparks.

The press grew immediately in international stature as a result of the merger. Each constituent brought its special publishing niche—the East-West Center Press in Asian studies and the UH Press in Hawaii and the Pacific. The two lists melded nicely and reflected the expanding academic strengths of the campus. Publications increased from an average of fifteen new titles per year to about twenty-five. A growing inventory and global interest in its titles led the press in 1972 to open a warehouse on Staten Island, New York (shared for several years with the University of California Press). Orders from this warehouse are shipped to the Americas, Europe, the United Kingdom, Africa, and the Middle East, while the Honolulu warehouse ships statewide, to Asia, and to the Pacific.

The 1970s positioned the merged press amidst the knowledge explosion generated by scholarship. The amount and diversity of scholarly material increased substantially. Instead of reviewing an average of 150 proposals per year, the number doubled—with no increase in editorial staff. With more projects to select from, many by top Asian and Pacific scholars, a new identity began to emerge—a press more fully reflecting the research and teaching interests of its parent university. Concentration on Hawaii, Asia, and the Pacific earned the distinction of being the most focused of all university presses, the only American university press to specialize on the Pan-Pacific region rather than focusing on Europe and the United States.

The merger brought the press one of its most financially rewarding projects: the *Learn Japanese: College Text* series. The four-volume series since 1972 has been among the most widely used Japanese language textbooks. Hundreds of thousands of students have learned Japanese from the series as the press generated income of more than $4 million, enabling it to publish important, but economically risky, scholarly works that otherwise would not have seen the light of day.

Development was checked during the mid-1970s by a slowdown in the vigorous economic growth and rising tax revenues that Hawaii had enjoyed since statehood. The press wanted to add experienced personnel to mount a global marketing effort, but a hiring freeze delayed the enterprise until the end of that decade. Sales were greatly stimulated, rising from approximately $100,000 in 1970 to almost $1,000,000 in 1980. The press was on its way to being a scholarly publisher with a global impact.

To save rent, the University in 1975 relocated the press to the mauka campus in Manoa Valley. Six "temporary" portable buildings that had housed the Institute for Astronomy on Kolowalu Street are still its "temporary" headquarters twenty years later.

Output began to stabilize in the 1980s at around forty books per year, in contrast to the 1970s' average of twenty-five to thirty. The number of submissions climbed with output. Each year the press was now vetting more than five hundred proposals, manuscripts, and query letters. Demands on the small editorial staff created evaluation backlogs often requiring two or three months to clear up.

In 1981, when the East-West Center withdrew its subsidy, the press name reverted to University of Hawai'i Press, reflecting its sole alliance with its parent university.

Despite limitations of staff size, the 1980s was a decade of unparalleled growth. The number of books and journals published each year increased, as did sales, providing the press with a degree of financial flexibility, allowing it to automate production with state-of-the-art typesetting and design equipment. In addition to publishing books and journals under its own imprint, the press began marketing books of local nonprofit groups and those of small scholarly and educational publishers from New Zealand, Australia, Southeast Asia, and East Asia that previously had no effective means of promoting their books abroad.

The press also began to develop a production-service program in order to utilize more fully its expensive equipment, continuously upgraded as technology improved. Dozens of University, community, and nonprofit organizations came to contract with the press for editing, book and cover design, typesetting, printing, and distribution services.

In 1985 director Sparks announced he would retire the following year, but continued part-time while the University recruited a successor. The third director, William Hamilton, began in August 1987. Hamilton, with twenty years of educational publishing experience, was the first mainland professional to be hired for the position, selected to bring a fresh perspective to the operation and to expand publishing opportunities. From 1987 through 1994 the press doubled its sales, increased its annual output to more than fifty books and forty issues of a dozen scholarly journals, and established itself as the world's premier scholarly publisher on Asia and the Pacific. It is the state's largest publisher.

The commitment to publishing important Hawaiiana continued into the 1990s. *The Manual of the Flowering Plants of Hawai'i* (1990), by Warren L. Wagner, Derral

R. Herbst, and S. H. Sohmer, copublished with the Bishop Museum, was a long-awaited publication, as were *Plants in Hawaiian Culture* (1993), by Beatrice Krauss, and *Ka Lei Ha'aheo: Beginning Hawaiian* (1992), by Alberta Pualani Hopkins. The inauguration of two new literature series in 1993 broadened the publishing base and created a new readership. One series presents in English translation outstanding fiction of this century from China. The second, *Talanoa: Contemporary Pacific Literature,* presents the fiction of indigenous Pacific Islanders.

From a beginning of one half-time position, the press now employs forty full-time staff, more than thirty freelance contractors, and about a dozen students. Annual operating budgets increased from $10,515 in 1947 to more than $5 million, mostly self-generated. Between fiscal year 1947–1948 and 1953, a total of 7,650 books were sold; now the press sells between 375,000 and 400,000 books each year. In its early years the press published primarily on Hawaii and the Pacific. In the 1990s the scope has widened: 50 percent of its titles are related to Asia, 30 percent to Hawaii, and 20 percent to the Pacific. Among its 1,200 books are works for people of all ages at every educational level. Dozens have won international, national, and local awards in a variety of categories: editorial excellence, design, best journal in its field, contribution to a particular field of knowledge, and so forth.

As it reached its fiftieth birthday, the central mission of the press remained the same as the day it was brought into existence: to publish books and journals of high merit that reflect the research and teaching interests of the University of Hawai'i.

PART III

BEYOND MANOA: HILO, WEST O‘AHU, THE COMMUNITY COLLEGES

18

THE UNIVERSITY OF HAWAI'I AT HILO

Frank T. Inouye

UNTIL 1970, the University of Hawai'i at Hilo (UHH) was a satellite of the Manoa campus that combined a two-year liberal arts curriculum with the offerings of a community college. This curious mixture of programs was the result of an ill-conceived move in 1965 to ensure the survival of a burgeoning and popular college curriculum on the Big Island.

Post–high school noncredit courses had been offered in Hilo as early as 1945 under the University's Adult Education Service, which became the UH Extension Division. Three years later, the Hilo Center was organized at Lyman Hall of the Hilo Boys School utilizing local instructors, who taught fifteen credit courses to fifty students.

An attempt in 1951 by Governor Oren E. Long to close the school as an economy measure led to the Big Island's first concerted effort on behalf of its only "college." The local community noted that the threatened closure was not opposed by the Manoa campus. This would be remembered.

An outpouring of support, spearheaded by influential Republican legislators in Hilo, resulted that same year in establishing the Hilo Branch as an integral (two-year) part of the University, its director reporting directly to Vice-President Paul S. Bachman. Edward T. White of the Manoa faculty was sent to serve as the first director of the school. He initiated the process that led to a full-fledged two-year undergraduate program. Much of the credit for the development of the Hilo Branch, however, goes to the Hilo chapter of the UH Alumni Association, whose active membership included most of the educational establishment on the island. It was through its efforts that the Hilo Branch was able to get funds and land, a thirty-acre parcel that is the present UHH campus.

In 1952, Bachman hired Frank T. Inouye, a young history instructor at Ohio State University, to succeed White as director. Inouye had been a graduate assistant under

In 1947 a Hilo Center of the University opened in Lyman Hall of the old Hilo Boarding School. In 1955 six new buildings were opened on 37 acres *mauka* of Hilo. The photograph (bottom) shows the cafetorium, now the Geology Department, under construction.

Allan Saunders, chairman of the Department of Government at Manoa, and was the first nisei to be hired by that department.

Within three years, the Hilo Branch had moved to its new campus and enlarged its faculty to serve a growing student body. Working closely with the UH Alumni Association, the island's legislators, and county officials, Inouye organized tours of all Big Island high schools to acquaint students with the advantages of attending the local branch.

By 1957 enrollment approximated two hundred, with a faculty and staff of twenty. That year, Bachman, newly installed as UH president and still supportive of the Hilo Branch, suddenly died. His successor, Laurence Snyder, was an outspoken critic of the school. He said that Hilo was a "fringe operation . . . which should not have been started and should not be kept going. . . ."[1] Snyder's opposition gave the Big Island community a political goal: the school should add a curriculum in agriculture and become a four-year college. The future of the Hilo Branch, according to the *Honolulu Star-Bulletin,* in 1960 had become the "hottest issue" on the Big Island. Support was widespread. Governor William Quinn asserted that "The State needs a small, four-year liberal arts college to round out its program of higher public education."[2]

In 1964 President Thomas Hamilton, a strong believer in centralized administration, released a feasibility study on creating a statewide system of community colleges operating as part of the University.[3] A key recommendation was to merge the Hilo Branch and the the Hawaii Technical School to create a community college in Hilo. The threat thus posed to the status of the Hilo Branch stimulated Big Island legislators to gain deletion of these recommendations from the 1966 statute creating the community college system. Instead, Hawaii Technical School was converted into Hawai'i Community College, under the state Department of Education, not the University. For economy, however, the college and the Hilo Branch of UH were to share campus facilities. This awkward arrangement was to plague both schools for two decades.

In 1969, as part of a University-wide effort to cut costs, UH Vice-President Richard Takasaki reduced the UH-Hilo budget allotment by $141,000, money that had been earmarked to begin the third year of instruction, the first, critical step toward becoming a college that granted bachelor's degrees. Only strident protests by students, faculty, and community spokesmen at a regents' meeting in Hilo saved the funds.

Thus, by 1970 the Hilo institution had survived three challenges to its development or even existence, all originating from Oahu and all deemed to be supported by UH at Manoa. These experiences left lasting anti-Manoa feelings not only within the Big Island community but also among the faculty and students of UH-Hilo, contributing to future problems of operating within the University system.

Harlan Cleveland, who succeeded Hamilton, pursued a directly contrary policy in respect to Hilo. He instituted a reorganization plan that elevated the top campus administrator to be chancellor, reporting to him. He then appointed Paul Miwa to the post. Kaoru Noda, the provost since 1965, was promoted to vice-chancellor and Charles Neff of the Manoa faculty was named provost. The Hilo campus was renamed Hilo College and, joined with Hawai‘i Community College, was given the collective name of the University of Hawai‘i at Hilo.

Miwa began his tenure with an almost visionary conception of UHH's future. His objective, he said, was to "build the University of Hawaii [at Hilo] into a major university complex."[4] At his inauguration in April 1970, he foresaw development of a "University Park" encompassing the Beaumont Agricultural Research Center, the Cooperative Extension Service, the Institute for Astronomy and Cloud Physics laboratory, a multiculture study center, an Institute of Tropical Studies, and a College of Continuing Education and Community services.

Miwa had come at a favorable time. In 1970 enrollment exceeded one thousand, having grown 10 to 20 percent annually in the preceding years. A bachelor's degree was now offered, capping development of a four-year curriculum that listed 154 courses taught by a staff of eighty-two. Hawai‘i Community College's growth was keeping pace. Its six hundred students were offered an associate degree program as well as vocational training.

Cleveland, anticipating the need to place some four thousand UH students on Neighbor Island campuses, in 1971 ordered a study of the liberal arts and vocational programs at Hilo. The report, "Toward Comprehensiveness," proposed a complete merger of Hilo College and Hawai‘i Community College. Like many another University plan, this one was written and announced without checking with those most affected—the students and faculty at Hilo. Their opposition and that of the Hawaii County Council caused the House of Representatives to castigate the UH administration for not consulting with the community college constituency, who saw the plan as a move to gut vocational education in favor of liberal arts. Cleveland conceded defeat in early 1973, agreeing with Miwa that the two schools must remain separate, except for joint use of physical facilities and campus services.

Miwa's tenure was marked by dissension. Abrupt cancellation of the contracts of five part-time instructors by Provost Neff in April 1972 set off a bitter dispute between faculty and administration, leaving feelings of mutual distrust. This carried over in 1973 to the case of Frank Nelson, a veteran professor who sought a year of service beyond the UH mandatory retirement age of sixty-five. It took a court decision, favoring Nelson, to resolve the conflict.

Neff, caught in a cross fire of criticism from administrative superiors and the faculty, resigned. Cleveland said an interim provost would be named, an action so strongly opposed by the college faculty that another serious confrontation threatened. It was averted by the appointment of Charles Fullerton, a respected Hilo-based faculty member, who directed the Cloud Physics Observatory.

Despite recurring crises, the Hilo institution continued to grow. Its first class of seniors, seventy-three in number, graduated in 1972. More than three thousand—an unprecedented number—were enrolled in both schools in 1973, when the regents approved a UHH master plan tripling the size of campus facilities, envisaging a combined student body of more than five thousand.

The resignation of Chancellor Miwa in 1975 was soon followed by that of Dean William Hildemann, leaving an administrative vacuum at Hilo College. Edwin Mookini, chairman of the Mathematics Department at Manoa, was appointed interim chancellor; he chose David Purcell as acting dean. Purcell's appointment raised the ire of Hilo faculty and students since he was not on the list of a campus selection committee. In a confrontation with the protesters, Mookini declared: "I'm the person who has to make the final judgment."[5]

He brought with him a "restructuring" plan that eliminated the top four pay steps for Hilo professors and put a limit on research time and more emphasis on community service. The faculty strongly opposed the plan, which it saw as a challenge to tenure and professional advancement, a threat to them and to the school itself. At campus and community meetings vigorous complaints were leveled against Mookini and UH-Manoa.

In April 1977, the Hilo faculty overwhelmingly resolved that it "censures and registers its lack of confidence in the central administration of the University and in the chancellor."[6] The fact that Mookini's restructuring plan would eliminate five study programs created fears that it presaged closing UHH, leading the Hawaii County Democratic Party, at its spring 1978 convention, to roundly criticize Mookini's management. This sealed his fate; his tenure ended that June.

Mookini was succeeded by Stephen Mitchell, from Western Michigan University, a man of enthusiasm. On his arrival, he made it known that Hilo College was "a great option," a fine alternative to UH-Manoa that by vigorous recruitment would expand its enrollment beyond Big Island residents. No sooner had the new chancellor organized his administration, however, than the Hilo campus was again up in arms, this time over a policy adopted by the regents requiring periodic review of all UH faculty members, including those already tenured. There was opposition to this perceived threat to faculty job security throughout the UH system but nowhere so strong as in Hilo. Most instructors refused the University's offer to consult on implementation of the policy, arguing that it was a matter for their union to handle through collective bargaining. When faculty members protested against the distribution to students of teaching evaluation forms, the University of Hawai‘i Professional Assembly filed a grievance on their behalf.

An unfavorable evaluation of the UHH Teachers College program by the state Department of Education (DOE) added to Mitchell's burden. The DOE's complaints dated back to 1978; it now cited the need for new courses in teaching methods and the shortage of education professors. Mitchell announced his resignation, effective in June 1984, saying that "it is time for new leadership." UH President Fujio Matsuda followed suit that same year, to be replaced by Albert Simone.

Concerning UH-Hilo, Simone was a visionary in the Cleveland mold. He unveiled a plan for a new state college system, of which UHH would be the "flagship." He called for a number of four-year colleges to fill the gap between the community colleges and Manoa. UHH and West O'ahu College would be "alternative" institutions, each serving five thousand students. In 1985 Simone released an ambitious UHH Academic Development Plan, which had been prepared under Matsuda. It proposed to move the school "into the forefront of the information technology movement" while achieving excellence in both vocational and liberal arts programs. Specifically, the plan called for strengthening geosciences, astronomy, and agriculture as well as articulating the liberal arts programs of Hilo College and of the community college.

The more immediate problems were money, following budget cuts over the last two biennia, and a decline in enrollment. Despite optimistic projections, the student body, which peaked at thirty-seven hundred in 1982, had dropped to thirty-two hundred in 1985. These critical losses prompted UHH supporters to propose a total separation of the school from the University system. A Hilo businessman, Bert Fraleigh, told the Hawaii County Council that the administration at Manoa treated UHH "like a colony." Were it independent, he said, UHH could have an enrollment of twenty thousand by 1990. State Representative Harvey Tajiri and many others called for autonomy of the local campus.[7]

So intense was the "separatist" movement that the 1985 legislature directed its Legislative Reference Bureau to study the feasibility of making Hilo College independent. The resulting report, while sympathetic to the school's needs, concluded that "a separate University of Hawai'i at Hilo would only create two mediocre institutions."[8]

Simone in 1986 appointed Edward Kormondy as chancellor, promising him a "completely free hand" without interference from Honolulu. Like his predecessor, Kormondy brought enthusiasm to his position, eagerly welcomed by the campus and community. At his inauguration he reiterated the dream of developing Hilo College as a scientific center. In February 1988 he proposed a major restructuring by forming colleges in general studies, professional studies, and vocational studies, while eliminating the community college. He argued that continuing the two schools under one roof would keep the community college "second class."

His plan, though brilliant in ending "class" distinctions between the students and faculties of the two units, was not well received. It was opposed by most Hawai'i Community College faculty members and, fatally, by the regents on the grounds that the community college would lose its identity and thereby its attraction to vocational students.

Instead, Simone proposed that UH at Hilo and Hawai'i Community College be separated. Over Kormondy's objection, the regents so ordered. The community college was thus moved from the UHH "umbrella" into the state community college system, where it should have been placed in 1965. UHH was left to consist of three units: Arts and Sciences; Tropical Agriculture and Human Resources; and a Center for Continuing Education and Community Service.

If UHH lost a major component, it gained another campus, in West Hawaii. Begun in 1987 as an "outreach" of the college, the Kona facility would serve the western side of Hawaii, planned eventually to be a separate four-year college, though under UHH management.

By 1990, it was evident that UHH had not needed a community college to justify its existence. Countering a temporary decline in student numbers, it offered a variety of new programs: a Hawaiian Language Center; Center for Gifted and Talented Native Hawaiian Children; Small Business Development Center; Social Sciences Training and Research Laboratory; and the long-studied project outlined by Chancellor Paul Miwa in 1970—the UHH Research and Technology Park.

The issue of independence from the University system would not die. It found a strong advocate in Big Island Senator Malama Solomon. Chair of the Higher Education Committee, she advocated "academic autonomy" for Hilo and that programs in Hawaiian, Asian, and Pacific Asian studies—as well as agriculture—be transferred there from Manoa. She had a key ally in Representative Brian Taniguchi, her counterpart in the other house. In 1989 Solomon persuaded the Senate to pass a bill separating UHH from the UH system. Taniguchi, however, questioned the need for two universities in a small state, and without his support the bill died.

Chancellor Kormandy resigned in August 1993. He had served seven years, the longest tenure of a chief executive since UHH was established in 1970. He was, in the words of a contemporary, "the most successful chancellor UHH had."[9] During his chancellorship the school had almost doubled its enrollment, reaching almost three thousand—of whom approximately five hundred came from the Pacific, Japan, and the U.S. mainland. UHH had proven itself more than a "local" institution, with about a third of its student body "imported" to the Big Island.

Encouraged by President Simone, Kormandy had brought to a troubled campus a talent for healing. By involving the faculty in solving problems, he greatly narrowed the divide between staff and administration, bringing unprecedented harmony to the school. His great disappointment, the result of what he termed "micromanagement" by legislators and regents, was failing to achieve the total merger of UHH and Hawai'i Community College.[10]

Kormondy was succeeded in 1993 by Kenneth Perrin, executive of a national educational accreditation agency and a former associate of newly appointed UH President Kenneth Mortimer. In announcing Perrin's appointment, Mortimer said that, in addition to acting as chancellor, he would also serve as a senior vice-president of the UH system with oversight of the Kona campus and West Oahu College.

In his inaugural address, Perrin set a goal of broadening the school's appeal, and enhancing its status as a university, by establishing selected graduate programs, using astronomy as an example. He pledged to strengthen the faculty with more permanent and fewer temporary positions, to complete the separation of UHH and Hawai'i Community College, and to clarify the role of the Kona Center.

How did it go? Interviewed in November 1994, Perrin discussed his first fifteen months of running UHH.[11] He admitted that the college suffered from a dearth of building funds, compared with Manoa's $190 million budget for capital improvements, but was optimistic about expanding programs in astronomy, tropical agriculture, and small-business development and in attracting conventions to the Hilo campus.

There was, however, a troubling problem. Although enrollment increased at a much faster rate than at the Manoa campus, the dropout rate among sophomores was a staggering 38 percent. A major reason, he said, was the absence of social activities on campus. Unlike Honolulu, with a reasonably good bus system and varied recreational and cultural events both on and off campus, Hilo had few such activities and limited public transportation service to reach them. His analysis suggested that without a massive infusion of funding for campus and community facilities, the further growth of UHH would be questionable.

For Perrin, as for his predecessors, UHH's future seemed inextricably tied to the scientific-technical programs with which the Big Island abounds, ranging from astronomy to aquaculture, geophysics to scientific farming. The development of the UHH Research and Technology Park, located on two hundred acres upland of the campus, attracted some base facilities supporting the astronomy projects atop Mauna Kea, which may expand as additional telescopes are added. However, there is a check to the growth of these support functions at Hilo imposed by the attractiveness of Waimea, where much of the astronomy community lives.

(The Hilo campus did find a lively student response to the offering of a language-focused baccalaureate in Hawaiian studies. In August 1996, the regents approved establishing a master's degree program in Hawaiian language and literature, the first in the nation.)

As UHH in 1995 began its twenty-fifth year as a college, it could look back at a full cycle of development, from a struggling two-year liberal arts branch of UH-Manoa into a four-year college, giving it major status within the UH system. It had fulfilled expectations of its supporters by providing an opportunity for higher education, alternative to Manoa, which emphasized the liberal arts, education, and agricultural and extension programs, with vocational and semiprofessional offerings for those seeking such training.

That history, rife with debate and struggle for more autonomy, well demonstrated the tensions in which a statewide university, dependent in large part on the support of the state government, must operate. Local needs and sensitivities, as those of the Neighbor Islands, were shown to be highly relevant to the success of the University's development. Hawaii politics, reflecting such needs, strongly shapes the institution.

19

THE UNIVERSITY OF HAWAI‘I–WEST O‘AHU

Daniel B. Boylan

THE UNIVERSITY STRAINED under the mounting demands of poststatehood Hawaii. With the main campus at Manoa already overcrowded, by the mid-1960s the wave of students seeking higher education forced UH administrators and downtown political leaders to consider the need for both a community college system and a second four-year campus. In 1966 the legislature funded a study to determine the feasibility of a four-year liberal arts college in Leeward Oahu. In the same year, UH *Academic Development Plan I* called for a second baccalaureate-granting campus on the island. After approval by the Manoa Faculty Senate, the Council of Deans, and President Thomas Hamilton, the Board of Regents accepted the proposal.[1]

West Oahu College was the result, but it took a decade for the school to open its borrowed doors. Arguably, no college ever began under more trying circumstances. In January 1976, would-be students coming to register for classes were met by a line of placard-carrying, leaflet-passing protesters from the environmental organization Life of the Land. Also on the picket line was a member of the state House of Representatives (and future U.S. congressman), Neil Abercrombie.

The opponents of the nascent college condemned it as yet another developer's rip-off, a ploy for rezoning the agricultural Leeward plain for commercial and residential development. Abercrombie, whose election district included the Manoa campus, led the opposition. In response to a *Honolulu Advertiser* article on the school, he characterized the "so-called West Oahu College" as an "academic fraud designed to be the lead dog on the development sled of Campbell Estate."[2]

Perhaps it was, but for UH professor and administrator Richard Kosaki, who became the first chancellor of West Oahu College (WOC) in 1973, the motives were mixed. "I accepted it on the proviso that the land issue was settled," he remembered a decade later. "President Harlan Cleveland assured me that it was." Kosaki's political mentor opposed a second campus on Oahu. "Governor Burns wanted a residential college; he'd sent his own kids to small colleges on the mainland. But he really wanted a college at Kamuela," Kosaki said. "He loved that coast of the Big Island and he thought Waimea would make a beautiful place to put a campus."[3]

The site issue had become complicated by the development of the Hilo campus into a four-year college in 1969. Hilo business and political leaders had long sought a full college for the state's second-largest city. Governor Burns, seeking reelection in 1966, endorsed the plan. In a speech at Hilo he said, according to longtime supporter Hiroshi "Scrub" Tanaka, "'Within my jurisdiction and power, in the next term I will work for a four-year college.' So . . . I knew we were going to get a four-year college because the man will never fail his statement."[4]

Hilo's four-year campus further complicated the issue for Oahu. "I wanted the second Oahu campus for its educational values," Kosaki said. "Manoa had grown too large. I envisioned a residential college with large senior classes and small freshman classes, the opposite of research institutions. But West Oahu got swallowed up in land and education politics."[5]

That it did. Every other campus within the University system, each feeling the economic pinch of the 1970s, expressed displeasure with talk of establishing a new one. *Ka Leo,* the Manoa student newspaper, spoke out against the proposed college. So did the Manoa Faculty Senate.

In the fall of 1975, Kosaki resigned the chancellorship. President Fujio Matsuda replaced him with the provost of Leeward Community College, Ralph Miwa. Miwa, a political scientist and former dean of the University's College of Continuing Education, would guide West Oahu for the next eleven years. A former aide to U.S. Senator Daniel Inouye, he was well connected politically and lobbied hard at the state legislature for West Oahu College.

In the spring of 1976, the embattled school and its full-time faculty of four began their nomadic first semester. For want of a site, classes were held at night and on weekends at three high schools: Campbell in Ewa Beach, Mililani, and Pearl City. Faculty members had neither office space nor secretarial help. Most taught four upper-division classes, with four different preparations. Often they were courses they had never taught before. Classes were small, sometimes comically so. One professor met his only student in a United States history course at McDonald's in Mililani. Faculty worked out of the trunks of their cars. The school's tiny administrative staff worked in a corner of the University System Planning Office far off in Manoa.

In the fall of 1976, West Oahu College entered leased space in the recently constructed Newtown Square Office Building in Aiea. It shared the building with chiropractors and optometrists, a few restaurants and a liquor store, a Straub Medical Center outreach facility, and a massage parlor. The college librarian crammed her growing collection into two of the eight rooms rented by WOC; the nine faculty members crowded their books, filing cabinets, desks, chairs, and selves into another. Three rooms provided teaching space for courses in business and public administration, history, English, philosophy, psychology, sociology, political science, economics, and anthropology. Enrollment doubled to 140 students, and in the spring of 1977 WOC graduated its first class—of seven.

From its inception, West Oahu considered routine what the rest of academe was coming to identify as the "nontraditional" student: older, working, usually interested in a practical education. The mean age in 1982 was 35.2 years; by 1992 it had fallen slightly to 33. In the latter year, more than two-thirds of the college's students were attending classes part-time.

A shift in gender makeup took place. Early in WOC's brief history, men, many of them using their Vietnam-era GI Bill benefits, composed more than half of the enrollment. By the 1990s, however, women were outnumbering them; in the fall of 1992 almost two-thirds of the students were females. More often than not, they were young mothers whose children had finally entered school, giving them time to resume the education they had interrupted to begin a family.

Despite using information booths at shopping centers, community carnivals, college fairs, and community colleges, manned by faculty, staff, and students, the new school suffered from underexposure. Few understood it; no one seemed to recognize it as a campus of the University of Hawai'i. To the mention of "West Oahu College," listeners would too often reply, "What's that?"

The college's first four years were unstable indeed. In 1978 Governor George Ariyoshi refused to approve building a campus on the two hundred acres of prime agricultural land in Leeward Oahu selected for the school. There was opposition within the University. The head of the Manoa Faculty Senate testified before the Ways and Means Committee of the state Senate that UH should shut down both West Oahu and Windward Community College, the newest campus of the community college system, to save money.

Three events in 1981 strengthened the position of WOC. First, it moved to a better academic neighborhood. The University provided West O'ahu with temporary quarters in two portable buildings on the Leeward Community College campus. Administrative offices filled one, faculty offices the other. Leeward lent space in its library and classrooms (grudgingly on the part of some Leeward faculty members). Close proximity to Leeward had an immediate effect: enrollment increased to 370 juniors and seniors.

That fall West Oahu also initiated its first outreach degree program—on Kauai. It was an immediate success. Courses, primarily in public and business administration, were offered on Friday nights and Saturdays for five weeks (later extended to six). Kaua'i Community College provided the classrooms, to which one or more West Oahu faculty members came. In 1986 WOC faculty also began spending

In 1977 West Oahu College rented eight rooms in an Aiea office building and moved into temporary buildings on the Leeward Community College campus in 1981.

long weekends teaching on Maui, where the outreach program proved equally successful.

Perhaps the most significant development of 1981 was the granting of accreditation by the Western Association of Schools and Colleges. During the previous five years, visiting accreditation teams had hesitated, citing insufficient library holdings or poor facilities as evidence of a lack of commitment on the part of the University to West Oahu College. In 1981, however, they finally conceded that the commitment existed.

But members of the Board of Regents and budget-conscious state legislators criticized having a full-time, generously paid (by academic standards) chancellor for such a miniscule school. In 1984 the board eliminated the West Oahu chancellorship, giving responsibility for the college to the chancellor of the University of Hawai'i at Hilo. The move may have made economic sense, but it deprived West Oahu of a full-time advocate during the time of good financial support that the University enjoyed in the late 1980s.

Despite West Oahu's bare-bones facilities—rented office space, temporary buildings, borrowed classrooms—its students seemed to think they were getting their money's worth. They valued the smallness of the school and its emphasis on undergraduate education. Said business administration major Hale Freitas in 1987: "They really want to educate you here. You're someone. . . . At UH [Manoa] you're a social security number, or row three, seat three."[6]

By West Oahu's tenth anniversary in 1986, enrollment, still limited to juniors and seniors, had risen to 480. The number of full-time faculty members, however, remained at fewer than a dozen. That anniversary year saw the appointment of Edward Kormondy, a seasoned university administrator from California, to the dual chancellorship of the Hilo and West Oahu campuses.

By 1989 it had become apparent that Leeward-area real estate developers had not needed the building of a college campus to stimulate growth and a consequent boom in land values. The prime agricultural land that Governor Ariyoshi had attempted to save from urban development was fast disappearing. Campbell Estate's "second city" of Kapolei was taking shape on the Leeward plain, replacing the sugarcane grown there for most of a century. Housing developments stretched from Mililani to Ewa Beach. Zero-lot zoning and massive new shopping centers were turning Leeward and Central Oahu into the fastest growing region in Hawaii—just as the early planning documents for the college had predicted. By 1990 more than 320,000 people resided in the West Oahu area, with a projected population of 420,000 by 2010.

The boom was a reality recognized even by the *Honolulu Advertiser,* long the most vocal editorial critic of the college. In a March 1989 editorial, the newspaper endorsed the decision of UH President Albert Simone to begin the search for a campus site, citing population growth in Ewa's "second city," traffic congestion on the freeway to Manoa, as well as the need for "nontraditional" programs as reasons for creating a West Oahu campus.

The Board of Regents responded by approving a plan prepared by Richard and Mildred Kosaki to expand West Oahu to include freshmen and sophomores. It called for a campus on three hundred to five hundred acres near Kapolei to include student dormitories and housing for both West Oahu and Manoa faculty. The emphasis on undergraduate teaching would continue. The regents also acted to clear up the long-standing uncertainty about whether West Oahu College had anything to do with the University; they renamed the school the University of Hawai'i-West O'ahu.

As the 1990s began, the future of the University of Hawai'i-West O'ahu looked promising. In anticipation of expanding to four years, the full-time faculty doubled, including the addition of a biologist to plan the natural-science curriculum the expanded program would require. In the fall of 1993, a committee of the regents held hearings on seven proposed campus sites. In December they announced their choice: a five-hundred-acre parcel of Campbell Estate land *makai* of the H-1 freeway near Kapolei. The following March, Governor John Waihee transferred the land to UH.

Eight months later, Hawaii's voters elected a new governor. Ben Cayetano launched his administration by announcing that the state faced the worst fiscal crisis in its thirty-five-year history. He directed that all state agencies, including the University, take deep cuts in their budgets. Further, Cayetano discovered that he disapproved of the land deal struck between the Waihee administration and the Campbell Estate. In the summer of 1995, he and members of his administration, notably the budget director and attorney general, began negotiations with the estate. They took on added urgency because the fledgling campus faced an accreditation visit that fall, and in previous reports the Western Association of Schools and Colleges had warned of pulling accreditation of the campus if the University did not make progress on providing it a site and adequate facilities.

At year's end, Cayetano announced a new agreement. The University of Hawai'i-West O'ahu would be built on 910 acres of Campbell hillside property *mauka* of the freeway near Makakilo, obtained in exchange for the state-owned Hawaii Raceway Park, a fifty-nine-acre parcel at Campbell Industrial Park. The state would sell the originally chosen five-hundred-acre-acre site for housing development. According to Cayetano, the sale would net $130 million with which to build the new campus.[7]

Although many observers praised the governor for his second-campus initiative, most questioned where, in the midst of the budget crisis, funds would come from to launch and operate a new campus. These questions persisted throughout the 1996 session of the state legislature. Ultimately, the legislature approved the land exchange, including a requirement that the University build the campus by 2011—allowing plenty of time, it was assumed, for the state's fiscal condition to improve. The legislature also appropriated $3.2 million to move nineteen portable buildings from Kapi'olani Community College to the Leeward Community College campus, which was to continue as the home of the University of Hawai'i-West O'ahu for the foreseeable future. University officials felt that the land exchange plus the expanded, if temporary, facilities, would satisfy the accrediting agency.[8]

But the college's future remained clouded. While the campus enjoyed the support of UH President Kenneth Mortimer, Governor Cayetano, the legislature, the editorial pages of both Honolulu daily newspapers, and an exploding Leeward Oahu population, it continued to face often bitter opposition from faculty, staff, and students at its financially strapped sister institutions in the University system. After two decades of operation and educating more than twelve hundred graduates, it still appeared that the University of Hawai'i-West O'ahu might be "swallowed up by educational politics."

20

THE COMMUNITY COLLEGES

Robert R. Fearrien and Ruth Lucas

HAWAII WAS LATE in beginning a system of community colleges, doing so only in 1964, when three-fourth of the states already had them in operation. The national community college movement began just after World War II, stimulated largely by the Veterans Re-adjustment Act of 1944—the GI Bill of Rights—which provided financial support for veterans resuming their interrupted schooling. President Truman's 1946 letter of appointment to the Commission on Higher Education called for

> opening of the doors of higher education to members of society who, throughout American history, had lingered on the periphery of the American dream for all: members of lower socioeconomic groups, blacks, women, working adults, and other segments of society.[1]

The commission proposed the establishment of community colleges readily available at minimal cost to the student.

ESTABLISHING THE UH COMMUNITY COLLEGES

Inspiration for establishing Hawaii's community colleges was derived from several academic studies, especially Teruo Ihara's 1959 Ph.D. dissertation. Ihara, a UH professor, was a stalwart of the Democratic Party and a close friend of its leader, John Burns. In 1961 the legislature authorized a study of the "Organization, relationships, and development planning of the University of Hawaii." Burns arranged for the U.S. Office of Education to do the work under the direction of S. V. Martorana. The report, published in November 1962, strongly recommended establishing six community colleges under UH. Offering "programs of general studies, freshman and sophomore level arts and sciences and occupational curriculums of up to 2 years of formal study," they would be created by improving and expanding Honolulu, Maui, and Kauai Technical Schools, moving Kapiolani Technical School to the Waipahu-Wahiawa area of central Oahu, combining the Hawaii Technical School with the Hilo branch of the University, and establishing a new community college in windward Oahu.[2]

Ihara, political science professor Richard Kosaki, and others discussed the concept of community colleges with gubernatorial candidate Burns during his 1962 campaign. Burns strongly favored the idea, and the Hawaii Democratic Party platform called for creating the colleges. Legislators overwhelmingly supported the proposal, but it was opposed by many administrators in the state Department of Education (DOE) and by teachers in its technical schools, who feared losing those schools to a college system. Opposition was also voiced by former UH Vice-President K. C. Leebrick, who headed the private Mauna Olu College on Maui, and by Big Island advocates of a four-year UH campus at Hilo, who thought a community college there would stymie that plan. Although there was no organized opposition from the University, some professors were skeptical about the academic standards of community colleges, from which students could transfer to the Manoa campus.

Three bills were introduced in the 1963 legislative session calling for community colleges on Kauai and windward and leeward Oahu. None came to a vote. Instead, the House by Resolution 245 asked the University to "develop plans for implementing a statewide community college system" and to make recommendations prior to the 1964 session. Fifty thousand dollars was appropriated, and UH President Thomas Hamilton asked Richard Kosaki to make the study. Kosaki reported that many high school graduates wished to continue their education but lacked the money. Only a fifth of them immediately entered UH. More than two-thirds of the 1964 senior class indicated that they would consider enrolling in a public two-year college if given the opportunity.[3]

Kosaki recommended that the technical schools be transferred to UH; they be expanded as community colleges offering curricula that included both college-transfer and vocational education, as well as community service and general education courses; they maintain an "open-door" policy, admitting all high school graduates and adults over eighteen years of age, who would be served by counseling and guidance services. At that time the technical schools made no charge and UH tuition was $170 per year. Kosaki proposed that annual tuition initially be set at $130 and, as a general rule, should not exceed 80 percent of Manoa's fee.[4]

A suggested timetable had Hawaii Technical School merged with the UH Hilo campus to form a community college offering classes as early as 1965. Kapiolani Technical School would be converted to a community college in 1965, followed by Honolulu and Maui in 1966, and a new campus opened in leeward Oahu in 1967. The feasibility of a college in windward Oahu was to be studied further.

Citing lack of interest among Kauai high school seniors, Kosaki recommended that Kauai Technical School be transferred administratively to the community college system but "retain its present designation" until a rise in student interest justified creating a community college. Kauai legislators, however, succeeded in having Kauai Tech included in the enabling legislation. House Bill 257, introduced by twenty-eight of the forty Democratic representatives, was approved on March 21, 1964, by a vote of forty-three to four. The Senate concurred a week later, and Burns signed the bill as Act 39 on April 23. It authorized the regents "to create community colleges [except on the island of Hawaii] and to provide for the inclusion of the technical schools of the department of education in such community colleges."

Protests from Hawaii business leaders, Hilo campus faculty members, and Big Island legislators had led to the exclusion of Hawaii Technical School. Its transfer was not authorized until 1969, when it was joined with Hilo College to become the University of Hawai'i at Hilo. In 1990, Hawai'i Community College was separated administratively from UH at Hilo and included in the community college system.

Act 39 made explicit the broad scope and multiple missions of the community colleges:

> The purposes of community colleges shall be to provide two-year college transfer and general education programs, semi-professional, technical, vocational, and continuing education programs, and such other educational programs and services as are appropriate to such institutions.

After initially proposing that local residents pay no tuition fees, the legislature allowed the regents to set rates for all students, which were put at $25 a semester. Although there were increases over the years, community college tuition fees were maintained at less than a third of those charged at Manoa.

The schools thus created were unique in several ways. Perhaps most important psychologically was that they were "community colleges" at a time when their mainland counterparts were still generally called "junior colleges." Another departure was the inclusion of the colleges within the University. In other states, similar schools were separate from the state university, many under county boards of education. Finally, the multipurpose curriculum serving community interests in Hawaii was from the onset exceptionally broad.

STARTING UP

The early history of Hawaii's community colleges was dominated by dealing with problems arising from the conversion of the technical schools to colleges. They had operated with high school courses, policies, and practices; as they converted, misunderstanding and miscommunication troubled both vocational and liberal arts facul-

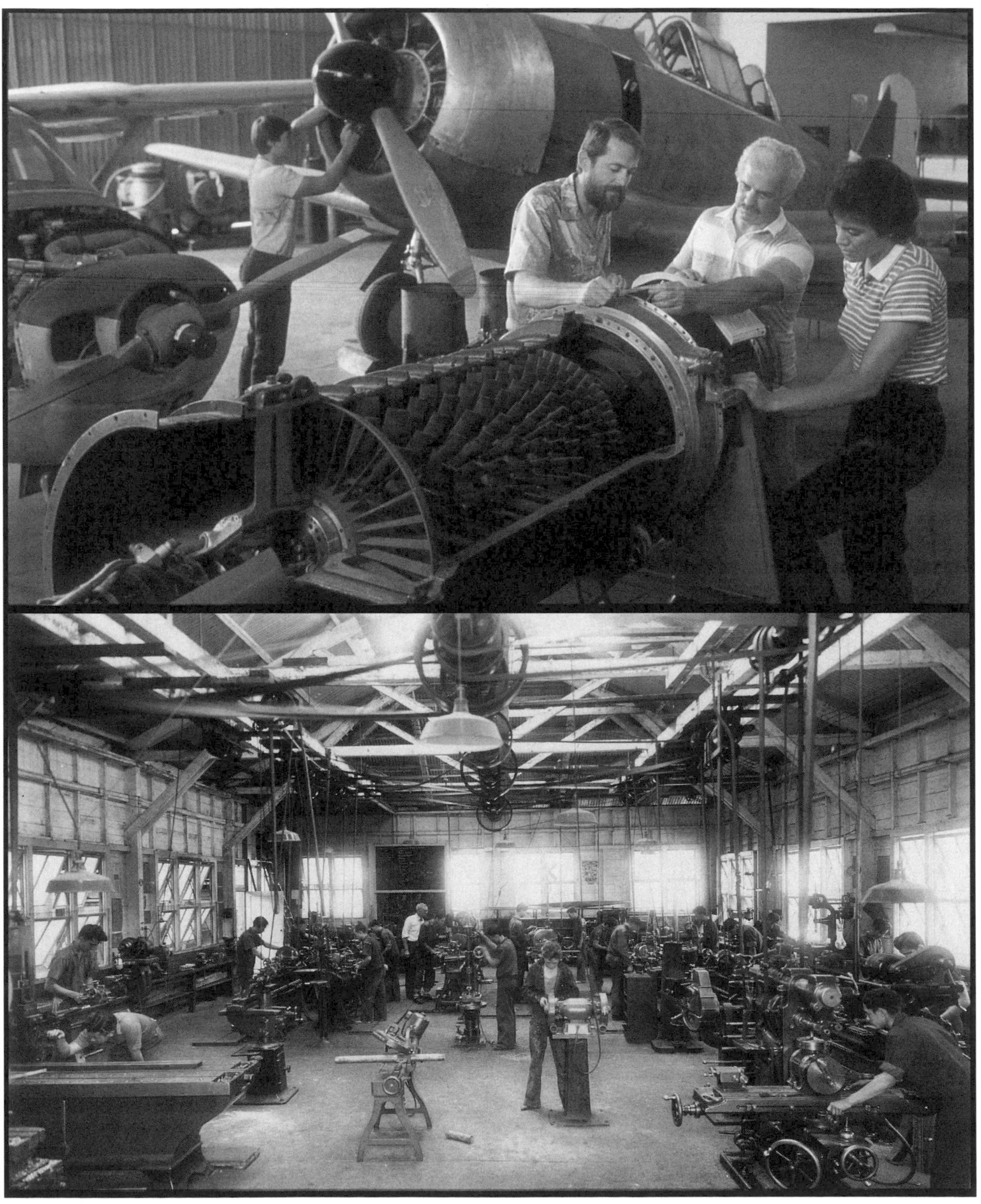

The 1938 machine shop of the Honolulu Technical School looks primitive compared with the contemporary aeronautics classroom of the college.

ties for several years. Faculty work hours, titles, roles in school governance, and expectations of and attitudes toward students vexed the new colleges.

Curricula had to change. The mission of the technical schools had been to provide vocational training. Their programs reflected job opportunities in mid-century Hawaii, such as in business education, carpentry, machine shop, electricity, drafting, welding, food services, cafeteria management, cosmetology, and commercial sewing. Courses in math and science, English, history, and other liberal arts subjects had to be added for graduates planning to go on to a university.

Creating community colleges from these technical schools also meant radical shifts in attitudes toward students and faculty. The tech school day had been 7:30 A.M. to 3:30 P.M., with both students and faculty members required to punch time clocks. Students were subjected to rigid discipline, including a strict dress code. For example, boys at the Hilo Technical School wore khaki shirts tucked in their trousers; girls had to wear dresses, stockings, and shoes with heels. This all changed quickly after conversion. Former technical school teachers had to accept that they were no longer teaching "kids," but "students." Bathroom doors that bore the words "Girls" and "Boys" were repainted "Ladies" and "Gentlemen."

Teachers accustomed to the culture of technical schools and those now recruited with liberal arts backgrounds had to learn to work with each other. Technical school faculty members without graduate degrees were apprehensive. Kosaki tried to persuade them that degrees were not necessary in all fields. "It was effective and updated teaching that we wanted and, in fact, we initially asked that they work more closely with the industries they were training students for."[5]

Qualifications of the vocational teachers did not fit the UH system of rank and salaries based on academic degrees. In order to retain well-qualified vocational instructors, local trade unions agreed to pay the differential between the salaries the vo-tech faculty members had been earning and what they received in contracts with the University.

Choosing titles for community college administrators and faculty members was a thorny task. Since "principal" was no longer appropriate in a college setting, the new title for the chief campus administrator was "provost," with deans for academic and student affairs. The three-step ranks of professorships used by universities was initially considered too elitist for the egalitarian philosophy of some of the colleges. In 1967 the regents decided that continuing to use the title of "instructor" exclusively would not preclude hiring faculty members with doctorates, as Kaua'i Community College already had done. This nomenclature was changed in 1992, however, when community college faculty members were given professorial titles.

Some technical school faculty resented the introduction of liberal arts faculty members who dressed casually, took up already limited classroom and office space, and lent strident voice to campus decision making—to which the vo-tech teachers were unaccustomed. Sometimes relationships between the two faculties were soured by the fact that different kinds of courses were held in different buildings. On Maui, the older technical school buildings were downhill from the newer liberal arts buildings and library, giving rise to the terms "lower campus" and "upper campus," with a not-so-subtly implied distinction in status. Kapiolani liberal arts faculty members resented having to teach in stuffy portables while business and food services classes were taught in air-conditioned comfort.

Former technical school teachers had to alter their views of themselves. Guy Fujiuchi, a faculty member at Kauai and later its dean of students, described how he and his colleagues felt:

> We were pretty ignorant about what community colleges were. You can imagine how the trade guys felt. We were scared of what would happen. Could we do what we were going to do? What would we be doing? What would be expected of us? There was a lot of apprehension. How do we find out? Who can help?[6]

To stimulate career development of the community college faculties, the University received a federal grant for "developing institutions." It was used to send faculty members to observe and receive training at community colleges in California. An outstanding exemplar of faculty development during the transition was Samson Shigetomi, an electronics instructor who became provost of Honolulu Community College, earned an Ed.D. from UCLA, and returned to serve as state director for vocational education.

Emphasis on quality was promoted with awards for excellence in teaching, begun in 1972. Technical faculty members were encouraged to take courses offered at Manoa and by visiting specialists on educational methodology, course preparation, presentation and evaluation, and the general nature of community colleges. Many faculty members earned advanced degrees that improved both skills and self-image. According to Fujiuchi, the result was a growth in self-confidence, a clarification of purpose, and realization that "We were doing the right thing already."

A 1967 regents' report stated, "An important educational concept [is] the idea of intermingling the technical, liberal arts and general students."[7] Intermingling of the staff was equally important. Liberal arts faculty members and administrators brought from the mainland and the University at Manoa, some with doctorates, had to be assimilated. One approach was placing offices and classrooms so that vo-tech instructors and classes would be next door to liberal arts instructors and their classes. Efforts were made to equalize roles in campus governance, to guard against discrimination in program support or new building construction, and to provide opportunity for faculty members of both groups to work together. These attempts were variously successful. Social events to which all faculty members were invited helped smooth faculty interaction, although isolated instances of personal differences and charges of "elitism" against liberal arts faculty remained.

Then there was the problem of translating the number of laboratory hours, which had defined technical school course requirements, into college credit hours. Neither students nor faculty were easily convinced that instruction in daily eight-hour classes could be equated with credits earned in classes that met three days a week for fewer hours. Kosaki attended some vocational classes and helped instructors separate "lecture" time from "shop" time, providing a more flexible schedule. A national expert helped prepare a guide to curriculum development.

The transition took time. Although the formal transfer of the technical schools to the UH system was made in 1965, college transfer courses were not taught at Maui and Kauai until 1967 and a year later at Honolulu and Kapiolani. Leeward Community College opened in improvised classrooms in 1968 and Windward Community College in 1972.

GAINING ACCEPTANCE; HELPFUL GRADS

Initially, the concept of community college education was not widely understood. Kosaki and others gave many explanatory speeches to business, labor, and community organizations. For years, many citizens continued to refer to the colleges as "Kapiolani Tech" and "Honolulu Tech." But gradually, "the idea took hold (especially when the Leeward campus made its imposing physical appearance), and the student enrollments quickly surpassed our projections." As students graduated, got jobs, demonstrated their capability, told others of the success of their education, and occasionally rose to prominence, their colleges became more respected by the community. Kosaki further commented:

> When wedding announcements in the newspapers started to regularly mention that the bride or groom was a graduate not only of X high school but also of Y Community College, I interpreted that to mean that the community colleges were accepted as respectable.[8]

A factor in this acceptance was the wide spectrum of community college students being served. Demographic studies of registrations revealed that, compared with Manoa, the community colleges were ethnically more representative of Hawaii's population, especially in the larger proportions of Hawaiian and Filipino students. Also, the average age was higher than that at Manoa. Although Honolulu Community College, with its emphasis on the trade and technical vocations, remained predominantly male, overall the colleges enrolled more women than men. Most community college students were fully or partially employed.

Students were not alone in promoting good public relations. Faculty members and administrators devoted hours to community service and lent effective support at legislative hearings. In addition, people from the community were invited to campuses for conferences and as classroom speakers and participants in public forums. Most important in spreading the word about the new college opportunities were students in short-term, noncredit classes. For example, while about 26,000 students were enrolled in credit classes in 1993, more than 107,000 participated in community college noncredit activities.

While striving for public acceptance, the community colleges also needed academic recognition, and the process of getting it stimulated their development. In 1970 and again in 1972, visiting accreditation teams from the Western Association of Schools and Colleges (WASC) made reports that highlighted problems and successes of the colleges. These reports, often critical of the physical facilities, provided leverage for colleges to lobby with the University administration and the legislature for funds needed to improve their campuses and resources.

Honolulu Community College's campus was described as "dingy" and "down-at-the-heels," and the 1970 WASC visiting team criticized its frequently changing administration. Faculty members told the team that they referred to their chief administrators as "Provost of the Month" and "Vanishing Dean." Inspectors were appalled to discover no schedule existed for replacing vocational training equipment vital to technical programs. They also criticized the college's reliance on trade unions for financial assistance. At Kapiolani, the team reported "a wide range in quality of instruction." Except for the business education and food services buildings, facilities at the old Pensacola Street campus were termed "totally inadequate." At Maui, the team found "a residue of sentiment among the vocational-technical staff that glamorized the 'good old days' of the technical school."[9]

Nor did the system's central administration escape criticism. A WASC team faulted it for devoting more resources to researching college operations than to providing leadership to the campuses. Both WASC teams recommended that only the vice-president for community colleges, and not the several provosts, report directly to the UH president, to be a "consistent advocate" for the colleges. Years were needed to work out a satisfactory administrative connection between the colleges and the central administration.

NEW AND BETTER CAMPUSES

A 1970 policy statement of the Board of Regents envisioned an ambitious future for the community colleges:

> The goals of the community colleges of the University of Hawaii are comprehensive programs, low tuition, open-door admission, education guidance, quality teaching and responsiveness to the community which each college serves.[10]

Reaching those goals required major work in campus development. The older campuses had a long way to go to become efficient and physically appealing. In the movie images of the time, Kosaki called run-down Honolulu Community College "Phyllis Diller before the face lift" and crowded Kapiolani on its cramped Pensacola Street site "Brigitte Bardot in Twiggy's clothing." The new Leeward campus, however, was "Elizabeth Taylor."[11] Under criticism by the WASC accrediting teams and demands by college students, faculties, and administrators, the legislature appropriated funds to build the facilities already planned for by the University. Following Leeward, new campuses for Kauai and Kapiolani arose. At Honolulu, Maui, Windward, and Hawaii colleges, existing buildings were renovated and new ones constructed. With these efforts, the colleges remarkably improved their appearance and attractiveness to students.

VARYING ADMINISTRATIVE LEADERSHIP

Differences between college administrators and faculties on the one hand and the UH central administration on the other were sometimes vexatious. From the beginning, college system administrators were located at Manoa, some authority coming from Bachman Hall and some from the college system offices nearby on Dole Street. Richard Kosaki served as vice-president for the community colleges during their formation into a system, until September 1969. He was succeeded by Harold Masumoto as interim director until Brett Melendy was named vice-president in 1970. The next year, President Harlan Cleveland issued a reorganization plan for the University in which college provosts reported directly to Stuart M. Brown, vice-president for academic affairs. Melendy complained that this reduced his authority to that of a staff person rather than a line administrator with decision-making power. Melendy championed comprehensive curricula for the colleges while Brown wanted them to concentrate on preparing lower division students for the four-year campuses. Abolition of a regents' Committee on Community Colleges removed Melendy from official participation in the board's meetings, leading to his stormy resignation in May 1973. Brown won the battle, but Melendy's approach later characterized the system's development.

For the next two years "strong provosts" reported directly to the president, each college operating somewhat independently under general policies set by the regents and the central administration. In 1975, however, President Fujio Matsuda reorganized the University to include a chancellor for community colleges, appointing education professor Shiro Amioka to the post. Long associate dean of the UH Summer Session and protégé of Dean Shunzo Sakamaki, Amioka was often referred to as the "Kakaako samurai." He had strong opinions on academic matters, tending to run roughshod over those who disagreed with him. This attitude had created problems when he was state superintendent of schools from 1971 to 1974 and soon got him into contention with the community college faculties.

Before Amioka, the central administration of the community college system had been primarily concerned with personnel management, planning, budgeting, and legislative reporting. Amioka decided to include oversight of academic affairs, but the colleges were determined to retain their individual authority. When he eliminated teaching-load reductions for Faculty Senate chairpersons on each campus, justified to allow them time to discharge their senate responsibilities, he encountered strong opposition. Several college Faculty Senates resolved they had "no confidence" in Amioka. The controversy led to his resignation in 1977.

Amioka was succeeded by Manoa mathematician Edwin Mookini, who was also somewhat authoritarian but in a less confrontational style, reflecting his Hawaiian culture. Unfortunately for the fulfillment of his vision for the colleges, Mookini died in 1979 before he had time greatly to influence their development.

Dewey Kim, who had filled a number of administrative roles in the University, then became chancellor and served until retirement in July 1983. Kim encouraged staff development and administrative internship programs, leading to the selection of faculty and staff members for administrative positions within the system. During his administration, new procedures for appointing administrators and faculty members helped end political interference from within as well as without the University. Adept in politics and public relations, Kim was largely responsible for the acquisition of the land and legislative permission to create the Diamond Head campus of Kapi'olani Community College.

In August 1983, Joyce Tsunoda, the first director of the system to be chosen from the ranks of the community college faculties, was named chancellor. In 1990 to that title was added senior vice-president in the University's central administration, giving the community college system an enhanced role in University-wide governance.

Another reorganization plan under President Albert Simone in 1985 gave more control to the chancellor and less to the UH vice-president for academic affairs. In turn, Chancellor Tsunoda delegated more responsibility to the provosts, deans, department chairs, and faculties. Although faculty senates already had recommending authority in matters of curriculum, academic policies, and faculty-student relations, such recommendations became more effective under Tsunoda. A Council of Provosts, meeting with the chancellor and her staff, coordinated intercollege relationships.

WORKING AS A SYSTEM

From time to time community college faculties and supporters continued to complain of being treated as stepchildren in comparison to the favoritism shown Manoa. There was pressure on legislators to separate the community colleges from the UH, but those efforts never succeeded. Under the UH umbrella, the colleges kept their individuality and a measure of autonomy, each with its own academic program, personality, style, and techniques of accommodation to the community.

Relationships between the community colleges and the four-year campuses of the University, as in transferring student credits, had to be worked out. Differing concepts and practices in grading led Manoa faculty members to assume that the community colleges were too lenient. Some of the colleges did have grading systems that omitted failing grades. Others for a time tried using letter designations that were not easily defined, such as Leeward's Q, given to students who, despite an honest effort, failed to pass. Consequently, at first the Manoa campus accepted community college credits but not the grades.

Then the equivalency of courses with similar titles and numbers taught throughout the UH system had to be worked out. Mike Rota, director of academic affairs for the community colleges, led negotiations for an agreement among the ten campuses of the University by which common courses would be articulated. A council representative of all campuses was established to coordinate the discipline-level committees that reviewed courses. Cooperation among campuses grew with opportunities for all faculties to discuss such defining issues as the UH graduation requirements. As more community college faculty members took graduate courses at Manoa and participated in faculty union activities, personal contacts among faculties of the various campuses grew, leading to increased recognition of the community colleges and their place in the state's system of higher education.

In another form of intercampus cooperation, Kaua'i and Maui Community Colleges for more than twenty years have provided facilities, equipment, advertising, and registration for upper-division and graduate extension courses offered by UH-Mānoa and West Oahu College to residents of those islands.

The most convincing evidence of articulation into a system, however, came with the success of students who transferred from the community colleges to Manoa. By 1989, fully a fourth of the juniors and seniors at Manoa were community college transfers, and their gradepoint average at graduation was not significantly different from those who began at Manoa as freshmen. Many graduated with honors. Conversely, many Manoa students, some with bachelor's degrees, transferred to the community colleges for vocational programs. The system was working for its students.

A RECORD OF GROWTH AND CHANGE

Commemorating the silver anniversary of the establishment of community colleges in Hawaii, the *Honolulu Advertiser* editorialized in 1989:

> With their easy accessibility to all comers, low-cost, nurturing attitudes, academic flexibility, and wide-ranging mission, the community colleges are one of the proudest legacies of Hawaii's social reform and growth in the last four decades.[12]

In those twenty-five years, the percentage growth in enrollment of the colleges far exceeded the state's increase in population. From its small beginning, community college enrollment became a major portion of the University's aggregate student body, in the 1990s well exceeding that of the Manoa campus.

Transformation from technical schools to comprehensive community colleges was reflected in the growing number of students selecting liberal arts majors. In the fall of 1968, for the entire system 3,100 students were enrolled in vocational programs and only 1,855 in liberal arts, but by 1993 the percentages were virtually reversed, with 8,199 in vocational programs compared with 14,258 in liberal arts. Of the total University enrollment in lower-division arts and sciences (students on a path leading to a baccalaureate degree), 72 percent were in the community colleges.

Within the vocational fields, major changes occurred in response to the job market. From an initial emphasis on agriculture and the construction trades, there was a steady shift to emerging technological fields and service industries. Health-related programs, food services, computer technology, tourism courses, leisure specialist training, and other emerging vocational fields were added, while some of the older craft and trade curricula were dropped.

Small classes under a faculty committed to teaching rather than research provided an effective alternative to traditional college education. The campuses attracted many nontraditional students. One of them, a Leeward Community College graduate, made the case for the community colleges in personal terms:

> As far as community college in my case, it was just the thing. I quit high school in the eleventh grade. . . . I broke my parents' heart. I really lacked self-confidence. Starting in community college built up my confidence. There was such an air of excitement. I forgot I was an old lady in the school. I thought I was a kid. The atmosphere was persuasive.[13]

The seven campuses of the community college system share this common history of struggle and achievement. Each, however, has its unique story of creation and growth. These are presented here necessarily without the scope that only a much larger volume would make possible, but they provide insight into the personality and development of each college.

Honolulu Community College

THE SCHOOL that is now Honolulu Community College is the oldest within the system. Opened in 1920 as the first of the technical schools under the territorial Department of Public Instruction (DPI), it was first located at Palama Settlement and was briefly at McKinley High School before moving to its present campus in Kalihi-Palama, acreage once used as a Chinese cemetery.[14] Its mission and curriculum always closely related to the community it serves, a neighborhood of blue-collar workers and immigrants, it offered trade-technical education, notably programs in automotive repair, carpentry, welding, cosmetology, and commercial baking that qualified its graduates for employment.

A boarding school in its earliest days, the administration strictly regulated behavior. All shop students had to keep their hair cut short and wear uniforms "so trouble-makers could be spotted." Only the electric shop students rebelled, wearing what they chose. But "if anybody did anything immoral, he was out." Little education was offered beyond a basic skills training.[15]

The DPI maintained tight financial reins over its technical schools. The Honolulu Technical School library book budget for the years 1962–1965 totaled $2,761. Only 386 books were purchased in those three years before the school was transferred to the University.[16] Buildings had so seriously deteriorated that the external walls of one were literally propped up. A history of inadequate funding was at the root of many of the problems that the school faced after it became Honolulu Community College.

The college continued the close ties the technical school had formed with the labor unions and the construction industry. Unlike the other community colleges, it was essentially two schools sharing a campus. In daylight, one set of faculty members taught the students enrolled in the vocational and liberal arts programs. At night, a different set of faculty members and students arrived for the apprenticeship training program. In the old administration building (destroyed by fire in 1974), one had to walk outside to get from the offices of the day programs to those of the apprenticeship program, a physical representation of their separation. The combined enrollment of these two sets of students gave the school for a number of years the largest enrollment of the UH community colleges.

Honolulu Technical School principal John Notham oversaw the transition from technical school to college and became its first provost. After his retirement in 1969, he was succeeded by four provosts in a span of four years. The lack of stable leadership and direction resulted in poor intracampus communication and little coherence in curricular planning. Emerging out of the chaotic situation was Clyde Yoshioka, a graduate of the carpentry program, who returned to teach mathematics and blueprint reading, then become dean of instruction, acting provost, and finally, in 1974, provost. Under his leadership, the school reshaped its organization, drawing the apprenticeship program into the college.

Honolulu Community College could rely on labor unions for friendly lobbying of the legislature. In 1970, however, when funding for a much-needed library and classroom building was slashed, other efforts were needed. Students marched on the state capitol with a black coffin symbolizing the death of the college. After this dramatic protest, supported by faculty members, union lobbyists, and sympathetic legislators, the funds were restored. The decrepit campus had a face-lift with the construction of a cosmetology facility in 1972, a new administration building in 1974, and a library and liberal arts classroom building in 1976. Completion of these projects in 1981 was the occasion for Yoshioka's retirement.

Program Development

Under Yoshioka, the college experimented with different curricular approaches. To supplement the associate in arts degree for liberal arts majors and the associate in science for vocational majors, he introduced an associate in general studies degree, awarded to students who chose courses from both vocational and liberal arts areas. Long-standing vocational programs were updated. The college's nationally certified automotive repair program used late-model cars donated by manufacturers, enabling students to become adept in modern auto technology. An important acquisition was an industrial computer, the Programmable Logical Controller, used in a number of automotive classes.[17]

The college had long offered aircraft mechanics training at an aircraft "boneyard" off Honolulu International Airport, using aged and discarded aircraft. Under Provost Peter Kessinger, appointed in 1983, that program obtained newer models for students to learn on. The airframe program was supplemented by advanced training for air traffic controllers and examiners for aircraft stress failures.

With the nearest boat engine repair shop in Seattle, Honolulu Community College met another local need with instruction in boat repair at a facility at Sand Island in Honolulu harbor. The $8.3 million project, on a par with the nation's leading marine facilities, prepared students for jobs in boat repair shops or in their own businesses.[18] The college's computer network, attached to the Internet, offered computer courses for hundreds of senior citizens through an anonymous million-dollar grant made in 1985, shared with Windward Community College and named in honor of UH President Emeritus Fujio Matsuda.

After the addition in 1968 of programs in liberal arts, enrollment shifted from predominantly vocational to a mixture of vocational and liberal arts. While liberal arts faculty members complained that the administration neglected liberal arts and did not provide the Kalihi-Palama neighborhood with artistic outlets such as a campus theatre, they took pride in the number of their students transferring to four-year campuses.[19]

The particular mission of the college, however, remained in vocational education. Helping its polyglot student body to attain rewarding career paths required a variety of approaches. Early on, Honolulu Community College recognized the need for improving students' language skills. Immigrants were offered intensive classes in English as a second language organized around the specific language needs of occupational subjects, incorporating the vocabulary used in vocational manuals, names of tools, the metric system, and so forth. They were trained in preparing résumés and coached in employment interviews. This developmental program, innovative for Hawaii, served as a general model for sister community colleges. Counselors advised students of what was needed in various vocations, encouraging them to try out some of the tasks they would face. College faculty members were offered workshops designed to increase awareness of cultural differences and expectations among students.

At the center of Honolulu, the school's programs attracted students from a wide area. In 1994–1995, 28 percent of its forty-seven hundred students were from its immediate neighborhood of Kalihi-Palama, 22 percent from Leeward Oahu, 11 percent from Windward Oahu, while 10 percent were from other Pacific Basin countries. The college drew heavily from its surrounding immigrant population. Twenty-one percent of the 1991 enrollment was Filipino, the largest ethnic group represented.

With its emphasis on the trades, enrollment remained predominantly male, even though women were actively recruited for traditionally male, trade-tech programs. A campus Physical Fitness Center was available for those needing development of the upper-body strength necessary for automotive and carpentry employment. In 1992, female students still made up only 39 percent of the enrollment, but their increase stimulated creation of a child-care center to accommodate student parents, many of them single mothers. The old Honolulu Technical School had been changed beyond recognition.

Kaua'i Community College

THE FIRST TECHNICAL SCHOOL to be founded on a Neighbor Island was begun in 1928 on the Kauai High School campus near Lihue. The Kauai Technical School (KTS) curriculum reflected the needs of the island's plantation economy. With the mechanization of sugar and the closing out of pineapple, however, Kauai's population declined from forty-five thousand to about twenty-five thousand by the mid-1960s. Many young people sought education and employment elsewhere. Surveys showed that Kauai youth were the least likely to attend a local institution of higher education.

Because standard models of community colleges assumed that a population base of 50,000 was necessary for adequate enrollment, the Kosaki feasibility study recommended against a college for Kauai. However, the politics of creating the community college system required the inclusion of KTS, and indeed in a few years the added enrollment of "hippies" attracted to the island and of a large number of Vietnam War veterans helped justify a new campus.

Where to place the campus readily became a political issue. Three sites were considered—Wailua on the northeast side of the island; central Lihue near the airport; and Puhi, near the population center and county seat at Lihue.[20] State Representative Tony Kunimura approached sugar planter Sam Wilcox of Grove Farm about obtaining a site at Puhi, and Wilcox donated two hundred acres of former sugar land for that purpose. No other community college in Hawaii has such an extensive land area, of which Kaua'i Community College has developed only about seventy acres.

Early Trials and Errors

Kauai's residents, basically rural and conservative, generally approved of the technical school's vocational curriculum and hoped the community college would retain its mission and methods relatively unchanged. These same residents watched with dismay the enrollment of mainland "hippies" whose lifestyle and drug culture presented a threatening intrusion and challenge to accustomed island life.

Into this setting came Mickey McCleery, an Antioch College political scientist, to spend his sabbatical year in 1965–1966. Growing familiar with Kauai's people and problems, he thought to resolve the culture conflict with a new kind of community college, drawing students from the island's scattered towns to join in serving its needs while learning new skills. To his college classmate, newly appointed community college director Richard Kosaki, McCleery sent a prospectus outlining his vision:

> The nature of life and work on this island has sustained a spirit of community in social life which is long lost and desperately sought. . . . This spirit is manifested in the mutual respect, cooperation and friendliness which mark human association here. Properly designed, the college can make this quality of human relationship a foundation for unique experience of learning.[21]

He suggested that the educational approach of the college be designed to encourage young people to remain on Kauai, as well as to attract a diverse student body from elsewhere, both to interact in service to the local population.

> To illustrate this approach, instruction in physics and electronics should examine the problems and employ the equipment of an "Automotive Diagnostic Center" . . . equipped with that use in mind. Students in retail management would be assigned responsibility for operating a school store designed to serve the entire community at a profit. A Community Research Center will give social science students experience in data collection, processing, and analysis. In . . . such programs, students working under faculty supervision will learn to meet the public, perform functions related to the solution of problems, and to understand the rationale of what they do.[22]

This prospectus intrigued Kosaki, and he appointed McCleery dean of instruction, authorized to implement his plan. McCleery arrived with supporting grants and sixteen students from Antioch and Goddard colleges to provide assistance and serve as role models. As well as teaching courses in political science and social research, McCleery directed the mainland students. He also housed and cooked for some of them.

The project was soon beset by problems, including the wreck of the van intended to serve the students in their community outreach; the culture shock and illnesses experienced by the mainlanders; and the intrusions of romantic liaisons into academic work plans. Such misadventures contributed to the collapse of the program. McCleery later wrote an instructive postmortem analysis that was also applicable to the transition then going on at the other former training schools.

> It is clear that a rude influx of outside administrators, faculty, and students in 1967, along with the ouster of the respected initial head of the Tech School-College [Kiyoshi Kubota, longtime principal, who was replaced as provost by UH Professor Walter Steiger], was seen as a threat to the workways and mission of the institution by its faculty, staff, and local employees. . . . The factions that emerged [included] the established faculty [who] took a conservative, inward if not backward looking position, defending their existing vocational curriculum and its students. Those brought in from outside attempted to impose a more academic, theoretical, outward or future oriented position.[23]

McCleery's vision, however, was not totally rejected. Guy Fujiuchi, instructor and administrator at Kauai, recognized as proper and necessary the goal of having a curriculum that served the community. And Dr. Richard Coller, an instructor at the school since 1967—who at first wondered, "How in the world are we going to do all this?"—later agreed that students needed an intercultural emphasis in their education.

The problems inevitable in converting a technical school into a college, intermingling trade school programs and teachers with new liberal arts curricula and faculty, were not always handled with tact. In the early years, relations between administrators and staff were especially discordant. Lawsuits filed against Provost Edward White (1972–1978) by faculty members who felt proper procedures had not been followed in selecting Dorothy Kohashi as dean of instruction, resulted in an injunction against her appointment. Neverless, three years later, even after a selection committee omitted Kohashi from its nominees for the post, White appointed her anyway.

More controversy arose out of White's attempt to fire instructors Jeanne Bunyan and Al Toda. The effect of the unrest was to leave faculty members wary of administrators for some years. (Despite White's controversial tenure, he left $350,000 to the college, designated for student activities, hiring of lecturers, faculty development, and the purchase of library books, all greatly needed.)

Each of the early provosts was appointed with a particular goal in mind: Philip Ige (1970–1972) to achieve accreditation; White to obtain a permanent campus site; Leroy King (1979–1981) to ease out Dorothy Kohashi. All achieved these goals. With the 1982 appointment of David Iha, who had roots and values firmly set in Kauai, the college was stabilized, morale no longer a serious problem, with faculty and staff energies more productively directed. Under Iha, the curriculum was expanded, and the general education and liberal arts courses that supplemented the technical school subjects were gradually adapted to local needs.

Hurricanes

The most drastic force hitting community colleges in Hawaii were the hurricanes that struck Kauai—Iwa in 1982 and Iniki in 1992. Kaua'i Community College sustained heavy damage each time. Iwa filled the flat roof of the library with water, causing its

Kaa La O Kauai (solar powered car) from Kaua'i Community College finishing ninth in a race from Arlington, Texas, to Minneapolis. Of the thirty-four participating colleges and universities, Kauai was the only community college. The University of Michigan winning car cost more than $2 million; *Kaa La* cost only $178,000. It was truly an interdisciplinary project, and Kauai won second place for artistic design and a special award for exemplifying the spirit of Sunrayce in the face of adversity—hurricane Iniki hit the college just as the students were completing the car.

Remains of the Hawaiian Studies Center after the 1992 hurricane. It had been built by faculty, staff, and students just eleven months before the 160 mph winds of Iniki hit the campus.

collapse; damage to books and furnishings was devastating. To save as many books as possible, they were removed to a refrigerated freight container to minimize mold damage. Before they could be reshelved when the library reopened, each volume had to be dried with a vacuum cleaner.

Iniki was much fiercer. In its destructive path, three wooden buildings housing the campus child-care center, the Hawaiian studies program, and the apprenticeship program, were entirely destroyed, and the theatre, then under construction, was severely damaged. The campus served as a shelter for two to three thousand evacuees, many of them tourists. Classes were canceled, and faculty members helped prepare and distribute food. The college reopened within two weeks, but with the loss of some students who chose to continue their educations in some calmer place. It was a month before commercial electric power could be restored to the campus. In the interim, the military brought a huge electric generator from Korea to provide temporary service. Provost Iha praised the "spirit of community among faculty and staff" in the emergency. "Living on a small island you just have to figure out a way to get along."[24] This linkage of effort by campus and island population manifested the community spirit that McCleery had said originally attracted him to Kauai.

Maui Community College

When Maui Technical School was established in 1930, its auto, carpentry, and machine shop programs served a rural island centered on the production of sugar and pineapple. The school got its real start when its first principal, Duncan Sinclair, visited the Maui Pineapple Company machine shop and saw no machines for repairing gears of the Ginaka machines used in pineapple processing. Shopmen were cutting the teeth by hand, and the replacement gears lasted for no more than two weeks. Sinclair said that his students could repair the gears.

> The engineer didn't think we could do it. . . . I suggested he give me a blank and the number of teeth, also a pitch of the chain. I picked it up the next [morning]. We worked on it and were back within two hours with the finished product. When I showed it to the engineer, he was flabbergasted and notified the management. We then got the job of cutting all the gears, 200 of them anywhere from 3″ to 20″ in diameter. That was the breakthrough we needed. We had gear work coming in from the neighbor islands. Industry was then interested, and we went on from there. Our boys were being placed in jobs and our enrollment increased.[25]

When Richard Kosaki was conducting his study of the feasibility of creating a system of community colleges, he encountered opposition to the idea of including the technical school from a variety of people, including Duncan Sinclair, some sugar plantation managers, and the private college president already referred to. Legislators and county officials, on the other hand, were generally supportive. When Kosaki later went before the Maui County Planning Board to ask for an additional sixty acres of public land adjoining the existing campus of the technical school in Kahului, he was "chastised for not asking for 100 acres."[26]

Aerial view of Maui Community College, with the old vocational school buildings to the right and the newer academic ones up the slope to the left.

Students and instructor in the Skybridge studio in 1993 provide instruction for students on Molokai and Lanai and in Hana.

Maui Community College (MCC) replaced the technical school in 1965, retaining a strong tie with the agricultural and business community on the three islands of Maui County. Its faculty members flew in single-engine planes to Lanai and Molokai to teach extension classes, dodging storms on occasion or swooping down to watch the whales before landing to stay at the Pau Hana Inn on Molokai. Classes over, their hospitable students sent them home with fresh fish and pineapples.

Maui was looked upon by some of its new faculty members as a tropical backwater, its people living in isolation. Geography professor Dick Mayer, who came to MCC in 1967, said that he was recruited partly because he had experience in the Peace Corps and accepted the offer because he thought he could survive Maui's presumed primitive conditions. "I half expected to live in a grass shack."[27]

When the college was preparing to offer a liberal arts program, there was disagreement on what the program should be. Longtime English professor Victor Pellegrino was refused an appointment because he did not have a Ph.D. when he first sought a position at MCC. The provost of that time wanted to pattern the college transfer program on the University of Chicago "Great Books" concept. Pellegrino felt that a curriculum that focused on great works of literature was "totally inadequate" for a community college on a small island.[28] Faculty members generally agreed, concluding that the Great Books concept revealed how out of touch with the community college philosophy that provost was.

Members of the faculty still talk of how they had to educate administrators in those early years. The reputed feistiness of the Maui faculty (a characteristic shared with the Leeward Community College faculty) was reflected in their belief that they had to provide leadership for the college. That feistiness was given full scope because, unlike the other colleges where the faculty senates were composed of departmental representatives, at MCC every instructor was a member of the senate.

Unionization of the faculty in 1972 caused a loss of "collegiality and creativity," Mayer says, resulting in an "us vs. them" mentality and adding to the general anti-administration attitude of the faculty. The subsequent mellowing of the faculty can be largely attributed to the stability and continuity provided by the tenures of Provosts Alma Cooper-Henderson (1980 to 1990) and Clyde Sakamoto (since 1990), as well as the leadership and calming influence of longtime instructor/professor Bruce Palmer, who twice served as dean of instruction.[29]

A different kind of controversy arose over the construction of the campus library. The architect proposed a central atrium, rising upward through all three floors. During the planning stages, head librarian Bea Kell sought to correct what she perceived as a mistake in the design. Finding that she was disregarded, she reluctantly resigned her position. When the building opened in 1970, users found that conversations and other sounds could be heard throughout the structure. A student described it at a public hearing as "the worst building ever built."[30] Later the noise was somewhat reduced by installing acoustical material.

During the height of the "hippie" era, the island of Maui attracted a number of social dissidents. Maui Community College provided a nonthreatening environment for those seeking to reenter mainstream society, even though some local residents tried to discourage them. One student wore a lava-lava and a flower behind his ear, and smoked marijuana, during the five years he lived on campus. His extended presence was evidence of a growing tolerance for a diverse student population.

In its early years, the college developed programs in nursing, home care, food services, and computer training. When Maui grew into a major tourist destination, MCC established a Visitor Industry Training and Educational Center, preparing students for employment in the tourist industry through the college's Community Services division. Its Food Services program was accredited by the American Culinary Food Services.

Maui Community College has the responsibility of serving all three islands of Maui County, since the small populations on Lanai and Molokai make it impractical for them to have campuses of their own. To meet their need, MCC created Skybridge, an interactive television network electronically linking not only the other islands but also the outlying areas of Hana and Kihei with the Kahului campus. Students at each of the locations participate in class discussions directed by faculty members from a studio in the campus library. Classes can also originate from any of the other centers. In addition to serving its own courses, MCC made Skybridge available for upper-division and graduate courses transmitted from UH at Mānoa and West Oahu College.

Course modifications at MCC reflected changing degree requirements and new forms of instruction through computer and television. The college developed competency-based courses in the occupational programs, stating specifically the skills and understanding students were expected to reach, allowing each student to progress individually. Some courses were given updated titles; for example, Apparel Design and Construction became Fashion Technology. Reflecting the change in Maui County's economic base to diversified agriculture and tourism, new courses were created in Landscape Plant Selection and Care, Pesticides and Safety, Interiorscapes, Tropical Fruits and Nuts, Organic Gardening, and Plant Breeding.

Maui Community College responded to community needs in a variety of ways. A program to provide nurses' training was initially funded through $30,000 raised in a 1992 tennis tournament cosponsored by the college. The college's facilities were used by Honolulu's Chaminade University from 1986 to 1990 in programs offering Maui residents elementary teacher certification and nursing training. In cooperation with Alexander & Baldwin, the leading Maui sugar producer, the campus housed a child-care center alongside Head Start facilities for preschool children. Upward

Bound, a six-week live-in program for at-risk high school students, utilized the MCC dormitories.

From time to time, Maui residents and the county government tried to persuade the Hawaii legislature to create a four-year campus on the island. Full enrollments in programs offered to Maui residents by Chaminade University and in upper-division courses offered by UH-Mānoa and West Oahu College were cited as evidence of the need. However, the limited size of the island's population and the state's continuing budget constraints make expansion of MCC to a four-year college seem unlikely in the near future.

Kapi'olani Community College

FROM A "CATERPILLAR" beginning at a crowded, noisy Pensacola Street site in central Honolulu, Kapi'olani Community College (KCC) became the "butterfly" of the UH community colleges. Not only did it acquire an attractive new campus when it moved to Diamond Head in 1975, but its curriculum underwent a metamorphosis to meet a changing Island scene.

Kapiolani Technical School had been created by merging a practical nursing program, started in 1947 in temporary shacks at the Pensacola site, with a hotel and restaurant program begun in 1946 at the Ala Wai Clubhouse, several blocks away. When the school opened in 1957, it added business education. In 1968, the food services program was moved from the clubhouse to new facilities on the Pensacola campus. With the introduction of liberal arts studies the same year, Kapi'olani became a comprehensive community college.

Physical conditions of the new college's five-acre campus were abysmal. The business and food services programs were in modest permanent buildings, but nursing classes, offered in a lounge adjoining the women's restroom, had to accommodate traffic en route to and from the busy toilets. Liberal arts classes were crammed into ramshackle portables equipped with air conditioners so noisy that they were often turned off, despite desperation to escape the heat. Broom closets were transformed into faculty offices, and one became a darkroom for the media center.[31] Twenty language arts instructors shared one large room divided into cubicles, also sharing one telephone. Kauai legislator Tony Kunimura toured the campus and described it as "the shittiest I've ever seen."[32]

Following the retirement of Ray Won, the holdover provost from technical school days, two provosts served briefly. During this unsettled time and throughout the college's beginnings, continuity was provided by longtime Dean of Instruction Harriet Nakamoto, a consummate mediator, who held the college together.

Conversion of the technical school into a community college in 1965 brought a rapid increase in enrollment, swamping the limited facilities. Very early it was apparent that the small site was insufficient to hold the burgeoning student enrollment, and Vice-President Richard Kosaki and University planner Hitoshi Mogi went to Schofield Barracks to talk with the commanding general about getting surplus federal land, particularly Fort Ruger, a former Army coastal artillery battery headquarters on fifty acres on the back slopes of Diamond Head. The general replied, "Take it all except the Cannon Club."[33]

When the federal government ultimately made available Fort Ruger and its barracks and officers' duplex housing, the University first considered using the land, which adjoined Leahi Hospital, for its medical school. However, when hospitals in the community agreed to accept medical students for practical training, the medical school no longer needed the site, and it was made available to Kapi'olani Community College.

Sensing the threat of other competing demands for the land, Provost Fred Haehnlen declared that the college had to "plant the flag" at Ruger. Using the existing Army buildings, classes began in the fall of 1975 for about half of the liberal arts students and four of the allied health programs. Other vocational programs and many of the liberal arts classes remained for the time at the old Pensacola campus.

Opposition to a permanent campus at Ruger from neighbors concerned about traffic and construction noise, joined by those interested in keeping the school at Pensacola Avenue, delayed legislative appropriation of funds to construct the new campus until 1981. Planned by the late Robert Matsushita, an architect praised for his imaginative design, a campus then slowly emerged, of low-rise earth-colored buildings placed in strikingly landscaped courtyards.

Development

Outside funds stimulated the growth of programs on the new campus and also its ability to gauge educational achievement. The school received a large five-year (1977–1982) federal grant to improve counseling services and to institute "competency-based" goals for students. Each program and course would have its required outcomes described as the specific skills or knowledge students were expected to gain. These were published as guidelines for students and faculty members. Kapi'olani was one of the first community colleges in the nation to set competencies for all of its courses and programs.

A second grant (1982–1986) allowed the college to pioneer a planning-management-evaluation system that linked evaluation by faculty and administration of pro-

Food preparation was one of the Kapi'olani programs that was carried over from the Technical School. Open to the public, its dining room continued as a prime place for fine food at both the Pensacola and Diamond Head campuses.

Moving from the cramped space on Pensacola Street to the campus on the *mauka* slopes of Diamond Head gave an opportunity to expand the curriculum to a wide range of academic and vocational fields. Shown here at the 1985 dedication of the new campus is former provost Fred Haehnlen (in chair marked "Reserved"), who "planted the flag at Fort Ruger."

grams, accreditation, planning and budgeting. This system became the prevailing pattern for the entire UH community college system.[34]

In 1980, Provost Joyce Tsunoda announced that the college would develop a Writing Across the Curriculum (WAC) program, which not only sought to improve students' writing skills but also used writing to facilitate learning in all courses. The WAC program was described by the director of the prestigious Iowa Institute on Writing, as "possibly the earliest, largest continuing, most carefully integrated, most energetically supported . . . and with the most widespread faculty participation" of any community college with which he was familiar.[35]

The WAC "selective emphasis" was followed by "across-the-curriculum" emphases in computer use, critical thinking, Asian and Pacific education, and mathematics. The Asian and Pacific emphasis was a recognition that many graduates would be employed in careers involving travel and trade in those regions. That emphasis was reflected in the foreign languages offered, which, in addition to the traditional courses in European languages, included Russian, Japanese, Mandarin, Korean, Tagalog, Samoan, and Hawaiian.

A grant from the Kellogg Foundation helped increase Kapi'olani Community College's role in international education. Directed by anthropology professor Bob Franco, the college published a set of booklets to guide instruction in international education and sponsored an international conference in Honolulu in 1992. An outcome of that conference was the creation of a computer network newsletter exchanging ideas and information with colleges across the mainland and the Pacific Basin. Kapiolani also established student exchanges, sister-college relationships, and consultancy contacts with colleges in Japan, China, Micronesia, Indonesia, and Malaysia. Faculty members organized and led educational tours of Europe, Asia, and the South Pacific.

One of KCC's earliest areas of emphasis was health-related services. To the limited training in practical nursing, a two-year nursing program was added in 1989. Subsequently, other programs were introduced for dental and medical assistants, long-term care and home health nurse's aides, medical laboratory technicians, in phlebotomy, occupational and physical therapy, radiological technology, respiratory care, and emergency medicine. A program in legal assisting begun in 1994 is unique in the UH system.

The original KCC food services program, which prepared students for employment in hotels and restaurants, received a major boost with a million-dollar gift from former Kauai hotelier Grace Guslander in 1989. That field was expanded to include hospitality education, hotel operations, and travel and tourism programs, all geared to help staff the industry on which the economy of Hawaii so heavily depended.

Leeward Community College

Since its founding in 1968, Leeward Community College (LCC) has taken seriously the "open-door" policy basic to the community college mission, trying to devise ways of educating all high school graduates who apply. Carved out of a kiawe bush–covered site beside West Loch at Pearl Harbor, Leeward was the first of the UH colleges to move onto an entirely new campus, the first not to start in life as a technical school. The innovative design of its complex structure, based on the concept of a shopping mall, was recognized by the American Association of Junior Colleges even before construction was completed.[36] Instrumental in the planning process were Richard Kosaki, University planner Hitoshi Mogi, Manoa professor Leonard Tuthill, who had been appointed as the founding provost, and John Prihoda, the first dean of educational services. Planning sessions often took place in the old Pearl City Tavern, just down the road from the campus site.[37]

While the college was still under construction, Tuthill began recruiting faculty members. One of the first he persuaded to join him was Joyce Tsunoda. Tuthill, then serving on Tsunoda's doctoral dissertation committee at Manoa, asked her, "How would you like to start a community college with me?" She replied, "What is a community college?" In his pickup truck, Tuthill drove her to Pearl City. As they sat on a rock overlooking the site, he said, "This is where I'm going to build a community college. We're going to use money for education that would otherwise be used for welfare." She told him, "But I don't know how to teach!" He answered, "That's the kind of teacher I want. I don't want someone with all those bad habits. You are going to start the chemistry lab." And she did.[38]

Tuthill's innovative philosophy was to permeate the LCC approach to education, initially taught by a faculty drawn largely from the ranks of Manoa instructors. He and Prihoda built support for the college by talking to community leaders to find their views on what the curriculum should be within the framework of a combined vocational/liberal arts college.

Nearly twice the anticipated number of students showed up on the first day of registration.

> All preparations but one—the new building—were made for Leeward's opening in the fall of 1968. . . . Unfortunately the construction time-line was delayed, and it was necessary to find other places to accommodate what we thought would be about 300 students. The Pearl City Kai elementary school [no longer in use] became "headquarters" and provided several classrooms. Churches, schools, and anything else we could lay our hands on (including the parking lot) were placed on "hold" until we had an idea about enrollment. We used it all when some 500 students enrolled.[39]

Before classes could be held in these makeshift quarters, they were scrubbed by a contingent of newly hired faculty members and community supporters. Opening day found instructors and students using blackboards designed for small children. Richard Aadland, a business professor well over six feet tall, remembers getting on his knees to write. Bathroom fixtures were equally pint-sized. Maisie Akana, a math professor, recalls storing books and supplies in the trunk of her car, as she had no office. When the rains came—as they did frequently—the parking lots turned to mud; cars stuck in the mire and had to be towed. Custodian Rose Hokoana remembers the only way to clean the classrooms was to hose them down. Other classes met in nearby churches. Concerts for the music classes were held in the Waipahu High School gym. This improvisation lasted for a semester, until the new building was opened.

Once fully open, Leeward became the bellwether of the Hawaii colleges in educational experimentation and in providing the system with academic administrators. Several deans, provosts, and a chancellor of the system began their careers there. It was also foremost in enrollment for nearly two decades until overtaken by Kapi'olani Community College.

Tuthill treated every faculty member as one vital to the college's success. He and his wife invited teachers to a series of dinners at their home, grouping guests by their zodiac signs. Early comers to campus would find Tuthill knocking on office doors to say "good morning" and to talk about his ideas for the college. "He kept us informed. He always let us know that faculty opinion mattered," says Akana.[40]

Tuthill and Prihoda's inspiration, along with the receptivity of the faculty, created a predilection for fresh educational approaches. A flexible calendar allowed students to enroll in courses at mid-semester. Objectives were specified for each course to make clear what students were expected to learn. The grading system used the traditional letter grades, but omitting the F and adding Q and N. Q, given to students who attended class regularly and made a conscientious effort to meet course objec-

Aerial view of LCC in the 1970s, with classrooms and administrative offices in the foreground, library in the center, and theatre beyond.

The dedication of Leeward Community College in 1969 shows (front row, left to right) faculty member Darrow Aiona, Provost Leonard Tuthill, Regent Robert Cushing, Governor John Burns, Vice-President Richard Kosaki, Dean of Instruction John Prihoda, and (in dark glasses) Vice-President Robert W. Hiatt.

tives but did not achieve the required level of competency, was designed to encourage students to take courses outside their major field without risk of a failing grade. Students who had not reached the minimum competencies and were continuing the course received an N. The rationale for not using Fs was explained in the college catalog: "The concepts of competition between students and the punitive grading or dismissal for slow or inadequate learning are not compatible" with LCC's mission of helping people to learn.

With experience Leeward's educational philosophy evolved, becoming more traditional in some respects. A reexamination of grading practices resulted in adding the F grade and dropping the Q.

Faculty members identified business, science, and mathematics as areas of special emphasis for a college curriculum largely devoted to liberal studies. An open-laboratory chemistry program, begun in 1980, assisted students with faculty-developed multimedia support for laboratory experiments. A Women in Transition and later a Men in Transition program were designed to enhance students' self-confidence and to help them explore career possibilities. In the early 1980s a program of "learning communities" was developed whereby small groups of students needing support took their classes together for peer reinforcement—"an ohana for learning." LCC was the first of the community colleges to employ a full-time specialist in learning disabilities, and its Komo Mai Center for disabled students has been nationally recognized as a model.

Leeward early embraced the performing arts. Its theatre program, the most fully developed in the community college system, furnished a well-equipped stage for nearly two hundred presentations each year, including student productions, national touring companies, dance concerts, film festivals, youth theater, jazz concerts, choral festivals, seminars, and meetings. Beginning in 1988, the college gave courses in commercial music and TV production, training many of the television technicians employed in Hawaii. Some of them won national and international awards for their work.

Because the leeward coast of Oahu had no college of its own, LCC operated a center offering individualized learning in reading, writing, and mathematics at Waianae. In cooperation with Kapi'olani Community College, the center also offered a con-centration in health education, including nursing.

Unconventional things had happened at LCC in its early years. The college, born in the late 1960s during an unpopular war and a time of social protest, attracted "hippie" students and faculty members. Students "streaked" bare-bottomed through hillside parking lots. A naked student presented an astonished Mayor Frank Fasi with a flower lei at a campus reception. Some veterans beat the system by enrolling in classes, failing to attend, but nevertheless collecting their government checks, thanks to LCC's lenient grading system. Students trashed lounges and gambled in the recreation room, forcing that room to be closed.

Out of this excess there arose a more settled institution serving an expanding student body in the most rapidly growing part of the state. With such modes as the "learning communities" of students with common interests, team-taught by professors representing different disciplines, it has continued its exploration of educational methods best suited to the diverse population it educates.

Windward Community College

Windward Community College (WCC), the youngest of the system, began classes in 1972 for three hundred students, using five plantation-style buildings that had served the Kaneohe State Hospital, whose grounds the college now shared with the mental-health facility. Like Leeward Community College, it began from scratch rather than evolving from a technical school. Located in a thriving suburb of Honolulu, the school was intended primarily for students living on Oahu's windward coast from Waimanalo to Kahuku and for personnel of the nearby Kaneohe Marine Corps Base.

According to its founding provost, John Prihoda, "The Windward concept was different from Leeward Community College in one important way: it was developed for those of the Hawaiian culture more than anyone else."[41] To help plan the teaching program, Prihoda and Dean of Instruction Melvyn Sakaguchi met with potential users and supporters of the college in the communities of windward Oahu.

> In a very short time, we spoke with many, many local people to determine what the college could do to help them, their children, and their communities. The flavor of their educational needs became the basis for the college's initial offering.[42]

Windward Community College began with a number of innovations, such as a grading system similar to Leeward's but, like Leeward, with experience it became more traditional.

In its early years, disturbed patients and ex-patients of the adjacent hospital still considered the campus to be their home. On discharge, they had been told, "When you need help, come back to Mahi Building." Even after Mahi was no longer part of the hospital, former patients would wander into classrooms—"coming home." A man ran into a classroom one day with a garbage bag over his head, threatening to "self-destruct." Another, a convicted rapist adjudged insane at the time of his crime, was released to enroll at the college, causing no little consternation among the students when he appeared in classes.[43]

WCC's proximity to the hospital led to the creation of a paramedical program offering short-term classes in psycho-social development. The direction of the relationship between the two institutions moved toward mutual support.

Because it "inherited" the old hospital buildings, WCC had difficulty in getting state funds for new classrooms, laboratories, library, or offices. The converted buildings, never extensively renovated, retained their "bubble-gum pink" walls, a color thought to be soothing to patients. Wire mesh covered the windows. There were anomalies, such as the music and science rooms being separated by a laundry. Test tubes for lab work had to be washed in a bathroom.

Starting-up experiences were memorable. The faculty fought mosquitoes, cleared rank vegetation from the grounds, and washed walls. Campus beautification took persistence and inventiveness. Trees donated by a local business were planted by faculty members, only to be flattened in a storm, then replaced. Flowers were planted in a derelict drinking fountain in the library.

Starting as a new school, its early curriculum made up predominantly of college transfer courses, Windward did not have the conflict between vocational and academic instructors experienced by some of the other UH community colleges. Coping with the problems of a do-it-yourself campus helped to create a close-knit faculty, student body, and staff. When asked in 1988–1989 for their reaction to their WCC experience, students sent in 250 letters praising it. "Students don't want to leave," said Provost Pete Dyer.[44]

The college continued to develop close ties with the neighboring population. Its small theatre was refurbished with community help and frequently used by community players. An art gallery was improvised in a basement.

WCC initially found it difficult to achieve the comprehensive curriculum characteristic of Hawaii's community colleges. When it opened, most of the major vocational programs planned for Oahu had been preempted by the other three colleges serving the island. Two popular programs, automotive mechanics and business, were duplicated at WCC, but distinctive vocational courses were sought. Someone suggested watch repair, but that was never taken seriously.

More appropriate options suggested themselves. Close to Kaneohe Bay and the Hawaii Institute of Marine Biology laboratory on Coconut Island, WCC in the mid-1970s began to offer the state's only aquaculture classes and a Marine Options program that provides students a concentration in ocean research and a certificate in marine skills. In a vacation state with many golf courses, WCC and Maui Community College offered the only turf-grass landscaping programs. The Windward faculty, with community assistance, in 1993 developed a three-hole golf course on which stu-

Capitalizing on the proximity of Kaneohe Bay and the Hawaii Marine Biology labs on Coconut Island, Windward developed aquaculture as a vocational and academic specialty. These ponds and tanks were part of that program in 1981.

The 1993 Institute of Hawaiian Studies Hoolaulea illustrates Windward's continuing emphasis on Hawaiian culture.

dents learn to monitor herbicides, pesticides, and water run-off. The links also provided a facility for research in growing grass.

Reflecting the large ethnic Hawaiian population in the surrounding area (a fourth of WCC's enrollment has been of Hawaiian descent), the college followed the direction originally set by Prihoda. Thirty-eight courses focus on Hawaiian culture, language, history, and religion, as well as such subjects as reefs, fish, volcanoes, and plants. Unique to WCC is a set of geology classes using field trips to each of the other islands. Providing an outreach counselor in the nearby Hawaiian homestead community of Waimanalo, the college worked with Alu Like, an organization assisting Hawaiians, to recruit students and to monitor their college program. In the early 1990s, WCC students, supervised by alumnus Kawehi Ryder, built a *loi* (taro patch) fronting the Waipa building on the campus. Annually, the college has hosted a taro festival and a *hoolaulea* (celebration), featuring Hawaiian crafts and music. *Ka'ohana,* the student newspaper, which strongly reflected views and interests of the college's Hawaiian enrollment, won several national awards.

The nearby communities of Kaneohe and Kailua, largest on the windward coast, were found to have many residents in need of assistance in making mid-life changes. For them, WCC developed the Windward Transition Program, with both daytime and evening classes. Originally designed to help women, it later came to serve both sexes.

In 1985 when Albert Simone became UH president, the newspapers reported that he was considering closing WCC to save money. The college faculty invited him to talk with them. Early one evening, soon after he took office, they spread blankets on the campus lawn and served popcorn and wine while Simone explained that his comments were taken out of context by the press. He agreed that Windward was a needed and contributing member of the University system.[45]

Discontent had been repeatedly voiced in the nearby communities that WCC received disproportionately small state funds for capital improvements. Supporters pointed to the fact that windward voters tend to vote Republican, and their representatives have little power in a Democratic legislature and state administration. Further, the area lacks any sizable industry or large labor union concentration, both factors that favorably influence priorities in state budgets.

Relief finally came. The first new building of the college, included in a 1985 campus master plan, was begun in 1995. It was designed by an architect who specialized in creating NASA structures. He paid attention to details of the windward setting, "even the way the wind crosses the roof." Housing the science classes, it includes a planetarium and an aerospace laboratory, already functioning off-campus to provide learning materials for school teachers. The aerospace program is directed by Professor Joseph Ciotti, who qualified as Hawaii's teacher-in-space nominee for the ill-fated *Challenger* flight.

As the twentieth century was ending, the college faced another challenge: providing New Age education not only for the windward side of the island but also to students from across Oahu who would be traveling the controversial H-3 highway in search of Windward Community College's brand of education. It would have ready for an expanded student body two more new structures. A science building and a humanities complex were under construction in 1996, in good time for the twenty-first century.

Hawai'i Community College

SURVIVOR OF TSUNAMIS and a twenty-year struggle for independence, Hawai'i Community College (HCC) was the last to join the system, in 1990. The origins of the program that ultimately became the college were vocational classes offered at Hilo public schools from 1941 to meet the needs of the island's sugar plantations. In 1943, organized as Hilo Technical School, it moved to its own campus, a cluster of modest shops beside Hilo Bay. Courses included automotive mechanics, carpentry, dressmaking, machine shop, and sheet metal and welding; later diesel mechanics and architectural drawing were added. Six years after the 1946 tsunami, the school was moved to a seventeen-acre site at Manono and Kaiwili Streets, where there was room further to expand the curriculum—food services, electricity, business education, automotive repairing, and finally electronics in 1966.

When the state legislature transferred all other technical schools from the state Department of Education to the University of Hawai'i in 1965, the Hilo school was excluded by statute. Big Island political and business interests wanted a baccalaureate degree-granting college and feared that creating a community college would dash hopes of converting the lower-division Hilo campus into a full college. The vocational school faculty argued that transferring the school to the University would diminish their programs by including a liberal arts component. UH-Hilo campus faculty thought academic standards would be compromised by turning the technical school into a community college with which they would have to compete.

Critics of the whole community college movement maintained that it was not necessary to train workers in a college. The *Honolulu Advertiser* editorial page disagreed:

> Do you send people to college to train as waitresses and gas-station attendants, the type of training that can be handled at Hilo Technical and other schools? The

> answer is yes. . . . The community college is a flexible concept that can handle training at levels from two-year degree programs down to short courses . . . and stimulate [students] to higher education.[46]

Not until 1969, when the Board of Regents authorized the UH-Hilo campus to offer third- and fourth-year courses and designated it as Hilo College, was Hilo Technical School transferred to the University as Hawai'i Community College. UH President Harlan Cleveland then placed it and Hilo College under an umbrella administrative unit called the University of Hawai'i at Hilo (UHH). The Board of Regents directed that the community college's course offerings should be "as comprehensive as possible while not unnecessarily duplicating other University programs at Hilo."[47] It also ordered that Hilo College "should provide the [liberal arts] 'transfer track' for Hawai'i Community College, rather than HCC developing it independently."[48] The community college continued to award certificates and associate in science degrees to students completing vocational-technical programs, but liberal arts students took their courses at Hilo College, about a half-mile from the Manono campus.

Although it offered vocational programs and some remedial courses, Hawai'i Community College was clearly not a part of the community college system. According to Mitsugu Sumada, principal of the technical school and provost of the college from 1964 to 1986, "every liberal arts course that HCC wished to initiate met with less than enthusiastic support of the chancellor and Hilo College staff."[49]

In 1973, the regents made UHH the official degree- and certificate-granting institution for both its component parts, "for the sake of consistency."[50] It also authorized an associate in arts degree, in which students were "encouraged" to take a fifth of their courses in vo-tech programs but were required to take a majority of their credits in "transfer-level" courses. UHH thus found itself in the odd position of conferring short-term certificates and two-year degrees as well as baccalaureate degrees.

Through the 1980s, UHH continued to struggle with reorganization plans. Sumada reported that his faculty "had no time at all to work on our overall curriculum design. . . . While other community colleges were . . . working on their curriculum and how to deliver services to students, we were engaged in a fruitless effort at organizing a university."[51]

After a College of Agriculture was created at UHH, Hawai'i Community College began an agricultural program in conjunction with the new college, a curriculum and facility long sought by Big Island legislators for their district. Nursing was added in 1974 and early childhood education in 1987. In 1985, HCC began the state's largest prison-inmate education program at Kulani Correctional Facility on the slopes of Mauna Loa, and in 1987 it offered courses to west Hawaii students at a Kealakekua outreach facility shared with UHH.

In May 1986, faculty staged a mock wedding of Hawai'i Community College and

Hawai‘i Community College carpentry students constructed a portable shed for use by heavy-equipment students in Hilo's rainy weather, 1977.

With sugar phasing out, agriculture students were led in new directions, here in developing backyard hydroponics techniques.

UHH in a Hilo nightclub. Miss Kapiolani-Mauka, dressed in a borrowed wedding gown, and Mr. Manono-Makai, in white shirt and red-sashed trousers, repeated their vows before a mock-minister. A two-tiered wedding cake, donated by a local bakery, was served to faculty guests, who toasted the "couple" with many a "banzai." "The marriage was doomed to failure, with family disagreements before, during, and after the ceremony."[52]

The "marriage" was in fact dissolved in 1990 when the regents severed HCC from UHH and put it under the chancellor for community colleges. This action, however, did not entirely separate the two institutions. HCC students continued to use the UHH library and media-production, computer, and learning centers. Students in some programs, notably liberal arts, continued to attend classes at the UHH campus. Faculty and students shuttled between the two campuses. Four coeducational resident halls, three at UHH and one at the Manono campus, served students who resided in other districts of the Big Island, on neighbor islands, or in foreign countries.

The separation found Hawai'i Community College with a leadership void and loss of faculty morale. Joanne Cooper, a Manoa professor who taught courses in the administration of higher education, wrote:

> Initial results showed confusion among faculty over institutional mission and priorities at both the community college and the university with the community college faculty split over the vision of the type of student they aim to produce and the university faculty struggling to balance a desire to appear friendly and open yet scholarly and learned, both institutions competing for the same students and yet having to cooperate in the use of shared resources.[53]

Into this situation came a new provost, Sandra Sakaguchi. In 1990 she began seeking funds to provide faculty and support services, formerly the responsibility of UHH. As the college set about finding its role in the community, it offered a program in Hawaiian leadership in conjunction with UHH, recruiting talented ethnic Hawaiians and facilitating their academic and leadership development. A curriculum in the Hawaiian language prospered. The college also set up "learning communities," which integrated interdisciplinary learning techniques and community activities to introduce small groups of students to a variety of academic disciplines.

No other community college in the system had HCC's struggle to seek and maintain its identity. Finally, however, after years of having its destiny decided by others, the college was able to develop its own philosophy and an expanded curriculum, which attracted an increasing number of students. Among the colleges of the Neighbor Islands it enrolled the largest number, approximately three thousand in 1995. Equally significant, its enrollment of students of Hawaiian and part-Hawaiian ancestry at more than eight hundred was the largest in the entire system of community colleges.

Employment Training Center

An important adjunct to the community college system is the Employment Training Center (ETC). Established in 1964 under the state Department of Education as the Manpower Training Office, it offered a basic skills curriculum, helping adults to prepare for employment. Although not originally perceived to be part of Hawaii's system of higher education, its goals fitted the community college open-door admission policies, and in 1968 it was transferred to the University with the ETC director reporting to the chancellor of the community colleges.

The focus of the center shifted, depending on the federal grant it was operating under. In 1971, its goal was to assist newly discharged Vietnam War veterans, persons on welfare, and others with special problems. At that time, 10 percent of its funding was provided by the state and 90 percent by the federal government. Its curriculum included basic English, English as a second language, arithmetic, carpentry, and cooking. Trainees entered any program on any Monday, beginning at any level and progressing at their own pace. They were allowed to stay for up to thirty weeks. Many worked toward earning a high school diploma.

Through the years, the programs and composition of the student body changed. Social agencies referred people to ETC for training, counseling and job placement. "At-risk" high school students were taught "how to work" as well as job skills. To the curriculum were added instruction in auto repair, office work, food preparation, school bus aide and driver training, motorcycle safety, and the like. In 1982 the center contracted with the state Department of Health to train emergency medical-care personnel for Oahu, a service it already provided for the other islands.[54]

ETC operated in various areas, including Nanakuli, Kalihi, and near Honolulu International Airport. Before moving to its present downtown location in 1993, it occupied the former site of Kapi'olani Community College on Pensacola Street. Other campus sites used by the center, and its course offerings there, included Honolulu Community College (heavy equipment, child care, cosmetology, and facility maintenance), Nanakuli High School (auto body repair), Sand Island and Leeward Community College (motorcycle safety education), and Schofield Barracks (military skills).

Beginning with two hundred students in 1964, enrollment grew to nearly six thousand in 1990. The end of some special programs, including the one serving the military, reduced that number. Also, leaving Pensacola Street apparently depressed ETC's enrollment, which dropped by a fourth after the move. Perhaps students missed the collegiality of a traditional campus that had been provided at the old Kapi'olani College location.

In the 1990s ETC began tailoring its applied mathematics and reading courses to the demands of particular jobs. Counselors were assigned to work with individual teachers at each program site. In addition, the center began interacting with individual community colleges so that its trainees, if they wished, could earn two-year degrees. Classes were put on a semester schedule rather than the open-entry and open-exit scheme. The more flexible schedules, however, remained in the office technology and food services programs at Kapi'olani Community College. According to Tim Craig, ETC director, these cooperative arrangements improved the student success rate, with three-quarters of the students completing their program in recent years.

SUMMING UP

THE UNIVERSITY OF HAWAI'I, unique as America's mid-ocean, tropical, multicultural university, also typifies the development of the nation's public institutions of higher learning from small colleges to large, research-centered "multiversities." Beginning, like most state colleges, as a school devoted to training agricultural specialists and engineers, it evolved into a university offering a broader liberal education (1920) and soon acquired its first professional school, Teachers College (1931).

Emphasis on undergraduate teaching continued through the middle of the century, even as the Manoa campus expanded after World War II to receive the wave of military veterans who transformed the student body. Three long-serving presidents—Dean, Crawford, and Sinclair—consecutively provided forty years of stability in leadership, guiding the school through the problems of getting started as a university, and surviving the Great Depression and the wartime occupation of the campus by the U.S. military. The foundation had been laid.

The subsequent rise of the University, in the thousands of students it served each year, the variety of programs it offered, the size and academic range of its faculty, the number of its campuses and buildings, was extraordinary. All across the United States an explosive growth in institutions of higher learning occurred in the mid-century, but in Hawaii that expansion was phenomenal. One comparison makes the point. For the nation as a whole, between 1951 and 1970 the enrollment in all institutions of higher learning increased from 2.1 million to 8.6 million—a quadrupling. During that same period the enrollment in the University of Hawai'i system rose from approximately five thousand to more than thirty-three thousand—a sixfold increase.

National and state policies supported an increasing expectation of students and their parents that an affordable college education would be available for all qualified applicants who presented themselves to a public university's admissions office. The federal government first offered education subsidies for World War II veterans under the GI Bill of Rights and then, in response to a perceived challenge in science and technology from the Soviet Union, made available a variety of grants to students and colleges under the National Defense Education Act of 1958. The government of Hawaii, especially after statehood was attained in 1959, generously supported the extraordinary growth of its University with appropriations that not only paid for its expansion but also enabled it to charge one of the lowest tuition rates in the nation.

In mid-century a transforming social change occurred nationally—probably more widespread in Hawaii than in any other state—as the result of coming to regard a college education as a natural right for all who were qualified. Hawaii responded to the change and the pent-up demand for education beyond high school by creating after 1965 a statewide system of higher education unique in the nation. To the Manoa and Hilo campuses the legislature added a network of community colleges, now seven in number, in each county, and then established the West Oahu campus, all under the administration of a single Board of Regents and president, but each given wide latitude for developing curricula designed to meet the differing requirements of its students and situation.

Stimulated by an expanded range of programs, ranging from the open-door, come-as-you-are, community colleges to highly selective professional schools and graduate studies, across the nation students poured into campus in numbers astonishing by pre–World War II standards. Young people of all ethnicities and economic levels saw career opportunities rarely envisioned by their parents and grandparents—especially in Hawaii, where most of those forebears had lived in plantation villages. Large organizations, corporations and governments alike, came to depend on colleges to train their white-collar workers—especially in Hawaii, with little industry and much government employment. An expanded middle class of white-collar workers and professionals was formed by the graduates of universities—especially in Hawaii, where by the last decade of the twentieth century more than a quarter of the resident population held bachelor's or graduate degrees, the fifth highest such ranking among the fifty states.

A rising flood of federal and state funds, augmented by grants from a growing number of private foundations, turned many land-grant colleges into "multiversities" that pursued research ever more widely and more deeply. So it was with the University of Hawai'i, beginning in the late 1950s, just before Hawaii was granted statehood. New research institutes at Manoa, starting with programs in ocean studies and geophysics, brought in federal grants and supported graduate degrees in ever increasing numbers and diversity. The establishment of the federally financed East-West Center on the campus gave strong stimulus to graduate studies in the humanities and social sciences, enabling the University to satisfy its abiding ambition to excel in studies concerning East Asia and the Pacific area.

A president of exceptional ability, Thomas Hamilton, led the confident expansion of the 1960s. In happy conjunction, Governor John Burns, then serving a long tenure as chief executive, strongly supported the expansion of the University's programs. They grew to include the community college system and an upper-division campus in West Oahu, as well as the elevation of the long-standing Hilo campus to a four-year college. A school of medicine and later a school of law were established.

Expansion continued after Hamilton, reacting to the first serious outcry of protest by students and faculty members in the University's history, resigned the presidency in 1968. However, in the early 1970s budgetary constrictions, last experienced in the decade leading up to statehood, forced the University system to check its growth and select those fields of teaching, research, and community service which it could best perform.

In a continuing quest for "selective excellence" of programs in which to distinguish itself, the University has had some notable successes, especially in the sciences. Its research programs in astronomy, ocean studies, and physics have earned international recognition. So have its exceptionally broad curricula in the history, languages, literature, social institutions, and business practices of much of Asia and its expertness in the theatre, dance, and music of East Asia.

The rise of graduate studies and research institutes after the 1960s rapidly changed the nature of the University. The range and variety of undergraduate courses continued to increase, but the academic departments at Manoa put greater weight on success in research and less on teaching in recruiting, retaining, and promoting their faculty members. This shift occurred across the United States as funds from the federal government and private foundations poured into research enterprise.

Responsibility for the instruction of undergraduates was increasingly assumed by the other campuses within the University system—Hilo, the community colleges around the state, and the West Oahu campus. Together, they annually enrolled more than half of the students within the University system. Each developed its own curricula and style, but all concentrated on teaching. The resulting differences between a Manoa faculty, much involved in research and graduate programs, and the other faculties created a tension. This became evident in the early 1970s, when the faculty members of the entire University system had to choose whether or not to create a collective bargaining unit to represent them in contract negotiations with the University administration and the state government. A negative attitude at Manoa was overcome by the "ayes" on the other campuses. The union of the several faculties remained strong, but a consequence of unionization was further to divide faculty from administration in working out solutions to the problems of growth and of diversity in a statewide system that chronically had to deal with budgetary crises.

What difference has this large, complex, expensive University made to Hawaii? What impact has it had on our society? One answer is obvious. The University of

Hawai'i has had a major role in the integration and democratization of Hawaii's people. Its low cost and receptive atmosphere brought to the campus children of all social ranks in the territory. This did not happen uniformly among ethnic groups, for in the student body at Manoa the proportion of Native Hawaiians, of Filipinos, and of other more recent immigrant groups continued to lag.

For all high school graduates, however, the existence of a local university fostered the aspiration to earn a college degree. Its benefits—marketable in qualifying for well-paying occupations, enriching in the discovery of broader intellectual horizons—became newly available to large numbers, those who could not afford to study at mainland colleges and those who, in earlier decades, would not necessarily have been welcomed there even if they could afford to go because they were of Oriental ancestry.

First of the non-Caucasians in Hawaii's population to come to the Manoa campus in relatively large numbers were the Chinese and the Japanese, although from the earliest years Native Hawaiians were enrolled in the school created with the strong support of Hawaiian legislators. Particularly after Teachers College was added to the University in 1931, professional careers became increasingly available to the school's racially diverse graduates—first in teaching, engineering, accounting, and agriculture, then in nursing, social work, and in the territorial and county civil service. Post-statehood creation of schools of medicine and law made special provision to enroll students of ethnic groups locally underrepresented in those professions. The community colleges and UH at Hilo were especially successful in reaching Hawaiians and Pacific Islanders.

In a different way from the offering of a liberal education and professional training, the University helped change the lives of its students and helped shape the culture of Hawaii. The admission policy of the College of Hawaii and of the University of Hawai'i was consciously set to encourage a multicultural student body. And that student body behaved in a way contrary to the society from which it came. It dropped the prevailing assumption of the early twentieth century that Caucasians were socially and intellectually superior, the natural leaders. As the campus organized itself, established a student government, formed theatre groups and vocational and social clubs, created a student newspaper, sport teams, later an ROTC unit, and so forth, a non-haole was as likely to be the president, the chairman, the captain, the editor as would a Caucasian student.

Carl A. Farden of the class of 1925, who later served on the Board of Regents, in a letter dated February 13, 1928, reflected on his experience as an undergraduate:

> Probably the greatest asset I have acquired or rather emphasized during my four years at the University of Hawaii is my ability to mingle and rub shoulders with the other races attending the institution, and existing in the Territory. I speak in

> this regard from the standpoint of the young generation, to whom ancestry in the Territory has handed the race problem for solution with more or less of the attitude of "posterity be damned." The younger generations will solve it, it is my firm belief, provided that ancestry keeps its hands out altogether. I learned this at the University as well as the reasoning which led to this belief.

The leadership given scope by the gradual spread, speeded by World War II, of the campus-nurtured attitude reflected by Farden has been impressive. Alumni of the University, rich in the variety of their ethnicity, have been prominent in tourism and many businesses, in all the professions and among the nonprofit social agencies of Hawaii. Especially have they taken leadership positions in public service. Since statehood, with very few exceptions, the governors and lieutenant governors of Hawaii, its representatives in Congress and its senators, have all been educated at the University of Hawai'i.

Change, the accelerating force speeding the world through the twentieth century, has been the invisible concern of institutions of higher learning everywhere. For Hawaii, its University has borne the chief responsibility for preparing people to cope with unremitting change.

As plantation agriculture peaked and then began to vanish, as the involuted oligarchical economy symbolized by the Big Five evolved into a competitive service economy linked to the worldwide corporate net, as technology was transmuted at a mounting speed, succeeding generations had to learn from the school system how to respond—gaining vocational skills, communication skills, and above all the ability to keep learning. The teaching was done by the schools of Hawaii, and at their head was the University.

So much, in brief, for the impact of the University system on the economic and political lives of the peoples of Hawaii. More pervasive is its impact on the unique multiculture of this state. Through its many campuses, UH has provided training and performance in the theatre, music, dance, and the visual arts. Only on University stages have been seen Kabuki and Noh drama, Chinese opera, Javanese dance with gamelan orchestra, all authentically presented. Instruction in a wide range of languages has given its students the opportunity to understand not only the European languages commonly offered on American campuses but also Tagalog and Ilokano, Vietnamese, Cambodian, Chinese, Japanese, Korean, Sanskrit, Lao, and other languages of East and Central Asia.

A critical contribution of this university was the creation more than seventy years ago of a sustained program in the Hawaiian language. That preserved Hawaiian from a progressive debasement that must have otherwise occurred for lack of the disciplined hold on grammar and pronunciation that in our culture only a school or academy can impose.

For many in Hawaii the University has been chiefly visible in competitive sports, on the football field, the baseball diamond, the basketball and volleyball courts, where over the decades the Manoa Rainbows and the Hilo Vulcans have maintained the tradition of collegiate athletic games. Others, listeners to public radio and viewers of public television, unknowingly benefit from the role of UH at Mānoa in providing a birthing place for noncommercial broadcasting in Hawaii.

The rainbow, symbol of the University, was appropriately chosen. This institution has raised its arch across Hawaii, providing broad, diverse bands of stimulus and enrichment. Like the rainbow, UH has shone brightly, although at times, as in this moment, it has been dimmed under clouds raised by budgetary uncertainty. Always it has reappeared, brighter and more promising than before.

APPENDIXES

Appendix 1

Presidents of the University of Hawai'i

Willis T. Pope, 1907–1908 (acting). B.S. 1898, Kansas State; M.S. 1916, California; D.Sc. 1926, Hawai'i.

John W. Gilmore, 1908–1913. B.S.A. 1898, M.S.A. 1906, Cornell.

John S. Donaghho, 1913–1914 (acting). A.B. 1889, A.M. 1897, Marietta.

Arthur L. Dean, 1914–1927. B.A. 1900, Harvard; Ph.D. 1902, Yale; LL.D. 1947, Hawai'i.

David L. Crawford, 1927–1941. B.A. 1911, LL.D. 1933, Pomona; M.A. 1912, Stanford; LL.D. 1947, Hawai'i.

Arthur R. Keller, 1941–1942 (acting). LL.B. 1907, National University Law School; M.S. 1916, MIT; Sc.D. 1942, Hawai'i.

Gregg M. Sinclair, 1942–1955. B.A. 1912, LL.B. 1949, Minnesota; LL.D. 1951, Ohio State; LL.D 1954, Columbia; LL.D. 1955, University of California, Berkeley; H.H.D. 1956, Hawai'i; D.Lit. 1960, Keio.

Paul S. Bachman, 1955–1957. B.S. 1922, Ohio State; M.A. 1925, Ph.D. 1927, Washington.

Willard Wilson, 1957–1958 (acting). B.A. 1929, LL.D. 1961, Occidental; M.A. 1930, Columbia; Ph.D. 1939, Southern California.

Laurence H. Snyder, 1958–1963. B.S. 1922, Sc.D. 1947, Rutgers; M.S. 1924, Harvard; Sc.D. 1960, Ohio State; H.H.D. 1962, North Carolina.

Thomas H. Hamilton, 1963–1968. B.A. 1936, LL.D. 1961, DePauw; M.A. 1940, Ph.D. 1947, Chicago; L.H.D. 1960, Alfred; LL.D. 1961, Rollins College; LL.D. 1961, Colgate; D.H. 1967, Oakland University (Michigan); LL.D. 1967, USC.

Robert W. Hiatt, 1968–1969 (acting). B.A. 1936, San Jose State; Ph.D. 1941, University of California, Berkeley.

Richard S. Takasaki, 1969 (acting). B.S. 1940, Hawai'i; M.A. 1949, Columbia; M.P.A. 1960, Harvard.

Harlan Cleveland, 1969–1974. A.B. 1938, Princeton; LL.D. 1956 Rollins College, 1960 Franklin and Marshall, 1962 Middlebury, 1962 Kent State, 1968 Arizona State, 1972 Korea University; L.H.D. 1958 Alfred, 1966 Kenyon; D.C.L. 1966, American; Litt.D. 1968, Pittsburgh.

Fujio Matsuda, 1974–1984. B.S. 1949, Rose Polytechnic Institute; Sc.D. 1952, Massachusetts Institute of Technology.

Albert J. Simone, 1984–1992. B.A. 1957, Tufts; Ph.D. 1962, Massachusetts Institute of Technology.

Paul C. Yuen, 1992–1993 (acting). B.S. 1952, Chicago; Ph.D. 1960, Illinois Institute of Technology.

Kenneth P. Mortimer, 1993–. A.B. 1960, M.B.A. 1962, Pennsylvania; Ph.D. 1969, University of California, Berkeley; L.H.D. 1985, Salisbury State College.

Appendix 2

Regents of the University of Hawaiʻi

1907–1914	Henry E. Cooper	1921–1933	Akaiko Akana
1907	Charles Franklin Eckart	1925–1932	Charles Byrant Cooper
1907–1909	Marston Campbell	1925–1935	George Ii Brown*
1907–1909	Walter Gifford Smith	1927–1941	David Livingston Crawford**
1907–1921	Alonzo Gartley	1932	Bruce Cartwright
1907–1914	Ralph Hosmer	1932–1937	Arthur Lyman Dean
1909	Morris Bissell	1933–1943	Carl Alexander Farden
1909	George W. Woodruff	1935–1946	Oren E. Long***
1909–1914	C. Montague Cooke	1937–1943	Herbert Ernest Gregory
1910	Arthur Ashford Wilder	1938–1943	Herbert Kealoha Keppler
1910–1940	Charles Reed Hemenway	1940	George Miles Collins
1914–1920	Wallace Rider Farrington	1940–1941	Alva Edgar Steadman
1914–1920	Jennie Robertson Ashford	1940–1943	Samuel N. Castle
1914–1917	Fred L. Waldron	1941–1943	J. Russell Cades
1918–1938	Arthur G. Smith	1941–1943	Ruth Emens Black
1920–1922	Richard Henderson Trent	1941–1943	Arthur L. Andrews
1920–1943	Mary Dillingham Frear	1942–1943	James Douglas Bond
1920–1925	Alatau L. C. Atkinson*	1943–1955	Gregg M. Sinclair**
1920–1927	Arthur Lyman Dean**	1943–1961	Philip E. Spalding

* Ex-officio, as president of Board of Agriculture and Forestry.

** Ex-officio, as president of the University.

*** Ex-officio, as superintendent of public instruction.

1943–1953	J. Frank McLaughlin
1943–1948	Willowdean Chatterton Handy
1943–1953	William Patterson Alexander
1943–1945	Marquis Fielding Calmes
1943–1951	Fred Kwai Lam
1943–1949	John Scott Boyd Pratt
1945–1946	E. Percy Lydgate
1946–1961	Katsuyuki Izumi
1946–1951	W. Harold Loper***
1949–1951	Benjamin O. Wist
1949–1961	Richard Penhallow
1952–1961	J. Garner Anthony
1952–1957	Clayton J. Chamberlin***
1953–1961	Hung Wai Ching
1953–1958	Jack Mizuha
1953–1957	Paul Bachman**
1957–1958	Willard Wilson**
1957–1961	Reynolds G. Burkland
1957–1961	Leslie Asa Hicks
1957–1958	Lloyd Kaapana
1959–1961	Ronald Toyofuku
1959–1962	Walton M. Gordon***
1959–1962	Laurence H. Snyder**
1961–1963	Abraham Akaka
1961–1963	Herbert C. Cornuelle
1961–1968	Robert L. Hind, Jr.
1961–1966	Robert H. Hughes
1961–1964	Arthur D. Lewis
1961–1968	Pete Tatsuo Okumoto
1961–1964	Lup Quon Pang
1961–1964	Morris Shinsato
1961–1963	Richard W. You
1962	R. Burl Yarberry***
1963	Thomas H. Hamilton**
1963–1967	Cornelius Clay Cadagan
1963–1968	George H. McPherson
1963–1970	Charles A. Kekumanu
1963–1968	Charles A. Harker
1964–1971	Edward H. Nakamura
1965–1974	Clarence Fong Chang
1966–1974	Charles S. Ota
1967–1974	Robert Cushing
1968–1974	Harold C. Eichelberger
1968–1971	Patrick M. Cockett
1968–1972	John Farias, Jr.
1969–1972	Herbert Monte Richards, Jr.
1971–1974	Stuart T. K. Ho
1971–1974	Brian L. Sakamaki
1971	Patsy L. Miyahara Young
1972–1981	Kiyoshi Sasaki
1972–1981	Harriet Mizuguchi
1974–1976	Sandra Ebesu
1974–1975	Roger C. Evans
1974–1982	Wallace S. Fujiyama
1974–1977	John A. Hoag
1974–1981	Ruth Oshiro
1974–1982	Tom T. Shibano
1975–1979	Anna Chung
1975–1983	Ambrose Rosehill
1975–1979	Scott Leithead
1976–1981	Carl A. Carlson, Jr.
1977–1978	Albert Mariano Felix
1977–1979	Bradley J. Mossman
1978–1982	Gerard A. Jervis
1979–1981	Michael Moriarty
1979–1986	Stanley Y. Mukai
1979–1985	Robert Fujimoto
1981–1982	Timothy Scott Farr

* Ex-officio, as president of Board of Agriculture and Forestry.

** Ex-officio, as president of the University.

*** Ex-officio, as superintendent of public instruction.

1981–1986 Stephen Bess
1981–1989 Julia A. Frohlich
1981–1989 Gregory Dela Cruz
1981–1985 Bert Tsuchiya
1982–1989 James F. Gary
1982–1991 Kenneth M. Kato
1982–1986 Walter Steiger
1983–1989 Gladys Brandt
1984–1986 Daniel M. Ishii
1984–1992 Robin Campiano
1985–1992 Herbert Monte Richards, Jr.
1985–1992 Dennis R. Yamada
1986–1987 Albert S. Nishimura
1987–1995 Howard Stephenson
1987–1995 John Ushijima
1987–1995 Edward Kuba
1987–1995 Ruth Ono
1987–1995 Roy Takeyama
1989–1993 Diane Plotts
1992–1993 Larry Tanimoto
1989–1997 Momi Cazimero
1989–(1998) Lee A. Ohigashi
1992–(2000) Joseph F. Blanco
1993–(2000) Clyde T. Kodani
1993–1997 Lily K. Yao
1995–(1999) John Hoag
1995–(1999) Shunichi Kimura
1995–(1999) Bert Kobayashi
1995–(1999) Ah Quon McElrath
1995–(1999) Donna Tanoue
1996–(1998) David Ramos

Parentheses show the years in which current appointments expire.

Appendix 3

Enrollment of Regular Students in the University of Hawai'i System

Academic Year	Manoa	Hilo	Community Colleges[a]	West Oahu	Total
1908–1909	41	-	-	-	41
1909–1910	64	-	-	-	64
1910–1911	112	-	-	-	112
1911–1912	160	-	-	-	160
1912–1913	128	-	-	-	128
1913–1914	121	-	-	-	121
1914–1915	105	-	-	-	105
1915–1916	105	-	-	-	105
1916–1917	110	-	-	-	110
1917–1918	139	-	-	-	139
1918–1919	145	-	-	-	145
1919–1920	242	-	-	-	242
1920–1921	397	-	-	-	397
1921–1922	404	-	-	-	404
1922–1923	496	-	-	-	496
1923–1924	674	-	-	-	674
1924–1925	618	-	-	-	618
1925–1926	738	-	-	-	738
1926–1927	874	-	-	-	874

Academic Year	Manoa	Hilo	Community Colleges[a]	West Oahu	Total
1927–1928	940	-	-	-	940
1928–1929	1,115	-	-	-	1,115
1929–1930	1,321	-	-	-	1,321
1930–1931	1,488	-	-	-	1,488
1931–1932	2,034	-	-	-	2,034
1932–1933	1,947	-	-	-	1,947
1933–1934	1,601	-	-	-	1,601
1934–1935	1,809	-	-	-	1,809
1935–1936	2,003	-	-	-	2,003
1936–1937	2,256	-	-	-	2,256
1937–1938	2,478	-	-	-	2,478
1938–1939	2,669	-	-	-	2,669
1939–1940	2,703	-	-	-	2,703
1940–1941	2,746	-	-	-	2,746
1941–1942	2,311	-	-	-	2,311
1942–1943	1,408	-	-	-	1,408
1943–1944	1,594	-	-	-	1,594
1944–1945	1,931	-	-	-	1,931
1945–1946	1,760	-	-	-	1,760
1946–1947	2,960	-	-	-	2,960
1947–1948	3,837	-	-	-	3,837
1948–1949	4,317	-	-	-	4,317
1949–1950	4,842	-	-	-	4,842
1950–1951	4,926	86	-	-	5,012
1951–1952	4,692	100	-	-	4,792
1952–1953	4,600	85	-	-	4,685
1953–1954	4,615	146	-	-	4,761
1954–1955	4,671	145	-	-	4,816
1955–1956	5,180	228	-	-	5,408
1956–1957	5,408	243	-	-	5,651

(continued)

Academic Year	Manoa	Hilo	Community Colleges[a]	West Oahu	Total
1957–1958	5,741	187	-	-	5,928
1958–1959	6,342	225	-	-	6,567
1959–1960	6,923	250	-	-	7,173
1960–1961	7,511	260	-	-	7,771
1961–1962	8,231	285	-	-	8,516
1962–1963	9,150	399	-	-	9,549
1963–1964	10,466	355	-	-	10,821
1964–1965	11,641	398	-	-	12,039
1965–1966	13,587	510	2,010	-	16,107
1966–1967	14,772	571	2,444	-	17,787
1967–1968	16,564	618	3,494	-	20,676
1968–1969	17,082	679	5,494	-	23,255
1969–1970	18,474	864	8,713	-	28,051
1970–1971	21,090	1,184	10,853	-	33,127
1971–1972	22,061	1,297	13,010	-	36,368
1972–1973	22,371	1,466	15,121	-	38,958
1973–1974	22,272	1,792	16,107	-	40,171
1974–1975	21,526	1,860	17,693	-	41,079
1975–1976	21,260	1,857	21,179	-	44,296
1976–1977	21,196	3,322	19,217	134	43,969
1977–1978	20,950	3,232	19,077	200	43,459
1978–1979	21,095	3,025	19,120	230	43,470
1979–1980	20,706	3,069	19,067	257	43,099
1980–1981	20,175	3,494	19,359	246	43,274
1981–1982	20,466	1,568[b]	22,706	365	45,085
1982–1983	20,880	1,658	24,264	408	47,210
1983–1984	20,966	1,628	23,214	433	46,241
1984–1985	19,965	1,506	21,903	435	43,809
1985–1986	19,606	1,447	21,750	443	43,246
1986–1987	18,918	1,594	21,690	480	42,682

Academic Year	Manoa	Hilo	Community Colleges[a]	West Oahu	Total
1987–1988	18,382	1,711	22,172	482	42,747
1988–1989	18,242	1,769	21,840	492	42,525
1989–1990	18,546	1,927	22,570	601	43,644
1990–1991	18,810	2,553	23,727	652	45,742
1991–1992	19,316	2,670	24,874	667	47,527
1992–1993	19,810	2,790	26,120	692	49,412
1993–1994	20,037	2,953	26,563	676	50,229
1994–1995	19,983	2,870	27,783	744	51,380
1995–1996	19,757	2,737	26,685	716	49,895

Sources: Robert C. Schmitt, *Historical Statistics of Hawaii* (Honolulu: University Press of Hawaii, 1977), Table 9.6; Institutional Research Office of the University, Nonduplicated annual enrollment through 1940–1941; fall semester enrollment in regular credit programs, including such special students as concurrent registrants and early admittees after 1958.

[a] For enrollment of individual community colleges, see *The State of Hawaii Data Book* for 1976 and subsequent years.

[b] Wide variation in enrollment data largely attributable to transfer of Hilo Community College, first to the Hilo campus and then to the community college system.

Appendix 4

Degrees Conferred by the University of Hawai'i

Academic Year	Bachelor's[a]	Master's[b]	Doctor's[c]	Associate[d]	Professional diplomas and certificates[e]
1908 to 1911	0	-	-	-	-
1911–1912	4	-	-	-	-
1912–1913	5	-	-	-	-
1913–1914	3	1	-	-	-
1914–1915	2	1	-	-	-
1915–1916	2	-	-	-	-
1916–1917	3	-	-	-	-
1917–1918	10	-	-	-	-
1918–1919	5	-	-	-	-
1919–1920	8	1	-	-	-
1920–1921	7	4	-	-	-
1921–1922	18	2	-	-	-
1922–1923	28	8	-	-	-
1923–1924	47	5	-	-	-
1924–1925	49	4	-	-	-
1925–1926	60	4	-	-	-
1926–1927	92	8	-	-	-
1927–1928	86	5	-	-	-

Academic Year	Bachelor's[a]	Master's[b]	Doctor's[c]	Associate[d]	Professional diplomas and certificates[e]
1928–1929	101	8	-	-	-
1929–1930	96	20	-	-	-
1930–1931	151	16	-	-	-
1931–1932	193	17	-	-	-
1932–1933	193	17	1	-	-
1933–1934	268	22	-	-	-
1934–1935	257	32	-	-	-
1935–1936	254	34	-	-	-
1936–1937	271	33	-	-	-
1937–1938	301	19	1	-	-
1938–1939	315	33	-	-	-
1939–1940	228	9	-	-	-
1940–1941	323	27	-	-	-
1941–1942	348	33	-	-	-
1942–1943	164	4	-	-	-
1943–1944	156	8	-	-	-
1944–1945	186	7	-	-	-
1945–1946	162	9	-	-	-
1946–1947	220	12	-	-	-
1947–1948	236	11	-	-	-
1948–1949	452	17	1	-	-
1949–1950	641	33	-	-	-
1950–1951	640	50	1	-	-
1951–1952	708	42	-	-	-
1952–1953	677	40	2	-	-
1953–1954	650	37	1	-	-
1954–1955	643	42	2	-	-
1955–1956	644	39	-	-	-
1956–1957	722	32	2	-	-

(continued)

Academic Year	Bachelor's[a]	Master's[b]	Doctor's[c]	Associate[d]	Professional diplomas and certificates[e]
1957–1958	704	45	3	-	-
1958–1959	755	71	4	-	-
1959–1960	881	81	3	-	-
1960–1961	832	109	7	-	-
1961–1962	869	112	2	-	-
1962–1963	894	252	15	-	-
1963–1964	983	304	14	-	-
1964–1965	1,183	362	20	-	-
1965–1966	1,444	427	29	129	-
1966–1967	1,515	555	28	232	-
1967–1968	1,833	819	47	448	-
1968–1969	1,961	982	58	448	-
1969–1970	2,329	1,018	53	647	-
1970–1971	2,681	1,103	78	854	-
1971–1972	2,976	1,167	80	1,108	-
1972–1973	3,205	1,272	98	1,251	-
1973–1974	3,406	1,165	109	1,403	-
1974–1975	3,365	1,110	94	1,638	-
1975–1976	3,232	1,132	116	1,857	-
1976–1977	not available				
1977–1978	not available				
1978–1979	3,087	1,063	244	2,288	735
1979–1980	3,067	969	238	2,109	691
1980–1981	2,919	968	267	2,081	646
1981–1982	2,794	993	248	2,197	715
1982–1983	2,923	938	252	2,302	697
1983–1984	3,022	945	232	2,322	719

Academic Year	Bachelor's[a]	Master's[b]	Doctor's[c]	Associate[d]	Professional diplomas and certificates[e]
1984–1985	2,899	914	275	2,193	710
1985–1986	2,960	837	263	2,163	778
1986–1987	2,941	794	267	2,107	683
1987–1988	2,837	830	237	1,991	652
1988–1989	2,674	833	281	1,897	501
1989–1990	2,760	804	227	2,006	538
1990–1991	2,721	835	261	2,028	546
1991–1992	2,767	932	256	2,104	518
1992–1993	2,997	1,088	262	2,135	628
1993–1994	3,019	1,018	299	2,022	725
1994–1995	3,156	1,070	276	2,107	920

Sources: For 1908–1909 to 1975–1976, Robert C. Schmitt, *Historical Statistics of Hawaii* (Honolulu: University Press of Hawaii, 1977), Table 9.6; for subsequent years, reports of Institutional Research Office, University of Hawai'i, on *Degrees, Diplomas and Certificates Earned,* excluding a small number identified in most years as "no data" as to type of degree awarded.

[a] Manoa campus only until 1950; thereafter also includes Hilo campus and, after 1976, the West Oahu campus as well.

[b] All graduate degrees were granted by the Manoa campus.

c Ph.D., Ed.D., Dr.P.H., and also first professional degrees, J.D. and M.D.

d In Nursing; Arts; Science.

e Includes Certificate in Education, Dental Hygiene, and community colleges' Certificate of Achievement; also Professional Diploma in Education from Manoa.

Appendix 5

Compensated Faculty and Staff University of Hawai'i System

Academic Year	Positions[a]	Total
1907–1908	2 (acting president and one other instructor); 1 librarian	
1908–1910	13 faculty (including president); 1 librarian	
1910–1912	19 faculty (including president); 1 librarian	
1912–1914	21 faculty (including president); 1 librarian	
1914–1920	21 to 23 faculty, plus unspecified no. of temporary lecturers and 1 librarian	
1920–1921	28 faculty; 1 librarian; 3 staff	32
1921–1922	38 faculty; 1 librarian; 8 staff	47
1922–1923[b]	48 faculty; 3 librarians; 14 officers and staff	65
1923–1924	47 faculty; 3 librarians; 18 officers and staff	68
1924–1925	50 faculty; 5 librarians; 18 officers and staff	73
1925–1926	62 faculty; 6 librarians; 29 officers and staff	97
1926–1927	61 faculty; 7 librarians; 35 officers and staff	103
1927–1928	69 faculty; 8 librarians; 39 officers and staff	116
1928–1929	79 faculty; 8 librarians; 53 officers and staff	140
1929–1930[c]	86 faculty; 8 librarians; 77 officers and staff	171
1930–1931	105 faculty; 10 librarians; 126 officers and staff	241
1931–1932[d]	175 faculty; 12 librarians; 91 officers and staff	278
1932–1933	176 faculty; 12 librarians; 117 officers and staff	305
1933–1934	145 faculty; 14 librarians; 103 officers and staff	262

Academic Year	Positions[a]	Total
1934–1935	143 faculty; 15 librarians; 114 officers and staff	272
1935–1936	153 faculty; 15 librarians; 145 officers and staff	313
1936–1937	143 faculty; 15 librarians; 174 officers and staff	332
1937–1938	195 faculty; 16 librarians; 183 officers and staff	394
1938–1939	209 faculty; 16 librarians; 170 officers and staff	395
1939–1940	248 faculty; 15 librarians; 172 officers and staff	435
1940–1941	175 faculty; 16 librarians; 171 officers and staff	362
1941–1942	171 faculty; 16 librarians; 184 officers and staff	371
1942–1943[e]	159 BOR appointees; 213 civil service	
1943–1944	132 faculty; 12 librarians; 162 officers and staff	306
1944–1945	150 faculty; 12 librarians; 186 officers and staff	348
1945–1946	244 BOR appointees; 275 civil service	
1946–1947	139 full-time equivalent teaching faculty	
1947–1948	not available	
1948–1949	not available	
1949–1950	358 faculty; 22 librarians; 271 officers and staff	651
1950–1951	not available	
1951–1952	not available	
1952–1953	271 faculty; 22 librarians; 350 officers and staff	643
1954–1955	515 BOR appointees; 359 civil service	
1955–1956	441 full-time equivalent faculty	
1956–1964	not available	

Academic Year	Board of Regents appointees	Civil Service	Total position count
1964–1965	1,187	724	1,911
1965–1966	1,497	829	2,326
1966–1967	1,749	903	2,652
1967–1968[f]	2,710	n.a.	n.a.
1968–1969	2,984	1,150	4,135

Academic Year	All Appointees			Full-time equivalent[h]
	Full-time	Part-time	Total[g]	
1969–1970	4,351	1,017	5,368	4,778
1970–1971	4,717	1,206	5,923	n.a.
1971–1972	4,828	1,276	6,104	n.a.
1972–1973	4,813	1,397	6,210	n.a.
1973–1974	4,668	1,322	5,990	n.a.
1974–1975	4,749	1,455	6,204	n.a.
1975–1976	4,873	1,590	6,463	n.a.
1976–1977[i]	4,764	1,727	6,491	5,306
1977–1978	4,758	1,567	6,425	5,255
1978–1979	4,841	1,643	6,484	5,350
1979–1980	4,742	1,647	6,389	5,245
1980–1981	4,851	1,621	6,472	5,330
1981–1982	4,803	1,774	6,577	5,310
1982–1983	4,852	1,810	6,662	5,364
1983–1984	4,770	1,785	6,555	5,290
1984–1985	4,812	1,836	6,648	5,342
1985–1986	4,807	1,907	6,714	5,364
1986–1987	4,909	1,989	6,898	5,489
1987–1988	4,987	1,986	6,973	5,558
1988–1989	5,166	2,002	7,168	5,741
1989–1990	5,222	2,164	7,386	5,849
1990–1991	5,542	2,248	7,790	6,196

Academic Year	All Appointees			Full-time equivalent[h]
	Full-time	Part-time	Total[g]	
1991–1992	5,719	2,309	8,028	6,411
1992–1993	5,930	2,305	8,235	6,625
1993–1994	5,994	2,295	8,289	6,699
1994–1995	6,102	2,291	8,393	6,823
1995–1996	5,775	2,178	7,953	6,490

Note: Between 1908, when the faculty was sufficiently small to be identifiable in one photograph, and 1976, when the UH Institutional Research Office began annual reports of faculty and staff numbers, there was no consistent definition of "faculty" (which came to include part-time lecturers, then graduate assistants and other groups of professional employees) and in most years no calculation of "full-time equivalents" whereby, for example, two half-time positions are reckoned as one FTE, the truer indication of staff size and budgetary needs. Because of the divergent sources from which the numbers prior to 1976 were derived (including annual reports of the president, personnel listings, campus phone books, and budget data). The figures for 1908 to 1976 should be used only for their intended purpose—to provide a numerical record, however variously measured, of how the University's human resources developed over the decades.

[a] Includes faculty members; researchers; specialists; librarians; extension agents; lecturers; positions classified as administrative, professional, and technical; executive and administrative staff; graduate assistants; and civil service positions.

[b] From this point includes staff of Experiment Station and, until 1945, of Hawaiian Pineapple Canners research organization on Manoa campus.

[c] For period 1929–1933 includes nonresidential instructional staff of University Extension Division.

[d] After 1931 includes personnel of Teachers College.

[e] Data for 1942–1943 and 1954–1955 from *Report of President University of Hawai'i 1955,* p. 7.

[f] Full-time equivalent positions of faculty and other professional staff, including Hilo and community colleges, East-West Center, Peace Corps, and other international programs.

[g] Total number of people employed.

[h] Total employment reduced by part-time appointments; for example, two half-time positions equal one full-time equivalent position.

[i] Data for 1976 forward from annual *Faculty and Staff Report* of the Institutional Research Office, University of Hawaii.

NOTES

Part I. The Manoa Campus and the University System

1. Origins and Early Years: 1907–1946

1. *Report of the Superintendent of Public Instruction on the Concurrent Resolution Adopted by the Legislature of the Territory of Hawaii,* 1905.
2. *Pacific Commercial Advertiser,* May 4, 1907, p. 1.
3. Charles Bouslog, "Ka Aina: Where the Land Came From," in *Building a Rainbow,* ed. Victor N. Kobayashi (Honolulu: University of Hawai'i Press, 1983), 182.
4. Arthur L. Dean, "Historical Sketch of the University of Hawaii" (University of Hawaii Occasional Paper No. 5, 1927), 8.
5. Beatrice Krauss, "Some of the Founders Reminisce," *Hawaii Alumnus,* March 25, 1937, 20.
6. Dean, "Historical Sketch," 11.
7. College of Hawaii Records, No. 16, Report of the Board of Regents to the Legislature, 1917, p. 6.
8. At p. 6.
9. William Kwai Fong Yap, *The Birth and History of the University of Hawaii* (Honolulu: privately published, 1933), 1.
10. Yap, *The Birth and History,* 4.
11. Yap, *The Birth and History,* 3.
12. Meeting of October 13, 1921, recorded in the notes of Willard Wilson.
13. U.S. Bureau of Education, *A Survey of Education in Hawaii* (Washington: Government Printing Office, 1920), 307.
14. Willard Wilson's note on Board of Regents reply of February 3, 1921.
15. *University of Hawaii Quarterly Bulletin* 5, no. 4 (1927):9.
16. *University of Hawaii Quarterly Bulletin* 9, no. 1 (1930):18.
17. *University of Hawaii Quarterly Bulletin* 12 (1931):21.
18. *University of Hawaii Quarterly Bulletin* 13 (1934):19.
19. For more on the merger, see Robert E. Potter and Linda Logan, *A History of Teacher Education in Hawai'i* (Honolulu: Hawaii Education Association, 1995).

20. *University of Hawaii Quarterly Bulletin* 9, no. 4 (1930):21.
21. Interview with Michiko Kodama-Nishimoto and Warren Nishimoto, April 19, 1991, typescript, p. 225. Oral History archives, University of Hawai'i at Mānoa.
22. Bruce White, "Teacher Education in Hawaii," *The Teachers College Journal* (Indiana State Teachers College, Terre Haute) 18, no. 3 (1946):64.
23. Judith R. Hughes, "The Demise of the English Standard School System in Hawai'i," *Hawaiian Journal of History* 27 (1993):73.
24. *Thirty Years: The University of Hawaii* (Honolulu, 1937), n.p.
25. *Honolulu Star-Bulletin,* October 14, 1941, p. 1.
26. *Honolulu Star-Bulletin,* October 17, 1941, p. 3.
27. From an interview with J. Russell Cades, a regent of that time, on December 17, 1994.
28. Data on the number and variety of courses and size of faculty, here and elsewhere in this chapter, are from annual reports of the president to the Hawaii legislature.

2. Becoming a Statewide System: 1947–1968

1. U.S. Office of Education, *The University of Hawaii and Higher Education in Hawaii* (Washington: Government Printing Office, 1962), 182.
2. John Griffin in *Honolulu Advertiser,* May 15, 1994, B4.
3. *Report of the President of the University of Hawaii, 1954–55,* 17.
4. *Honolulu Star-Bulletin,* June 25, 1955, 4:1.
5. U.S. Office of Education, *The University of Hawaii,* 7, 80, 128, 133,140–141.
6. Tom Coffman, *Catch a Wave: A Case Study of Hawaii's New Politics* (Honolulu: University Press of Hawaii, 1973), 65.
7. This discussion is largely based on the unpublished "Summary History of the Origin, Conception, Birth and Early Development of the Center for Cultural and Technical Interchange Between East and West" by Professor Emeritus Murray Turnbull, dated October 19, 1990. Copies are in Hamilton Library and in the University Archives.
8. Turnbull, "Summary History," 22b.
9. An intimate, incisive history of the John A. Burns Medical School, written by its former dean, Terence A. Rogers, is in the University Archives.
10. *Honolulu Star-Bulletin*, February 12, 1963, 2:1.
11. *Honolulu Star-Bulletin,* February 13, 1963, 7:7.
12. Oral History Interview, Tape 21-23-91, University of Hawai'i Oral History Program, transcription, pp. 287–290.
13. Account by Richard S. Takasaki, then vice-president for business affairs, on April 15, 1994.
14. For a recent account of the work of one secretary, Jean Imada, see David Yount, *Who Runs the University? The Politics of Higher Education in Hawaii, 1985–1992* (Honolulu: University of Hawai'i Press, 1996), 34–35.
15. David Kittelson, "University of Hawaii Library," *Hawaii Library Association Journal* 41 (1984):59. Kittelson's closely researched, comprehensive history of the university library appeared serially in issues of the *Journal* for 1971, 1973, 1983, and 1984.
16. *Honolulu Advertiser*, April 1, 1966, A-8:1.

3. Experiencing Maturity: 1969–1995

1. *Honolulu Advertiser,* May 24, 1968, A-8.
2. *Honolulu Advertiser,* May 15, 1969, A-14.
3. *Honolulu Advertiser,* January 27, 1972, F-8.

4. *Honolulu Star-Bulletin,* August 8, 1971, F-12.
5. *Honolulu Advertis*er, October 16, 1969, A-15.
6. *Honolulu Advertiser,* October 16, 1969, A-10.
7. *Honolulu Advertiser,* May 8, 1970, A-6.
8. Letter from Kenneth Lau, December 4, 1995, p. 3.
9. Letter to Dean Godfrey, November 11, 1966, filed in the UH Law School Library.
10. Conversation between Wallace Fujiyama and Robert Potter in 1972.
11. *Honolulu Advertiser,* September 9, 1973, A-1.
12. *Honolulu Advertiser,* January 15, 1970, A-10.
13. Robert W. Hiatt in an interview with Robert Potter, January 10, 1992.
14. Senate Resolution 223.
15. Arthur Goodfriend, "New College, September 8, 1970–August 9, 1973: The Life, Death and Legacy of Yet Another Experiment in Innovative Education" (Honolulu: University of Hawai'i at Mānoa, 1974), 2:98.
16. Report to the Faculty Senate Executive Committee from Its Task Force on Administration, April 2, 1973, p. 16.
17. Faculty Senate minutes, April 5, 1973, p. 2.
18. *Honolulu Advertiser,* March 9, 1973, A-1.
19. *Honolulu Advertiser,* March 10, 1973, A-1.
20. Letter from Gorter to Cleveland, May 16, 1974. Copy provided by Gorter.
21. Letter from Meller to Robert Potter, April 27, 1994.
22. *Honolulu Advertis*er, July 25, 1974, A-1.
23. WASC Team Report, 1985, pp. 3–4.
24. *Honolulu Advertiser,* August 3, 1985, A-1, 4.
25. WASC Team Report, fall 1990, pp. 4, 79.
26. WASC Team Report, fall 1990, pp. 42–44.
27. *Honolulu Star-Bulletin,* April 28, 1995, A-1; *Honolulu Advertiser,* April 29, 1995, A-3.
28. *Honolulu Advertiser,* July 14, 1995, A-1.
29. *Honolulu Star-Bulletin,* November 2, 1995, A-4.
30. Minutes of special meeting of the Board of Regents, November 3, 1995.
31. Kenneth H. Ashworth, "Point of View: Virtual Universities Could Produce Only Virtual Learning," *Chronicle of Higher Education,* September 6, 1996.

Part II. Manoa Colleges and Programs

5. The Pacific Islands Program

1. Agnes Quigg, "The History of the Pacific Islands Study Program at the University of Hawaii" (M.A. thesis, University of Hawai'i, 1986).

6. Asian Programs and Linkages

1. U.S. Bureau of Education, *A Survey,* 301–302.
2. See Paul H. Hooper, *Elusive Destiny: The Internationalist Movement in Modern Hawaii* (Honolulu: University Press of Hawaii, 1980), 79 ff., for a detailed account of these organizations and their involvement with the University.
3. Hooper, *Elusive Destiny,* 145.
4. Hooper, *Elusive Destiny,* 150.
5. Terence A. Rogers and Gardiner B. Jones, "John A. Burns School of Medicine, University of

Hawaii," reprinted from *New Medical Schools at Home and Abroad*, ed. John Z. Bowers and Elizabeth F. Purcell (New York: Josiah Macy, Jr. Foundation, 1978). For later examples, see Roland J. Fuchs, "International Studies and Programs at the University of Hawaii, 1985–87," mimeo (Honolulu: Office of University of Relations, University of Hawai'i, November 1987), 17–18.

6. Fuchs, "International Studies."

9. Arts and Sciences after Statehood

1. Memorandum, Cleveland to Gorter, January 3, 1974.

12. The Biological Sciences

1. *College of Hawaii Records, Annual Catalog,* 1909–1910.
2. *College of Hawaii Records,* Ser. 1, *Report of the Board of Regents to the Legislature, 1909.*
3. *College of Hawaii Records,* No. 5, "Botany and Horticulture at the College of Hawaii," 1910.
4. *College of Hawaii Records,* No. 9, *Report of the Board of Regents to the Legislature, 1913.*
5. A. K. Chock, "J. F.Rock 1884–1962," *Taxon* 12, no. 3 (1963):89–102.
6. *College of Hawaii Records, Annual Catalog,* 1909–1910.
7. *College of Hawaii Records,* No. 12, *Report of the Board of Regents to the Legislature, 1913.*
8. *College of Hawaii Records,* No. 16, *Report of the Board of Regents to the Legislature, 1917.*
9. *College of Hawaii Records,* No. 12, *Report of the Board of Regents to the Legislature, 1913.*
10. Bishop Museum Spec. Publ. 22, 1933.
11. P. H. Buck, "An Introduction to Polynesian Anthropology," *Bishop Museum Bulletin* (1945), 187.
12. G. D. Carr, "The Later Publications of Harold St. John," *Pacific Science* 48 (1944):188–192.
13. Volume I, Introduction.

13. Astronomy

1. Walter Steiger, "A Brief History of Astronomy in Hawaii," mimeo, n.d., 6.
2. Steiger, " A Brief History," 9.
3. *Hawaii Herald,* June 7, 1991, p. 1. For a discussion of political problem solving in establishing the Mauna Kea site, see chapter 11.
4. Quoted from Kevin Krisciunas, *Astronomical Centers of the World* (Cambridge: Cambridge University Press, 1988), 227.
5. Krisciunas, *Astronomical Centers,* 231.
6. M. Mitchell Waldrop, "Mauna Kea (1): Halfway to Space," *Science* 214 (November 1981): 1012.
7. M. Mitchell Waldrop, "Mauna Kea (II): Coming of Age," *Science* 214 (December 1981): 1110.

15. Theatre and Dance

1. "Training and Performance in Japanese No and Kyogen," *Theatre Topics* 3, no. 2 (September 1993):101.

2. "Japanese Tradition: Search and Research," *International Conference Journal*, 1981 Asian Performing Arts Summer Institute, University of California at Los Angeles, p. 75.
3. "Kennedy Theatre: The Early Years," undated mimeographed article prepared by the Department of Drama and Theatre, based on reminiscenses of emeriti professors Earle Ernst, Joel Trapido, and Edward Langhans, all former department chairmen who were "colleagues-in-arms" during the construction and preparation of Kennedy Theatre.

Part III. Beyond Manoa: Hilo, West O'ahu, the Community Colleges

18. The University of Hawai'i at Hilo

1. *Honolulu Advertiser,* January 24, 1959.
2. *Honolulu Star-Bulletin,* July 4, 1962.
3. Richard H. Kosaki, "Feasibility of Community Colleges in Hawaii." 1964.
4. *Honolulu Advertiser,* August 27, 1970.
5. *Honolulu Advertiser,* September 23, 1976.
6. *Honolulu Advertiser,* April 20, 1977.
7. *Honolulu Advertiser,* July 4, 1985.
8. Joyce D. Kahane, *The Establishment of an Independent University of Hawaii at Hilo* (Honolulu: Legislative Reference Bureau, 1986), 43.
9. Charles M. Fullerton, interview in Honolulu, April 22, 1995.
10. Edward Kormondy, "UHH: Whence and Whither," unpublished memoirs dated June, 1955, p. 4.
11. *Hawaii Business Magazine,* November 1994, p. 37.

19. The University of Hawai'i–West O'ahu

1. My sincere thanks to May Asato and June Tanabe of the University of Hawai'i–West O'ahu chancellor's office for access to their comprehensive collection of newspaper clippings on West O'ahu. They, Dean Fred Mayer, and Executive Vice-Chancellor Bruce Bergland also provided me with two chronologies and a file full of statistics on the history of the school.
2. *Honolulu Advertiser,* October 23, 1975.
3. Interview of Kosaki by the author, October 16, 1981.
4. Interview of Hiroshi "Scrub" Tanaka by author, July 25, 1977, John A.Burns Oral History Project, Tape #2, p. 8.
5. Kosaki interview.
6. Carol Clark, *Leeward Sun Press,* March 26, 1987.
7. Mike Yuen, "State will swap land for UH-West O'ahu Campus," *Honolulu Star-Bulletin,* December 20, 1995, A-1, 8.
8. *Imua! The Newsletter of the UH-West Oahu Campus,* May, 1996.

20. The Community Colleges

1. George B. Vaughan, "Historical Perspective: President Truman Endorsed Community College Manifesto," *Community and Junior College Journal* 53, no. 7 (April 1983):21.
2. S. V. Martorana and Ernest V. Hollis, *The University of Hawaii and Higher Education in Hawaii,* Hawaii State Department of Budget and Review, November 1962, p. 281.
3. *Feasibility of Community Colleges in Hawaii* (Honolulu: University of Hawai'i, February 1964).
4. *Feasibility of Community Colleges,* 90.

5. Letter from Kosaki, November 15, 1995.
6. Interview with Fujiuchi, January 30, 1995.
7. Board of Regents minutes, March 16, 1967, p. 13.
8. Kosaki letter, November 15, 1995.
9. Western Association of Schools and Colleges Accreditation Team Report, March 1970. UH Archives.
10. "Controlled Growth for the University of Hawaii: Community Colleges," policy statement of the Board of Regents, fall 1970, pp. 15–16.
11. *Sunday Star-Bulletin and Advertiser,* February 23, 1969, A-6.
12. *Honolulu Advertiser,* October 24, 1989, A-4.
13. Diane Fry, speaking on a videotaped program, *LCC 25th Anniversary Retrospective,* an LCC Educational Media Center production, 1993.
14. William McCartney, "History of the Honolulu Technical School," *Artisan* (HTS annual), 1960, 40–44.
15. Interview with Honolulu Community College faculty, June 2, 1993.
16. From information supplied by Violet Lai, Honolulu Community College librarian, in 1993.
17. Tom Mikulski, "Honolulu Paves the Way for PLCs in Hawai'i," *University of Hawai'i Community Colleges* 29, no. 3 (October 1993):8.
18. "Sand Island Boat Repair Project Begins," *Honolulu Advertiser,* March 16, 1994, A-5.
19. University of Hawai'i Community Colleges, *1991–92 Annual Report,* 26.
20. "Site Analysis Study, Kauai Community College," prepared for the University of Hawai'i by Donald Wolbrink and Associates, Inc., July 1971.
21. *A Prospectus for Kauai Community College*, September 1966, published by the UH Community College System, p. 2.
22. *A Prospectus for Kauai Community College,* 8.
23. Letter from McCleery to Frank Inouye, August 7, 1994.
24. Interview with Iha, August 10, 1993.
25. Duncan Sinclair, "History of the Maui Vocational School from 1930 to 1965," *Maui News,* July 21, 1976, A10.
26. Letter from Kosaki to authors, November 15, 1995.
27. Interviews with Mayer, June 26, 1993, and October 23, 1993.
28. Interview with MCC faculty, July 9, 1993.
29. Interview with Professor Jean Pezzoli, assistant dean of instruction, January 5, 1994.
30. Interview with MCC faculty, July 9, 1993.
31. Interview with KCC faculty, August 11, 1993.
32. Interview in 1993 with KCC faculty member who conducted a campus tour for Kunimura in the early 1970s.
33. Letter from Richard Kosaki, November 15, 1995, p. 3.
34. Interview with KCC Dean of Instruction Dr. Leon Richards, October 5, 1993.
35. "Writing Institute Founder Lauds Kapi'olani's Writing Across The Curriculum Program," *University of Hawaii Community Colleges,* January-February 1988.
36. *Junior College Journal* 38, no. 1 (1967):13–15.
37. Interview with LCC faculty, Pearl City Tavern, May 26, 1993.
38. Interview with Joyce Tsunoda, April 27, 1993.
39. Letter from Dr. John Prihoda to Fearrien, June 20, 1993.
40. Interview with LCC faculty members, Pearl City Tavern, May 26, 1993.

41. Letter from Prihoda to Fearrien, June 20, 1993.
42. Letter from Prihoda to Fearrien, June 20, 1993.
43. Interview with WCC faculty, May 1, 1993.
44. Interview with Provost Peter Dyer, May 28, 1993.
45. Interview with WCC faculty, May 1, 1993.
46. Editorial, *Honolulu Advertiser,* May 3, 1965.
47. Board of Regents minutes, November 24, 1970, p. 16.
48. Board of Regents minutes, June 20, 1971, p. 13.
49. Letter from Sumada to Fearrien and Lucas, December 3, 1993.
50. Board of Regents minutes, May 10, 1973, p. 6.
51. Sumada letter.
52. Typescript of Hawai'i Community College 50th Anniversary Production, July 15, 1991.
53. ERIC abstract of Joanne Cooper paper, "A Case Study of Institutional Divorce: The Separation of a Community College from a University," presented at a meeting of the Association for the Study of Higher Education, Boston, October 30–November 3, 1991.
54. Interview with Tim Craig, ETC director, August 31, 1993.

A NOTE ON SOURCES

In the major sections of this history, we have compromised on footnoting, seeking a middle ground between so many references that they distract the reader and too few to indicate sources of quotations and opinions of others. Authors of the shorter articles were free to attribute sources in their own manner.

The principal authors have all had long associations with the University of Hawai'i. Kamins and Potter have been on the Manoa faculty since 1947 and 1962 respectively. Fearrien and Lucas were at Kapi'olani Community College from 1968 and 1970 until their retirements in 1993 and 1988, respectively. The late Frank Inouye was director of the Hilo Branch from 1952 to 1957, and Boylan, after teaching at Manoa for six years, has been at West O'ahu since it opened on January 1, 1976. Our experiences as participants and deeply interested observers were primary sources for many events we reported as well as providing background for our reports.

Other major primary sources were the University's general catalogs, annual reports of the presidents, regents' minutes, and other official papers in the University Archives and the Hamilton Library Hawaiian Collection. Legislative journals, *Hawaii Revised Statutes,* governors' papers, and other government documents were also primary sources. Reports of visiting accreditation teams from the Western Association of Schools and Colleges and surveys done by the U.S. Office of Education and other consultants gave outside views. Interviews in the local newspapers, particularly the *Honolulu Star-Bulletin* and *Honolulu Advertiser,* provided many quotations and corroborations of our personal recollections. *Ka Palapala* (UH-Mānoa student yearbook), *Ka Leo,* and other campus newspapers gave student impressions. Oral interviews, informal conversations, letters, written notes, and the like from former administrators, retired and senior faculty members, alumni, and political leaders added illuminating details.

Other Sources

Andrews, Arthur. "Early Days." Manuscript in Hawaiian Collection, Hamilton Library.

Bouslog, Charles. "*Kai Aina:* Where the Land Came From," in *Building a Rainbow,* edited by Victor N. Kobayashi, 182–187 (Honolulu: University of Hawai'i Press,

1984). Describes early land acquisition for the Manoa campus. Bouslog was a longtime member of the Manoa English Department.

Bouslog, Charles, et al. *Manoa, the Story of a Valley (by Manoa Valley residents).* Honolulu: Mutual Publishing, 1994.

Carr, Norma, and Lenore Johnson. *Women's Campus Club, University of Hawai'i: 1920–1995.* 1995. Distributed by the Women's Campus Club on its seventy-fifth anniversary. Brief history of the club with personal accounts of campus living in the 1940s.

Dean, Arthur Lyman. "Historical Sketch of the University of Hawaii." University of Hawai'i Occasional Paper No. 5, 1927.

Farrington, Wallace R. "Memo of Reminiscence." UH Archives.

George, William H. "The University of Hawaii, A Short History" [n.d.]. Copy in Hawaiian Collection, Hamilton Library.

Gilmore, John. "The University of Hawaii: Its Work and Outlook," *The Hawaiian Forester and Agriculturist* 6, no. 1 (1909):1–13.

Hardy, Thornton Sherbourne. *Wallace Rider Farrington.* Honolulu: Star-Bulletin, 1935 (chapter 6, "The University of Hawaii," pp. 74–91).

Kittelson, David. "Founding the College of Hawaii," *Hawaii Historical Review* (July 1968):461–464.

———. "The History of the College of Hawaii." Master's thesis, University of Hawai'i, 1966.

———. "The History of Hilo College." Typescript in UH Library Hawaiian Collection, 1976. 4 p. Kittelson was librarian for the Hilo College and later UH archivist.

———. "The University of Hawaii Library, 1907–1920," *Hawaii Library Association Journal* 28, no. 2 (1971):3–9.

———. "The University of Hawaii Library, 1920–1941," *Hawaii Library Association Journal* 30, no. 1/2 (1973):15–26.

———. "The University of Hawaii Library, 1941–1961," *Hawaii Library Association Journal* 40, no. 1 (1983):53–65.

———. "The University of Hawaii Library, 1960–1983," *Hawaii Library Association Journal* 41 (1984):59–70.

Kobayashi, Victor N., editor. *Building a Rainbow.* Honolulu: University of Hawai'i Press, 1984. Accounts of buildings on the Manoa campus and how they were named. Many photographs.

———. "Summer Session at the University of Hawai'i at Manoa," *Educational Perspectives* 27, no. 2 (1990):15–20. Kobayashi is dean of the UH-Mānoa Summer Session.

Kosaki, Richard H. *Feasibility of Community Colleges in Hawaii.* Community College Study Project, UH, 1964. Report to the legislature. Contains many charts, tables, and graphs.

Krauss, Beatrice. "Some of the Founders Reminisce," *Hawaii Alumnus,* March 25, 1937.

Martorana, S. V., and Ernest V. Hollis. *The University of Hawaii and Higher Education in Hawaii.* Washington: U. S. Office of Education, Dept. of Health, Education and Welfare, 1962.

Nickerson, Thomas. *University of Hawaii, 1907–1957.* Honolulu: UH Office of Publication and Information [1958]. Photos and map.

Peterson, Vincent Z. "History of the UH-Manoa Physics Department." Typescript, 1994. 11 pp.

Potter, Robert E. "Academic Freedom or Academic Entrapment: The Oliver M. Lee Case," *Phi Delta Kappan* 50, no. 4 (1968):208–213.

———. *Autonomy and Accountability at the University of Hawai'i: A Review of the Significance and Implementation of the 1978 Constitutional Amendment.* Honolulu: College of Education, University of Hawai'i at Mānoa, 1984. 42 p. (ERIC ED240–968). A review of outside interference with the responsibilities of the Board of Regents.

———. "The Evolution of Summer Sessions for Teachers in Hawai'i," *Educational Perspectives* 27, no. 2 (1990):26–34.

———. "The Stiles Style, or Who Cuts the Pattern for Teacher Education for Hawai'i," *Educational Perspectives* 5, no. 3 (1965).

———. *The University of Hawai'i Board of Regents, 1907–1982: Its Composition and Roles Compared with Other Boards Governing Public Universities.* Honolulu: College of Education, University of Hawai'i at Mānoa, 1983. (ERIC ED227–811.) A history of the Board of Regents with a listing of regents up to 1982.

Potter, Robert E., and Linda Logan. *A History of Teacher Education in Hawai'i.* Honolulu: Hawaii Education Association, 1995. Contains chapters on the merger of the Territorial Normal School and the University of Hawai'i, Teachers College, and College of Education. Also a brief section on the UH-Hilo teacher education program.

Stone, Scott C. S., and Russell Fujita. *East-West Center, The First 25 Years.* Honolulu: East-West Center Office of Public Affairs [1985].

Turnbull, Murray. "Summary History of the Origin, Conception and Birth of the Center for Cultural and Technical Interchange Between East and West." Typescript [1990]. Copies in Hawaiian Collection, Hamilton Library, and in UH Archives.

Weaver, Herbert B. *University of Hawaii Department of Psychology: 1939–1989.* Distributed by the Department, 51 pp.

Wilson, Willard. *The Professor's Briefcase: The Wit and Wisdom of Willard Wilson,* edited by Amos Leib, Elizabeth Carr, and Thomas Nickerson. Honolulu: UH Office of University Relations and Development, 1975. Essays by Wilson.

Yap, William Kwai Fong. *The Birth and History of the University of Hawaii.* Honolulu: privately published, 1933. In English plus a version in Chinese. Yap's own record of his efforts to get the College of Hawaii expanded into a university.

Yount, David. *Who Runs the University? The Politics of Higher Education in Hawaii, 1985–1992.* Honolulu: University of Hawai'i Press, 1996. An insider's report, centered on the administration of President Albert Simone.

ILLUSTRATION CREDITS

Pages 10–11
Farrington, Cooper: Hawaii State Archives. Gilmore: UH University Relations. Faculty, football team: UH Archives.

Page 19
Yap: Thomas Brown, Preservation, UH Libraries. Wise: Star-Bulletin Printers. Dean, Hemenway: UH University Relations.

Pages 24–25
Aerial view, graduation: Bishop Museum. Library, gym class, men's dormitory: UH University Relations.

Page 28
Kapalapala yearbook, 1926.

Page 33
UH University Relations.

Pages 36–37
Varney Circle, Andrews Outdoor Theatre: Hawaii State Archives. Library: UH Archives. Aerial view: UH University Relations.

Page 44
Mrs. Thomas P. Gill.

Pages 48–49
Bomb shelter: UH Archives. Varsity Victory Volunteers: Hawaii State Archives. Men's barracks: UH University Relations.

Page 56
Tomi K. Knaefler.

Page 61
Ralph Toyota.

Page 66
Both photos: UH Archives.

Pages 72–73
Aerial view, band: UH Archives. Convocation, beauty contest, *Ka Leo* staff: UH University Relations. Dance: Tomi K. Knaefler.

Page 78
Sinclair and Asian scholars, groundbreaking: UH University Relations. Spoehr and Turnbull: Francis Haar.

Page 81
Waipio Valley: UH Archives. Bystrom, Nose, and Yuen and Tonga: PEACESAT, UH.

Pages 92–93
Aerial view, Klum Gym, Varsity Theatre: UH University Relations. Snack bar: UH Archives.

Pages 98–99
Gilmore Hall, student debate: UH University Relations. Liberation Hall: *Honolulu Star-Bulletin,* courtesy of Tomi K. Knaefler. Counter-demonstration: UH Archives.

Page 101
Hamilton and Wilson: UH University Relations.

Pages 120–121
All photos: UH University Relations.

Pages 130–131
All photos: UH University Relations.

Page 142
Beckley: Thomas Brown, Preservations, UH Libraries. Elbert and Morris, Hawaiian Studies facility, UH University Relations.

Pages 160–161
Maui Experiment Station: UH Archives. Krauss: Beatrice Krauss. Papaya, engineering class: UH University Relations. Electronic sensors: UH College of Engineering.

Pages 204–205
Bryan, Aquarium, Coconut Island, Enewetak: UH University Relations, courtesy of Alison Kay. Hiatt and others: Hawaii Institute of Marine Biology.

Page 212
Kaimuki observatory: Bishop Museum. Mauna Kea: Richard J. Wainscoat, UH Institute for Astronomy.

Pages 218–219
Kahananui: Dale Hall. Smith, gamelan: UH Archives. Sulu dance: UH Department of Theatre and Drama.

Pages 224–225
Mink: UH Archives. Ernst, *Benten Kozo:* UH Department of Theatre and Dance.

Page 236
Both photos: University of Hawai'i Press.

Page 224
Both photos: University of Hawai'i at Hilo Library.

Page 255
Both photos: UH University Relations.

Page 262
Machine shop: Office of Public Relations, UH Community College System. Aeronautics: UH University Relations.

Page 278
Hurricane damage: Office of Public Relations, UH Community College System. Car: Celeste Miyashiro, courtesy of Office of Public Relations, UH Community College System.

Page 281
Both photos: Gail Ainsworth, Maui Community College Library.

Page 287
Convocation: Rebekah Luke, courtesy of the Office of Public Relations, UH Community College System. Campus view: Office of Public Relations, UH Community College System.

Page 291
Both photos: Office of Public Relations, UH Community College System.

Page 296
Both photos: Office of Public Relations, UH Community College System.

Page 301
Shed on wheels: Rebekah Luke, courtesy of the Office of Public Relations, UH Community College System. Hydroponics: Office of Public Relations, UH Community College System.

CONTRIBUTORS

Daniel B. Boylan, Professor of History, University of Hawai'i–West O'ahu.

Oswald A. Bushnell, Emeritus Professor of Medical Biology and Medical History, University of Hawai'i.

Robert R. Fearrien, Associate Professor of Social Sciences (retired), Kapi'olani Community College.

Thomas P. Gill, attorney and former Hawaii legislator, lieutenant governor, and U.S. congressman.

Dale E. Hall, Associate Professor of Music, University of Hawai'i.

William Hamilton, Director, University of Hawai'i Press.

Robert W. Hiatt, late Emeritus Vice-President and Senior Professor of Zoology, University of Hawai'i; former President, University of Alaska.

Wilfred J. Holmes, late Dean, College of Engineering, University of Hawai'i.

Frank T. Inouye, late Director of the Hilo Campus, University of Hawai'i.

Rubellite K. Johnson, Emeritus Professor of Hawaiian, University of Hawai'i.

Robert M. Kamins, Emeritus Professor of Economics, University of Hawai'i.

E. Alison Kay, Professor of Zoology, University of Hawai'i.

Tomi K. Knaefler, journalist and author.

Victor N. Kobayashi, Dean of Summer Session, University of Hawai'i.

James R. Linn, Emeritus Professor of Speech, University of Hawai'i.

Ruth Lucas, Co-cordinator, Writing-across-the-Curriculum program (retired), Kapi'olani Community College.

Norman Meller, Emeritus Professor of Political Science, University of Hawai'i.

Wallace C. Mitchell, late Professor of Entomology, University of Hawai'i.

Deane E. Neubauer, Professor of Political Science, University of Hawai‘i.

Robert E. Potter, Emeritus Professor of Education, University of Hawai‘i.

Ralph Toyota, retired businessman.

Willard Wilson, late Professor of English; Dean of College of Arts and Sciences, of Student Personnel, of Faculties; Vice-President and Acting President; Provost; and Corporate Secretary of the University of Hawai‘i.

INDEX